CABLE AND X-FORCE

VENDETTA

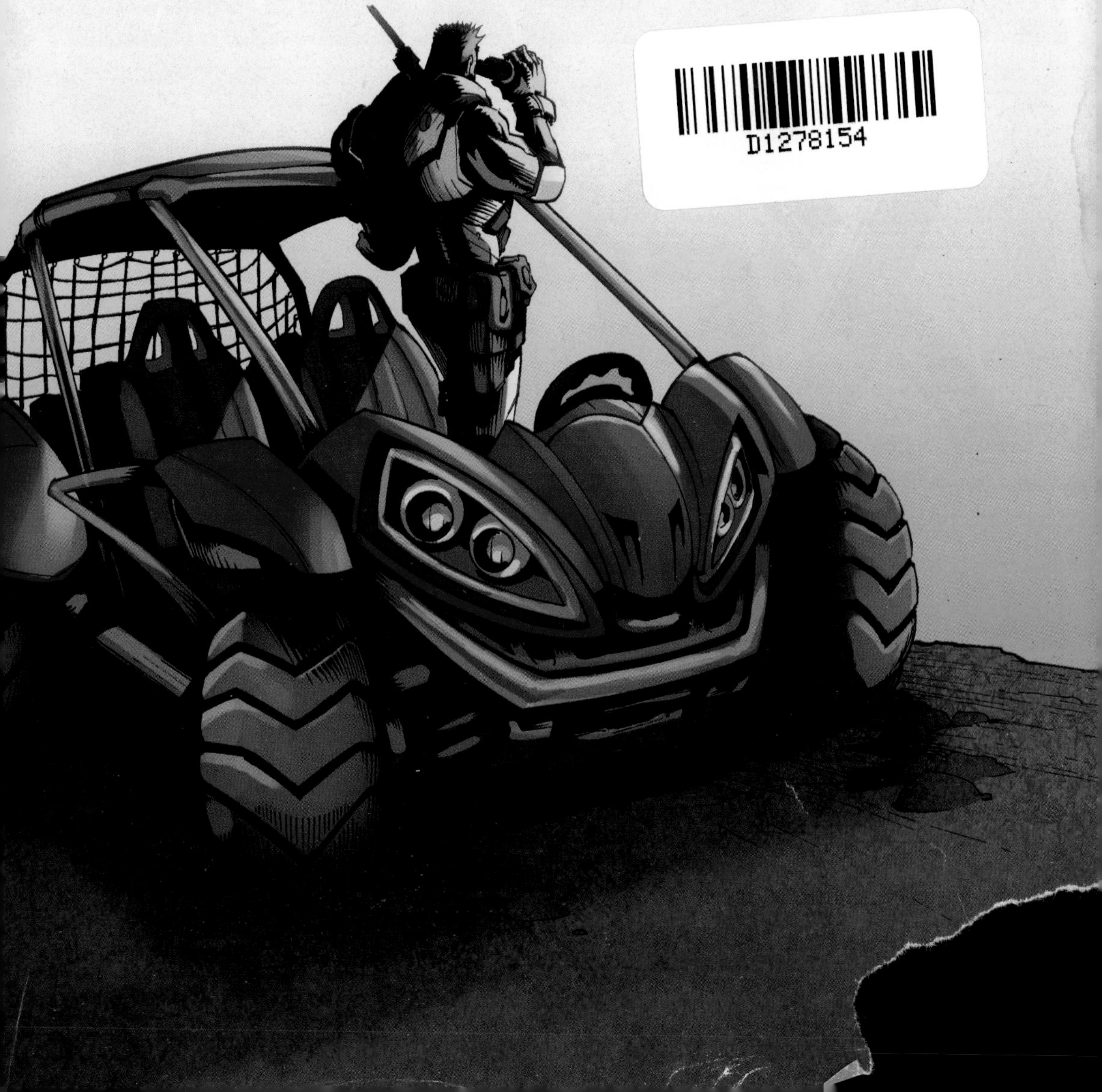

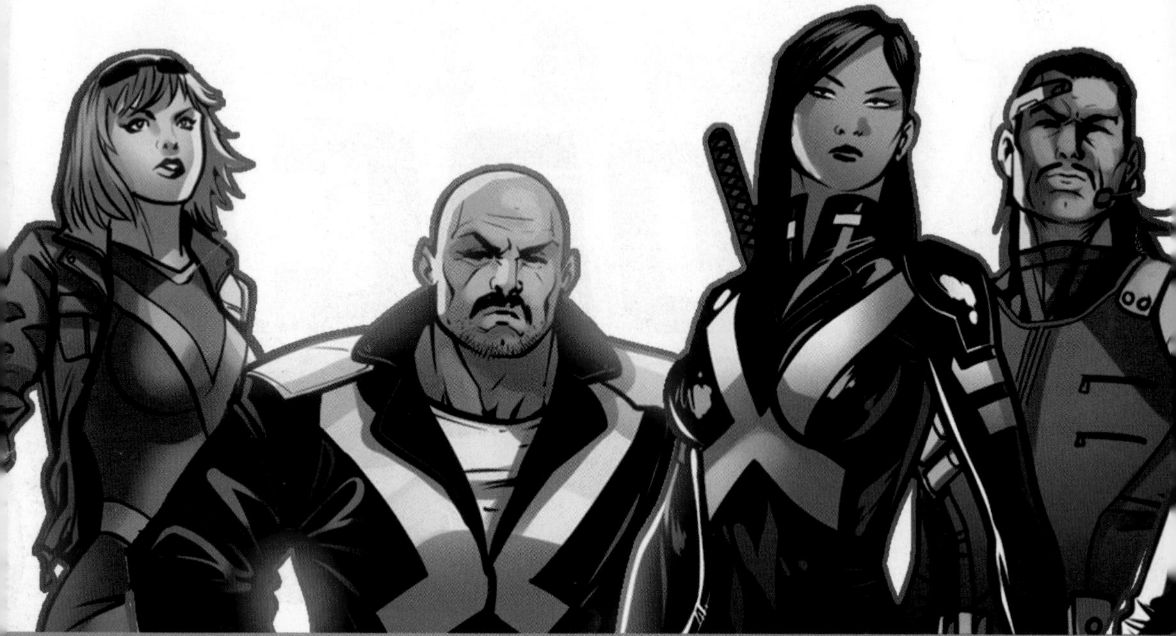

CABLE AND X-FORCE
VENDETTA

COLLECTION EDITOR: **ALEX STARBUCK** • EDITORS, SPECIAL PROJECTS: **JENNIFER GRÜNWALD & MARK D. BEAZLEY**
SENIOR EDITOR, SPECIAL PROJECTS: **JEFF YOUNGQUIST**
SVP PRINT, SALES & MARKETING: **DAVID GABRIEL**
COVER DESIGN: **JEFF POWELL** • INTERIOR DESIGN: **NELSON RIBEIRO**

EDITOR IN CHIEF: **AXEL ALONSO** • CHIEF CREATIVE OFFICER: **JOE QUESADA**
PUBLISHER: **DAN BUCKLEY** • EXECUTIVE PRODUCER: **ALAN FINE**

CABLE AND X-FORCE VOL. 4: VENDETTA. Contains material originally published in magazine form as CABLE AND X-FORCE #15-19 and UNCANNY X-FORCE #16-17. First printing 2014. ISBN# 978-0-7851-8946-6. Published by MARVEL WORLDWIDE, INC., a subsidiary of MARVEL ENTERTAINMENT, LLC. OFFICE OF PUBLICATION: 135 West 50th Street, New York, NY 10020.
...AN FINE, EVP - Office of the President, Marvel Worldwide, Inc. and EVP & CMO Marvel Characters B.V.; DAN BUCKLEY, Publisher & President - Print, Animation & Digital Divisions; JOE QUESADA, ... TOM BREVOORT, SVP of Publishing; DAVID BOGART, SVP of Operations & Procurement, Publishing; C.B. CEBULSKI, SVP of Creator & Content Development; DAVID GABRIEL, SVP Print, Sales ... of Operations & Logistics; DAN CARR, Executive Director of Publishing Technology; SUSAN CRESPI, Editorial Operations Manager; ALEX MORALES, Publishing Operations Manager; ...formation regarding advertising in Marvel Comics or on Marvel.com, please contact Niza Disla, Director of Marvel Partnerships, at ndisla@marvel.com. For Marvel subscription ... **anufactured between 1/31/2014 and 3/10/2014 by R.R. DONNELLEY, INC., SALEM, VA, USA.**

CABLE AND X-FORCE

WRITER
DENNIS HOPELESS

ARTISTS
GERARDO SANDOVAL (#15-17)
& ANGEL UNZUETA (#18-19)

COLOR ARTIST
RACHELLE ROSENBERG

LETTERER
VC'S JOE SABINO

COVER ART
SALVADOR LARROCA & FRANK D'ARMATA
AND RAMON PEREZ

UNCANNY X-FORCE

WRITER
SAM HUMPHRIES

PENCILERS
HARVEY TOLIBAO & DEXTER SOY

INKERS
DEXTER SOY, ED TADEO,
CRAIG YEUNG & ROLAND PARIS

COLOR ARTIST
DAVID CURIEL

LETTERER
VC'S CORY PETIT

COVER ART
RAMON PEREZ

ASSISTANT EDITOR
XANDER JAROWEY

EDITOR
DANIEL KETCHUM

X-MEN GROUP EDITOR
NICK LOWE

CABLE AND X-FORCE

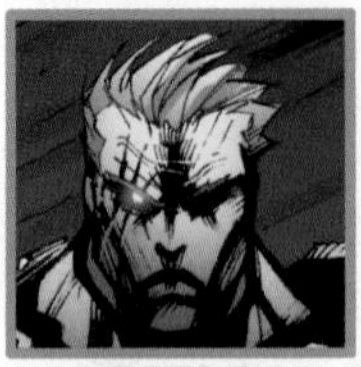

CABLE

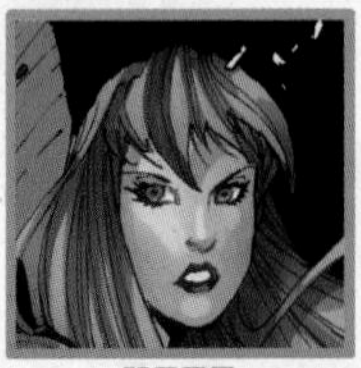

HOPE

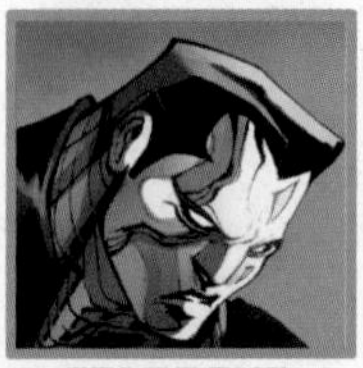

COLOSSUS

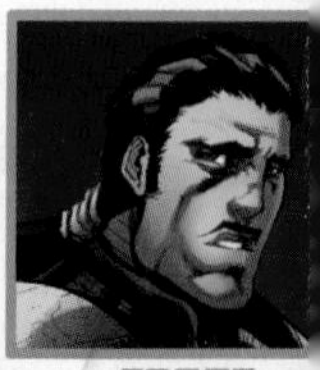

FORGE

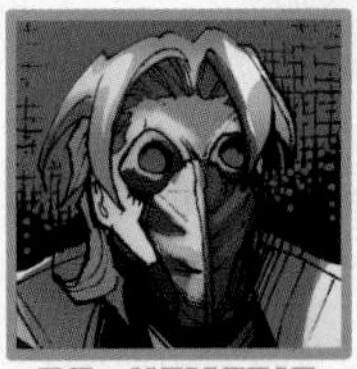

DR. NEMESIS

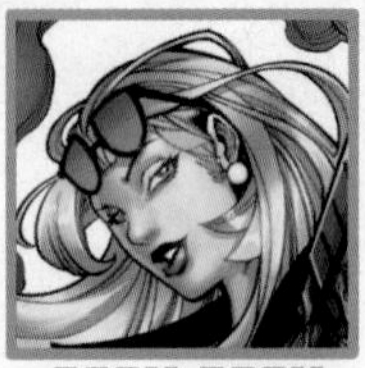

BOOM BOOM

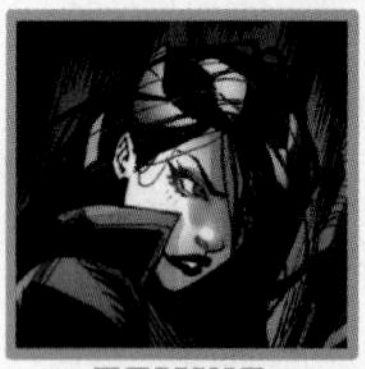

DOMINO

UNCANNY X-FORCE

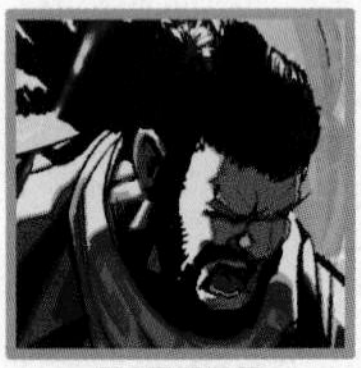

BISHOP

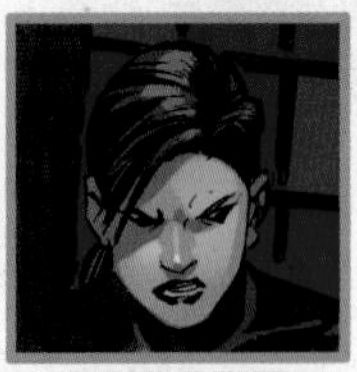

PSYLOCKE

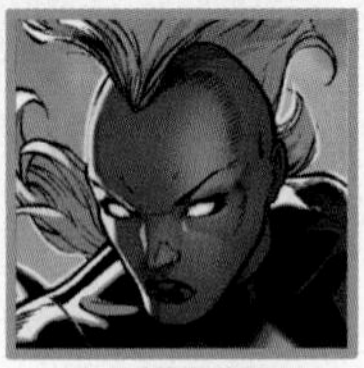

STORM

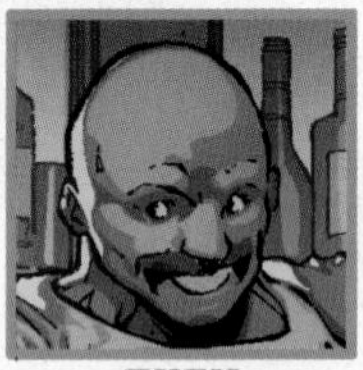

PUCK

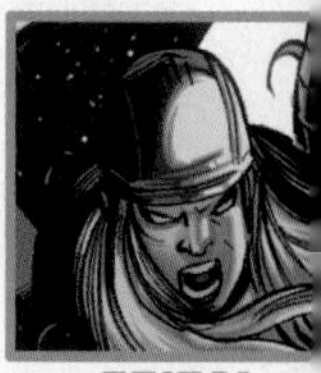

SPIRAL

PREVIOUSLY...

Cable's telepathy has evolved into something more: precognition. Forced to view premonitions of a dark future, he collected a team to combat these visions. Though his mind is racked with seizures caused by the evolution of his powers, Cable and his X-Force team continue to preemptively intercept those believed to be responsible for this dystopian future.

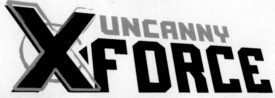

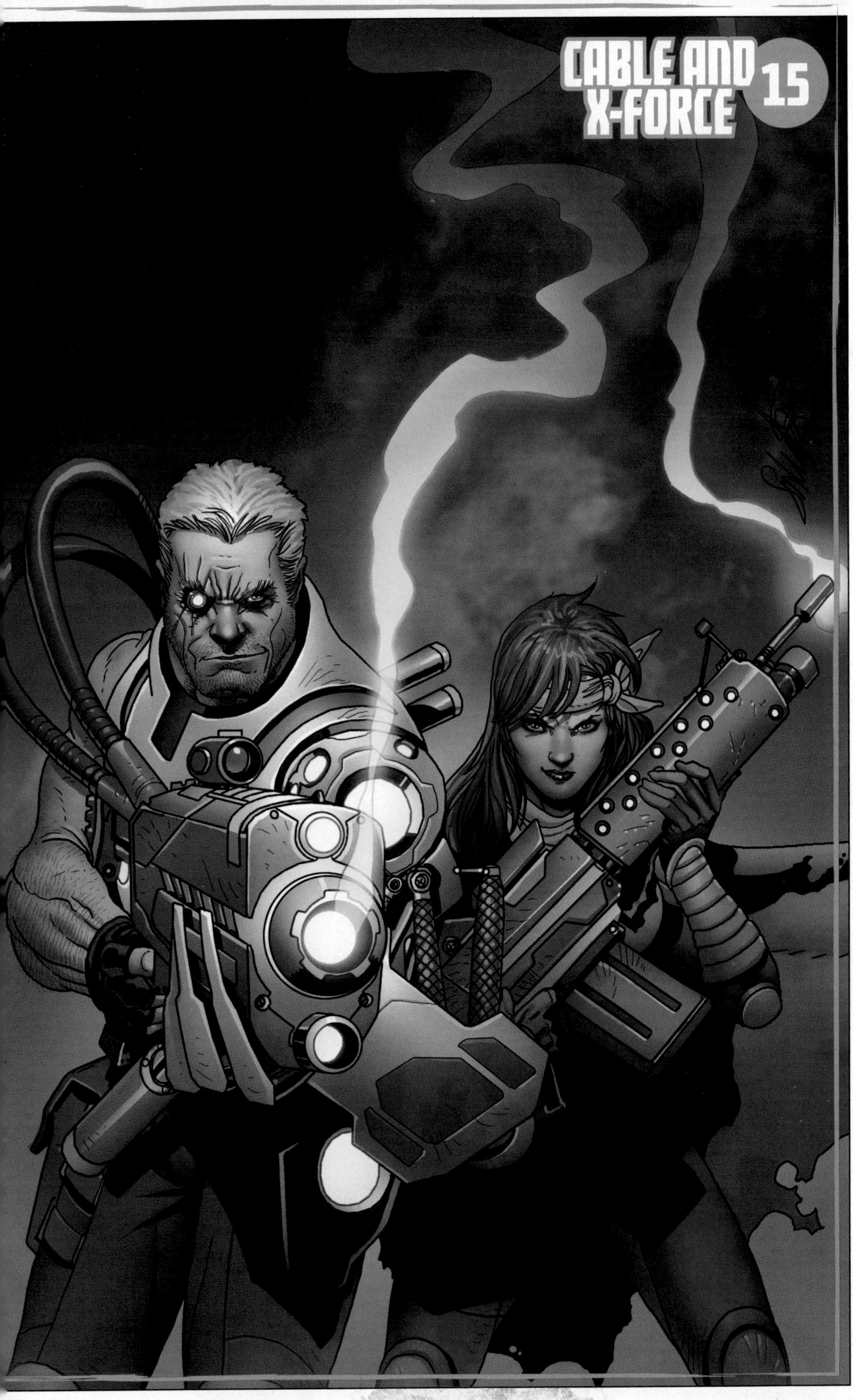
CABLE AND X-FORCE
15

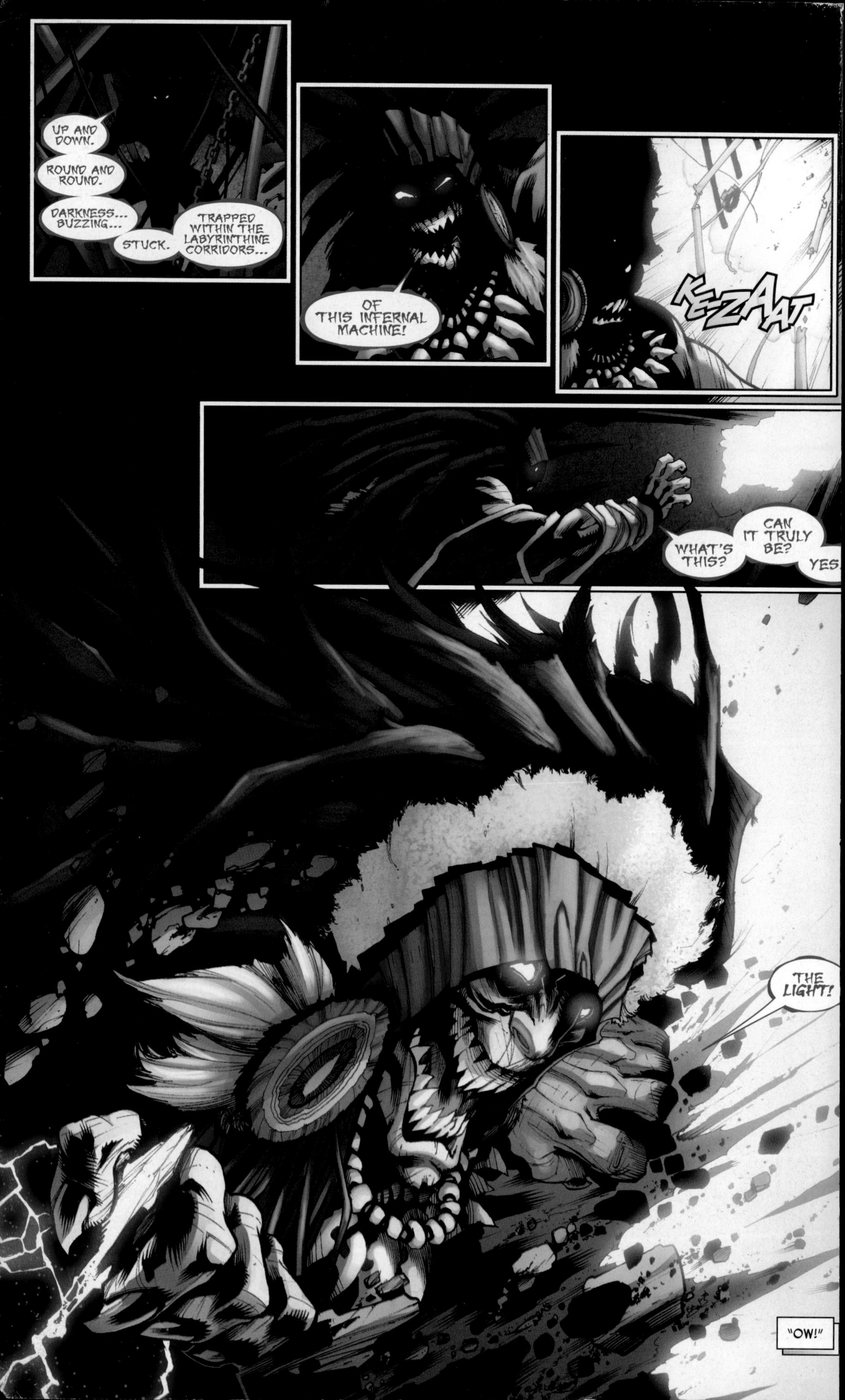

UP AND DOWN.
ROUND AND ROUND.
DARKNESS... BUZZING...
STUCK.
TRAPPED WITHIN THE LABYRINTHINE CORRIDORS...
OF THIS INFERNAL MACHINE!
KE-ZAAAT
WHAT'S THIS?
CAN IT TRULY BE?
YES.
THE LIGHT!
"OW!"

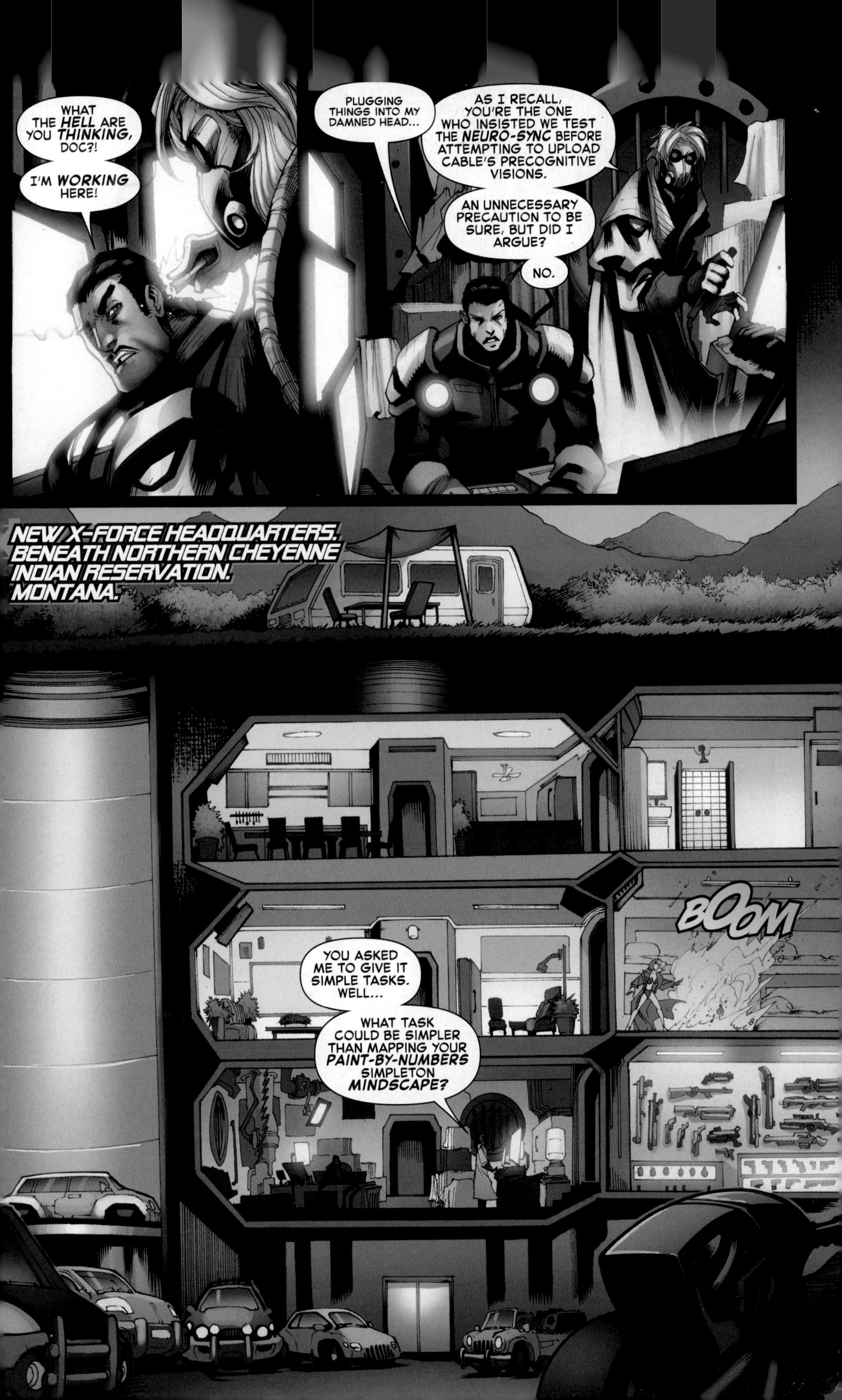
WHAT THE HELL ARE YOU THINKING, DOC?!
I'M WORKING HERE!
PLUGGING THINGS INTO MY DAMNED HEAD...
AS I RECALL, YOU'RE THE ONE WHO INSISTED WE TEST THE NEURO-SYNC BEFORE ATTEMPTING TO UPLOAD CABLE'S PRECOGNITIVE VISIONS.
AN UNNECESSARY PRECAUTION TO BE SURE, BUT DID I ARGUE?
NO.
NEW X-FORCE HEADQUARTERS. BENEATH NORTHERN CHEYENNE INDIAN RESERVATION. MONTANA.
BOOM
YOU ASKED ME TO GIVE IT SIMPLE TASKS. WELL...
WHAT TASK COULD BE SIMPLER THAN MAPPING YOUR PAINT-BY-NUMBERS SIMPLETON MINDSCAPE?

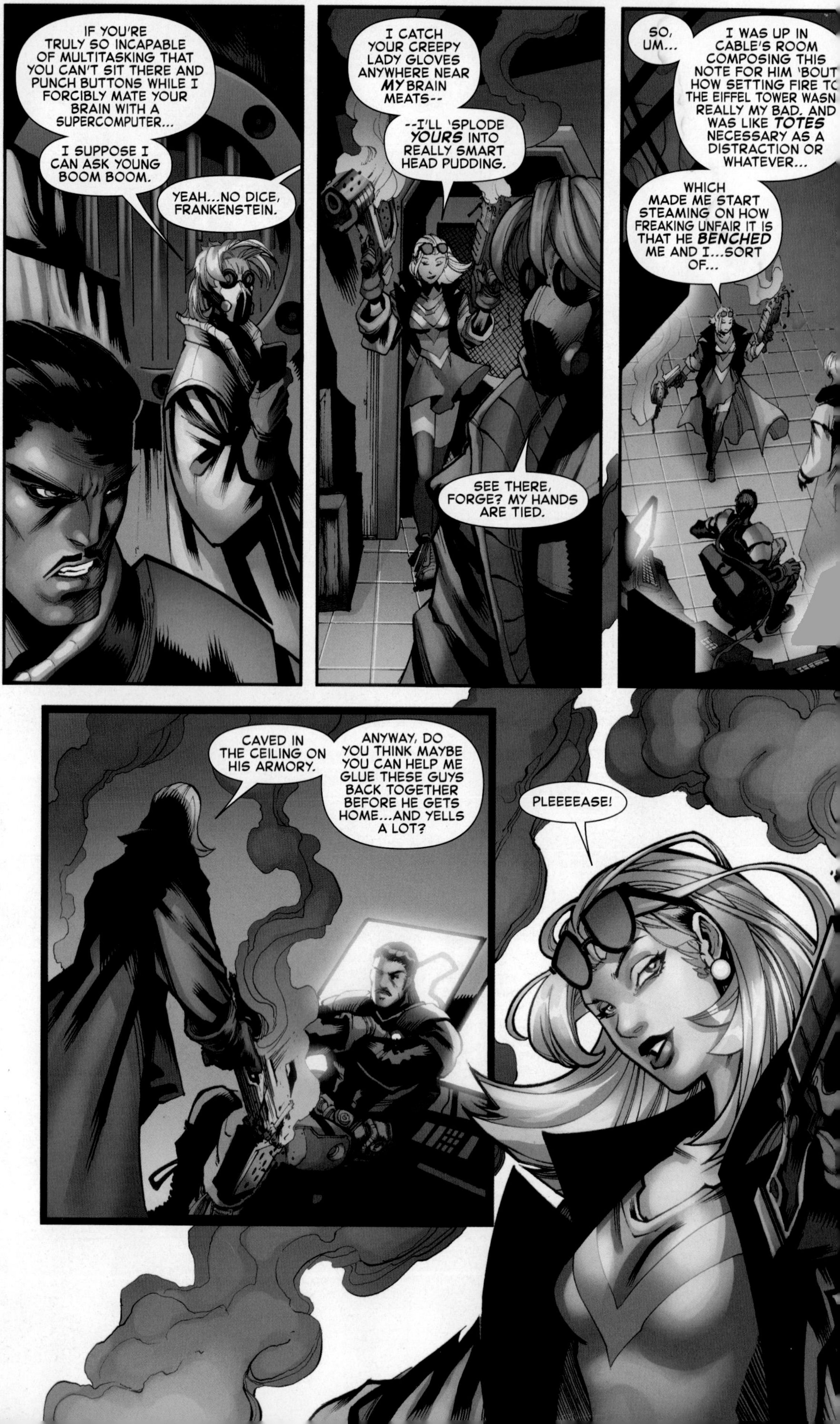

IF YOU'RE TRULY SO INCAPABLE OF MULTITASKING THAT YOU CAN'T SIT THERE AND PUNCH BUTTONS WHILE I FORCIBLY MATE YOUR BRAIN WITH A SUPERCOMPUTER...
I SUPPOSE I CAN ASK YOUNG BOOM BOOM.
YEAH...NO DICE, FRANKENSTEIN.
I CATCH YOUR CREEPY LADY GLOVES ANYWHERE NEAR MY BRAIN MEATS--
--I'LL 'SPLODE YOURS INTO REALLY SMART HEAD PUDDING.
SEE THERE, FORGE? MY HANDS ARE TIED.
SO, UM...
I WAS UP IN CABLE'S ROOM COMPOSING THIS NOTE FOR HIM 'BOUT HOW SETTING FIRE TO THE EIFFEL TOWER WASN REALLY MY BAD. AND WAS LIKE TOTES NECESSARY AS A DISTRACTION OR WHATEVER...
WHICH MADE ME START STEAMING ON HOW FREAKING UNFAIR IT IS THAT HE BENCHED ME AND I...SORT OF...
CAVED IN THE CEILING ON HIS ARMORY.
ANYWAY, DO YOU THINK MAYBE YOU CAN HELP ME GLUE THESE GUYS BACK TOGETHER BEFORE HE GETS HOME...AND YELLS A LOT?
PLEEEEASE!

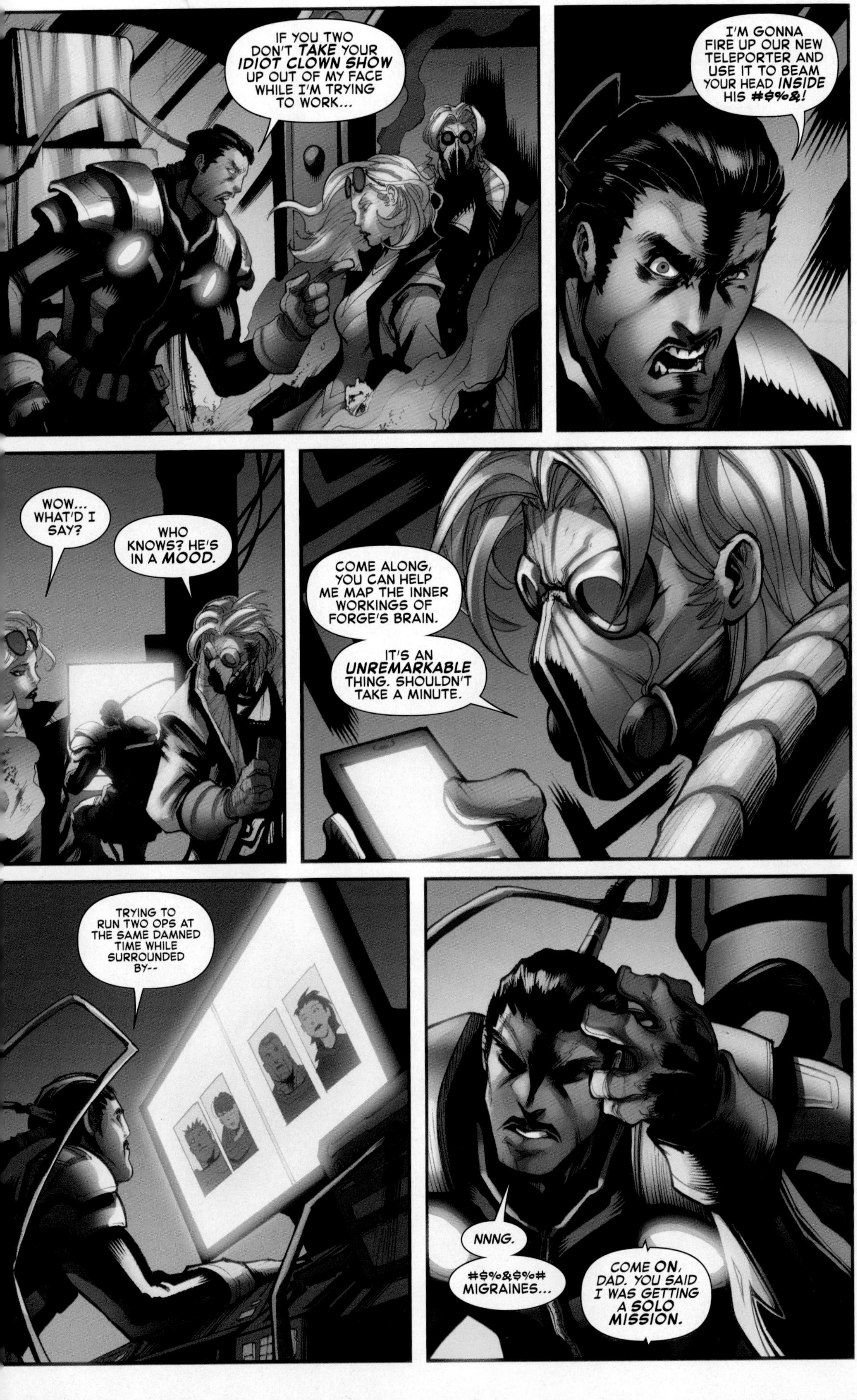
IF YOU TWO DON'T TAKE YOUR IDIOT CLOWN SHOW UP OUT OF MY FACE WHILE I'M TRYING TO WORK...
I'M GONNA FIRE UP OUR NEW TELEPORTER AND USE IT TO BEAM YOUR HEAD INSIDE HIS #$%&!
WOW... WHAT'D I SAY?
WHO KNOWS? HE'S IN A MOOD.
COME ALONG, YOU CAN HELP ME MAP THE INNER WORKINGS OF FORGE'S BRAIN.
IT'S AN UNREMARKABLE THING. SHOULDN'T TAKE A MINUTE.
TRYING TO RUN TWO OPS AT THE SAME DAMNED TIME WHILE SURROUNDED BY--
NNNG.
#$%&$%# MIGRAINES...
COME ON, DAD. YOU SAID I WAS GETTING A SOLO MISSION.

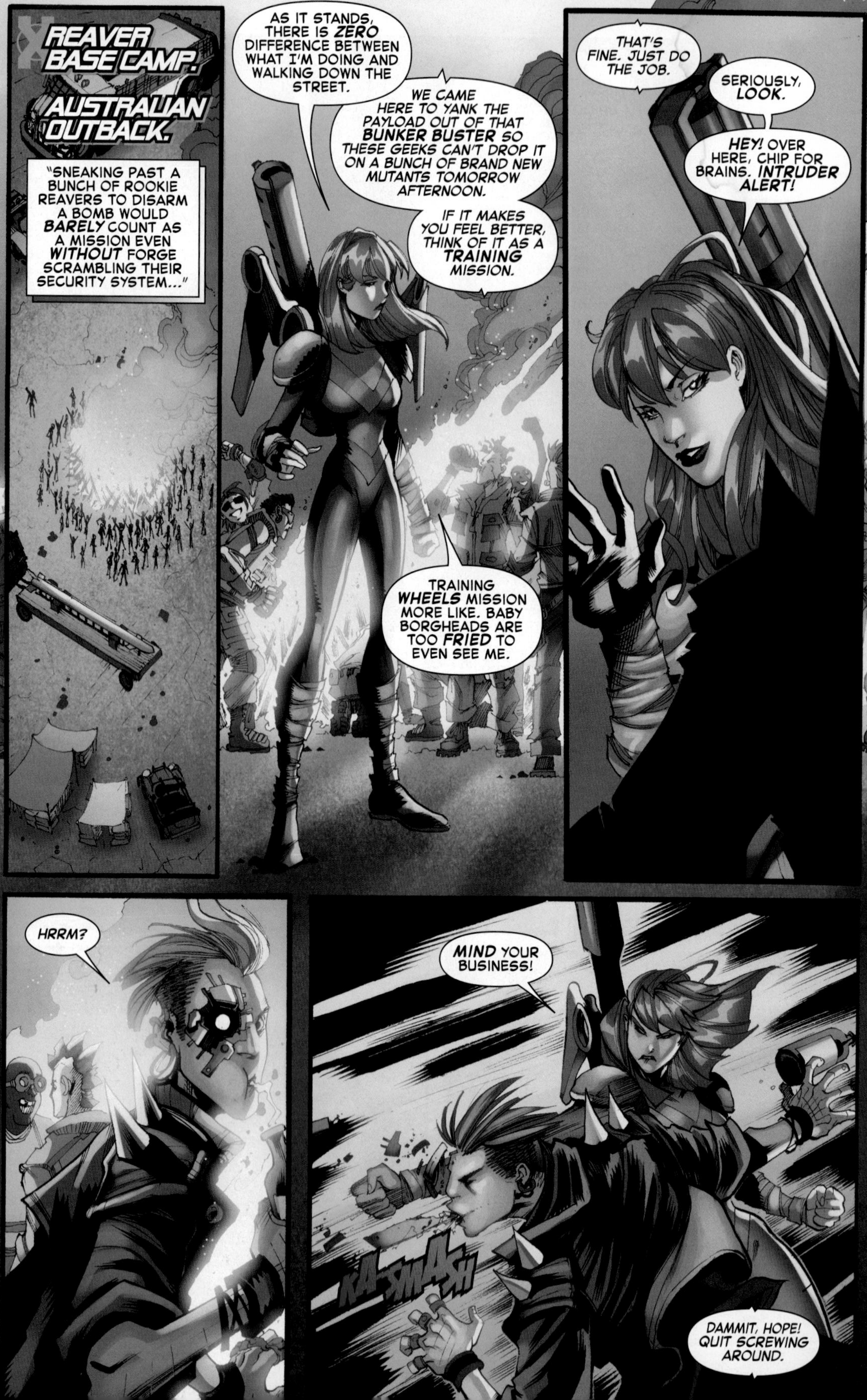
REAVER BASE CAMP.
AUSTRALIAN OUTBACK.
"SNEAKING PAST A BUNCH OF ROOKIE REAVERS TO DISARM A BOMB WOULD BARELY COUNT AS A MISSION EVEN WITHOUT FORGE SCRAMBLING THEIR SECURITY SYSTEM..."
AS IT STANDS, THERE IS ZERO DIFFERENCE BETWEEN WHAT I'M DOING AND WALKING DOWN THE STREET.
WE CAME HERE TO YANK THE PAYLOAD OUT OF THAT BUNKER BUSTER SO THESE GEEKS CAN'T DROP IT ON A BUNCH OF BRAND NEW MUTANTS TOMORROW AFTERNOON.
IF IT MAKES YOU FEEL BETTER, THINK OF IT AS A TRAINING MISSION.
TRAINING WHEELS MISSION MORE LIKE. BABY BORGHEADS ARE TOO FRIED TO EVEN SEE ME.
THAT'S FINE. JUST DO THE JOB.
SERIOUSLY, LOOK.
HEY! OVER HERE, CHIP FOR BRAINS. INTRUDER ALERT!
HRRM?
MIND YOUR BUSINESS!
KA-SMASH
DAMMIT, HOPE! QUIT SCREWING AROUND.

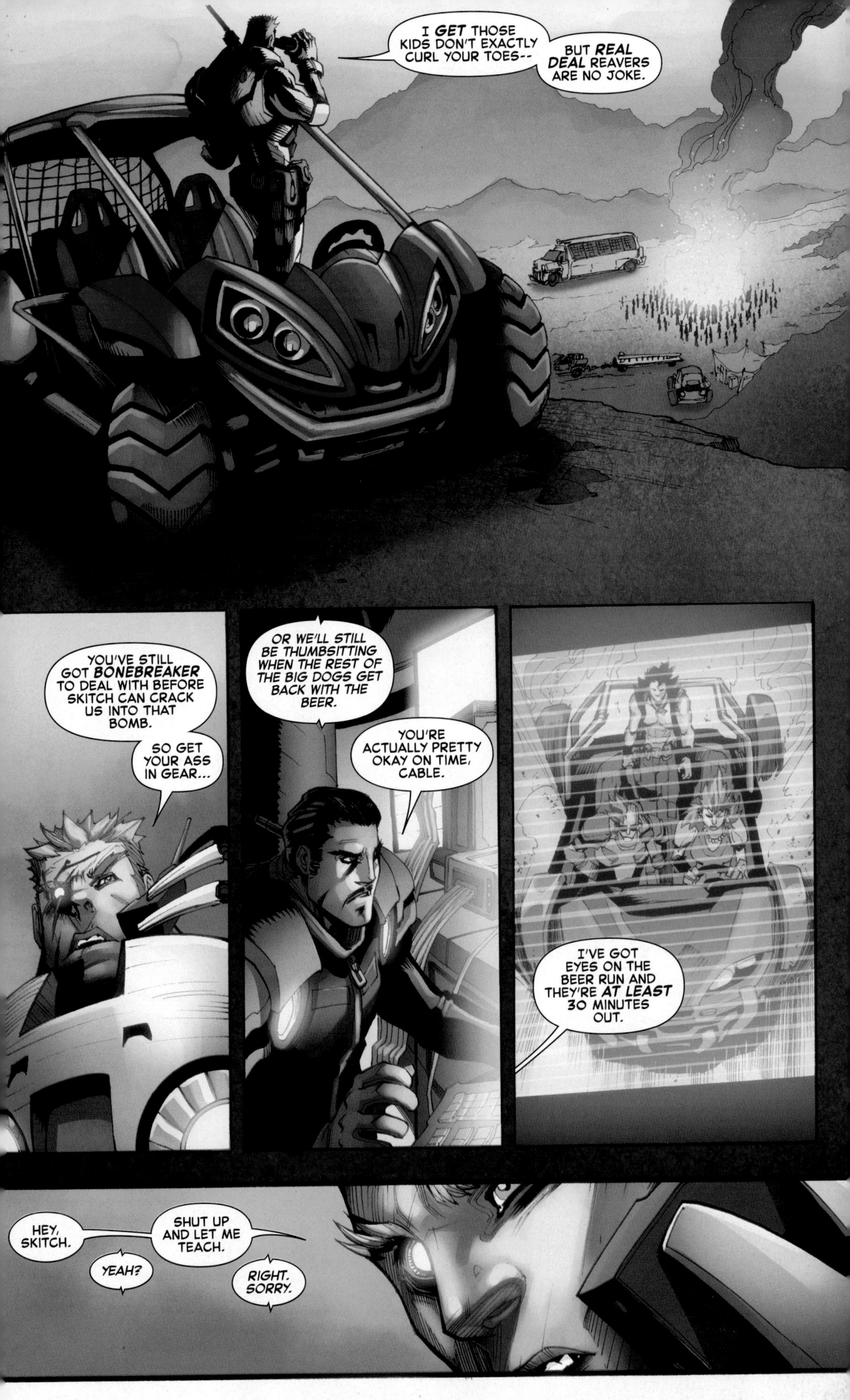
I GET THOSE KIDS DON'T EXACTLY CURL YOUR TOES--
BUT REAL DEAL REAVERS ARE NO JOKE.
YOU'VE STILL GOT BONEBREAKER TO DEAL WITH BEFORE SKITCH CAN CRACK US INTO THAT BOMB.
SO GET YOUR ASS IN GEAR...
OR WE'LL STILL BE THUMBSITTING WHEN THE REST OF THE BIG DOGS GET BACK WITH THE BEER.
YOU'RE ACTUALLY PRETTY OKAY ON TIME, CABLE.
I'VE GOT EYES ON THE BEER RUN AND THEY'RE AT LEAST 30 MINUTES OUT.
HEY, SKITCH.
YEAH?
SHUT UP AND LET ME TEACH.
RIGHT. SORRY.

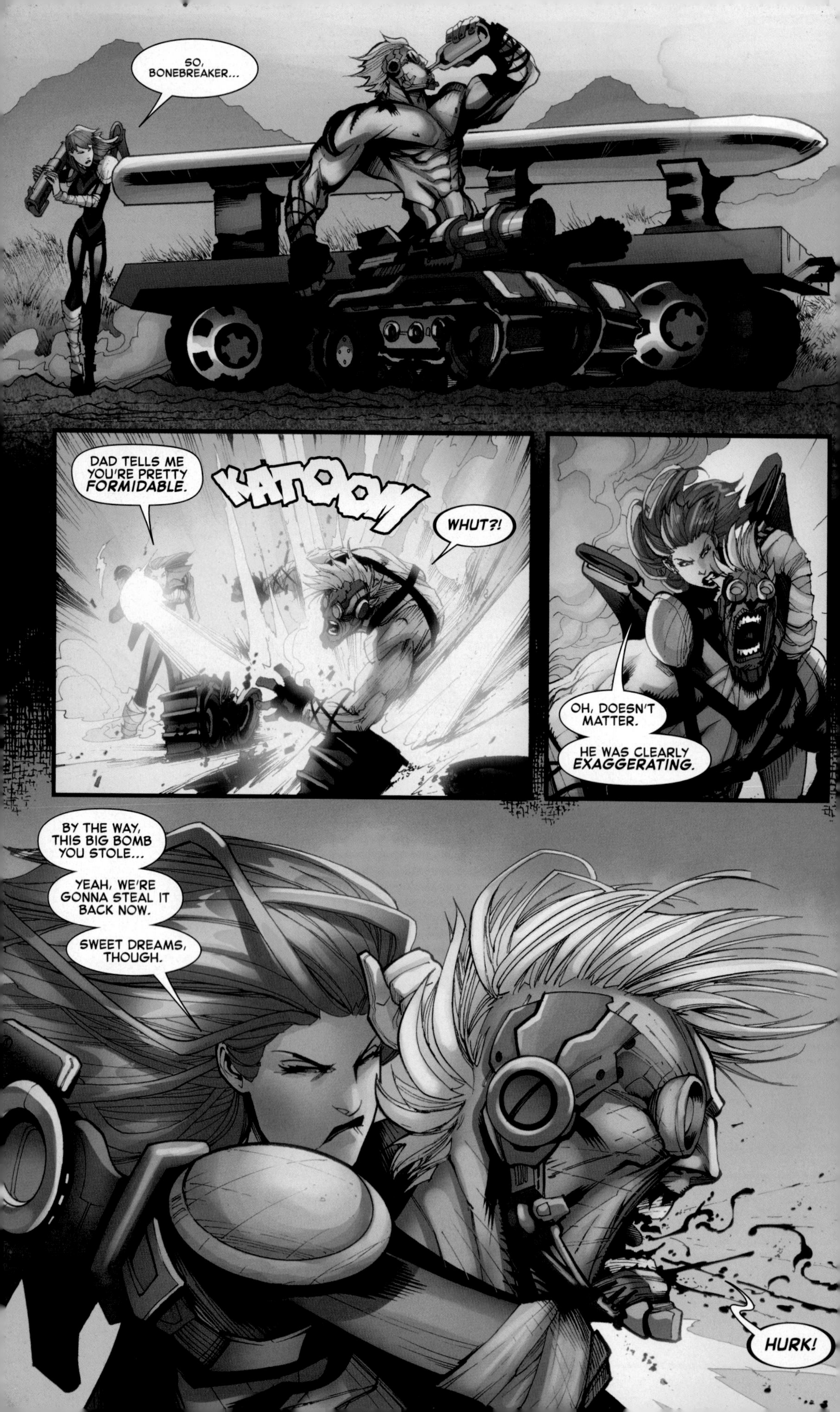

SO, BONEBREAKER...
DAD TELLS ME YOU'RE PRETTY *FORMIDABLE.*
KATOOOM
WHUT?!
OH, DOESN'T MATTER.
HE WAS CLEARLY *EXAGGERATING.*
BY THE WAY, THIS BIG BOMB YOU STOLE...
YEAH, WE'RE GONNA STEAL IT BACK NOW.
SWEET DREAMS, THOUGH.
HURK!

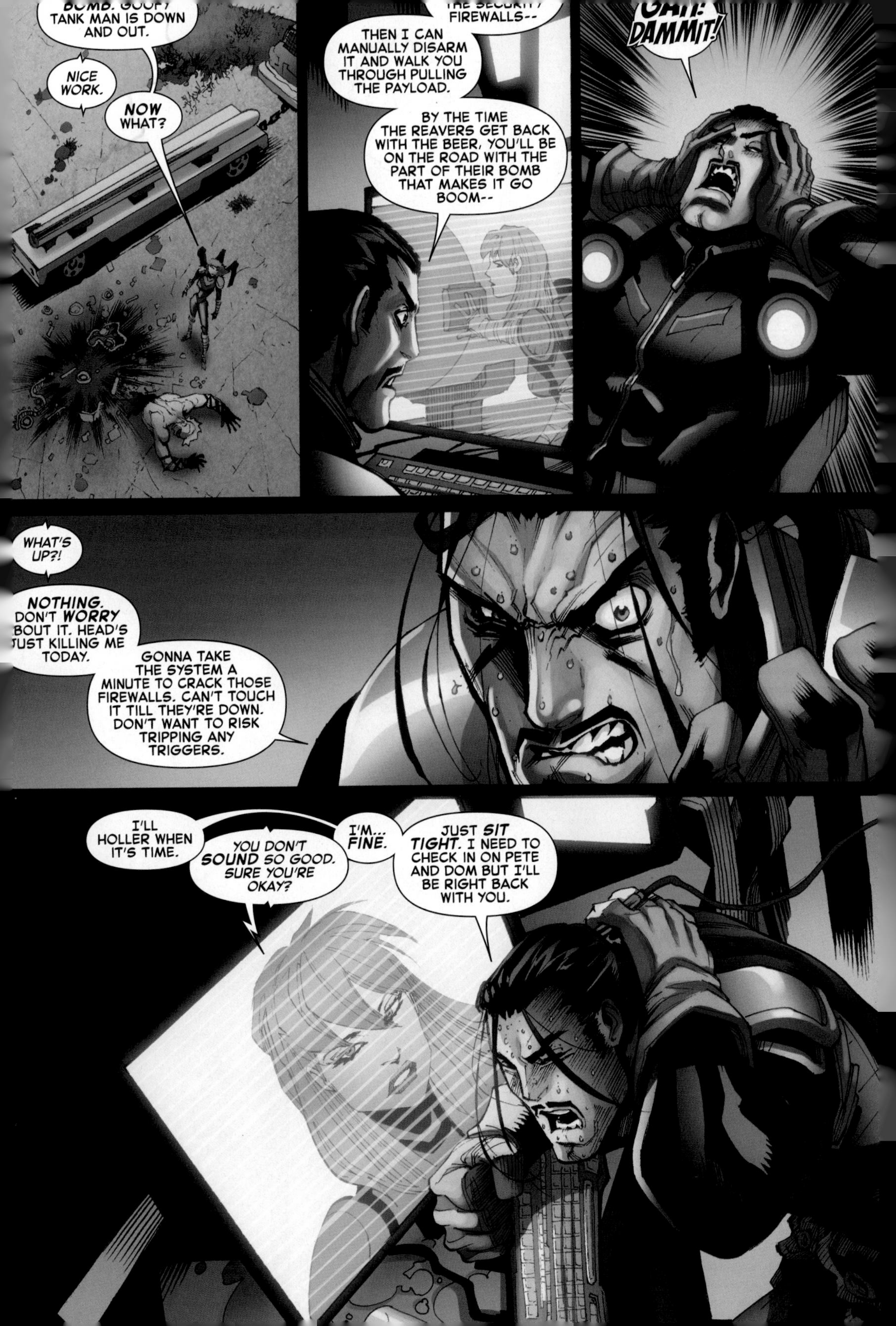
TANK MAN IS DOWN AND OUT.
NICE WORK.
NOW WHAT?
FIREWALLS--
THEN I CAN MANUALLY DISARM IT AND WALK YOU THROUGH PULLING THE PAYLOAD.
BY THE TIME THE REAVERS GET BACK WITH THE BEER, YOU'LL BE ON THE ROAD WITH THE PART OF THEIR BOMB THAT MAKES IT GO BOOM--
DAMMIT!
WHAT'S UP?!
NOTHING. DON'T WORRY BOUT IT. HEAD'S UST KILLING ME TODAY.
GONNA TAKE THE SYSTEM A MINUTE TO CRACK THOSE FIREWALLS. CAN'T TOUCH IT TILL THEY'RE DOWN. DON'T WANT TO RISK TRIPPING ANY TRIGGERS.
YOU DON'T SOUND SO GOOD. SURE YOU'RE OKAY?
I'M... FINE.
I'LL HOLLER WHEN IT'S TIME.
JUST SIT TIGHT. I NEED TO CHECK IN ON PETE AND DOM BUT I'LL BE RIGHT BACK WITH YOU.

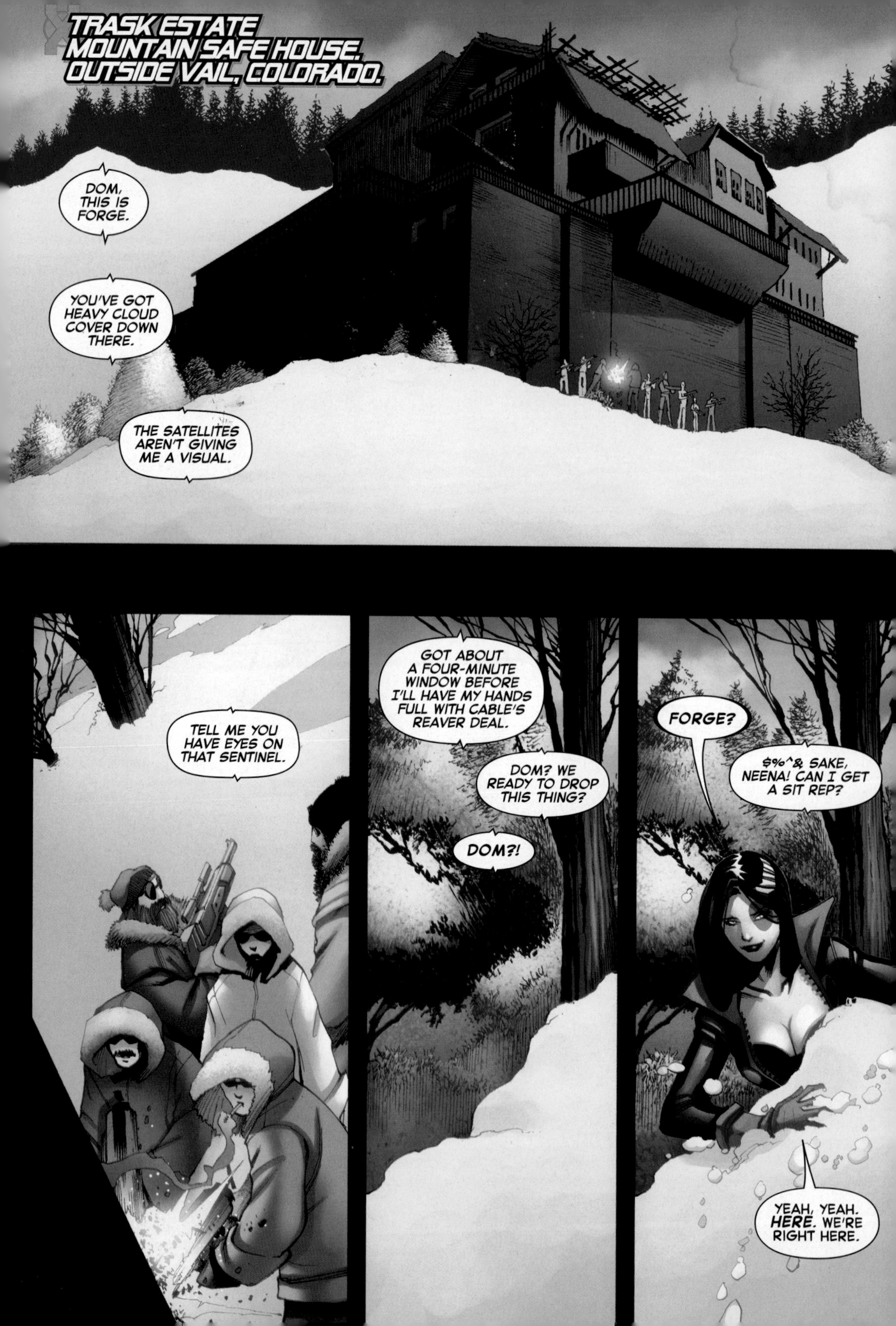
TRASK ESTATE
MOUNTAIN SAFE HOUSE.
OUTSIDE VAIL, COLORADO.
DOM, THIS IS FORGE.
YOU'VE GOT HEAVY CLOUD COVER DOWN THERE.
THE SATELLITES AREN'T GIVING ME A VISUAL.
TELL ME YOU HAVE EYES ON THAT SENTINEL.
GOT ABOUT A FOUR-MINUTE WINDOW BEFORE I'LL HAVE MY HANDS FULL WITH CABLE'S REAVER DEAL.
DOM? WE READY TO DROP THIS THING?
DOM?!
FORGE?
$%^& SAKE, NEENA! CAN I GET A SIT REP?
YEAH, YEAH. HERE. WE'RE RIGHT HERE.

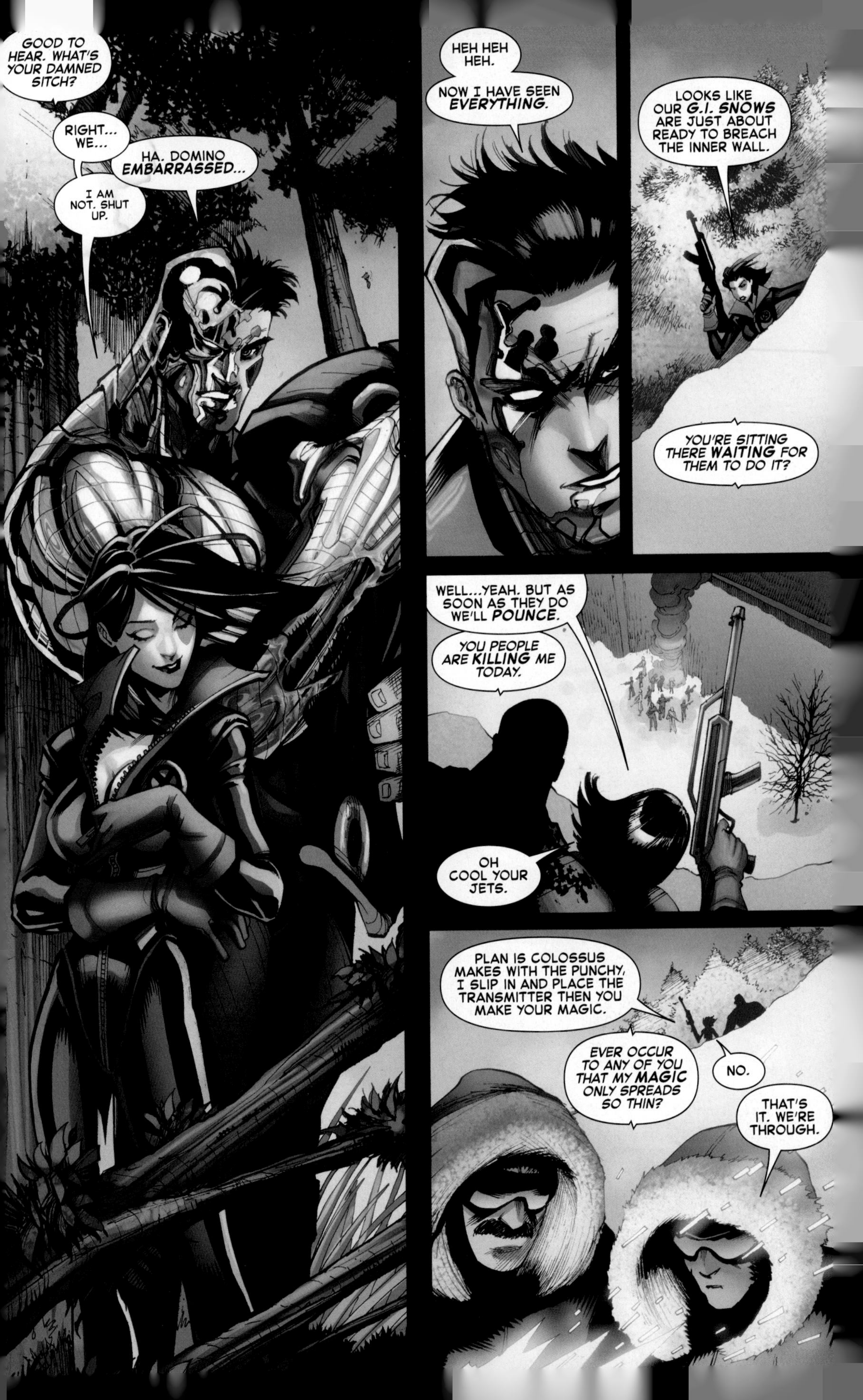
GOOD TO HEAR. WHAT'S YOUR DAMNED SITCH?
RIGHT... WE...
HA. DOMINO EMBARRASSED...
I AM NOT. SHUT UP.
HEH HEH HEH.
NOW I HAVE SEEN EVERYTHING.
LOOKS LIKE OUR G.I. SNOWS ARE JUST ABOUT READY TO BREACH THE INNER WALL.
YOU'RE SITTING THERE WAITING FOR THEM TO DO IT?
WELL...YEAH. BUT AS SOON AS THEY DO WE'LL POUNCE.
YOU PEOPLE ARE KILLING ME TODAY.
OH COOL YOUR JETS.
PLAN IS COLOSSUS MAKES WITH THE PUNCHY, I SLIP IN AND PLACE THE TRANSMITTER THEN YOU MAKE YOUR MAGIC.
EVER OCCUR TO ANY OF YOU THAT MY MAGIC ONLY SPREADS SO THIN?
NO.
THAT'S IT. WE'RE THROUGH.

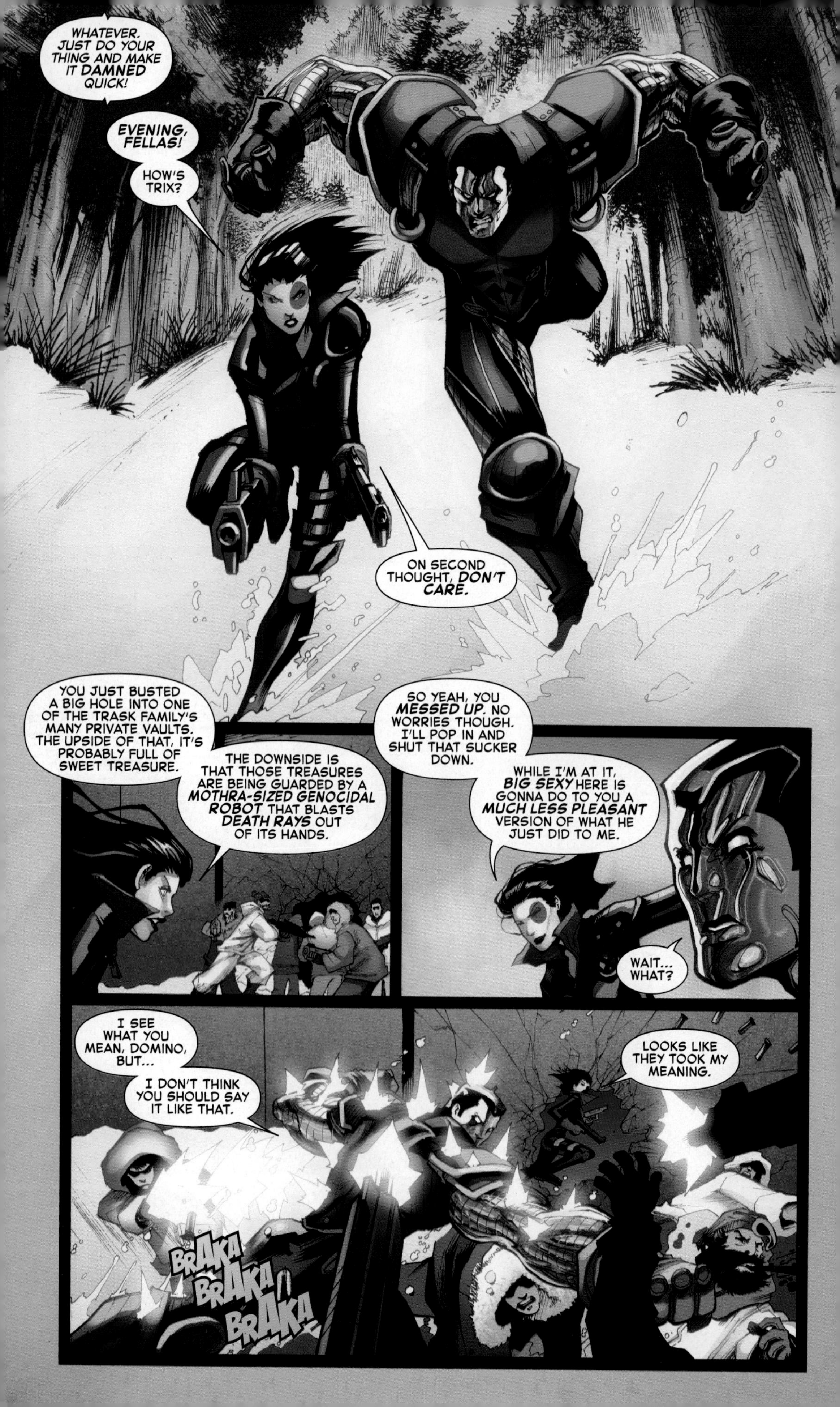
WHATEVER. JUST DO YOUR THING AND MAKE IT DAMNED QUICK!
EVENING, FELLAS!
HOW'S TRIX?
ON SECOND THOUGHT, DON'T CARE.
YOU JUST BUSTED A BIG HOLE INTO ONE OF THE TRASK FAMILY'S MANY PRIVATE VAULTS. THE UPSIDE OF THAT, IT'S PROBABLY FULL OF SWEET TREASURE.
THE DOWNSIDE IS THAT THOSE TREASURES ARE BEING GUARDED BY A MOTHRA-SIZED GENOCIDAL ROBOT THAT BLASTS DEATH RAYS OUT OF ITS HANDS.
SO YEAH, YOU MESSED UP. NO WORRIES THOUGH. I'LL POP IN AND SHUT THAT SUCKER DOWN.
WHILE I'M AT IT, BIG SEXY HERE IS GONNA DO TO YOU A MUCH LESS PLEASANT VERSION OF WHAT HE JUST DID TO ME.
WAIT... WHAT?
I SEE WHAT YOU MEAN, DOMINO, BUT...
I DON'T THINK YOU SHOULD SAY IT LIKE THAT.
LOOKS LIKE THEY TOOK MY MEANING.
BRAKA
BRAKA
BRAKA

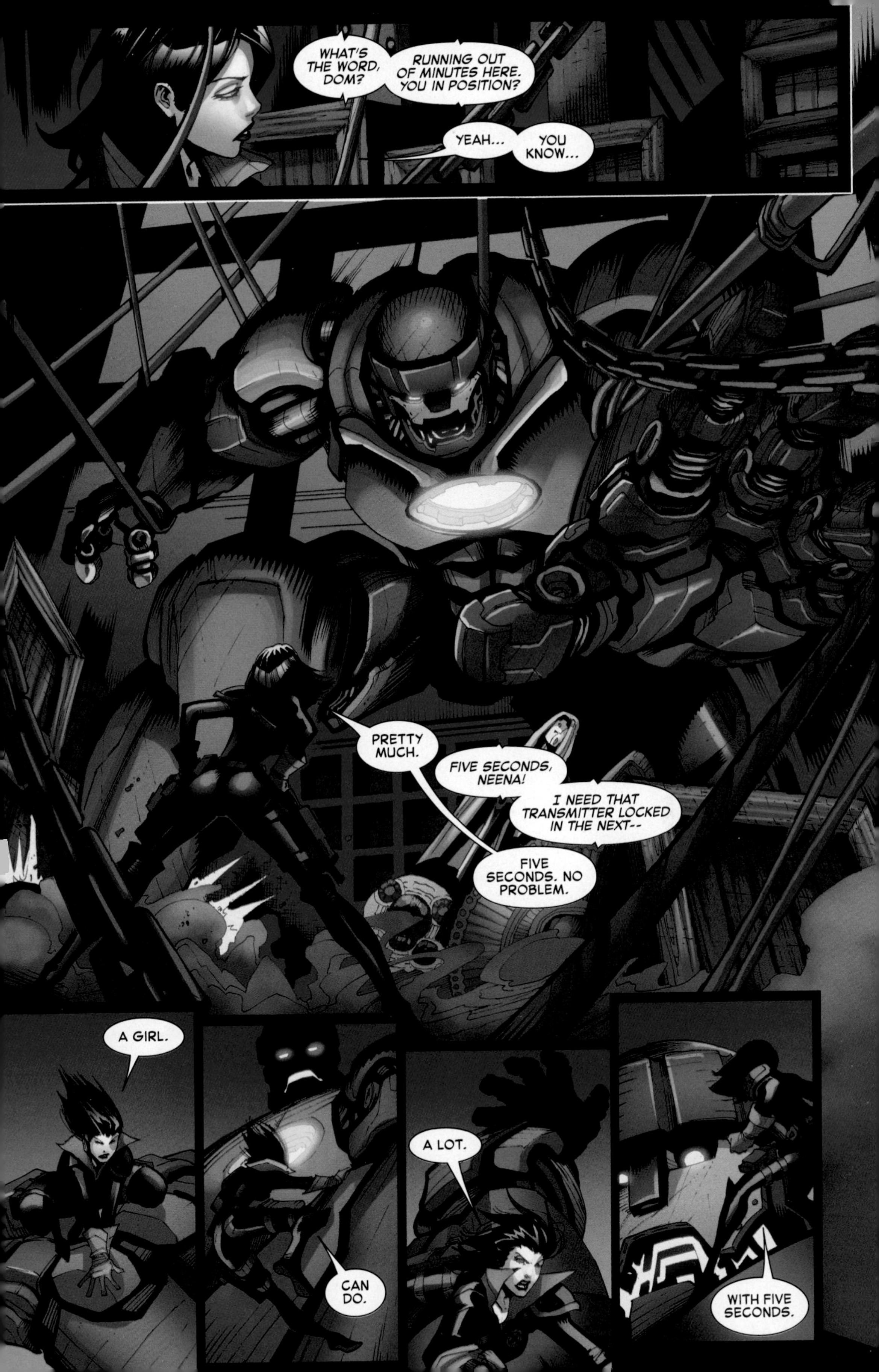

WHAT'S THE WORD, DOM?
RUNNING OUT OF MINUTES HERE. YOU IN POSITION?
YEAH... YOU KNOW...
PRETTY MUCH.
FIVE SECONDS, NEENA!
I NEED THAT TRANSMITTER LOCKED IN THE NEXT--
FIVE SECONDS. NO PROBLEM.
A GIRL.
CAN DO.
A LOT.
WITH FIVE SECONDS.

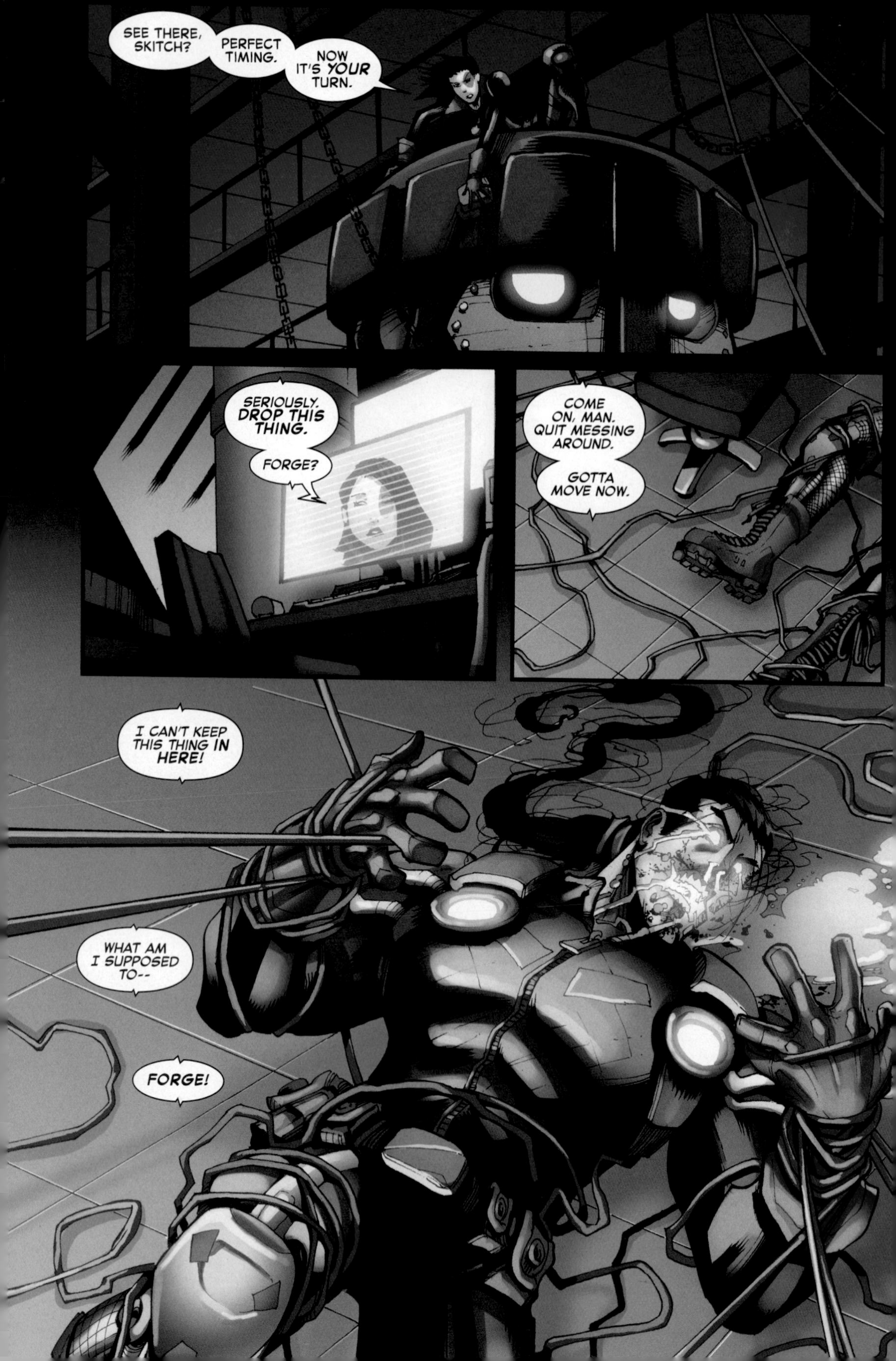
SEE THERE, SKITCH?
PERFECT TIMING.
NOW IT'S *YOUR* TURN.
SERIOUSLY. **DROP THIS THING.**
FORGE?
COME ON, MAN. QUIT MESSING AROUND.
GOTTA MOVE NOW.
I CAN'T KEEP THIS THING **IN HERE!**
WHAT AM I SUPPOSED TO--
FORGE!

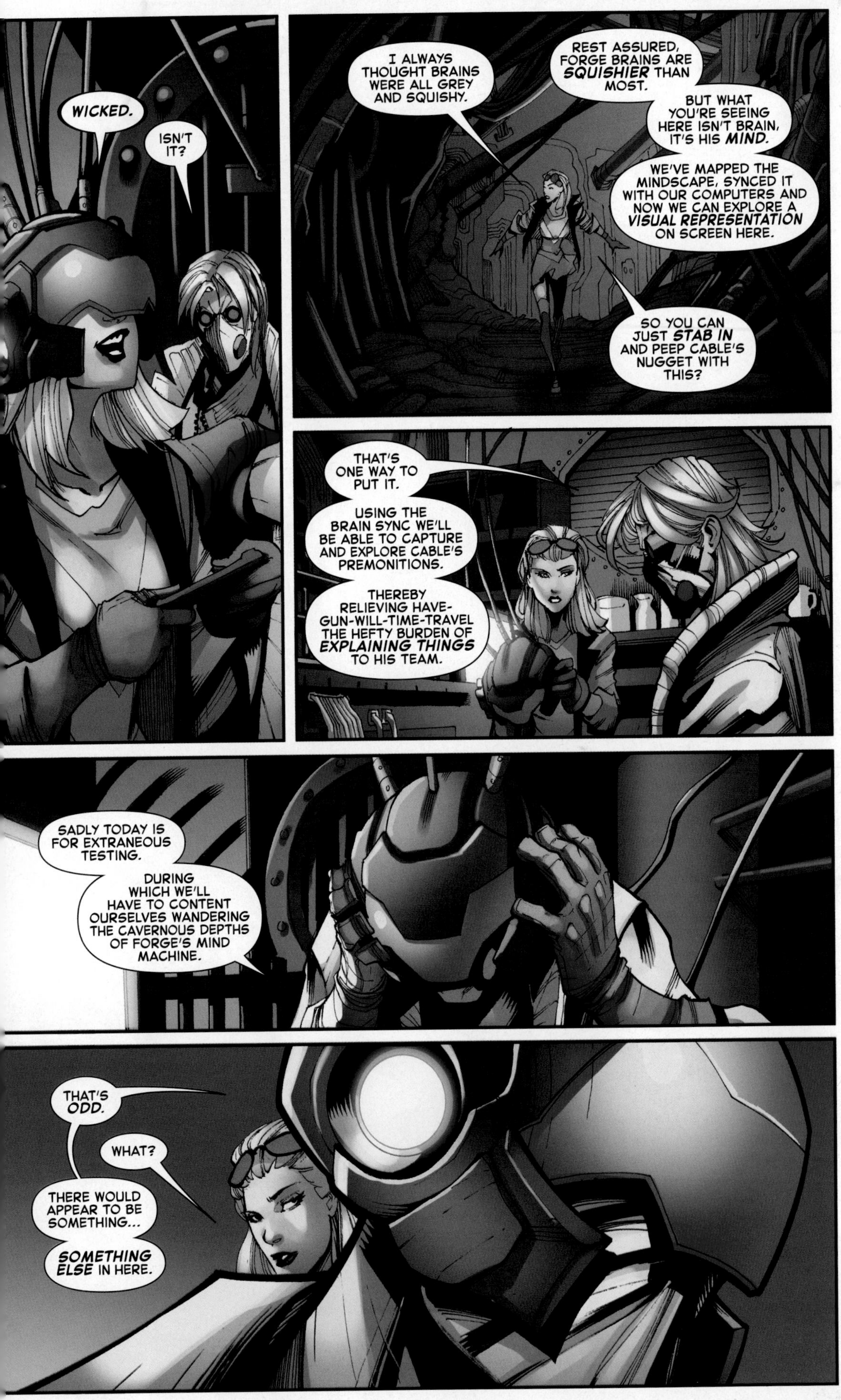
WICKED.
ISN'T IT?
I ALWAYS THOUGHT BRAINS WERE ALL GREY AND SQUISHY.
REST ASSURED, FORGE BRAINS ARE SQUISHIER THAN MOST.
BUT WHAT YOU'RE SEEING HERE ISN'T BRAIN, IT'S HIS MIND.
WE'VE MAPPED THE MINDSCAPE, SYNCED IT WITH OUR COMPUTERS AND NOW WE CAN EXPLORE A VISUAL REPRESENTATION ON SCREEN HERE.
SO YOU CAN JUST STAB IN AND PEEP CABLE'S NUGGET WITH THIS?
THAT'S ONE WAY TO PUT IT.
USING THE BRAIN SYNC WE'LL BE ABLE TO CAPTURE AND EXPLORE CABLE'S PREMONITIONS.
THEREBY RELIEVING HAVE-GUN-WILL-TIME-TRAVEL THE HEFTY BURDEN OF EXPLAINING THINGS TO HIS TEAM.
SADLY TODAY IS FOR EXTRANEOUS TESTING.
DURING WHICH WE'LL HAVE TO CONTENT OURSELVES WANDERING THE CAVERNOUS DEPTHS OF FORGE'S MIND MACHINE.
THAT'S ODD.
WHAT?
THERE WOULD APPEAR TO BE SOMETHING...
SOMETHING ELSE IN HERE.

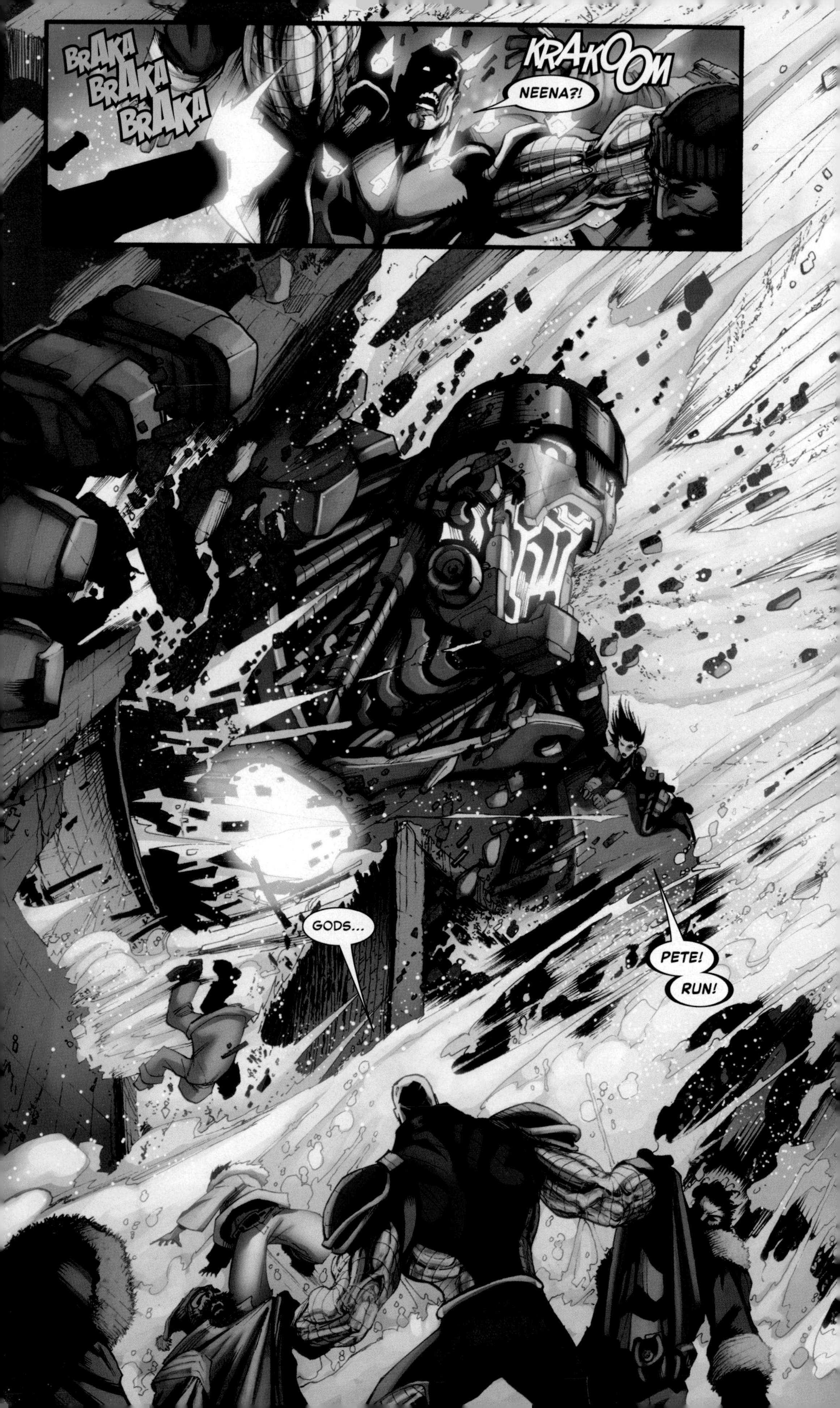
BRAKA
BRAKA
BRAKA
KRAKOOM
NEENA?!
GODS...
PETE!
RUN!

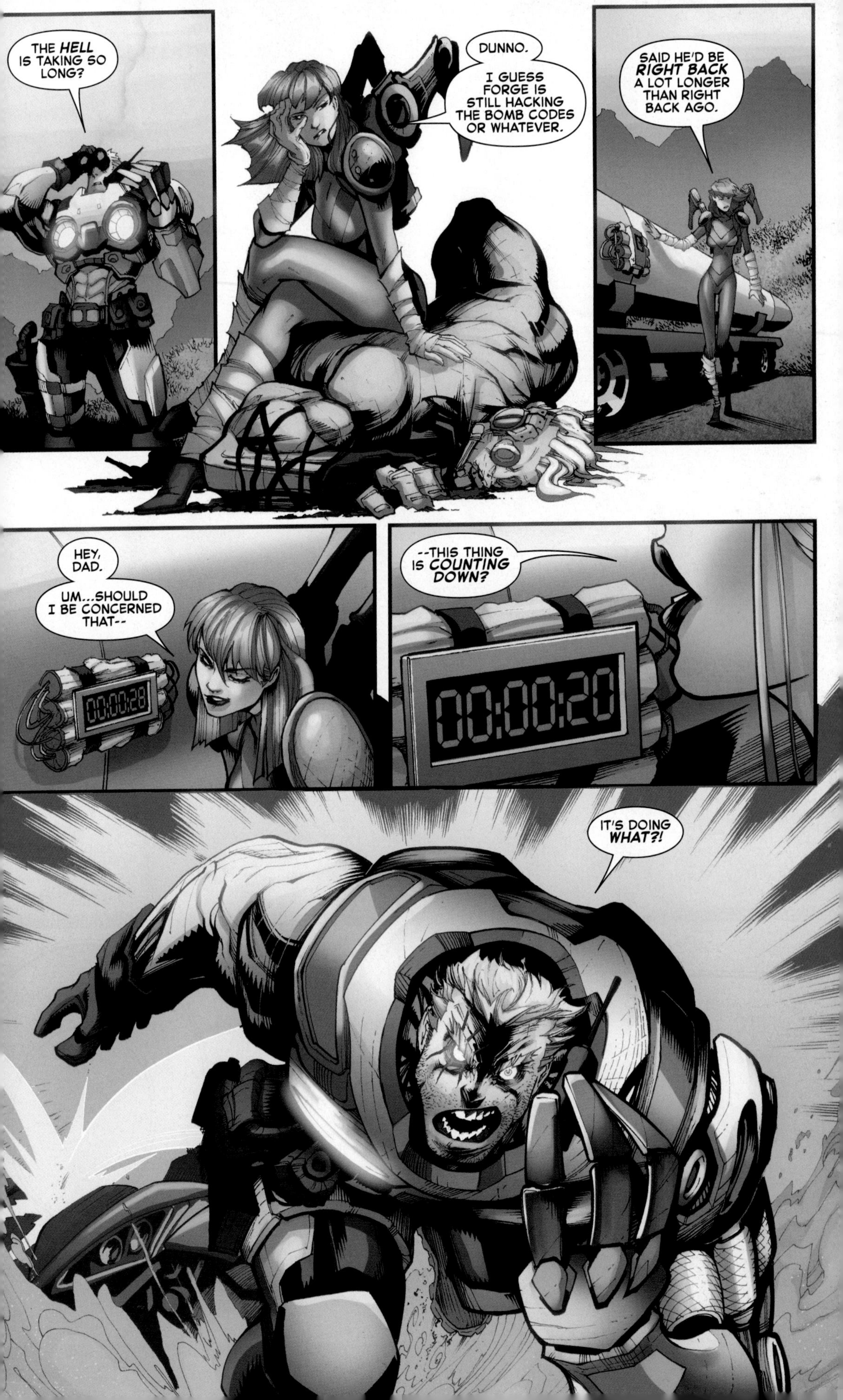
THE HELL IS TAKING SO LONG?
DUNNO.
I GUESS FORGE IS STILL HACKING THE BOMB CODES OR WHATEVER.
SAID HE'D BE RIGHT BACK A LOT LONGER THAN RIGHT BACK AGO.
HEY, DAD.
UM...SHOULD I BE CONCERNED THAT--
00:00:28
--THIS THING IS COUNTING DOWN?
00:00:20
IT'S DOING WHAT?!

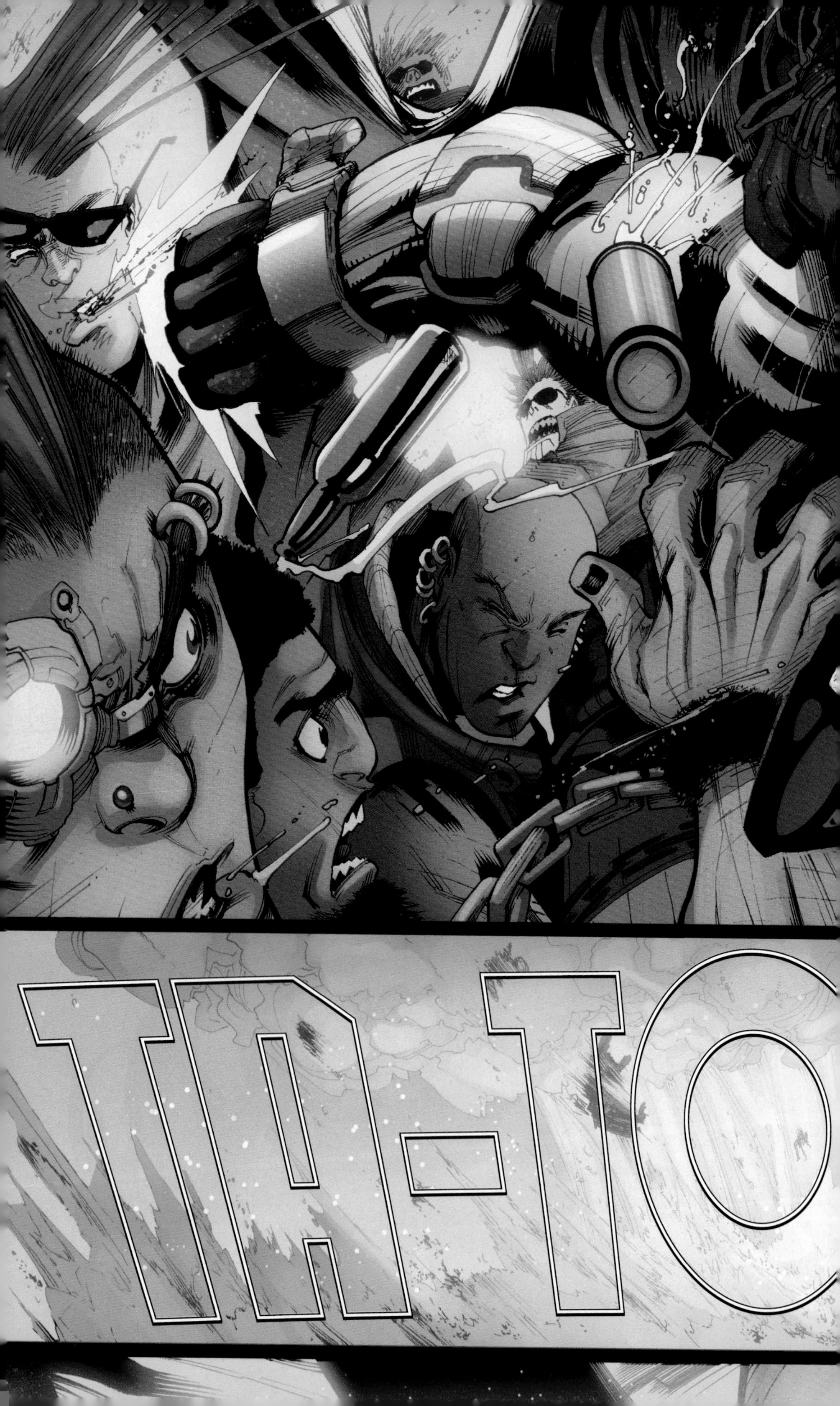
TA-TO

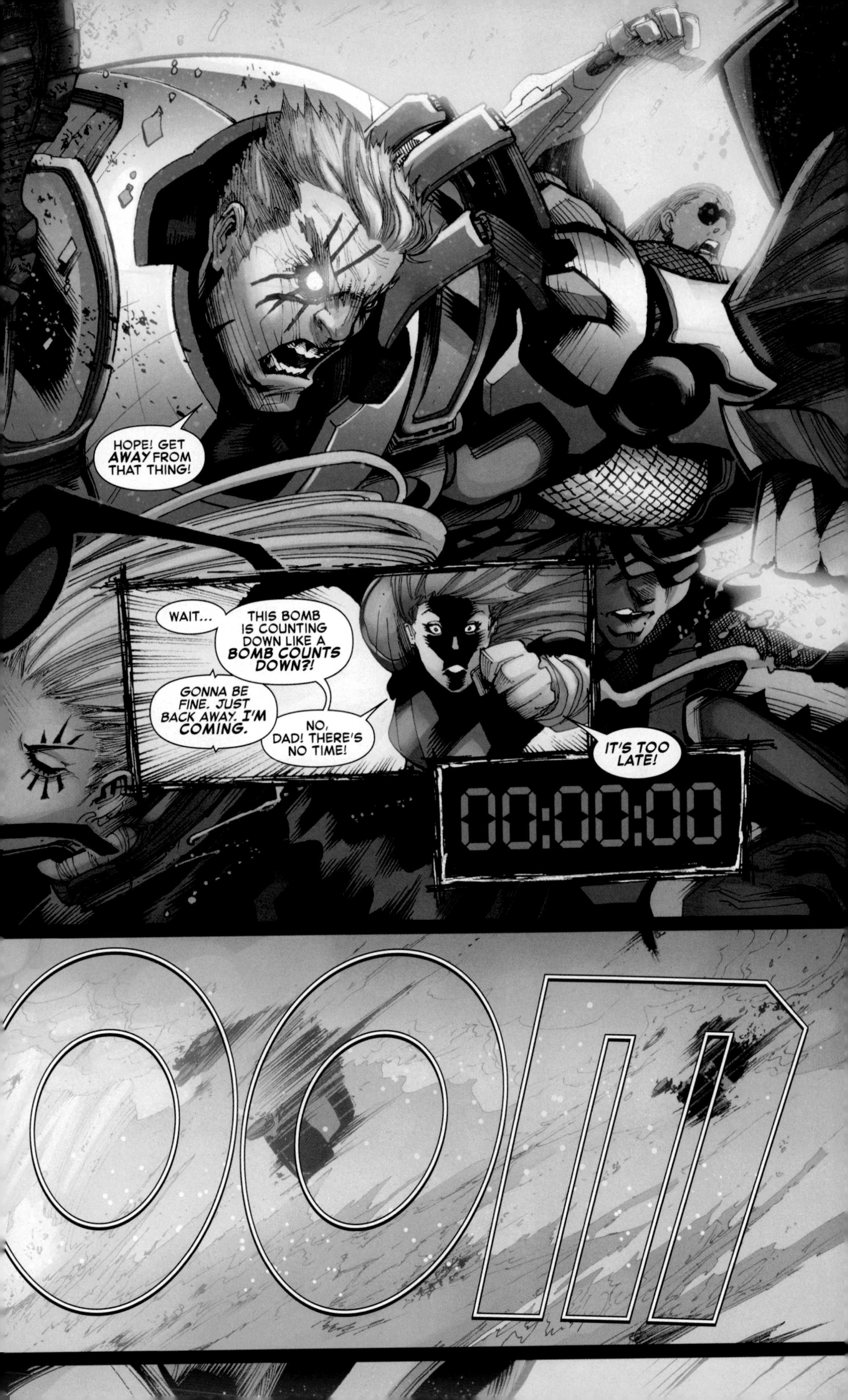
HOPE! GET AWAY FROM THAT THING!
WAIT...
THIS BOMB IS COUNTING DOWN LIKE A BOMB COUNTS DOWN?!
GONNA BE FINE. JUST BACK AWAY. I'M COMING.
NO, DAD! THERE'S NO TIME!
IT'S TOO LATE!
00:00:00
OOM

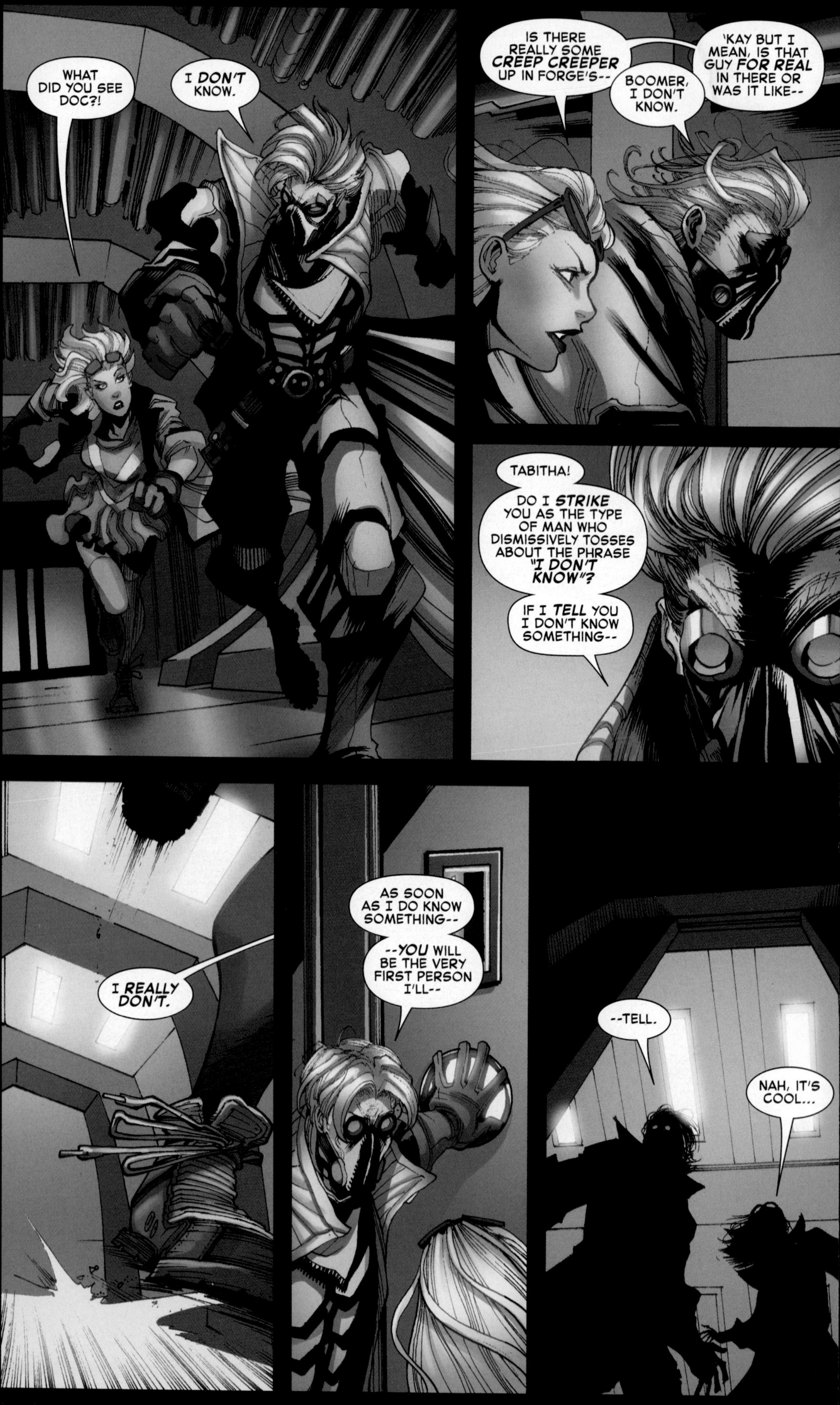

WHAT DID YOU SEE DOC?!
I *DON'T* KNOW.
IS THERE REALLY SOME ***CREEP CREEPER*** UP IN FORGE'S--
BOOMER, I DON'T KNOW.
'KAY BUT I MEAN, IS THAT GUY ***FOR REAL*** IN THERE OR WAS IT LIKE--
TABITHA!
DO I ***STRIKE*** YOU AS THE TYPE OF MAN WHO DISMISSIVELY TOSSES ABOUT THE PHRASE ***"I DON'T KNOW"?***
IF I ***TELL*** YOU I DON'T KNOW SOMETHING--
I ***REALLY DON'T.***
AS SOON AS I DO KNOW SOMETHING--
--***YOU*** WILL BE THE VERY FIRST PERSON I'LL--
--TELL.
NAH, IT'S COOL...

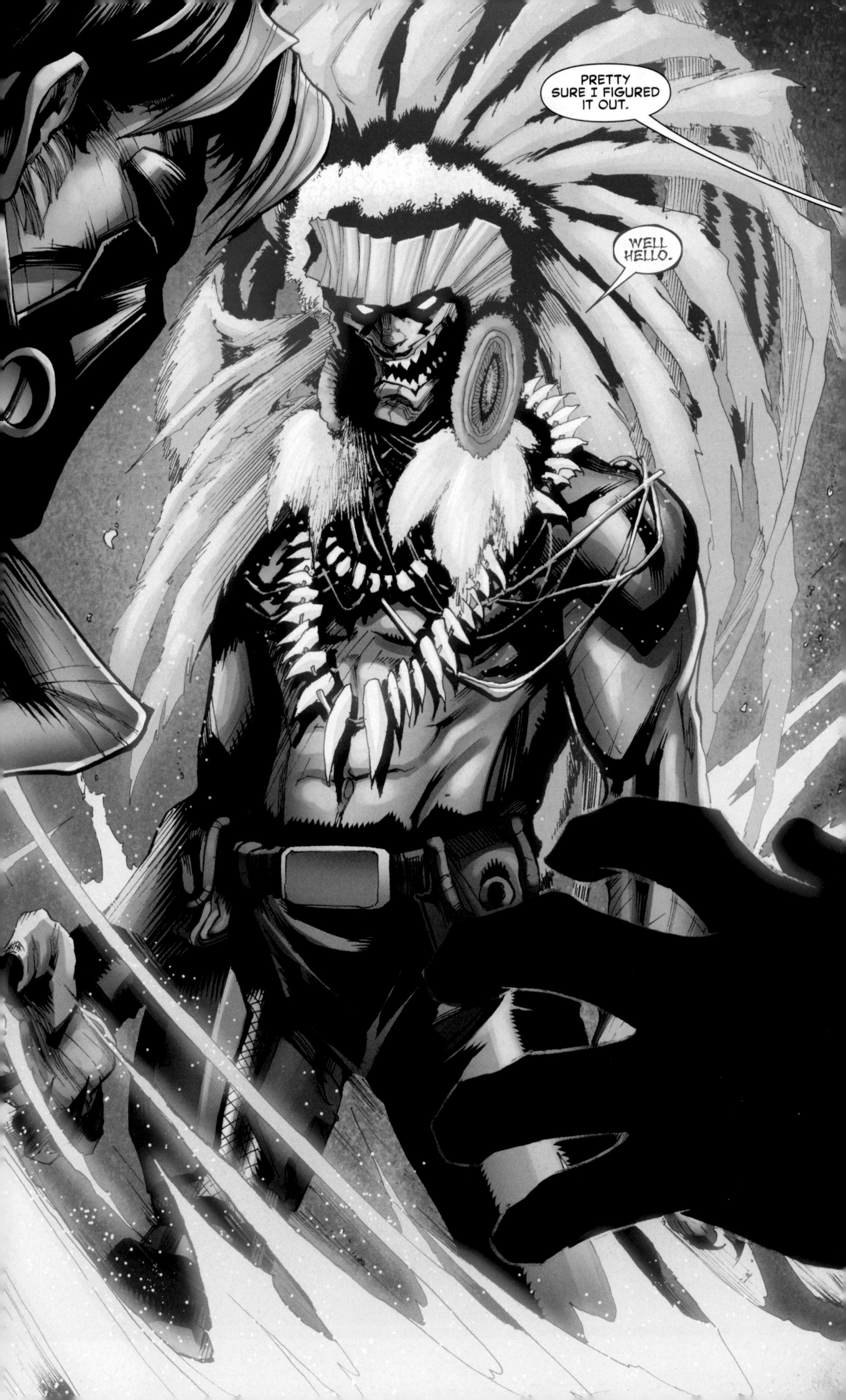
PRETTY SURE I FIGURED IT OUT.
WELL HELLO.

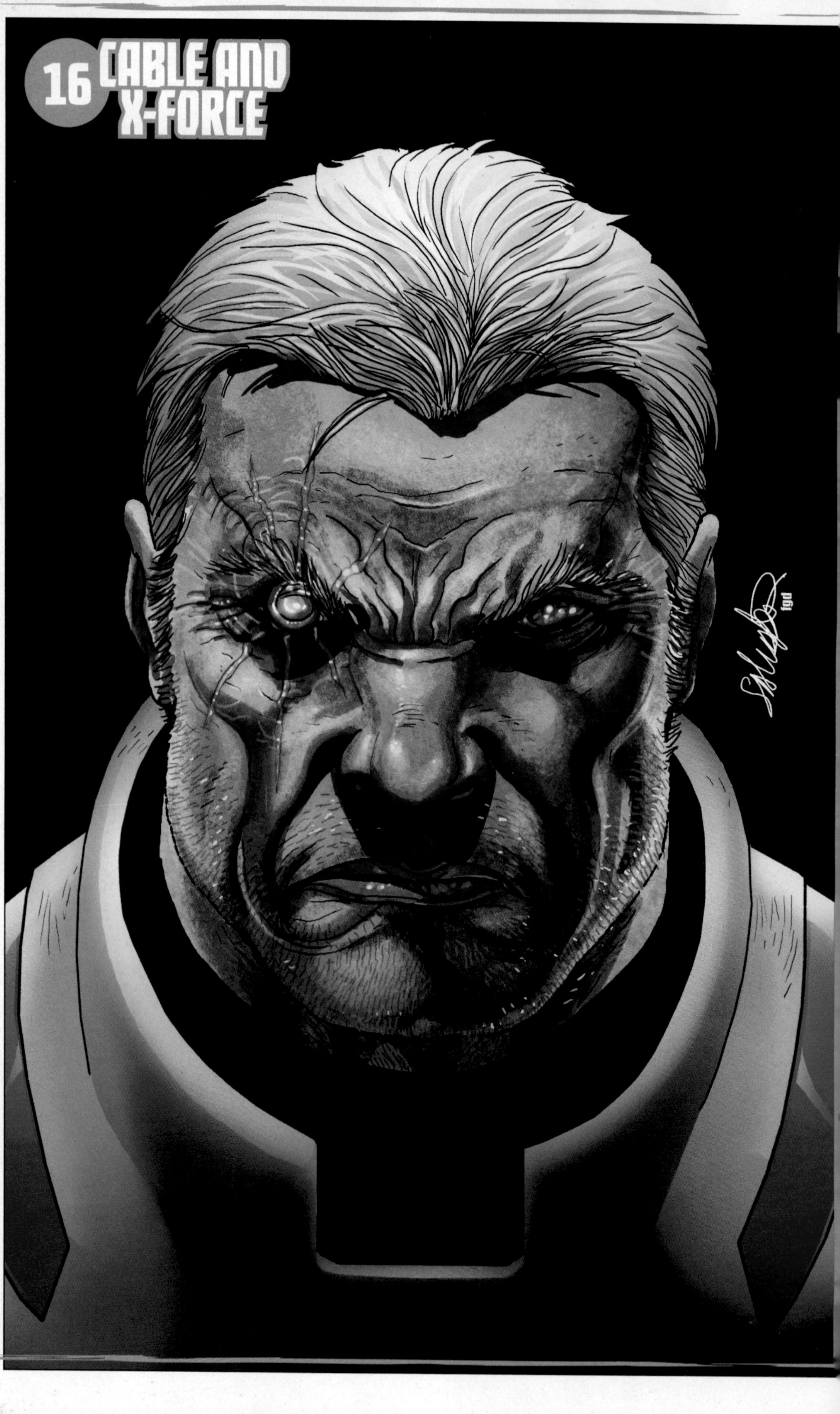
16
CABLE AND
X-FORCE

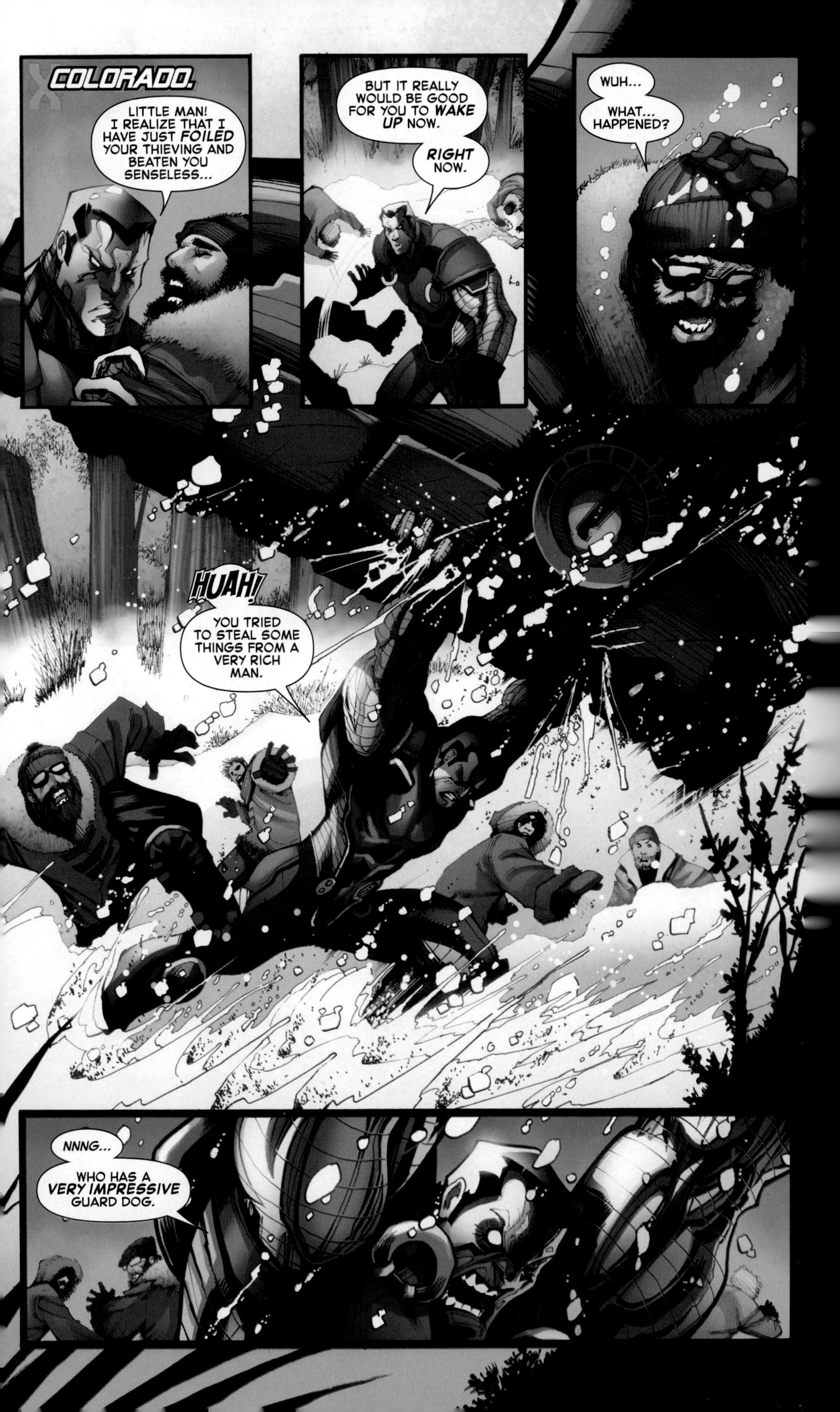
COLORADO.
LITTLE MAN! I REALIZE THAT I HAVE JUST FOILED YOUR THIEVING AND BEATEN YOU SENSELESS...
BUT IT REALLY WOULD BE GOOD FOR YOU TO WAKE UP NOW.
RIGHT NOW.
WUH...
WHAT... HAPPENED?
HUAH!
YOU TRIED TO STEAL SOME THINGS FROM A VERY RICH MAN.
NNNG...
WHO HAS A VERY IMPRESSIVE GUARD DOG.

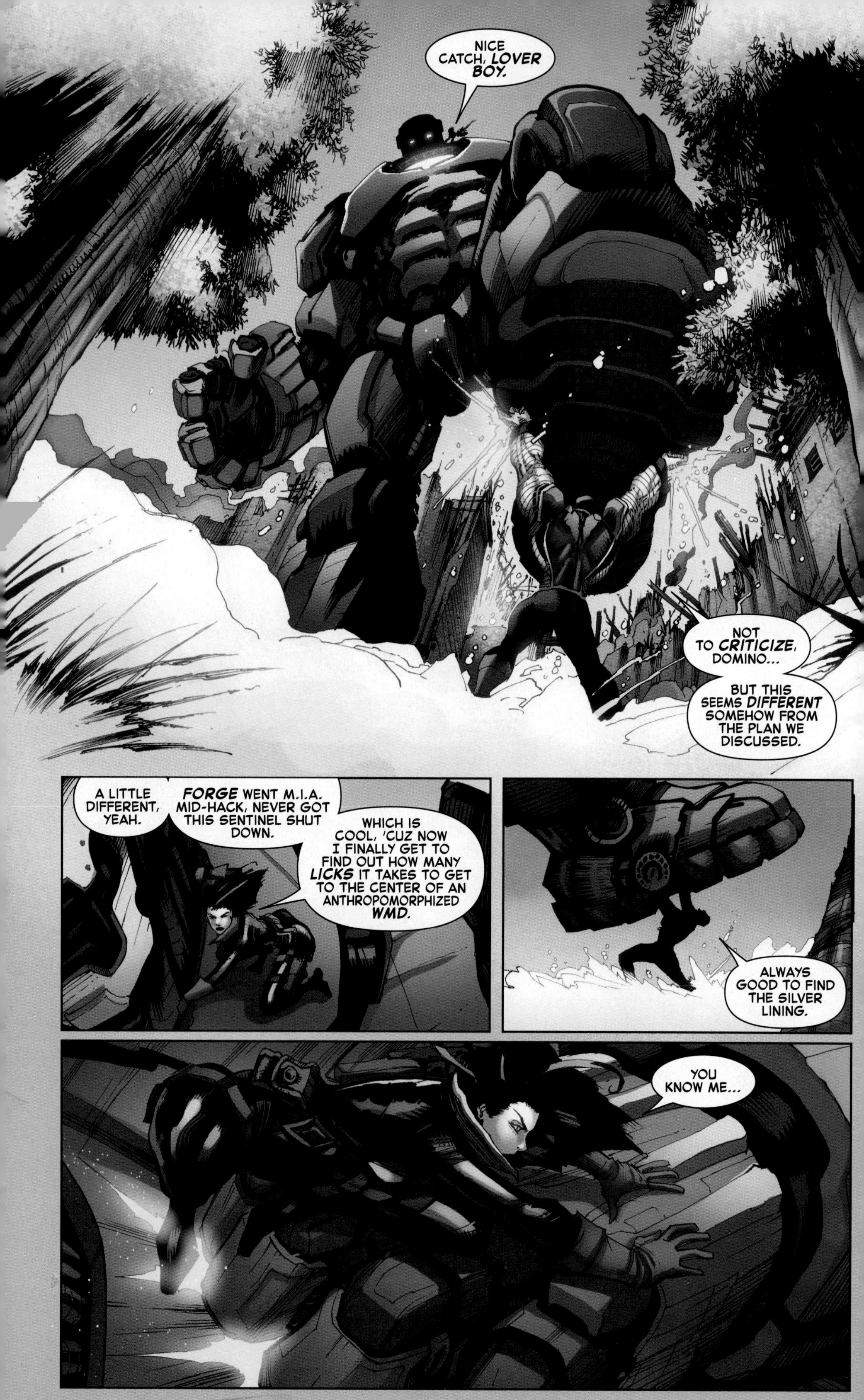
NICE CATCH, LOVER BOY.
NOT TO CRITICIZE, DOMINO...
BUT THIS SEEMS DIFFERENT SOMEHOW FROM THE PLAN WE DISCUSSED.
A LITTLE DIFFERENT, YEAH.
FORGE WENT M.I.A. MID-HACK, NEVER GOT THIS SENTINEL SHUT DOWN.
WHICH IS COOL, 'CUZ NOW I FINALLY GET TO FIND OUT HOW MANY LICKS IT TAKES TO GET TO THE CENTER OF AN ANTHROPOMORPHIZED WMD.
ALWAYS GOOD TO FIND THE SILVER LINING.
YOU KNOW ME...

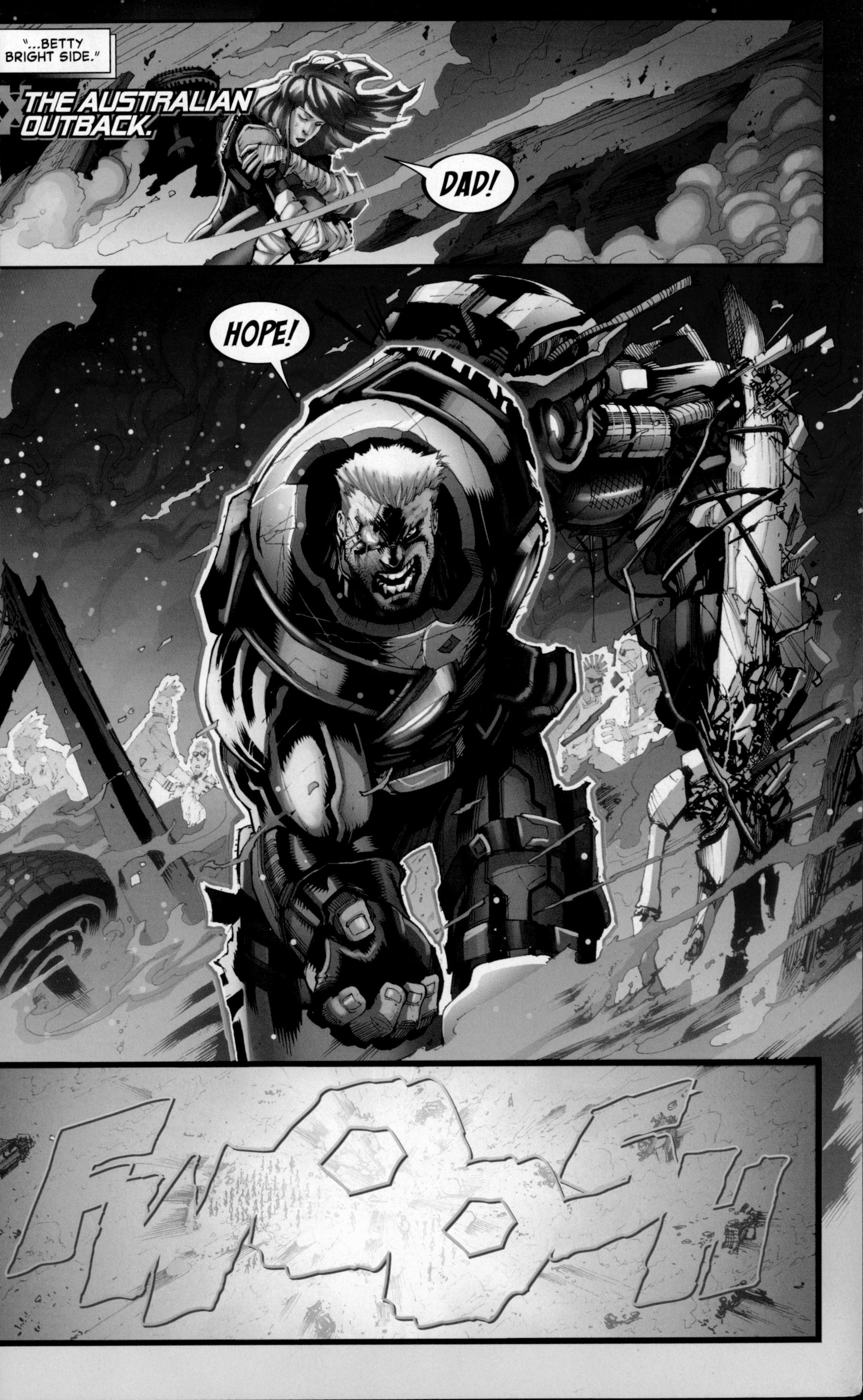
"...BETTY BRIGHT SIDE."
THE AUSTRALIAN OUTBACK.
DAD!
HOPE!

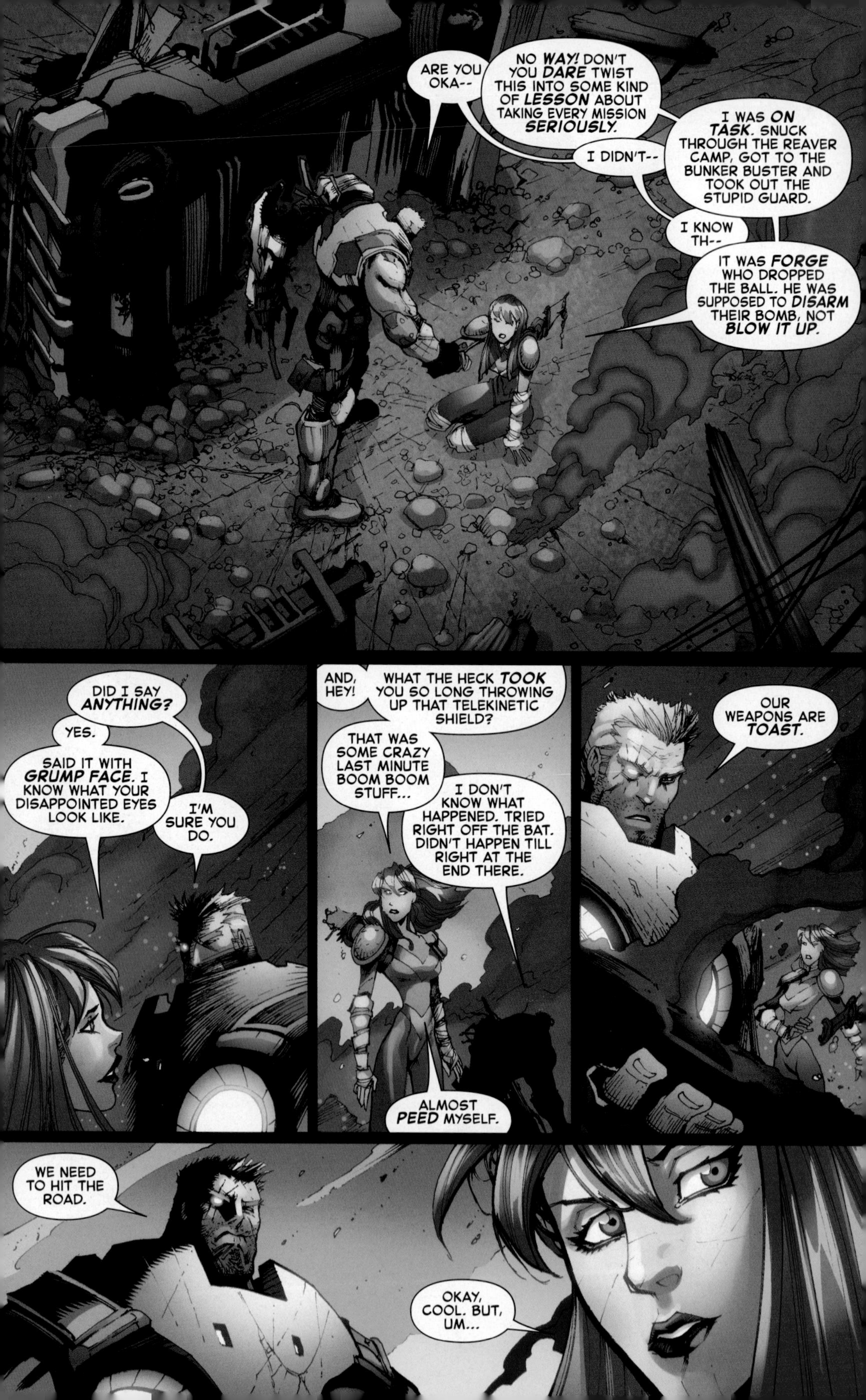
ARE YOU OKA--
NO WAY! DON'T YOU DARE TWIST THIS INTO SOME KIND OF LESSON ABOUT TAKING EVERY MISSION SERIOUSLY.
I DIDN'T--
I WAS ON TASK. SNUCK THROUGH THE REAVER CAMP, GOT TO THE BUNKER BUSTER AND TOOK OUT THE STUPID GUARD.
I KNOW TH--
IT WAS FORGE WHO DROPPED THE BALL. HE WAS SUPPOSED TO DISARM THEIR BOMB, NOT BLOW IT UP.
DID I SAY ANYTHING?
YES.
SAID IT WITH GRUMP FACE. I KNOW WHAT YOUR DISAPPOINTED EYES LOOK LIKE.
I'M SURE YOU DO.
AND, HEY!
WHAT THE HECK TOOK YOU SO LONG THROWING UP THAT TELEKINETIC SHIELD?
THAT WAS SOME CRAZY LAST MINUTE BOOM BOOM STUFF...
I DON'T KNOW WHAT HAPPENED. TRIED RIGHT OFF THE BAT. DIDN'T HAPPEN TILL RIGHT AT THE END THERE.
ALMOST PEED MYSELF.
OUR WEAPONS ARE TOAST.
WE NEED TO HIT THE ROAD.
OKAY, COOL. BUT, UM...

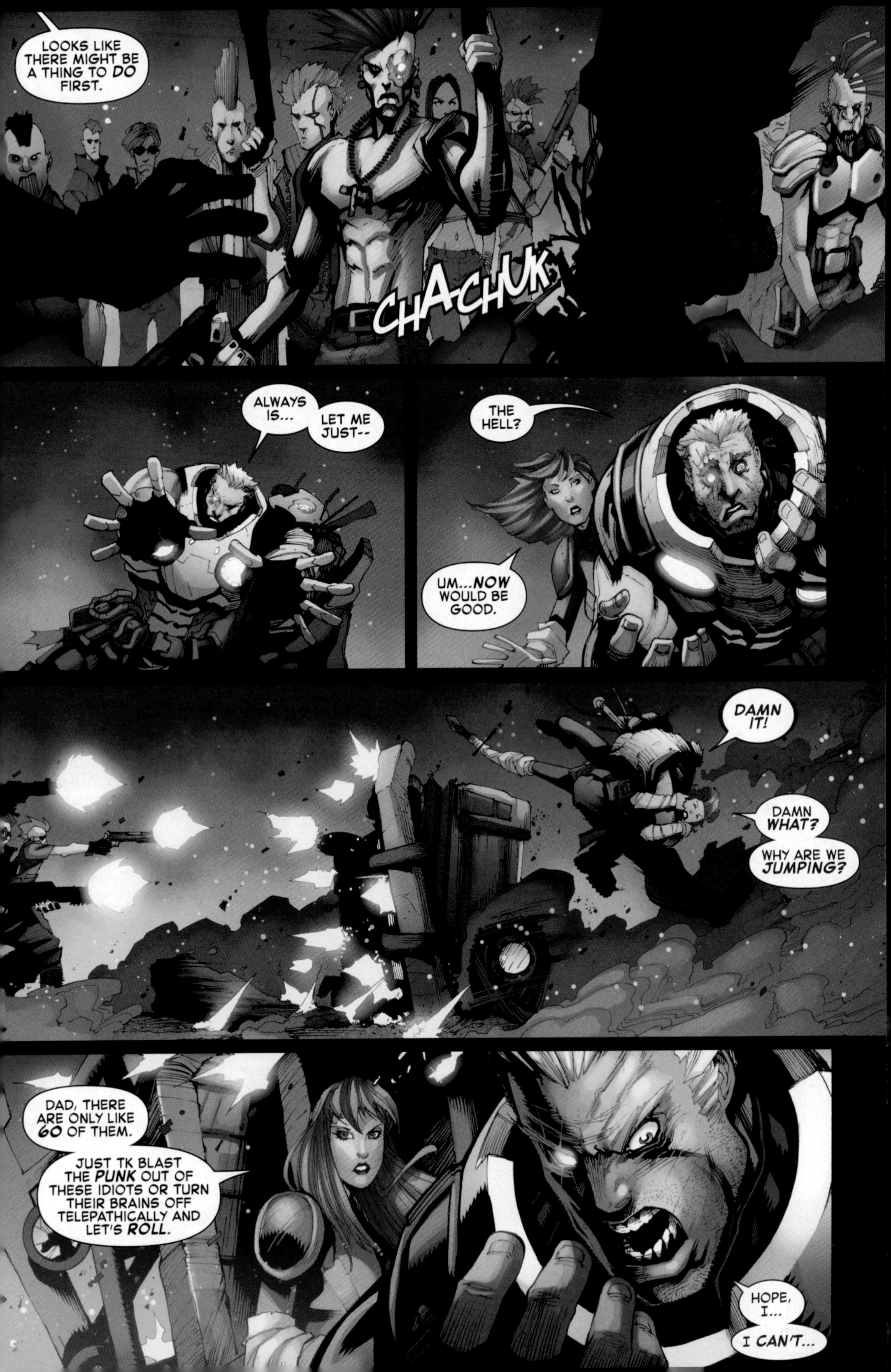
LOOKS LIKE THERE MIGHT BE A THING TO DO FIRST.
CHA-CHUK
ALWAYS IS...
LET ME JUST--
THE HELL?
UM...NOW WOULD BE GOOD.
DAMN IT!
DAMN WHAT?
WHY ARE WE JUMPING?
DAD, THERE ARE ONLY LIKE 60 OF THEM.
JUST TK BLAST THE PUNK OUT OF THESE IDIOTS OR TURN THEIR BRAINS OFF TELEPATHICALLY AND LET'S ROLL.
HOPE, I...
I CAN'T...

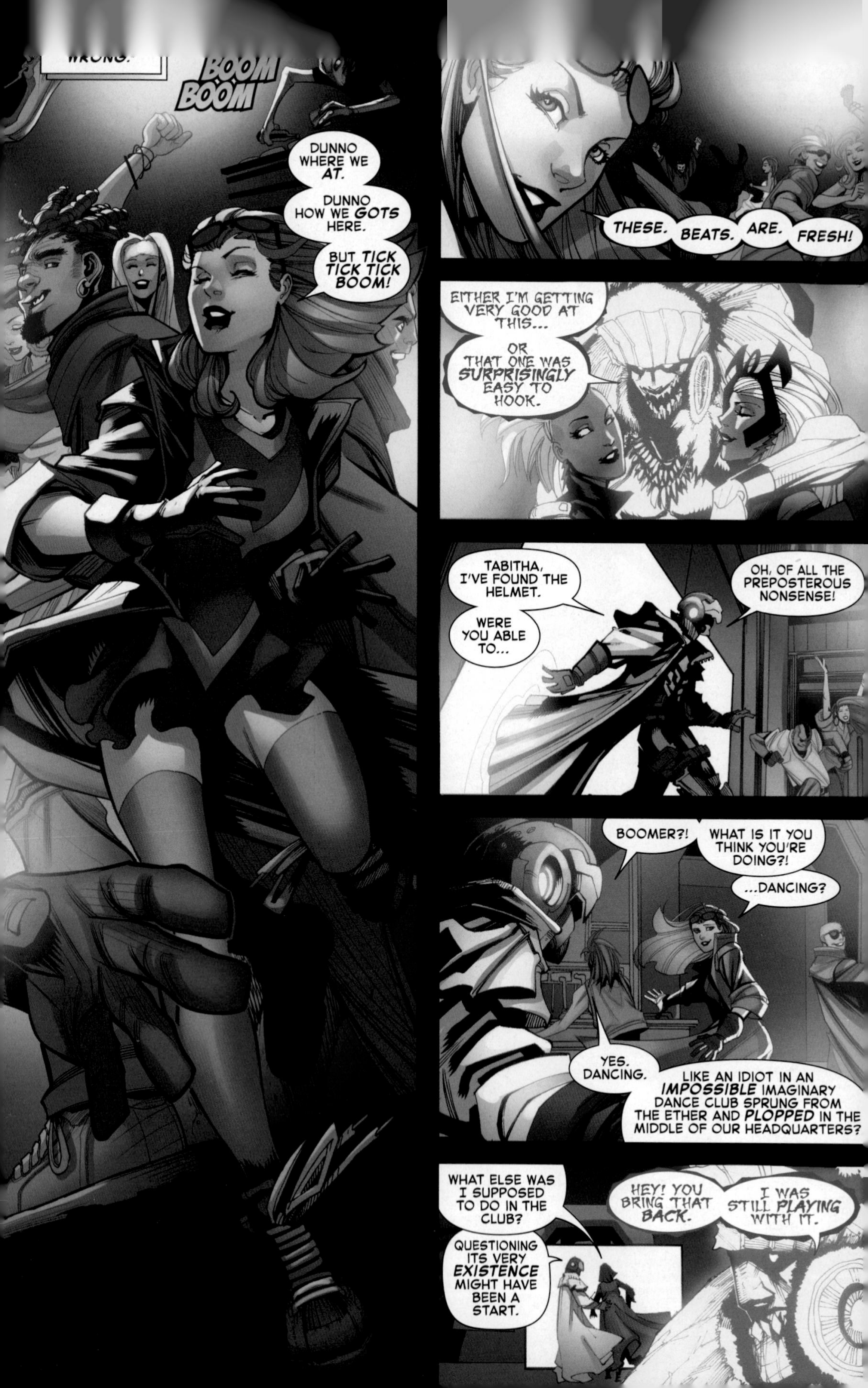
WRONG.
BOOM BOOM
DUNNO WHERE WE AT.
DUNNO HOW WE GOTS HERE.
BUT TICK TICK TICK BOOM!
THESE.
BEATS.
ARE.
FRESH!
EITHER I'M GETTING VERY GOOD AT THIS...
OR THAT ONE WAS SURPRISINGLY EASY TO HOOK.
TABITHA, I'VE FOUND THE HELMET.
WERE YOU ABLE TO...
OH, OF ALL THE PREPOSTEROUS NONSENSE!
BOOMER?!
WHAT IS IT YOU THINK YOU'RE DOING?!
...DANCING?
YES. DANCING.
LIKE AN IDIOT IN AN IMPOSSIBLE IMAGINARY DANCE CLUB SPRUNG FROM THE ETHER AND PLOPPED IN THE MIDDLE OF OUR HEADQUARTERS?
WHAT ELSE WAS I SUPPOSED TO DO IN THE CLUB?
QUESTIONING ITS VERY EXISTENCE MIGHT HAVE BEEN A START.
HEY! YOU BRING THAT BACK.
I WAS STILL PLAYING WITH IT.

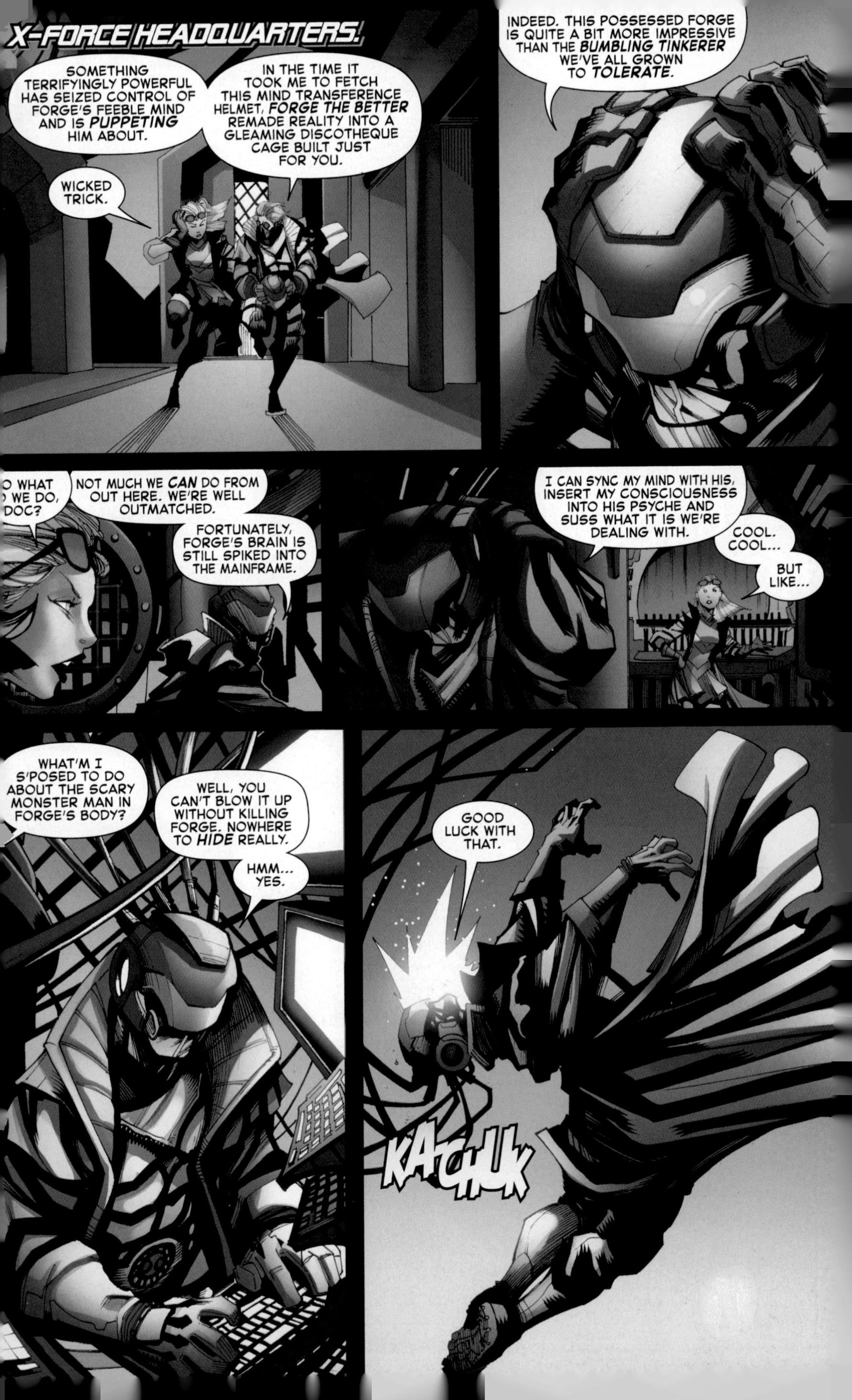
X-FORCE HEADQUARTERS.
SOMETHING TERRIFYINGLY POWERFUL HAS SEIZED CONTROL OF FORGE'S FEEBLE MIND AND IS PUPPETING HIM ABOUT.
IN THE TIME IT TOOK ME TO FETCH THIS MIND TRANSFERENCE HELMET, FORGE THE BETTER REMADE REALITY INTO A GLEAMING DISCOTHEQUE CAGE BUILT JUST FOR YOU.
WICKED TRICK.
INDEED. THIS POSSESSED FORGE IS QUITE A BIT MORE IMPRESSIVE THAN THE BUMBLING TINKERER WE'VE ALL GROWN TO TOLERATE.
WE DO, DOC?
NOT MUCH WE CAN DO FROM OUT HERE. WE'RE WELL OUTMATCHED.
FORTUNATELY, FORGE'S BRAIN IS STILL SPIKED INTO THE MAINFRAME.
I CAN SYNC MY MIND WITH HIS, INSERT MY CONSCIOUSNESS INTO HIS PSYCHE AND SUSS WHAT IT IS WE'RE DEALING WITH.
COOL. COOL...
BUT LIKE...
WHAT'M I S'POSED TO DO ABOUT THE SCARY MONSTER MAN IN FORGE'S BODY?
WELL, YOU CAN'T BLOW IT UP WITHOUT KILLING FORGE. NOWHERE TO HIDE REALLY.
HMM... YES.
GOOD LUCK WITH THAT.
KA-CHUK

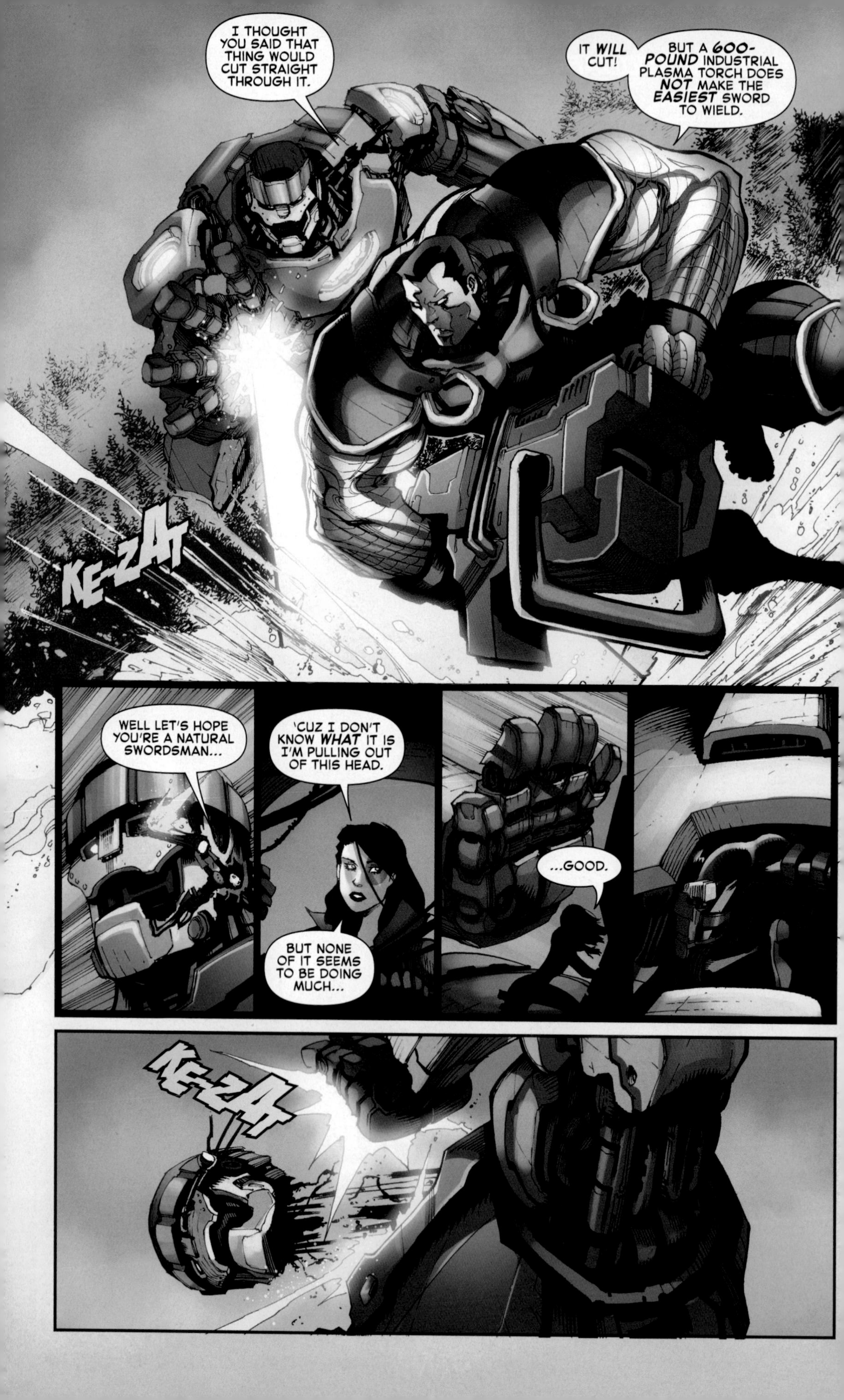
I THOUGHT YOU SAID THAT THING WOULD CUT STRAIGHT THROUGH IT.
IT WILL CUT!
BUT A 600-POUND INDUSTRIAL PLASMA TORCH DOES NOT MAKE THE EASIEST SWORD TO WIELD.
KE-ZAT
WELL LET'S HOPE YOU'RE A NATURAL SWORDSMAN...
'CUZ I DON'T KNOW WHAT IT IS I'M PULLING OUT OF THIS HEAD.
BUT NONE OF IT SEEMS TO BE DOING MUCH...
...GOOD.
KE-ZAT

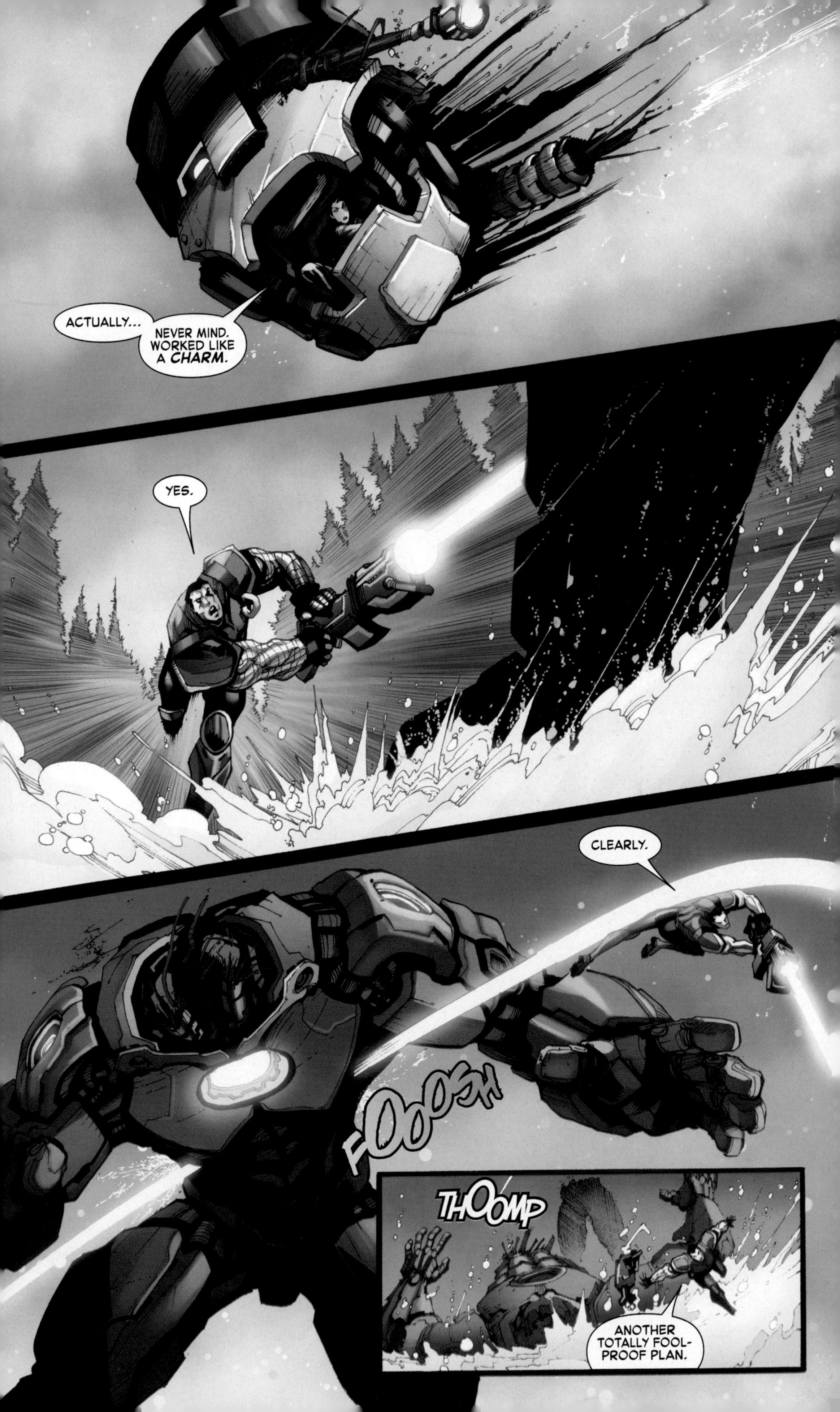
ACTUALLY...
NEVER MIND. WORKED LIKE A CHARM.
YES.
CLEARLY.
FOOOSH
THOOMP
ANOTHER TOTALLY FOOL-PROOF PLAN.

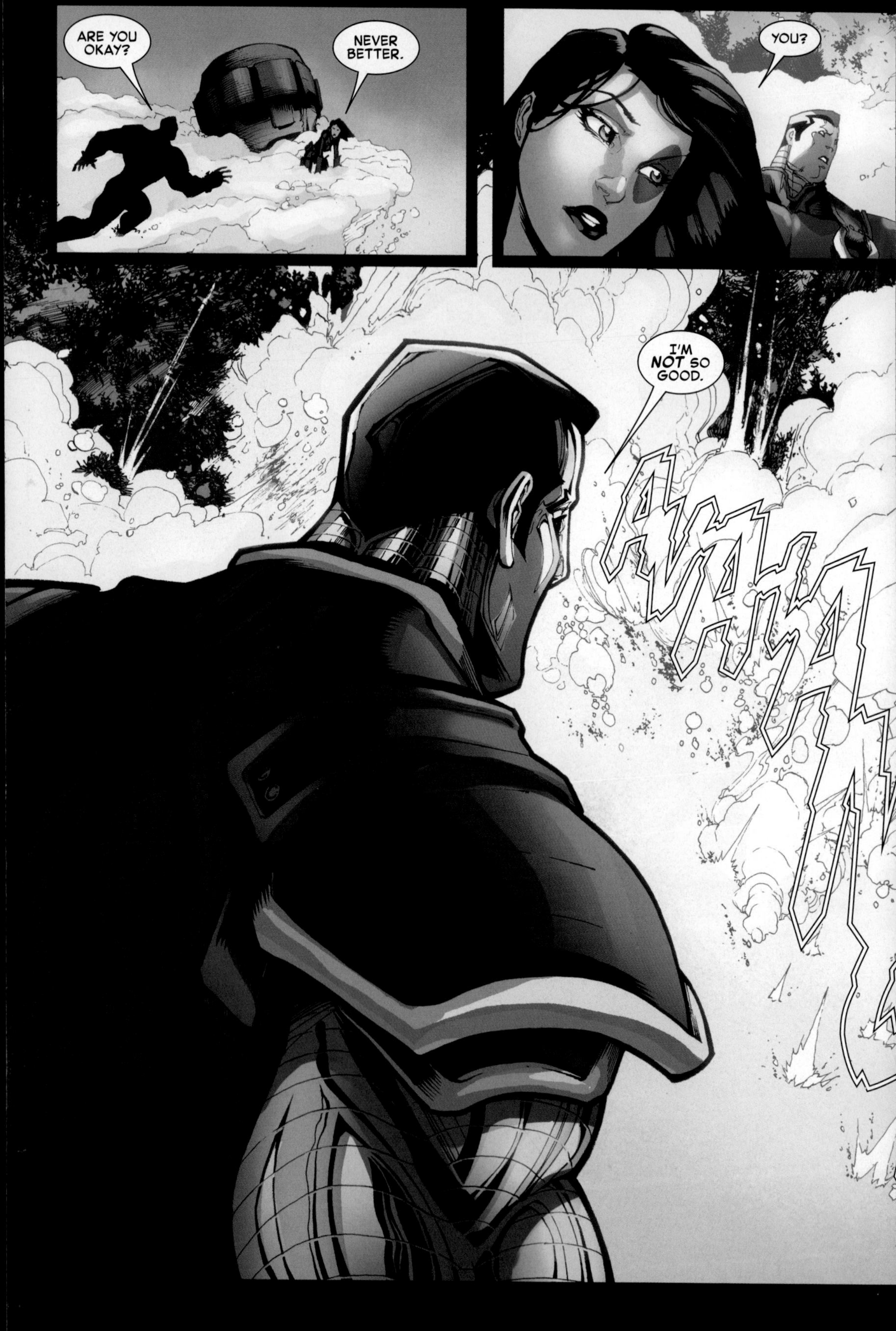
ARE YOU OKAY?
NEVER BETTER.
YOU?
I'M NOT SO GOOD.

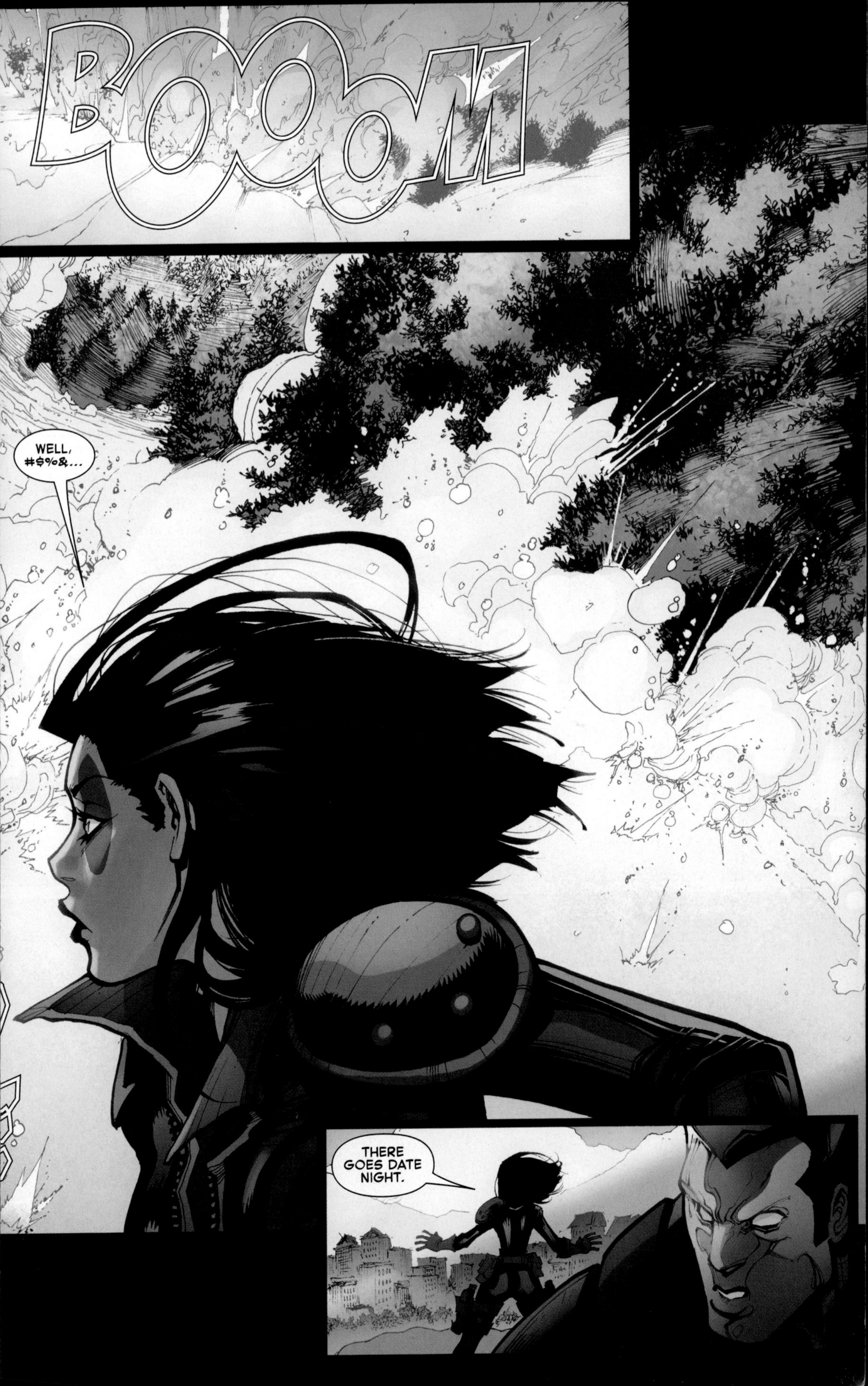
BOOOOM
WELL, #$%&...
THERE GOES DATE NIGHT.

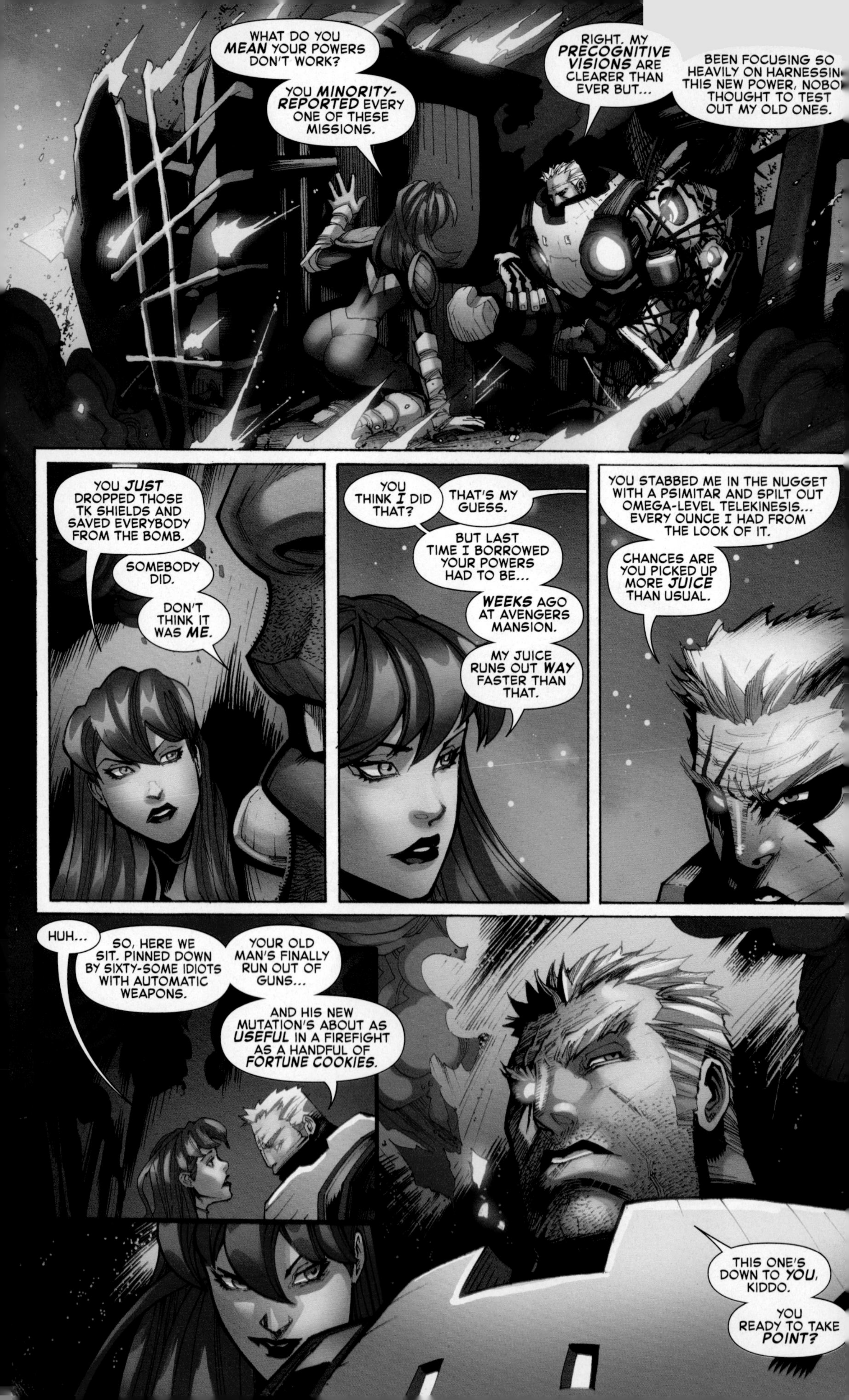
WHAT DO YOU MEAN YOUR POWERS DON'T WORK?
YOU MINORITY-REPORTED EVERY ONE OF THESE MISSIONS.
RIGHT. MY PRECOGNITIVE VISIONS ARE CLEARER THAN EVER BUT...
BEEN FOCUSING SO HEAVILY ON HARNESSIN THIS NEW POWER, NOBO THOUGHT TO TEST OUT MY OLD ONES.
YOU JUST DROPPED THOSE TK SHIELDS AND SAVED EVERYBODY FROM THE BOMB.
SOMEBODY DID.
DON'T THINK IT WAS ME.
YOU THINK I DID THAT?
THAT'S MY GUESS.
BUT LAST TIME I BORROWED YOUR POWERS HAD TO BE...
WEEKS AGO AT AVENGERS MANSION.
MY JUICE RUNS OUT WAY FASTER THAN THAT.
YOU STABBED ME IN THE NUGGET WITH A PSIMITAR AND SPILT OUT OMEGA-LEVEL TELEKINESIS... EVERY OUNCE I HAD FROM THE LOOK OF IT.
CHANCES ARE YOU PICKED UP MORE JUICE THAN USUAL.
HUH...
SO, HERE WE SIT. PINNED DOWN BY SIXTY-SOME IDIOTS WITH AUTOMATIC WEAPONS.
YOUR OLD MAN'S FINALLY RUN OUT OF GUNS...
AND HIS NEW MUTATION'S ABOUT AS USEFUL IN A FIREFIGHT AS A HANDFUL OF FORTUNE COOKIES.
THIS ONE'S DOWN TO YOU, KIDDO.
YOU READY TO TAKE POINT?

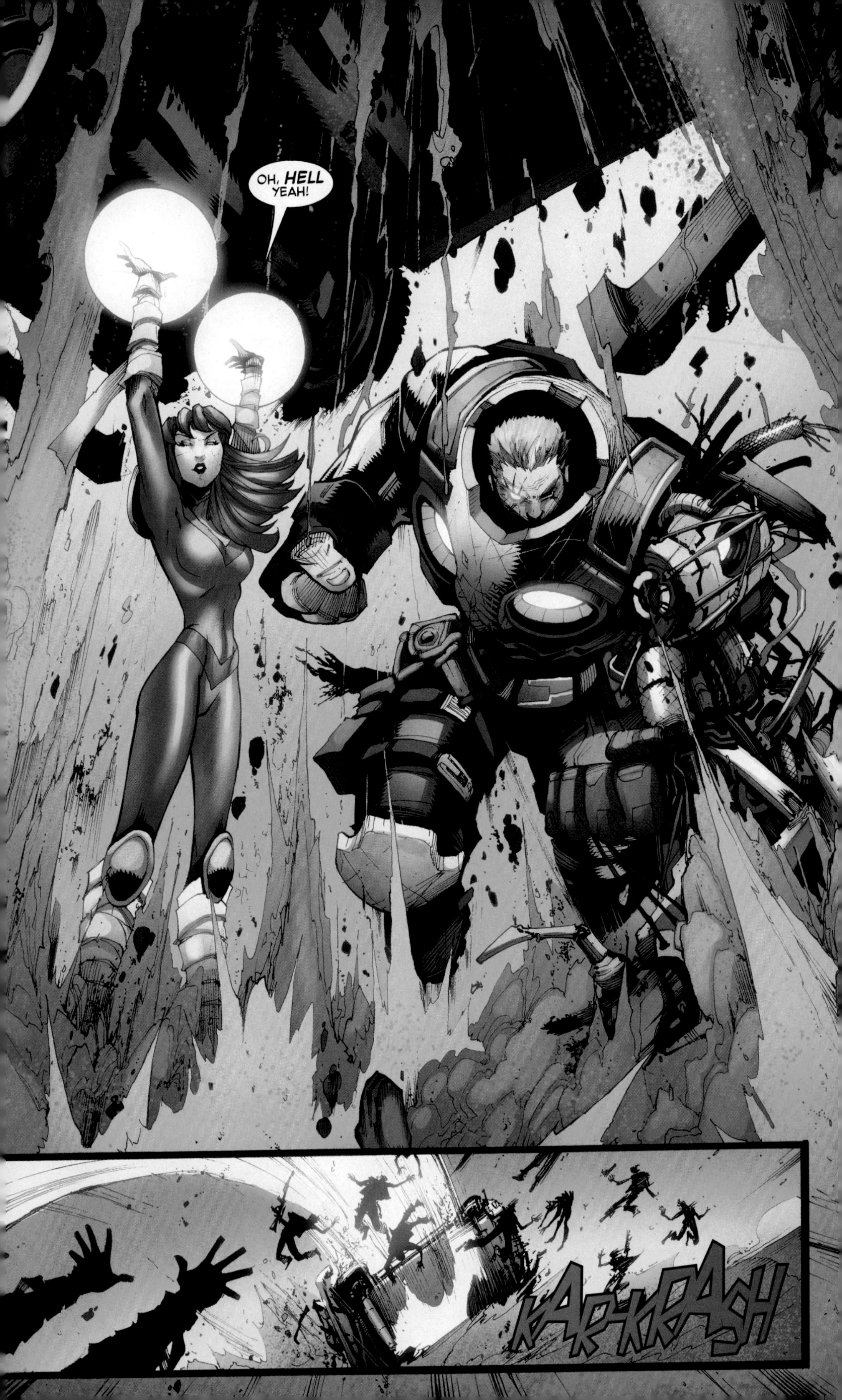

OH, HELL YEAH!
KA-KRASH

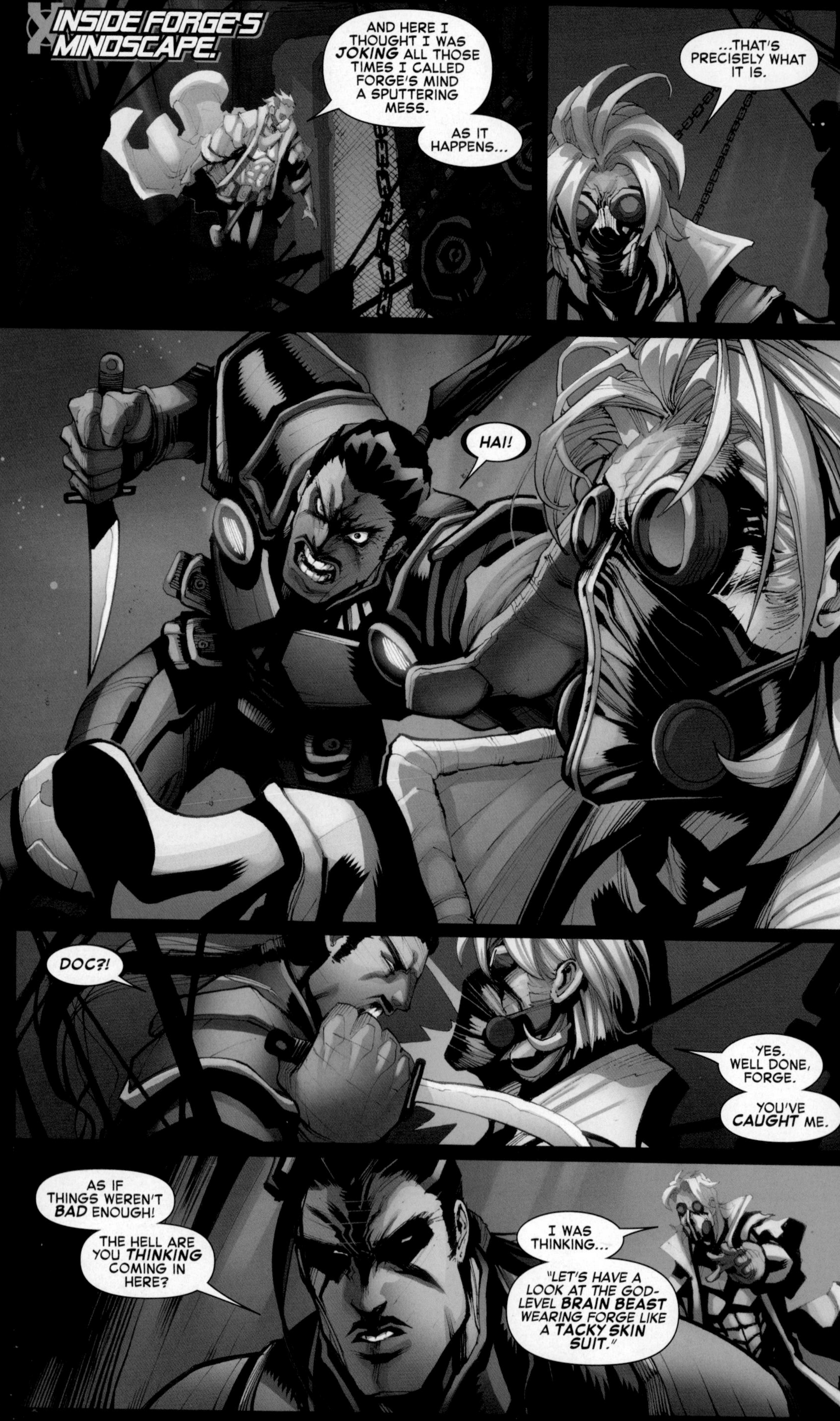
INSIDE FORGE'S MINDSCAPE.
AND HERE I THOUGHT I WAS JOKING ALL THOSE TIMES I CALLED FORGE'S MIND A SPUTTERING MESS.
AS IT HAPPENS...
...THAT'S PRECISELY WHAT IT IS.
HAI!
DOC?!
YES. WELL DONE, FORGE.
YOU'VE CAUGHT ME.
AS IF THINGS WEREN'T BAD ENOUGH!
THE HELL ARE YOU THINKING COMING IN HERE?
I WAS THINKING...
"LET'S HAVE A LOOK AT THE GOD-LEVEL BRAIN BEAST WEARING FORGE LIKE A TACKY SKIN SUIT."

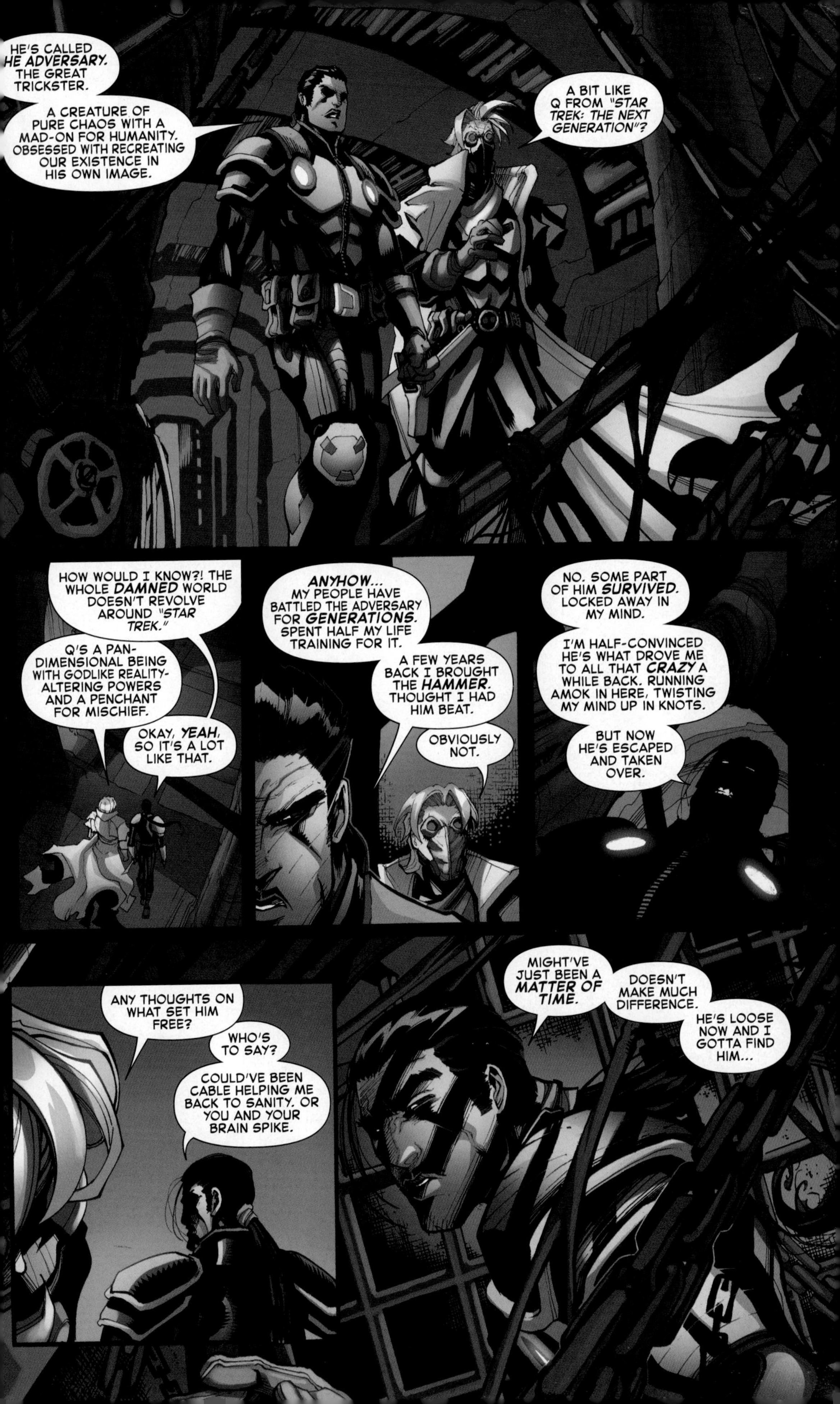
HE'S CALLED HE ADVERSARY. THE GREAT TRICKSTER.
A CREATURE OF PURE CHAOS WITH A MAD-ON FOR HUMANITY. OBSESSED WITH RECREATING OUR EXISTENCE IN HIS OWN IMAGE.
A BIT LIKE Q FROM "STAR TREK: THE NEXT GENERATION"?
HOW WOULD I KNOW?! THE WHOLE DAMNED WORLD DOESN'T REVOLVE AROUND "STAR TREK."
Q'S A PAN-DIMENSIONAL BEING WITH GODLIKE REALITY-ALTERING POWERS AND A PENCHANT FOR MISCHIEF.
OKAY, YEAH, SO IT'S A LOT LIKE THAT.
ANYHOW... MY PEOPLE HAVE BATTLED THE ADVERSARY FOR GENERATIONS. SPENT HALF MY LIFE TRAINING FOR IT.
A FEW YEARS BACK I BROUGHT THE HAMMER. THOUGHT I HAD HIM BEAT.
OBVIOUSLY NOT.
NO. SOME PART OF HIM SURVIVED. LOCKED AWAY IN MY MIND.
I'M HALF-CONVINCED HE'S WHAT DROVE ME TO ALL THAT CRAZY A WHILE BACK. RUNNING AMOK IN HERE, TWISTING MY MIND UP IN KNOTS.
BUT NOW HE'S ESCAPED AND TAKEN OVER.
ANY THOUGHTS ON WHAT SET HIM FREE?
WHO'S TO SAY?
COULD'VE BEEN CABLE HELPING ME BACK TO SANITY. OR YOU AND YOUR BRAIN SPIKE.
MIGHT'VE JUST BEEN A MATTER OF TIME.
DOESN'T MAKE MUCH DIFFERENCE.
HE'S LOOSE NOW AND I GOTTA FIND HIM...

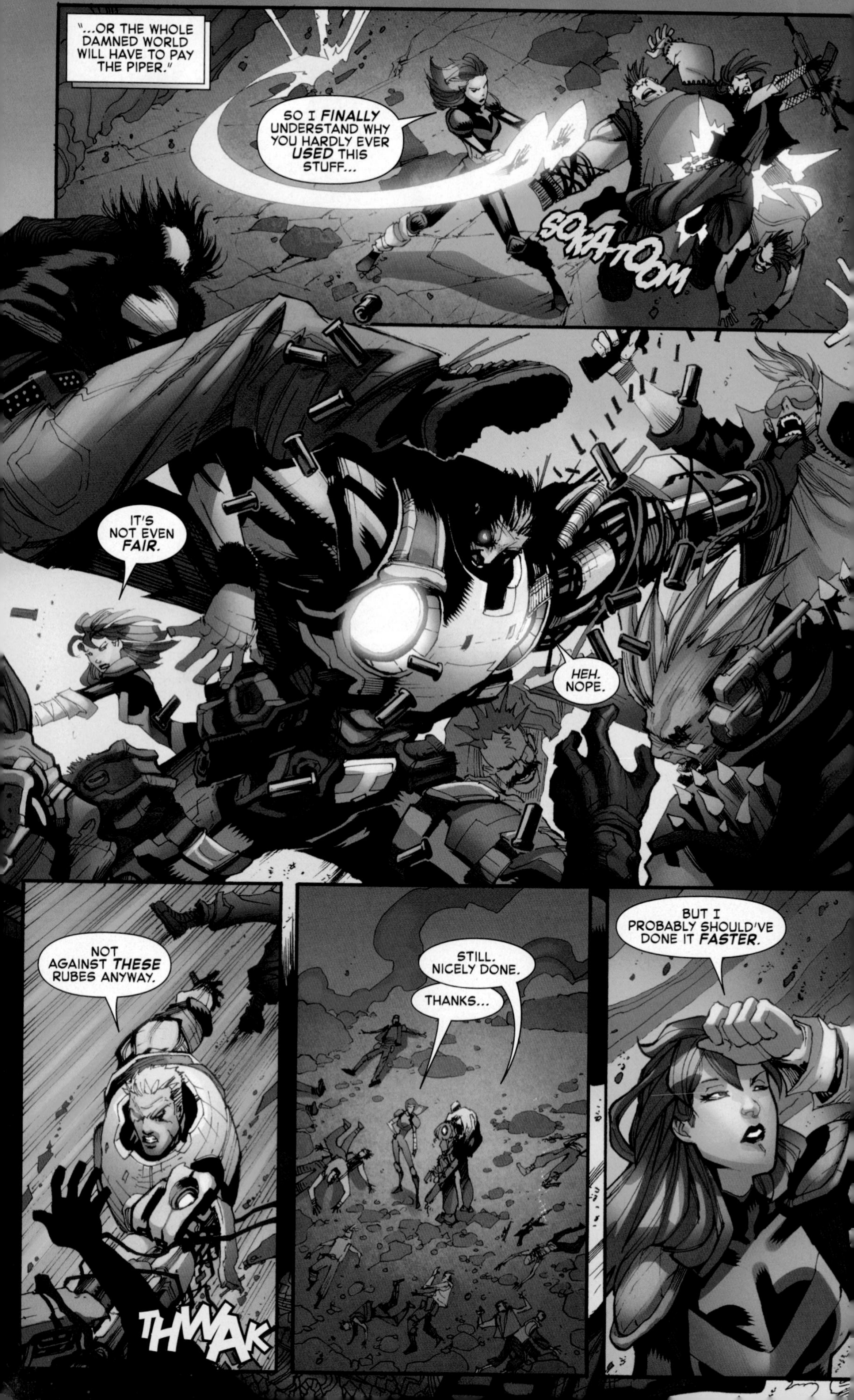
"...OR THE WHOLE DAMNED WORLD WILL HAVE TO PAY THE PIPER."
SO I FINALLY UNDERSTAND WHY YOU HARDLY EVER USED THIS STUFF...
SKA-TOOM
IT'S NOT EVEN FAIR.
HEH. NOPE.
NOT AGAINST THESE RUBES ANYWAY.
THWAK
STILL. NICELY DONE.
THANKS...
BUT I PROBABLY SHOULD'VE DONE IT FASTER.

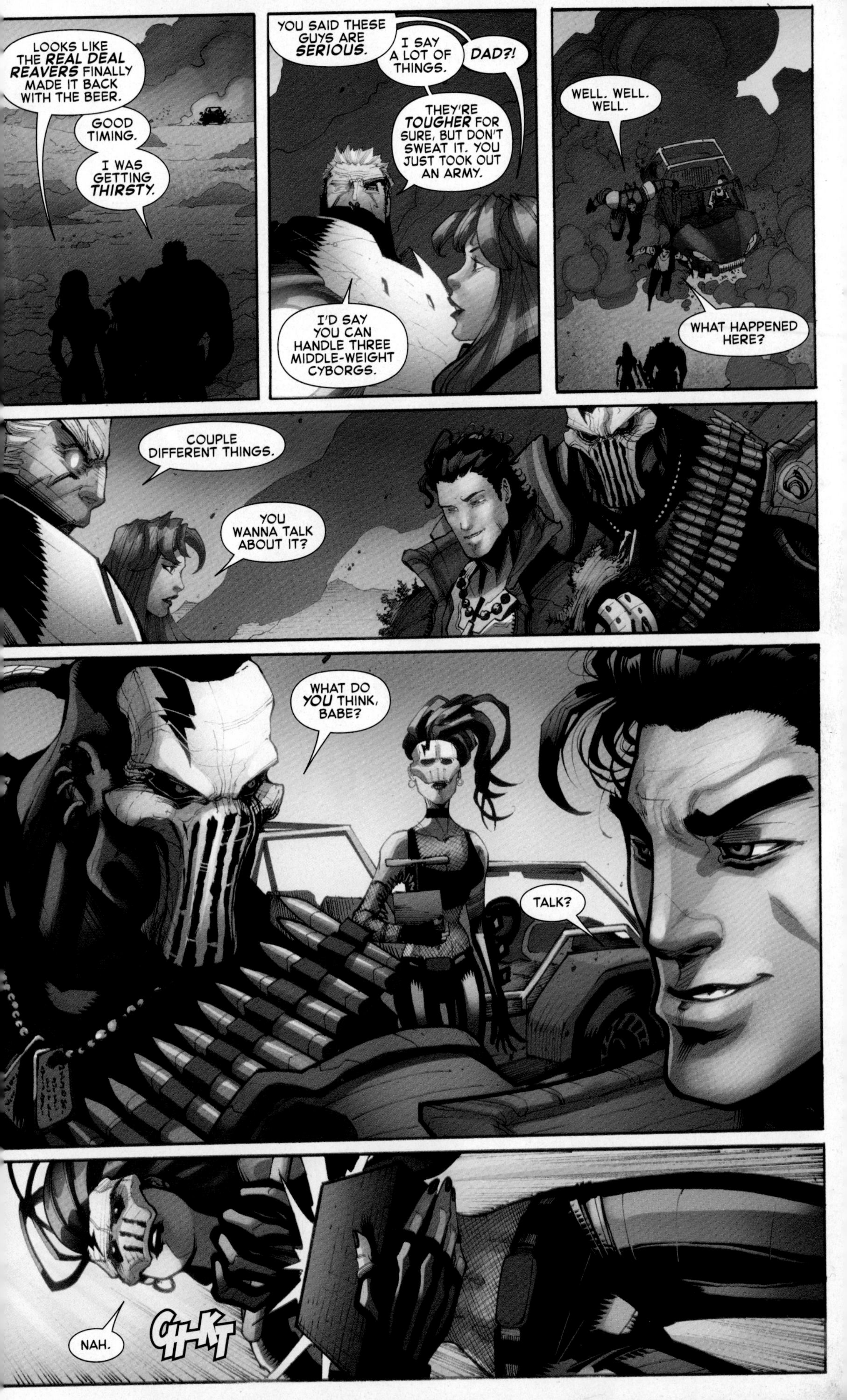
LOOKS LIKE THE REAL DEAL REAVERS FINALLY MADE IT BACK WITH THE BEER.
GOOD TIMING.
I WAS GETTING THIRSTY.
YOU SAID THESE GUYS ARE SERIOUS.
I SAY A LOT OF THINGS.
DAD?!
THEY'RE TOUGHER FOR SURE, BUT DON'T SWEAT IT. YOU JUST TOOK OUT AN ARMY.
I'D SAY YOU CAN HANDLE THREE MIDDLE-WEIGHT CYBORGS.
WELL. WELL. WELL.
WHAT HAPPENED HERE?
COUPLE DIFFERENT THINGS.
YOU WANNA TALK ABOUT IT?
WHAT DO YOU THINK, BABE?
TALK?
NAH.
CH-KT

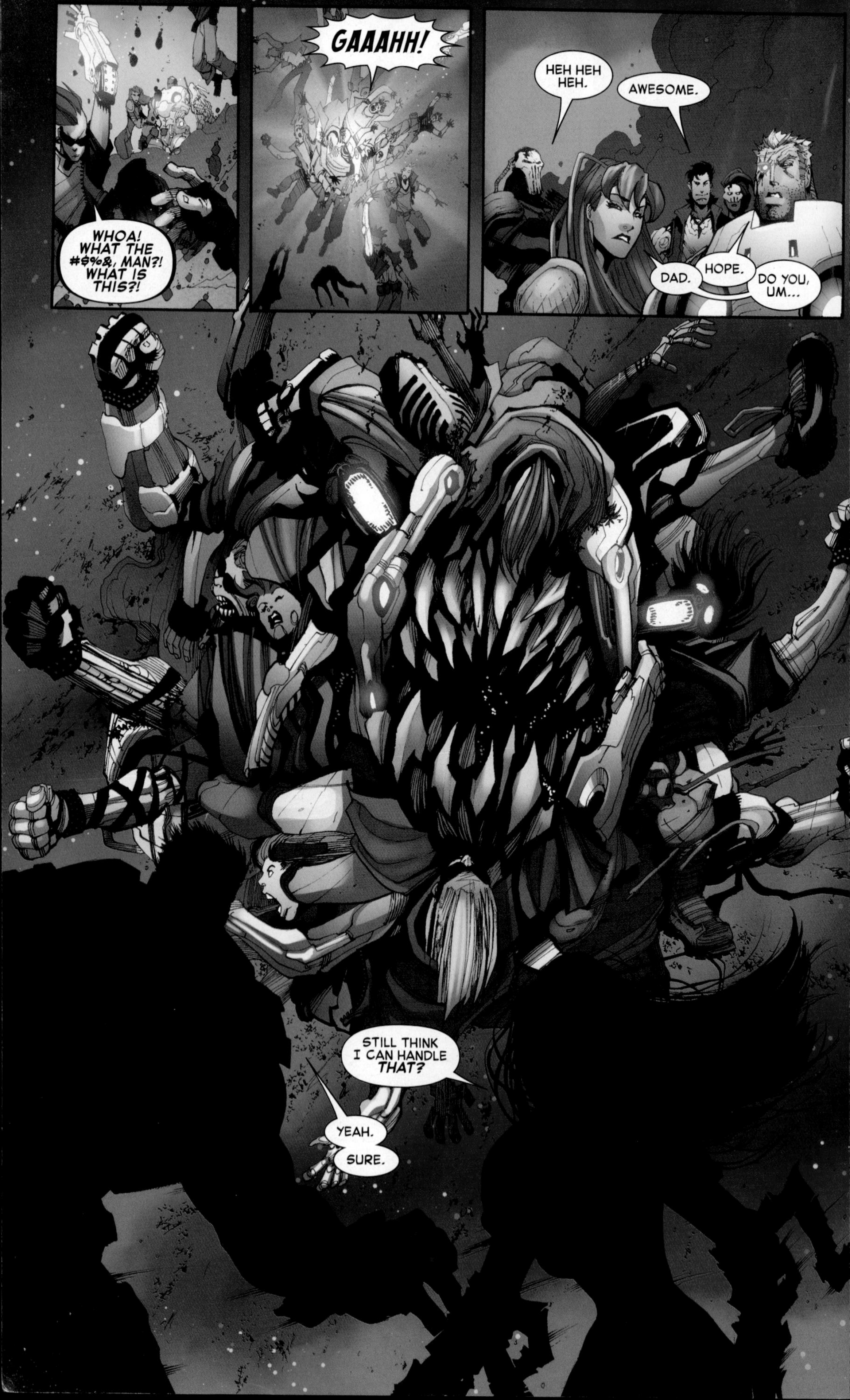

WHOA! WHAT THE #$%&, MAN?! WHAT IS THIS?!
GAAAHH!
HEH HEH HEH.
AWESOME.
DAD.
HOPE.
DO YOU, UM...
STILL THINK I CAN HANDLE THAT?
YEAH.
SURE.

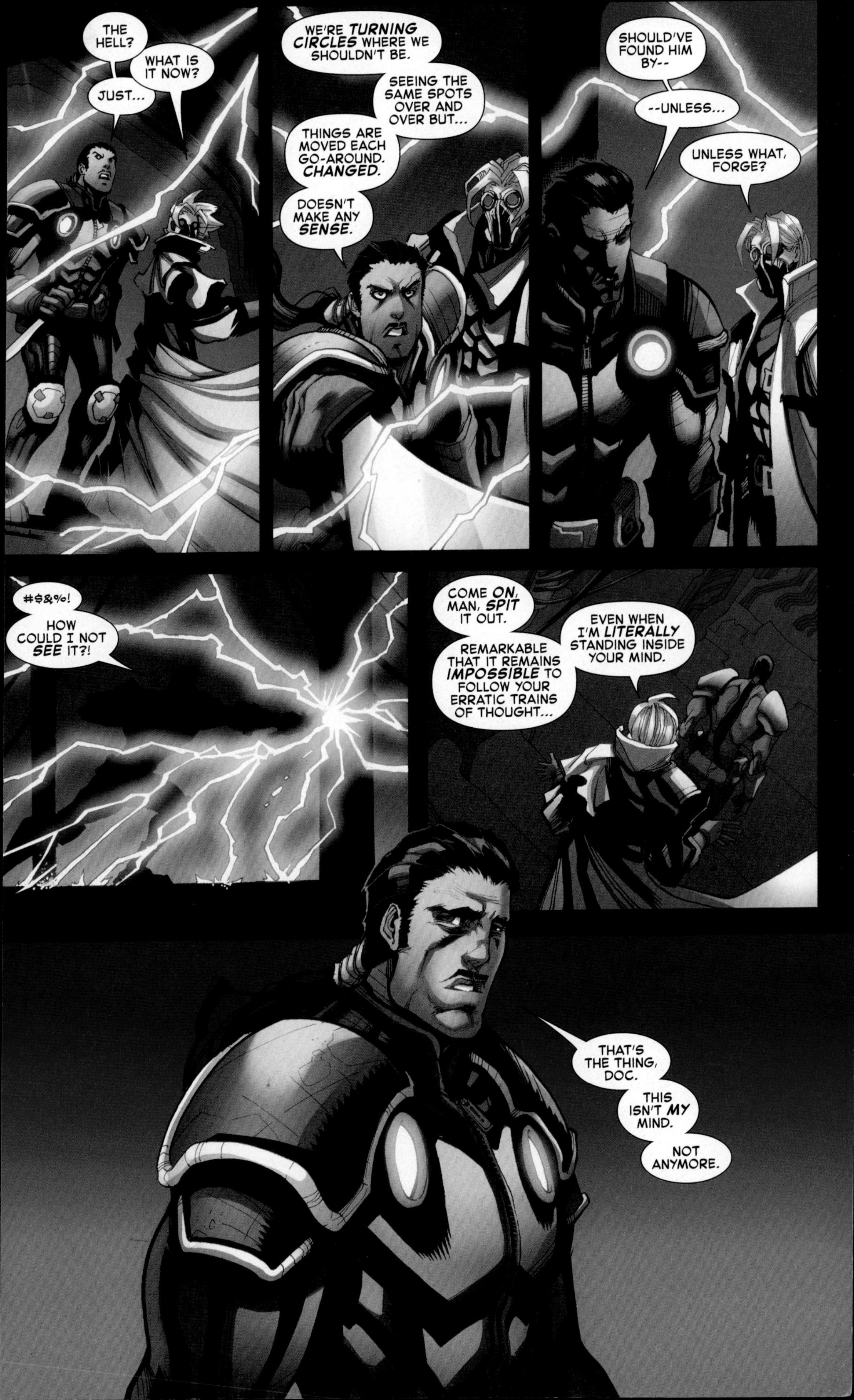
THE HELL?
WHAT IS IT NOW?
JUST...
WE'RE TURNING CIRCLES WHERE WE SHOULDN'T BE.
SEEING THE SAME SPOTS OVER AND OVER BUT...
THINGS ARE MOVED EACH GO-AROUND. CHANGED.
DOESN'T MAKE ANY SENSE.
SHOULD'VE FOUND HIM BY--
--UNLESS...
UNLESS WHAT, FORGE?
#$&%! HOW COULD I NOT SEE IT?!
COME ON, MAN, SPIT IT OUT.
REMARKABLE THAT IT REMAINS IMPOSSIBLE TO FOLLOW YOUR ERRATIC TRAINS OF THOUGHT...
EVEN WHEN I'M LITERALLY STANDING INSIDE YOUR MIND.
THAT'S THE THING, DOC.
THIS ISN'T MY MIND.
NOT ANYMORE.

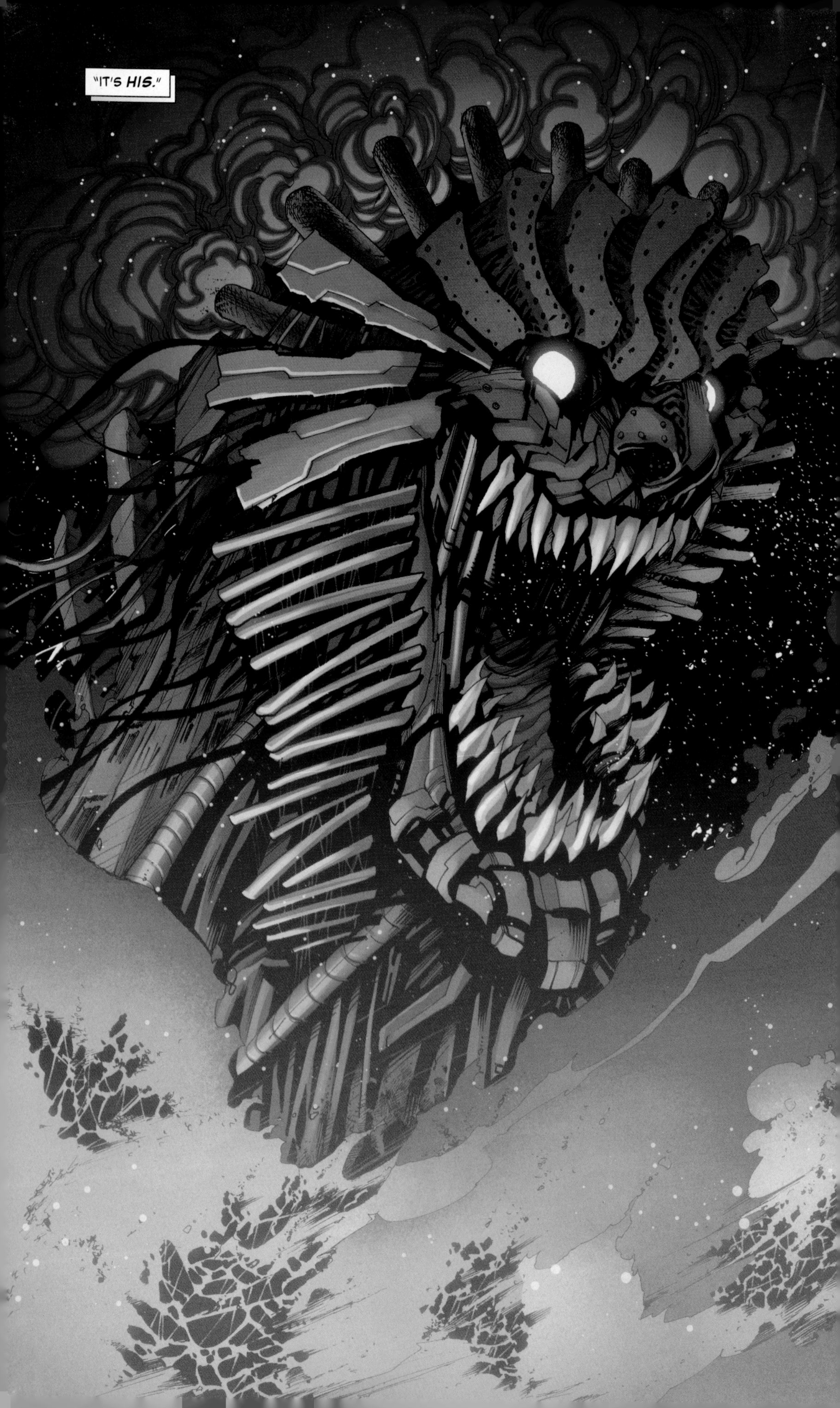
"IT'S *HIS.*"

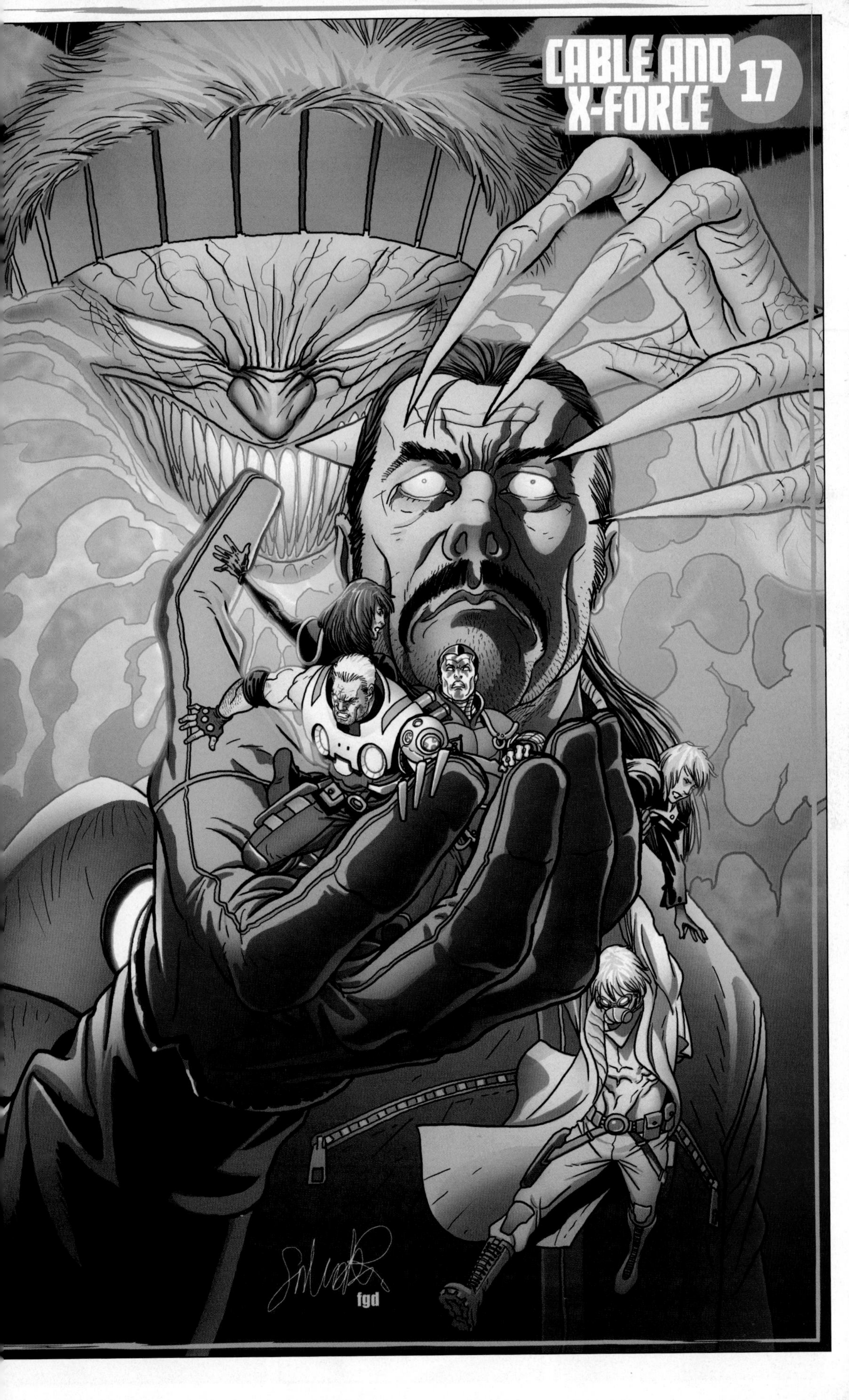
CABLE AND X-FORCE
17
fgd

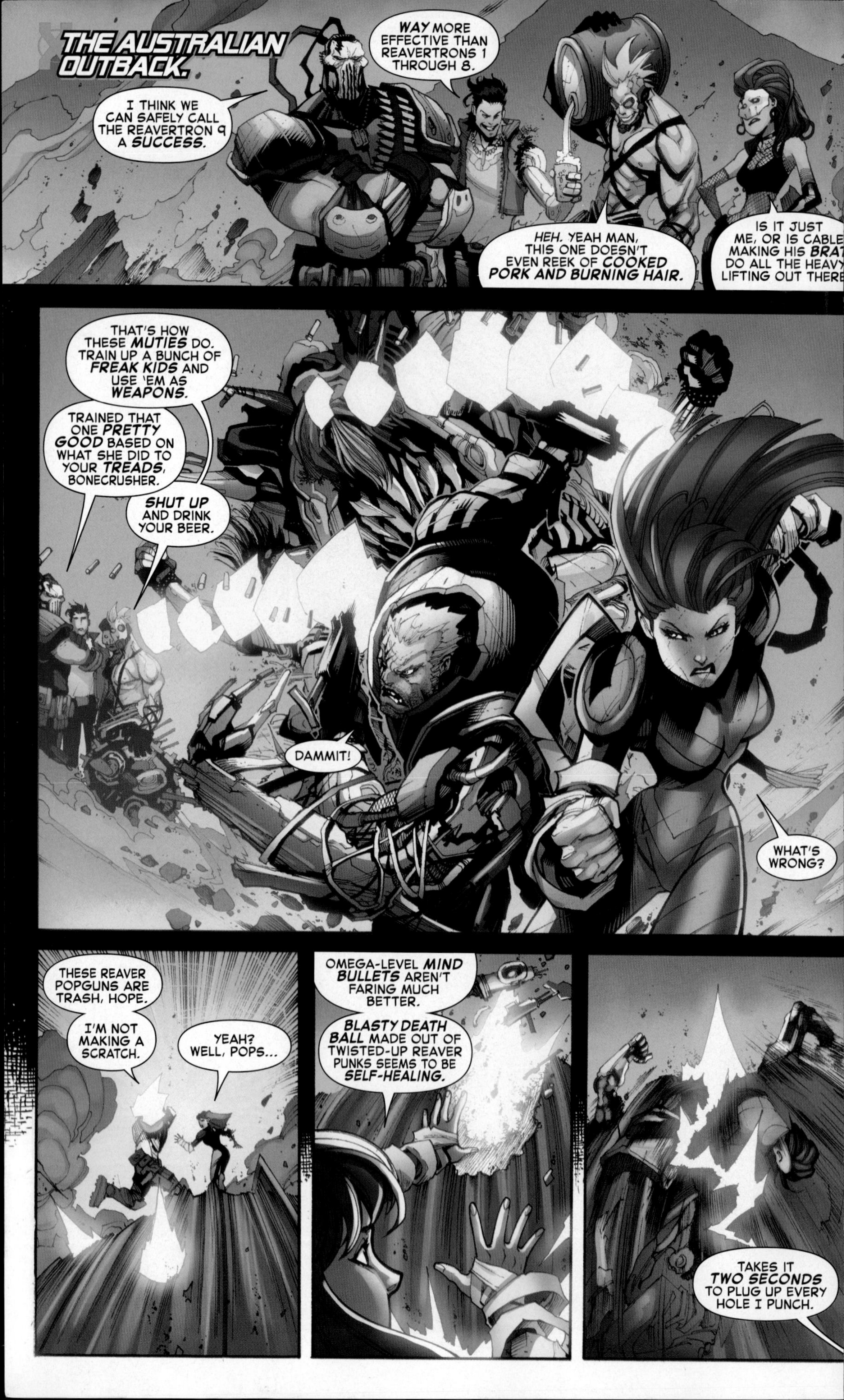
THE AUSTRALIAN OUTBACK.
I THINK WE CAN SAFELY CALL THE REAVERTRON 9 A SUCCESS.
WAY MORE EFFECTIVE THAN REAVERTRONS 1 THROUGH 8.
HEH. YEAH MAN, THIS ONE DOESN'T EVEN REEK OF COOKED PORK AND BURNING HAIR.
IS IT JUST ME, OR IS CABLE MAKING HIS BRAT DO ALL THE HEAVY LIFTING OUT THERE
THAT'S HOW THESE MUTIES DO. TRAIN UP A BUNCH OF FREAK KIDS AND USE 'EM AS WEAPONS.
TRAINED THAT ONE PRETTY GOOD BASED ON WHAT SHE DID TO YOUR TREADS, BONECRUSHER.
SHUT UP AND DRINK YOUR BEER.
DAMMIT!
WHAT'S WRONG?
THESE REAVER POPGUNS ARE TRASH, HOPE.
I'M NOT MAKING A SCRATCH.
YEAH? WELL, POPS...
OMEGA-LEVEL MIND BULLETS AREN'T FARING MUCH BETTER.
BLASTY DEATH BALL MADE OUT OF TWISTED-UP REAVER PUNKS SEEMS TO BE SELF-HEALING.
TAKES IT TWO SECONDS TO PLUG UP EVERY HOLE I PUNCH.

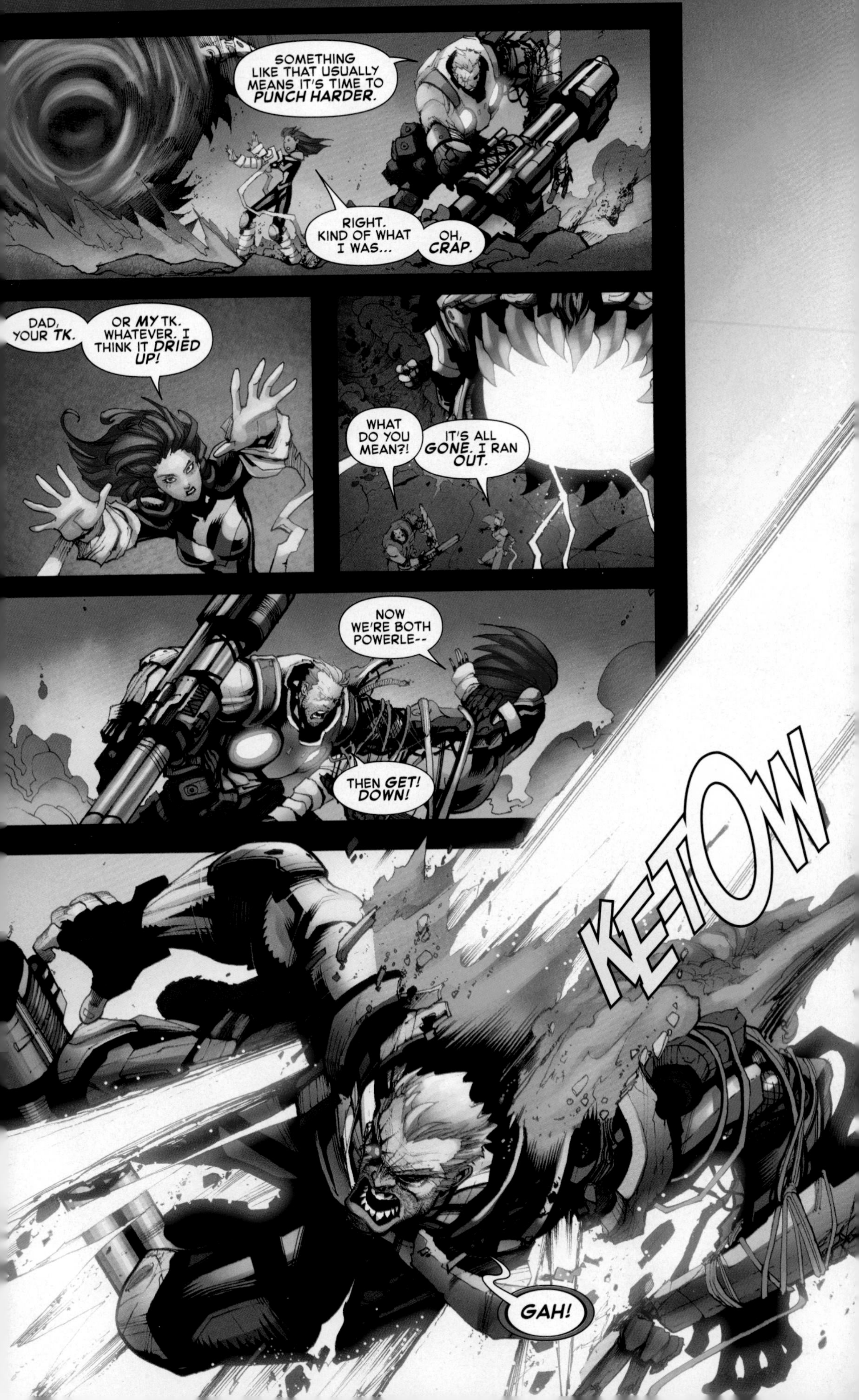

SOMETHING LIKE THAT USUALLY MEANS IT'S TIME TO PUNCH HARDER.
RIGHT. KIND OF WHAT I WAS...
OH, CRAP.
DAD, YOUR TK.
OR MY TK. WHATEVER. I THINK IT DRIED UP!
WHAT DO YOU MEAN?!
IT'S ALL GONE. I RAN OUT.
NOW WE'RE BOTH POWERLE--
THEN GET! DOWN!
KE-TOW
GAH!

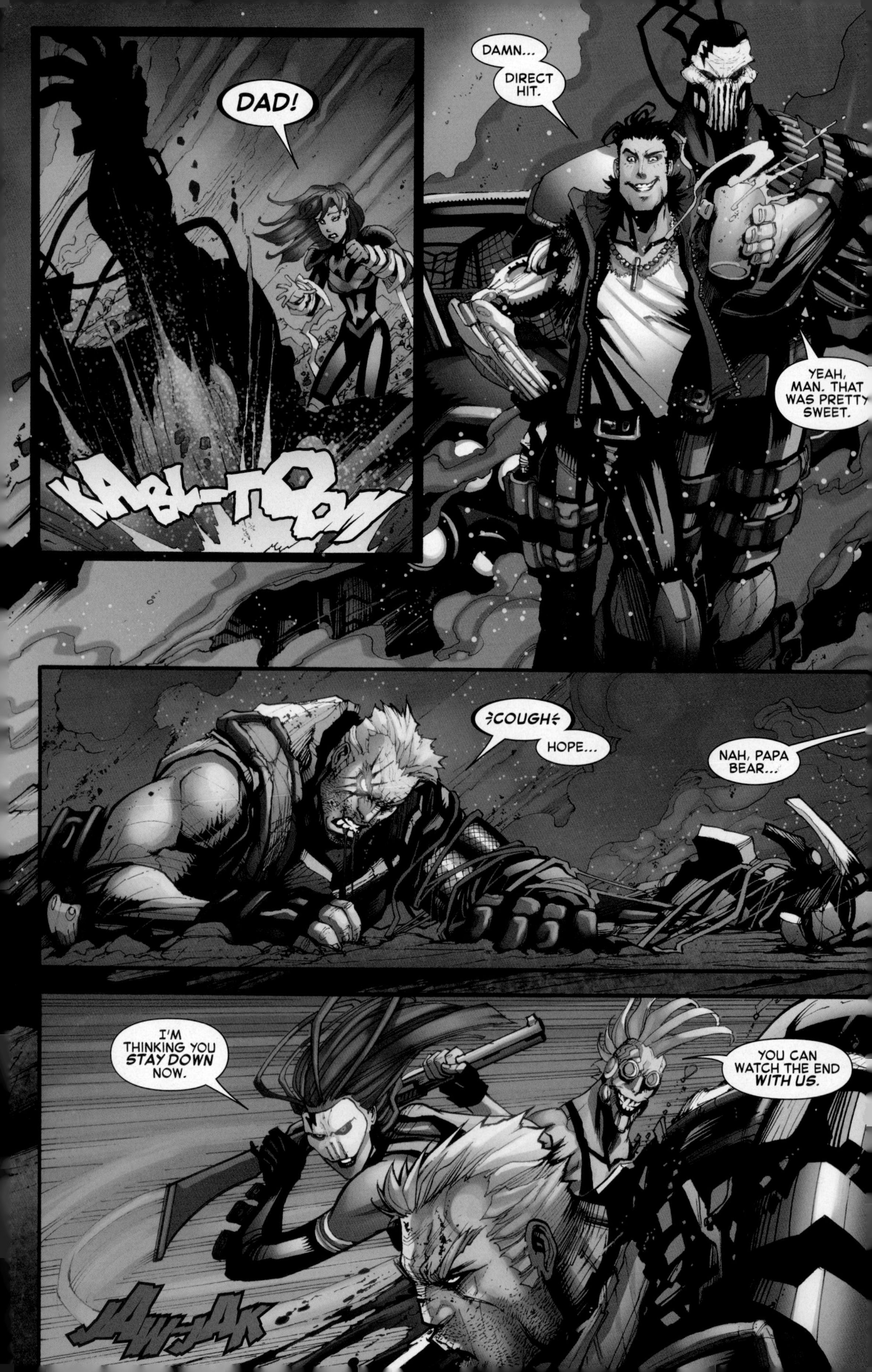
DAD!
KABL-TOOM
DAMN...
DIRECT HIT.
YEAH, MAN. THAT WAS PRETTY SWEET.
COUGH
HOPE...
NAH, PAPA BEAR...
I'M THINKING YOU STAY DOWN NOW.
YOU CAN WATCH THE END WITH US.
JAW-JAK

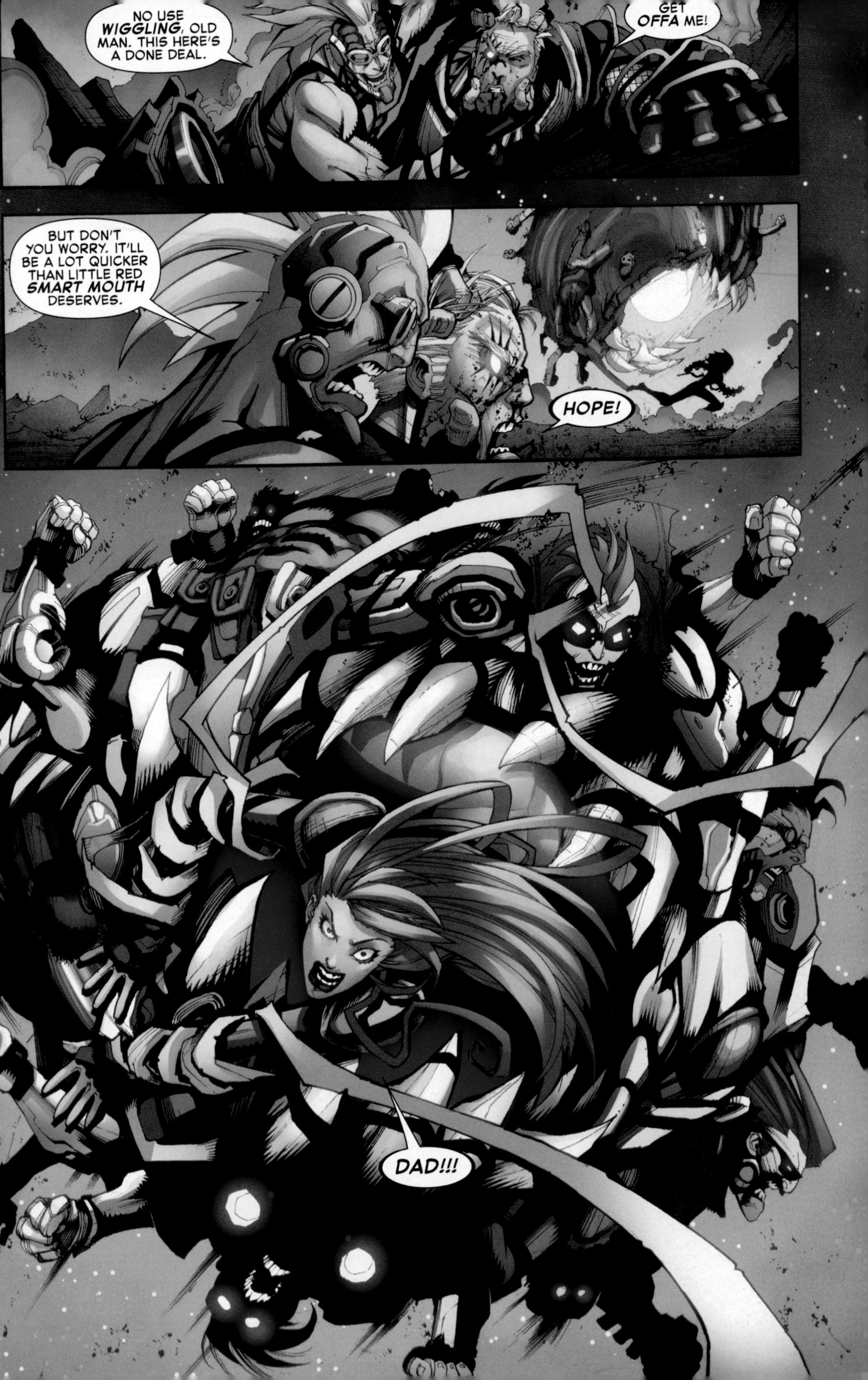
NO USE WIGGLING, OLD MAN. THIS HERE'S A DONE DEAL.
GET OFFA ME!
BUT DON'T YOU WORRY. IT'LL BE A LOT QUICKER THAN LITTLE RED SMART MOUTH DESERVES.
HOPE!
DAD!!!

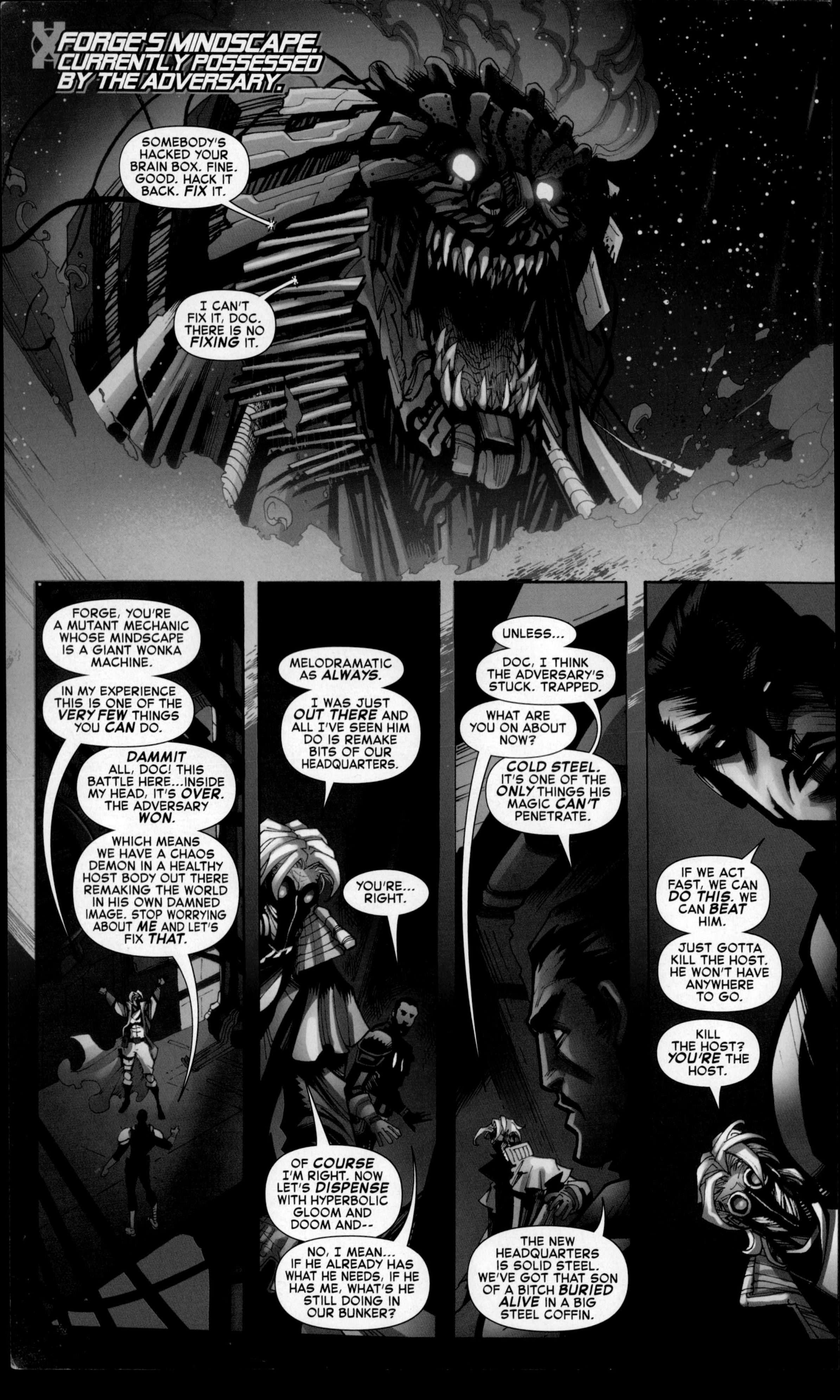
FORGE'S MINDSCAPE. CURRENTLY POSSESSED BY THE ADVERSARY.
SOMEBODY'S HACKED YOUR BRAIN BOX. FINE. GOOD. HACK IT BACK. FIX IT.
I CAN'T FIX IT, DOC. THERE IS NO FIXING IT.
FORGE, YOU'RE A MUTANT MECHANIC WHOSE MINDSCAPE IS A GIANT WONKA MACHINE.
IN MY EXPERIENCE THIS IS ONE OF THE VERY FEW THINGS YOU CAN DO.
DAMMIT ALL, DOC! THIS BATTLE HERE...INSIDE MY HEAD, IT'S OVER. THE ADVERSARY WON.
WHICH MEANS WE HAVE A CHAOS DEMON IN A HEALTHY HOST BODY OUT THERE REMAKING THE WORLD IN HIS OWN DAMNED IMAGE. STOP WORRYING ABOUT ME AND LET'S FIX THAT.
MELODRAMATIC AS ALWAYS.
I WAS JUST OUT THERE AND ALL I'VE SEEN HIM DO IS REMAKE BITS OF OUR HEADQUARTERS.
YOU'RE... RIGHT.
OF COURSE I'M RIGHT. NOW LET'S DISPENSE WITH HYPERBOLIC GLOOM AND DOOM AND--
NO, I MEAN... IF HE ALREADY HAS WHAT HE NEEDS, IF HE HAS ME, WHAT'S HE STILL DOING IN OUR BUNKER?
UNLESS...
DOC, I THINK THE ADVERSARY'S STUCK. TRAPPED.
WHAT ARE YOU ON ABOUT NOW?
COLD STEEL. IT'S ONE OF THE ONLY THINGS HIS MAGIC CAN'T PENETRATE.
THE NEW HEADQUARTERS IS SOLID STEEL. WE'VE GOT THAT SON OF A BITCH BURIED ALIVE IN A BIG STEEL COFFIN.
IF WE ACT FAST, WE CAN DO THIS. WE CAN BEAT HIM.
JUST GOTTA KILL THE HOST. HE WON'T HAVE ANYWHERE TO GO.
KILL THE HOST? YOU'RE THE HOST.

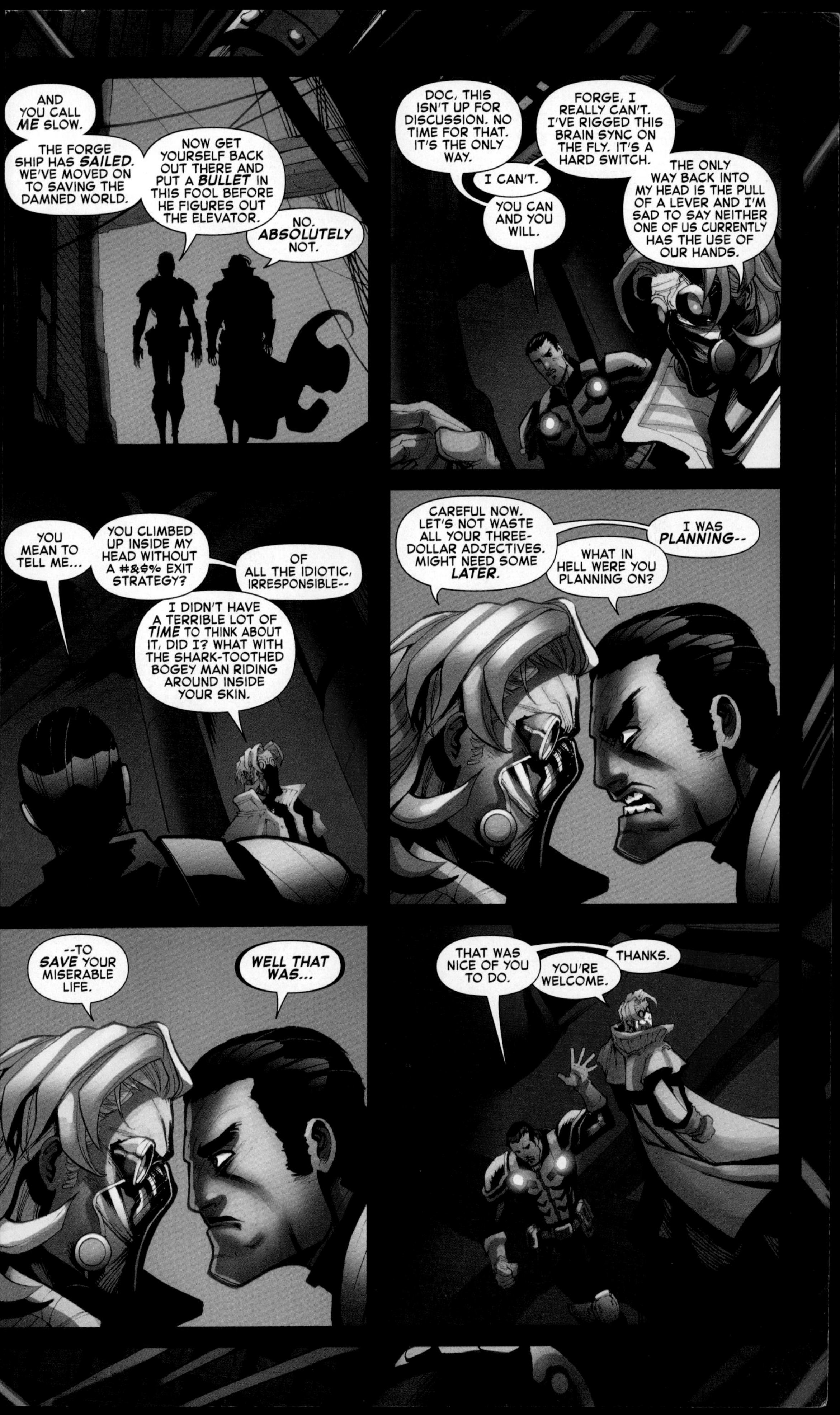
AND YOU CALL ME SLOW.
THE FORGE SHIP HAS SAILED. WE'VE MOVED ON TO SAVING THE DAMNED WORLD.
NOW GET YOURSELF BACK OUT THERE AND PUT A BULLET IN THIS FOOL BEFORE HE FIGURES OUT THE ELEVATOR.
NO. ABSOLUTELY NOT.
DOC, THIS ISN'T UP FOR DISCUSSION. NO TIME FOR THAT. IT'S THE ONLY WAY.
FORGE, I REALLY CAN'T. I'VE RIGGED THIS BRAIN SYNC ON THE FLY. IT'S A HARD SWITCH.
I CAN'T.
YOU CAN AND YOU WILL.
THE ONLY WAY BACK INTO MY HEAD IS THE PULL OF A LEVER AND I'M SAD TO SAY NEITHER ONE OF US CURRENTLY HAS THE USE OF OUR HANDS.
YOU MEAN TO TELL ME...
YOU CLIMBED UP INSIDE MY HEAD WITHOUT A #&$% EXIT STRATEGY?
OF ALL THE IDIOTIC, IRRESPONSIBLE--
I DIDN'T HAVE A TERRIBLE LOT OF TIME TO THINK ABOUT IT, DID I? WHAT WITH THE SHARK-TOOTHED BOGEY MAN RIDING AROUND INSIDE YOUR SKIN.
CAREFUL NOW. LET'S NOT WASTE ALL YOUR THREE-DOLLAR ADJECTIVES. MIGHT NEED SOME LATER.
I WAS PLANNING--
WHAT IN HELL WERE YOU PLANNING ON?
--TO SAVE YOUR MISERABLE LIFE.
WELL THAT WAS...
THAT WAS NICE OF YOU TO DO.
THANKS.
YOU'RE WELCOME.

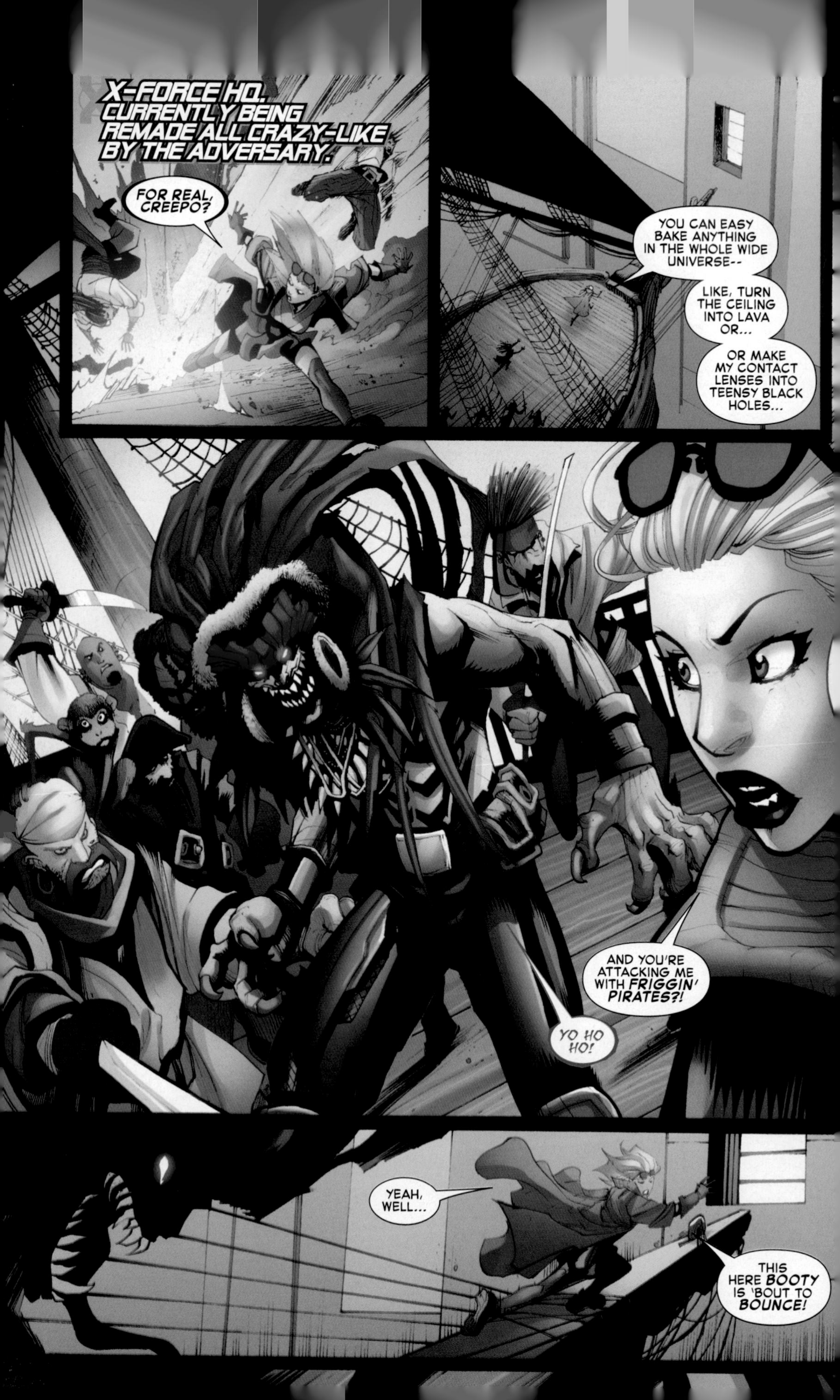
X-FORCE HQ. CURRENTLY BEING REMADE ALL CRAZY-LIKE BY THE ADVERSARY.
FOR REAL, CREEPO?
YOU CAN EASY BAKE ANYTHING IN THE WHOLE WIDE UNIVERSE--
LIKE, TURN THE CEILING INTO LAVA OR...
OR MAKE MY CONTACT LENSES INTO TEENSY BLACK HOLES...
AND YOU'RE ATTACKING ME WITH *FRIGGIN' PIRATES?!*
YO HO HO!
YEAH, WELL...
THIS HERE *BOOTY* IS 'BOUT TO *BOUNCE!*

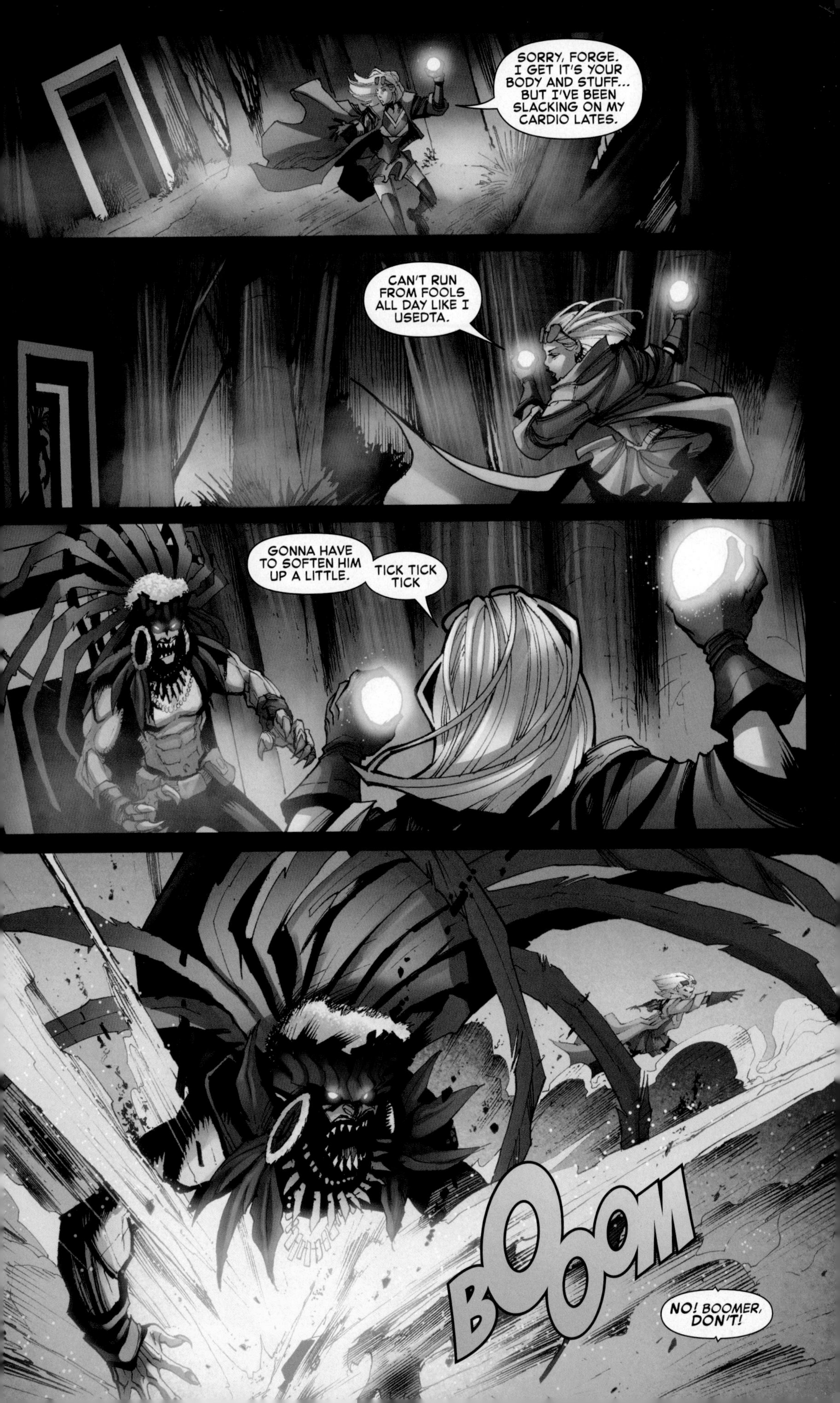
SORRY, FORGE. I GET IT'S YOUR BODY AND STUFF... BUT I'VE BEEN SLACKING ON MY CARDIO LATES.
CAN'T RUN FROM FOOLS ALL DAY LIKE I USEDTA.
GONNA HAVE TO SOFTEN HIM UP A LITTLE.
TICK TICK TICK
BOOOM
NO! BOOMER, DON'T!

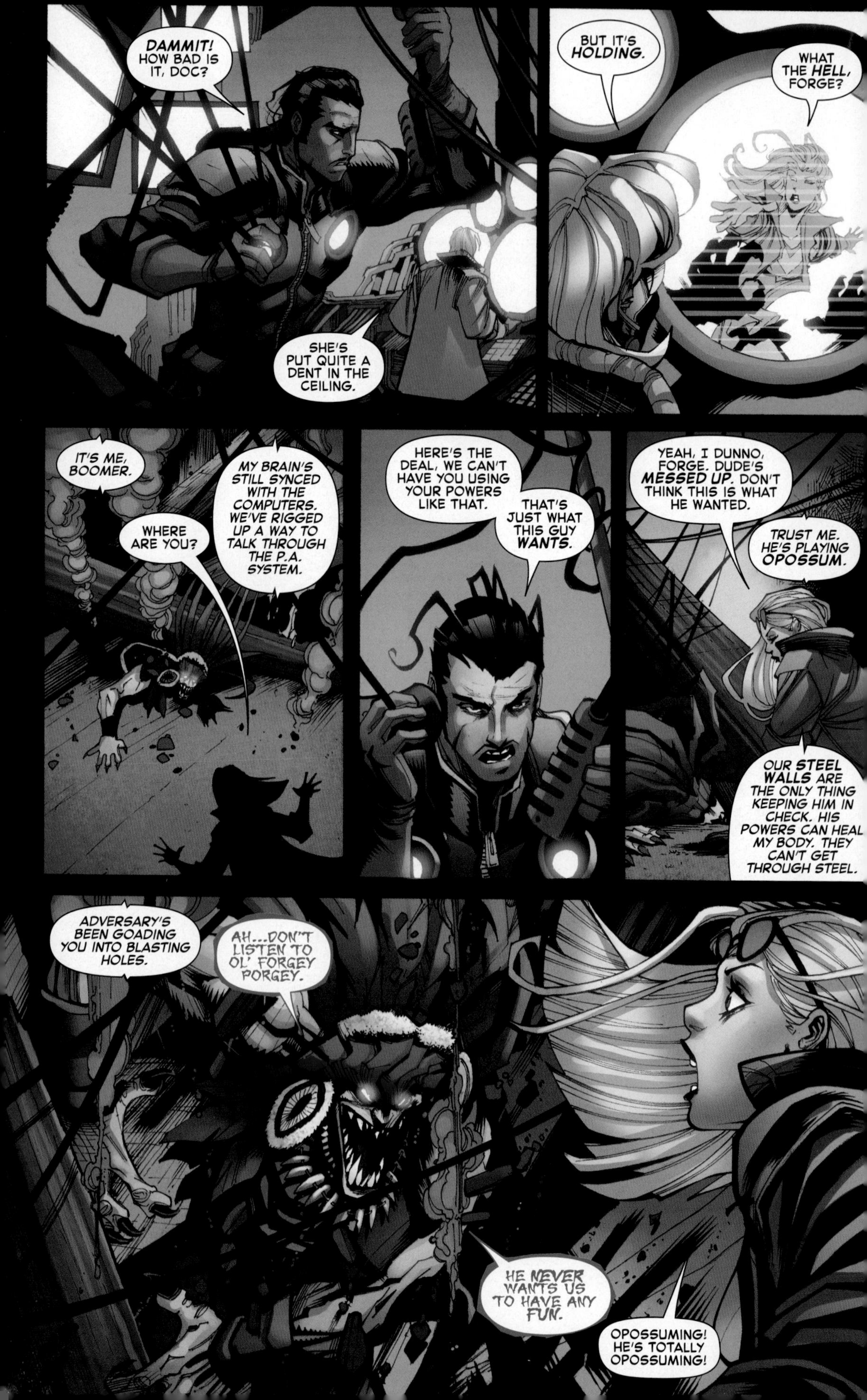

DAMMIT! HOW BAD IS IT, DOC?
SHE'S PUT QUITE A DENT IN THE CEILING.
BUT IT'S HOLDING.
WHAT THE HELL, FORGE?
IT'S ME, BOOMER.
WHERE ARE YOU?
MY BRAIN'S STILL SYNCED WITH THE COMPUTERS. WE'VE RIGGED UP A WAY TO TALK THROUGH THE P.A. SYSTEM.
HERE'S THE DEAL, WE CAN'T HAVE YOU USING YOUR POWERS LIKE THAT.
THAT'S JUST WHAT THIS GUY WANTS.
YEAH, I DUNNO, FORGE. DUDE'S MESSED UP. DON'T THINK THIS IS WHAT HE WANTED.
TRUST ME. HE'S PLAYING OPOSSUM.
OUR STEEL WALLS ARE THE ONLY THING KEEPING HIM IN CHECK. HIS POWERS CAN HEAL MY BODY. THEY CAN'T GET THROUGH STEEL.
ADVERSARY'S BEEN GOADING YOU INTO BLASTING HOLES.
AH...DON'T LISTEN TO OL' FORGEY PORGEY.
HE NEVER WANTS US TO HAVE ANY FUN.
OPOSSUMING! HE'S TOTALLY OPOSSUMING!

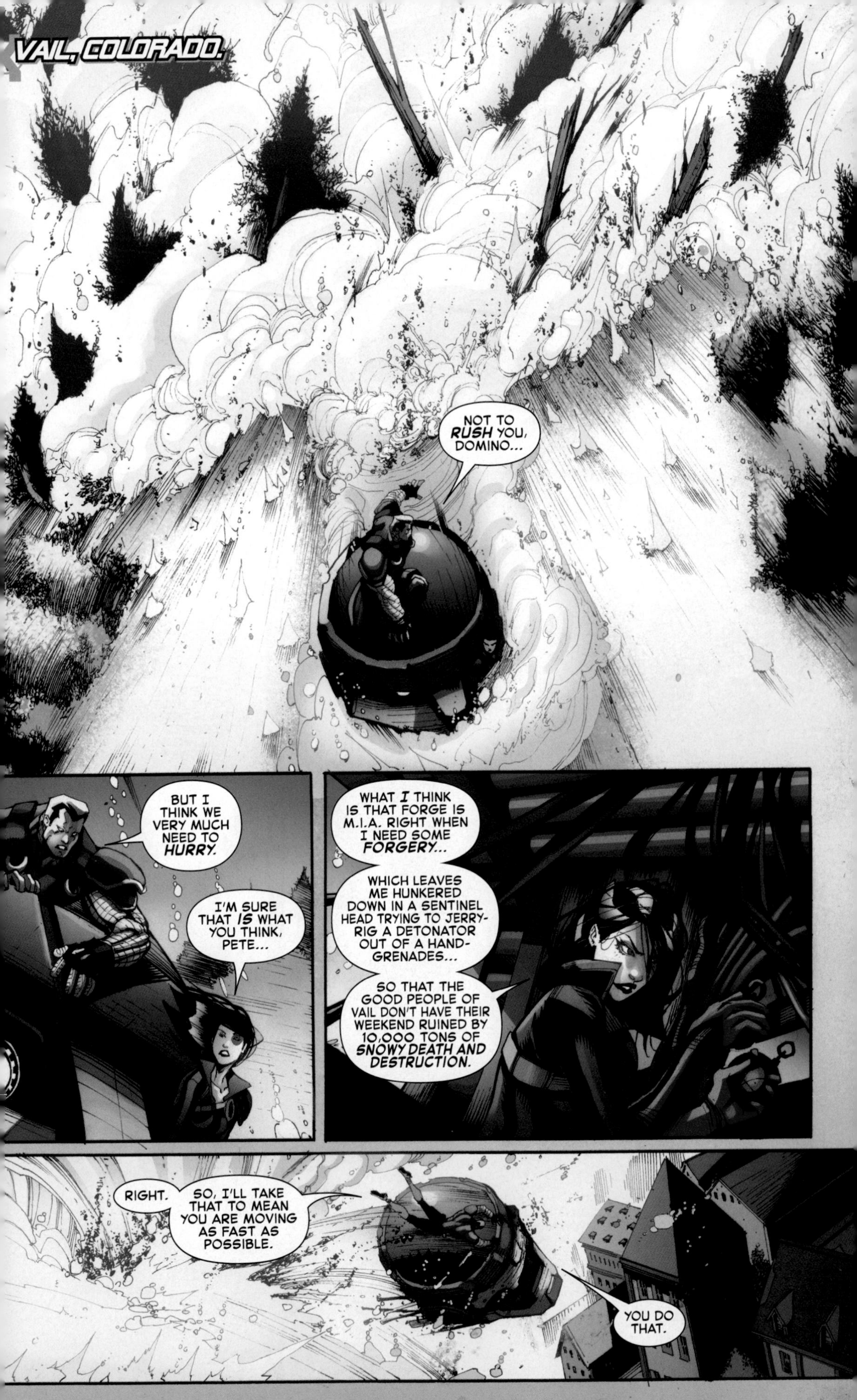
VAIL, COLORADO.
NOT TO RUSH YOU, DOMINO...
BUT I THINK WE VERY MUCH NEED TO HURRY.
I'M SURE THAT IS WHAT YOU THINK, PETE...
WHAT I THINK IS THAT FORGE IS M.I.A. RIGHT WHEN I NEED SOME FORGERY...
WHICH LEAVES ME HUNKERED DOWN IN A SENTINEL HEAD TRYING TO JERRY-RIG A DETONATOR OUT OF A HAND-GRENADES...
SO THAT THE GOOD PEOPLE OF VAIL DON'T HAVE THEIR WEEKEND RUINED BY 10,000 TONS OF SNOWY DEATH AND DESTRUCTION.
RIGHT.
SO, I'LL TAKE THAT TO MEAN YOU ARE MOVING AS FAST AS POSSIBLE.
YOU DO THAT.

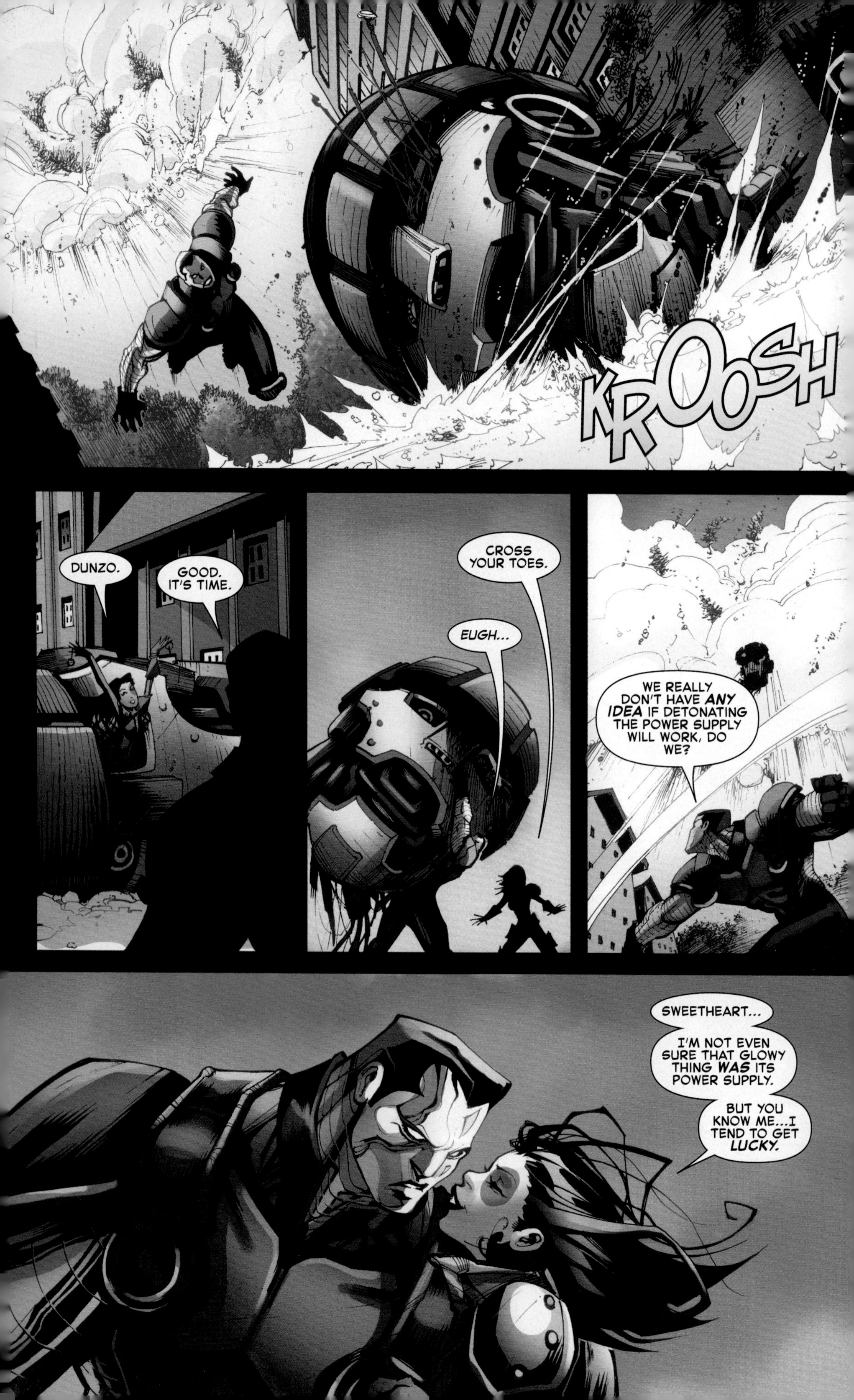
KROOSH
DUNZO.
GOOD. IT'S TIME.
CROSS YOUR TOES.
EUGH...
WE REALLY DON'T HAVE ANY IDEA IF DETONATING THE POWER SUPPLY WILL WORK, DO WE?
SWEETHEART...
I'M NOT EVEN SURE THAT GLOWY THING WAS ITS POWER SUPPLY.
BUT YOU KNOW ME...I TEND TO GET LUCKY.

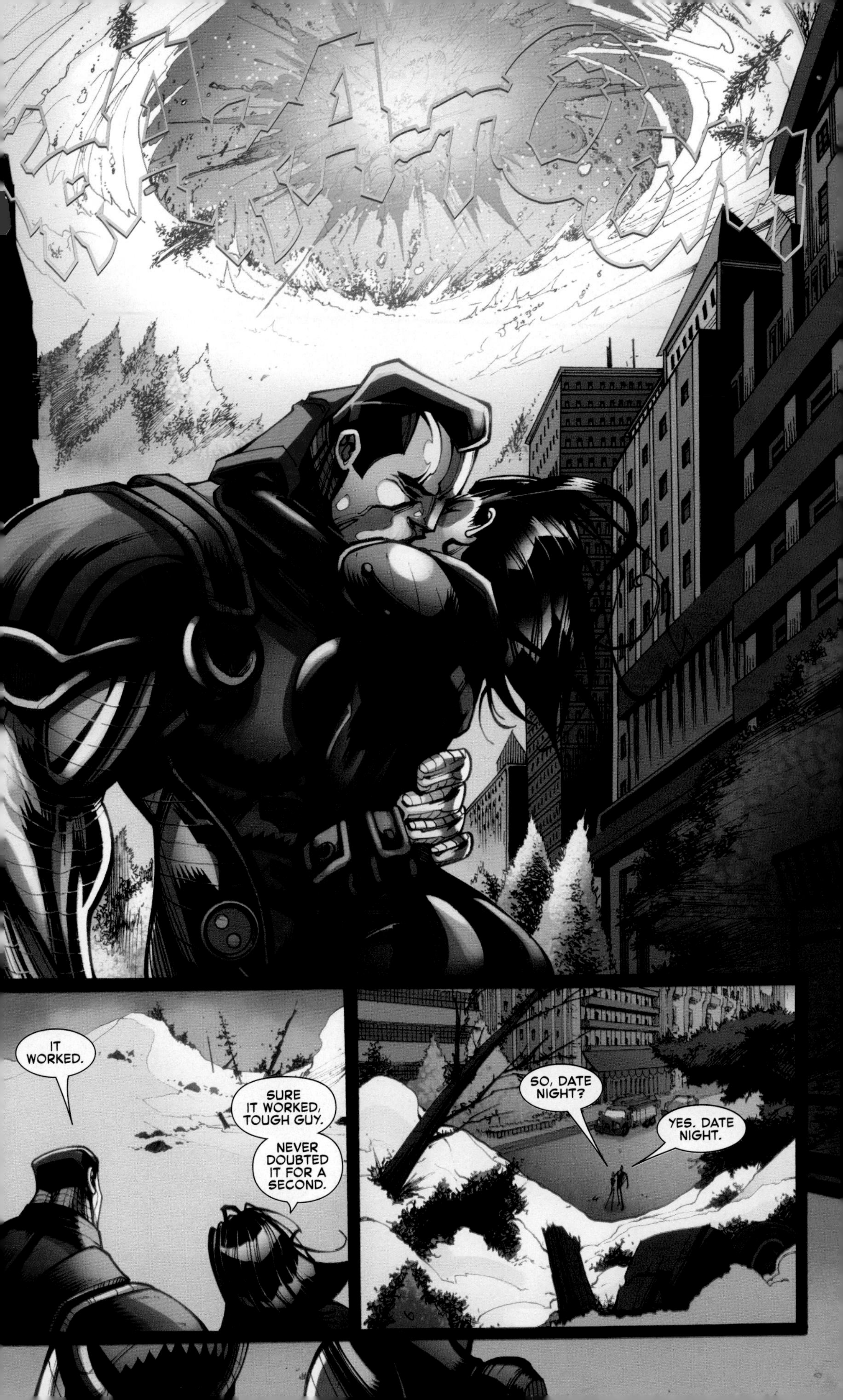
IT WORKED.
SURE IT WORKED, TOUGH GUY.
NEVER DOUBTED IT FOR A SECOND.
SO, DATE NIGHT?
YES. DATE NIGHT.

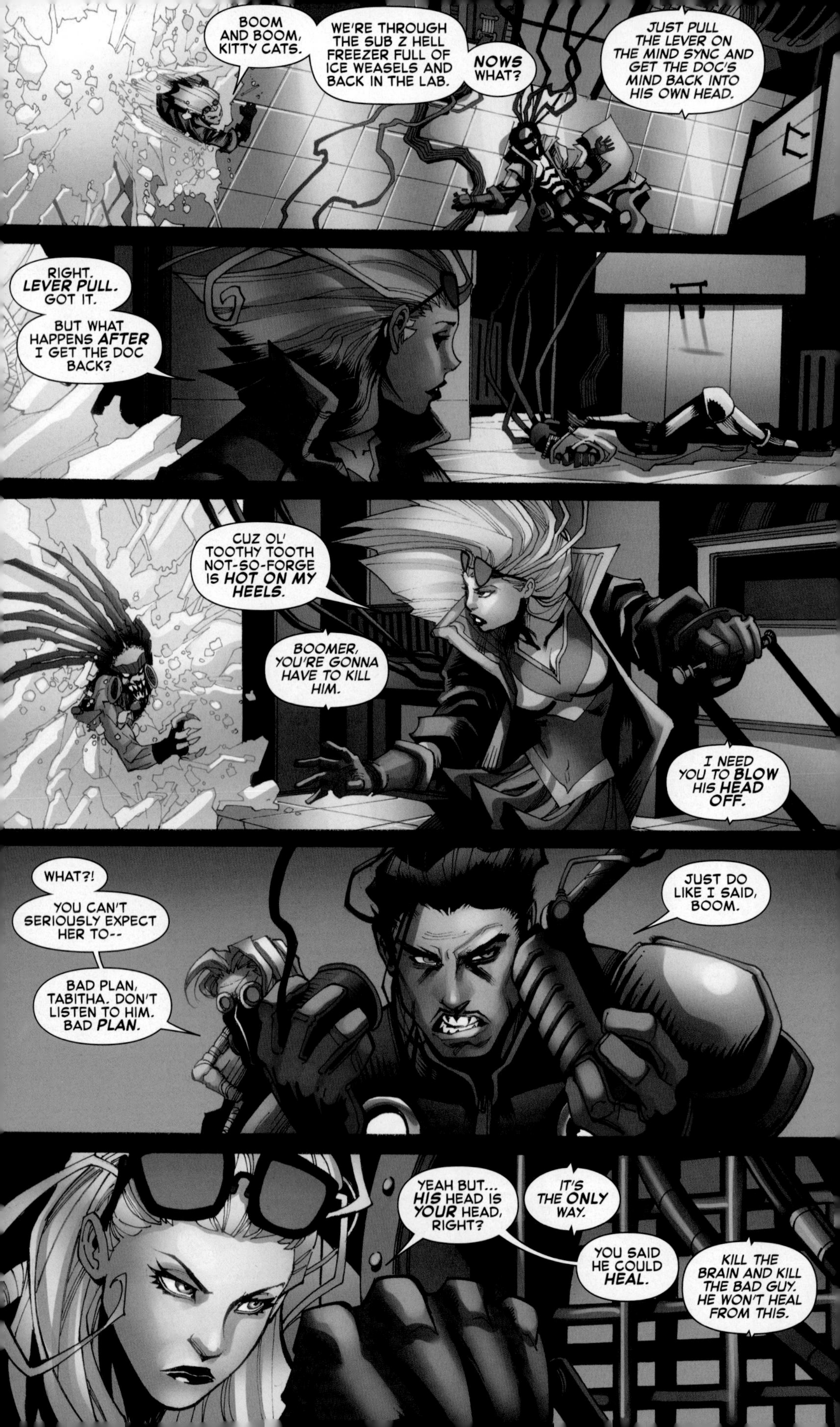
BOOM AND BOOM, KITTY CATS.
WE'RE THROUGH THE SUB Z HELL FREEZER FULL OF ICE WEASELS AND BACK IN THE LAB.
NOWS WHAT?
JUST PULL THE LEVER ON THE MIND SYNC AND GET THE DOC'S MIND BACK INTO HIS OWN HEAD.
RIGHT. LEVER PULL. GOT IT.
BUT WHAT HAPPENS AFTER I GET THE DOC BACK?
CUZ OL' TOOTHY TOOTH NOT-SO-FORGE IS HOT ON MY HEELS.
BOOMER, YOU'RE GONNA HAVE TO KILL HIM.
I NEED YOU TO BLOW HIS HEAD OFF.
WHAT?!
YOU CAN'T SERIOUSLY EXPECT HER TO--
BAD PLAN, TABITHA. DON'T LISTEN TO HIM. BAD PLAN.
JUST DO LIKE I SAID, BOOM.
YEAH BUT... HIS HEAD IS YOUR HEAD, RIGHT?
IT'S THE ONLY WAY.
YOU SAID HE COULD HEAL.
KILL THE BRAIN AND KILL THE BAD GUY. HE WON'T HEAL FROM THIS.

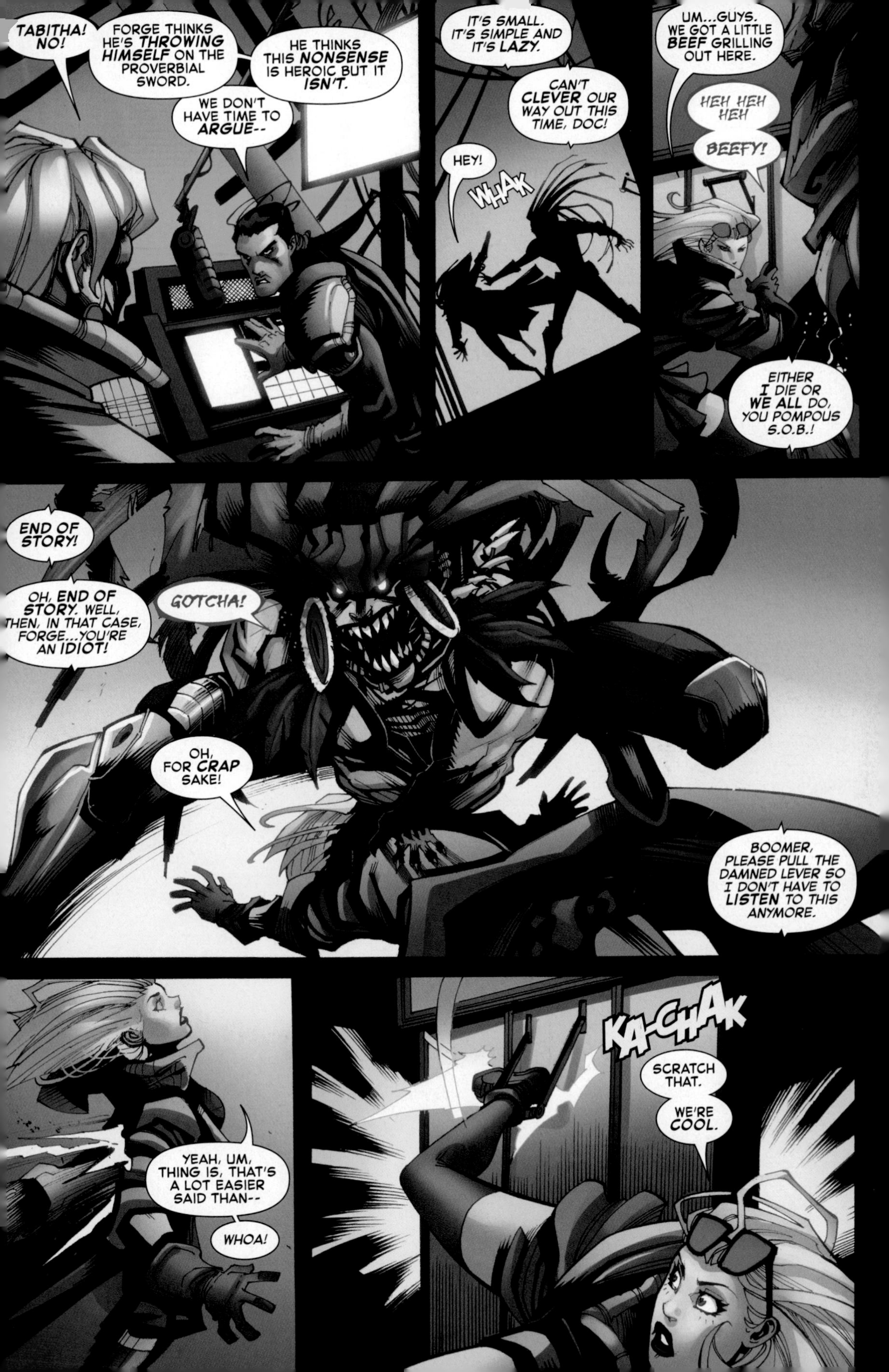
TABITHA! NO!
FORGE THINKS HE'S THROWING HIMSELF ON THE PROVERBIAL SWORD.
HE THINKS THIS NONSENSE IS HEROIC BUT IT ISN'T.
WE DON'T HAVE TIME TO ARGUE--
IT'S SMALL. IT'S SIMPLE AND IT'S LAZY.
CAN'T CLEVER OUR WAY OUT THIS TIME, DOC!
HEY!
WHAK
UM...GUYS. WE GOT A LITTLE BEEF GRILLING OUT HERE.
HEH HEH HEH
BEEFY!
EITHER I DIE OR WE ALL DO, YOU POMPOUS S.O.B.!
END OF STORY!
OH, END OF STORY. WELL, THEN, IN THAT CASE, FORGE...YOU'RE AN IDIOT!
GOTCHA!
OH, FOR CRAP SAKE!
BOOMER, PLEASE PULL THE DAMNED LEVER SO I DON'T HAVE TO LISTEN TO THIS ANYMORE.
YEAH, UM, THING IS, THAT'S A LOT EASIER SAID THAN--
WHOA!
KA-CHAK
SCRATCH THAT.
WE'RE COOL.

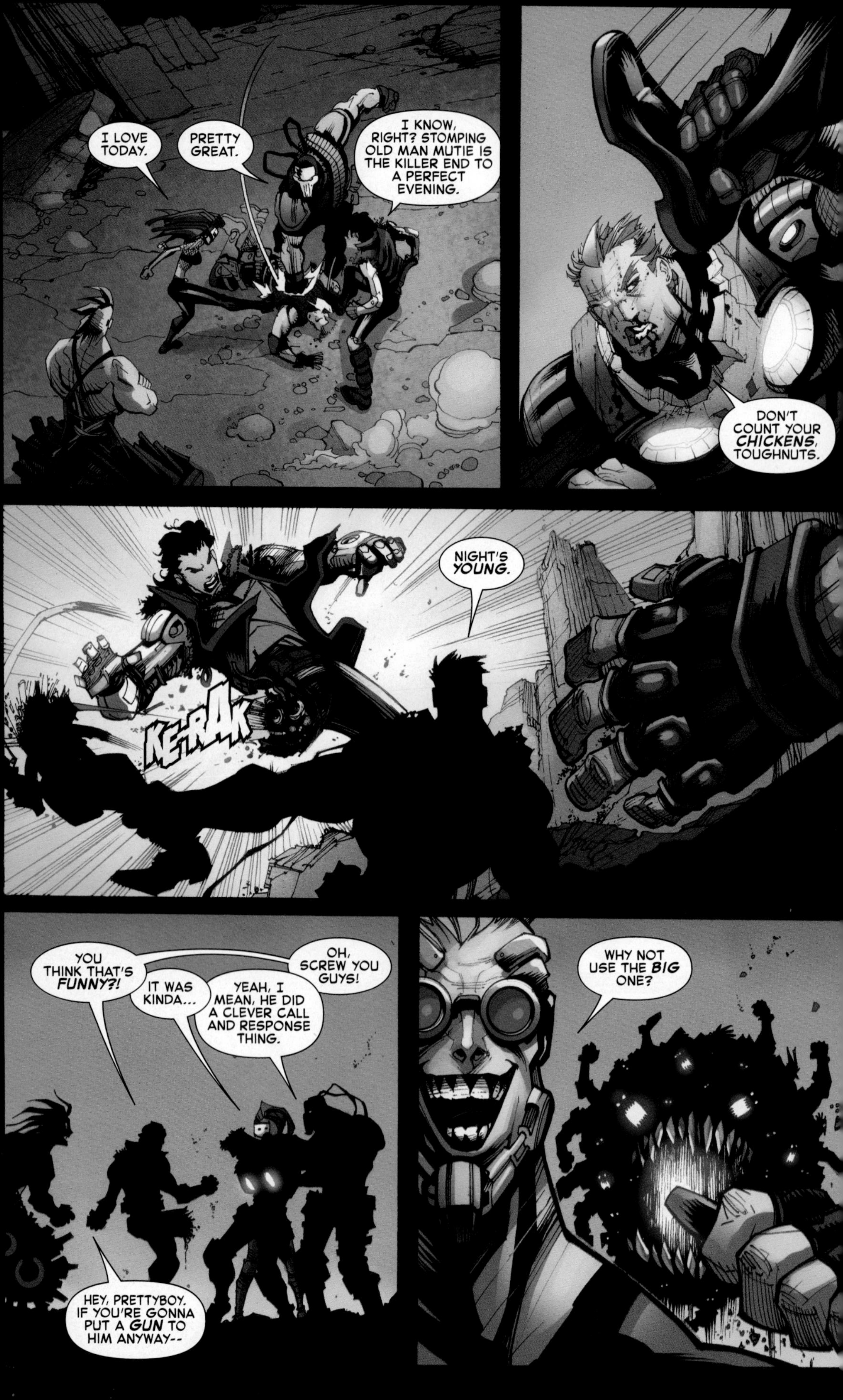
I LOVE TODAY.
PRETTY GREAT.
I KNOW, RIGHT? STOMPING OLD MAN MUTIE IS THE KILLER END TO A PERFECT EVENING.
DON'T COUNT YOUR CHICKENS, TOUGHNUTS.
NIGHT'S YOUNG.
KE-RAK
YOU THINK THAT'S FUNNY?!
OH, SCREW YOU GUYS!
IT WAS KINDA...
YEAH, I MEAN, HE DID A CLEVER CALL AND RESPONSE THING.
HEY, PRETTYBOY. IF YOU'RE GONNA PUT A GUN TO HIM ANYWAY--
WHY NOT USE THE BIG ONE?

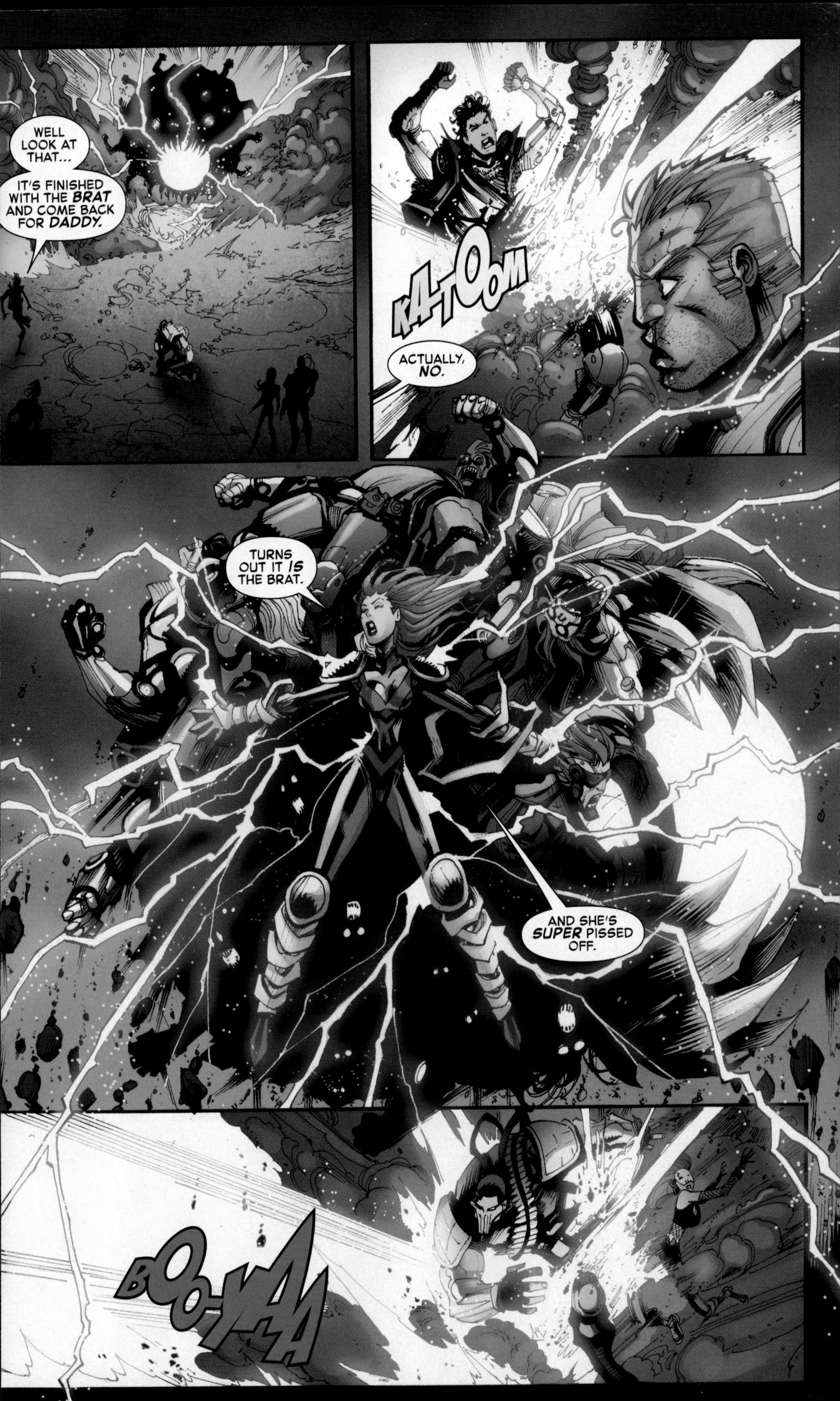
WELL LOOK AT THAT...
IT'S FINISHED WITH THE BRAT AND COME BACK FOR DADDY.
KA-TOOOM
ACTUALLY, NO.
TURNS OUT IT IS THE BRAT.
AND SHE'S SUPER PISSED OFF.
BOO-YAA

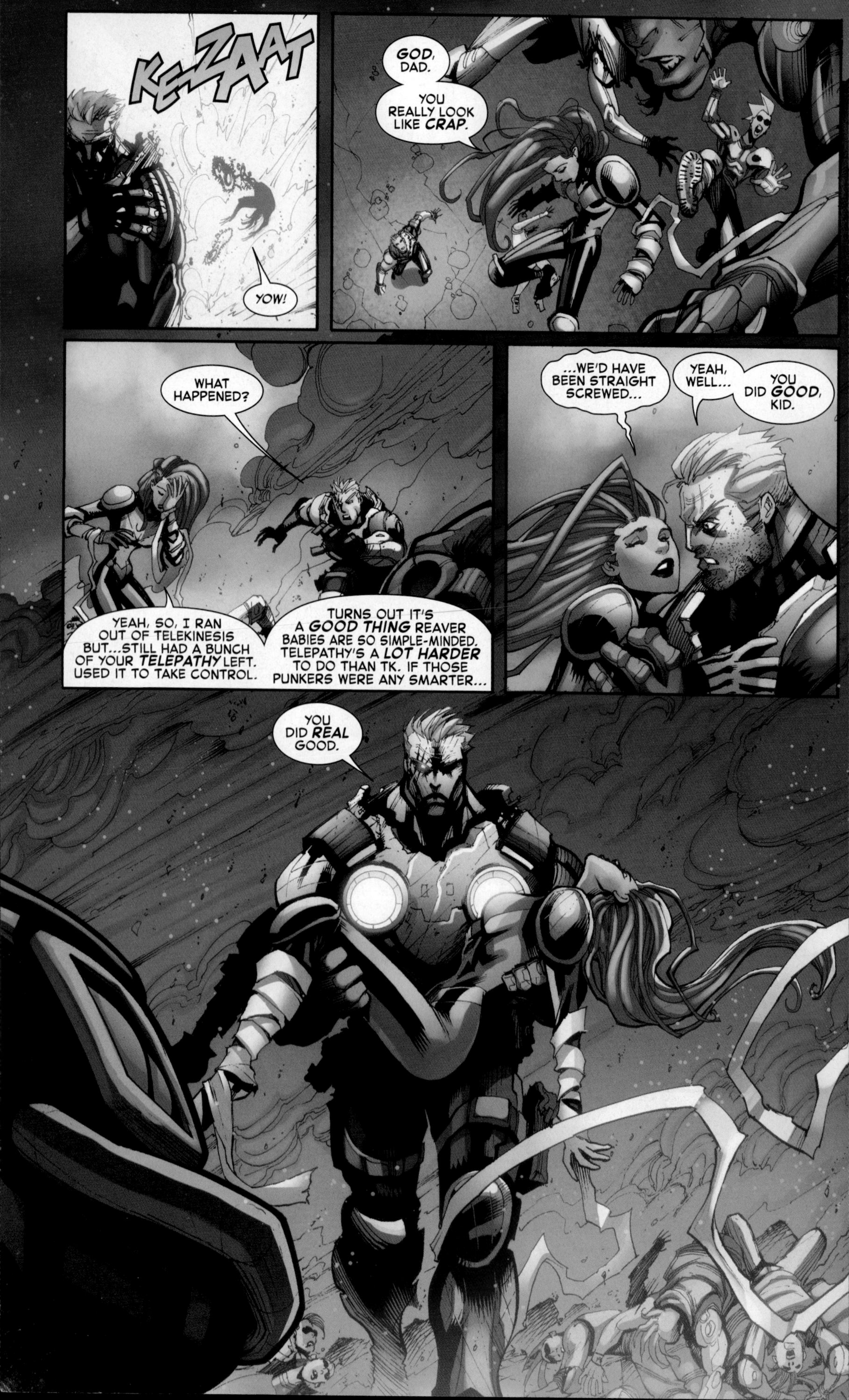
KE-ZAAT
YOW!
GOD, DAD.
YOU REALLY LOOK LIKE CRAP.
WHAT HAPPENED?
YEAH, SO, I RAN OUT OF TELEKINESIS BUT...STILL HAD A BUNCH OF YOUR TELEPATHY LEFT. USED IT TO TAKE CONTROL.
TURNS OUT IT'S A GOOD THING REAVER BABIES ARE SO SIMPLE-MINDED. TELEPATHY'S A LOT HARDER TO DO THAN TK. IF THOSE PUNKERS WERE ANY SMARTER...
...WE'D HAVE BEEN STRAIGHT SCREWED...
YEAH, WELL...
YOU DID GOOD, KID.
YOU DID REAL GOOD.

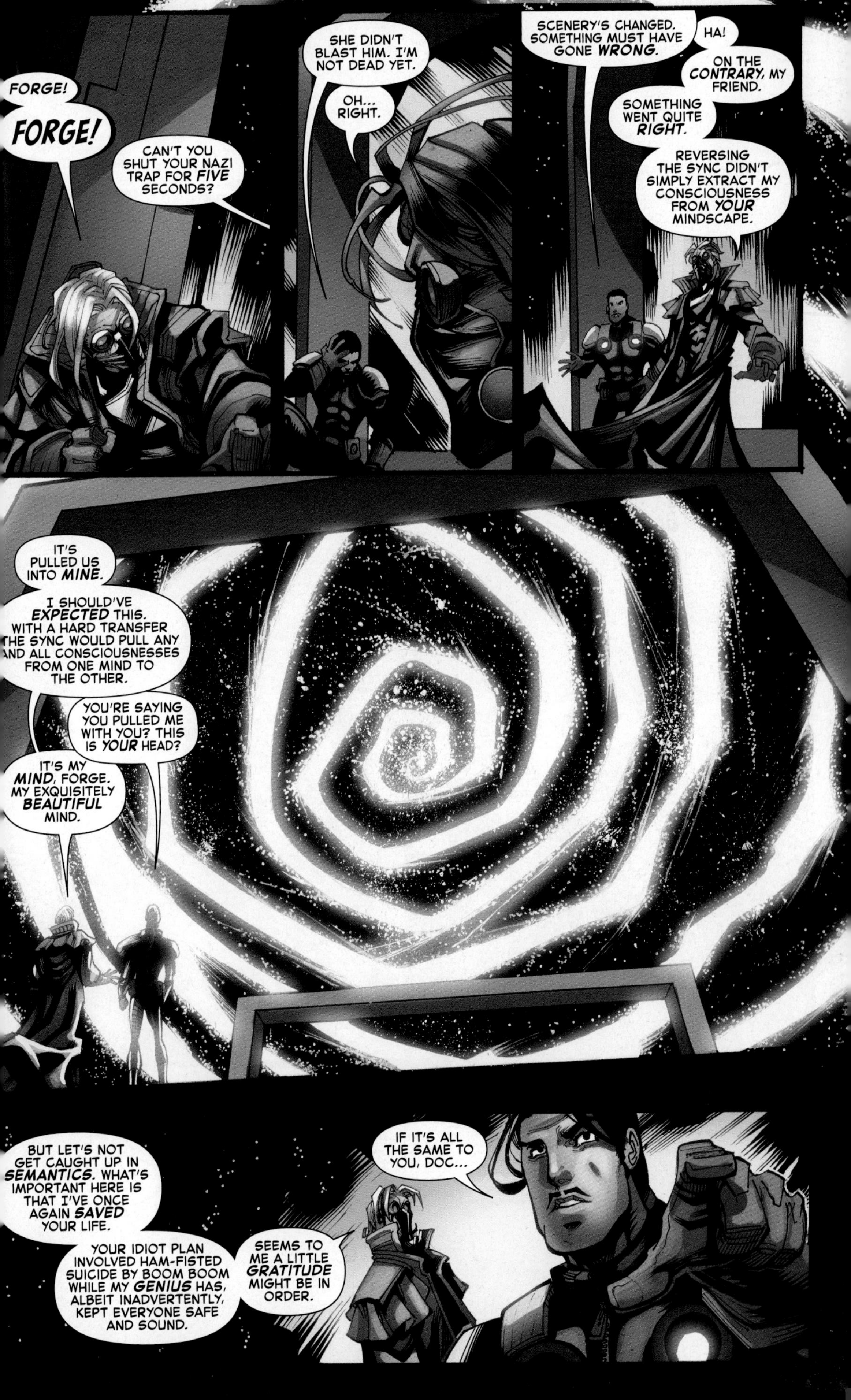
FORGE!
FORGE!
CAN'T YOU SHUT YOUR NAZI TRAP FOR FIVE SECONDS?
SHE DIDN'T BLAST HIM. I'M NOT DEAD YET.
OH... RIGHT.
SCENERY'S CHANGED. SOMETHING MUST HAVE GONE WRONG.
HA!
ON THE CONTRARY, MY FRIEND.
SOMETHING WENT QUITE RIGHT.
REVERSING THE SYNC DIDN'T SIMPLY EXTRACT MY CONSCIOUSNESS FROM YOUR MINDSCAPE.
IT'S PULLED US INTO MINE.
I SHOULD'VE EXPECTED THIS. WITH A HARD TRANSFER THE SYNC WOULD PULL ANY AND ALL CONSCIOUSNESSES FROM ONE MIND TO THE OTHER.
YOU'RE SAYING YOU PULLED ME WITH YOU? THIS IS YOUR HEAD?
IT'S MY MIND, FORGE. MY EXQUISITELY BEAUTIFUL MIND.
BUT LET'S NOT GET CAUGHT UP IN SEMANTICS. WHAT'S IMPORTANT HERE IS THAT I'VE ONCE AGAIN SAVED YOUR LIFE.
YOUR IDIOT PLAN INVOLVED HAM-FISTED SUICIDE BY BOOM BOOM WHILE MY GENIUS HAS, ALBEIT INADVERTENTLY, KEPT EVERYONE SAFE AND SOUND.
SEEMS TO ME A LITTLE GRATITUDE MIGHT BE IN ORDER.
IF IT'S ALL THE SAME TO YOU, DOC...

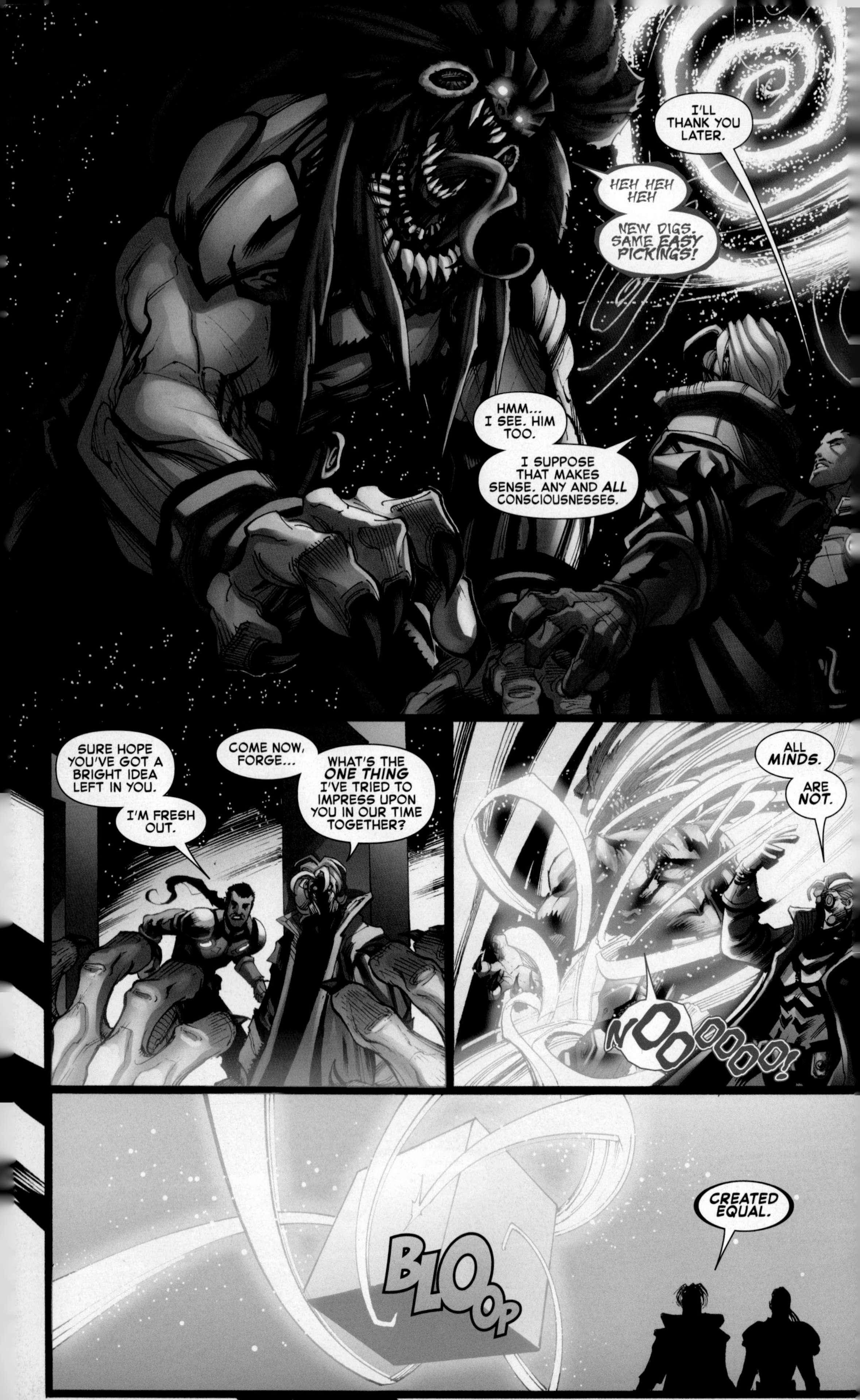
I'LL THANK YOU LATER.
HEH HEH HEH
NEW DIGS. SAME EASY PICKINGS!
HMM... I SEE. HIM TOO.
I SUPPOSE THAT MAKES SENSE. ANY AND ALL CONSCIOUSNESSES.
SURE HOPE YOU'VE GOT A BRIGHT IDEA LEFT IN YOU.
I'M FRESH OUT.
COME NOW, FORGE...
WHAT'S THE ONE THING I'VE TRIED TO IMPRESS UPON YOU IN OUR TIME TOGETHER?
ALL MINDS.
ARE NOT.
NOOOOOO!
CREATED EQUAL.
BLOOP

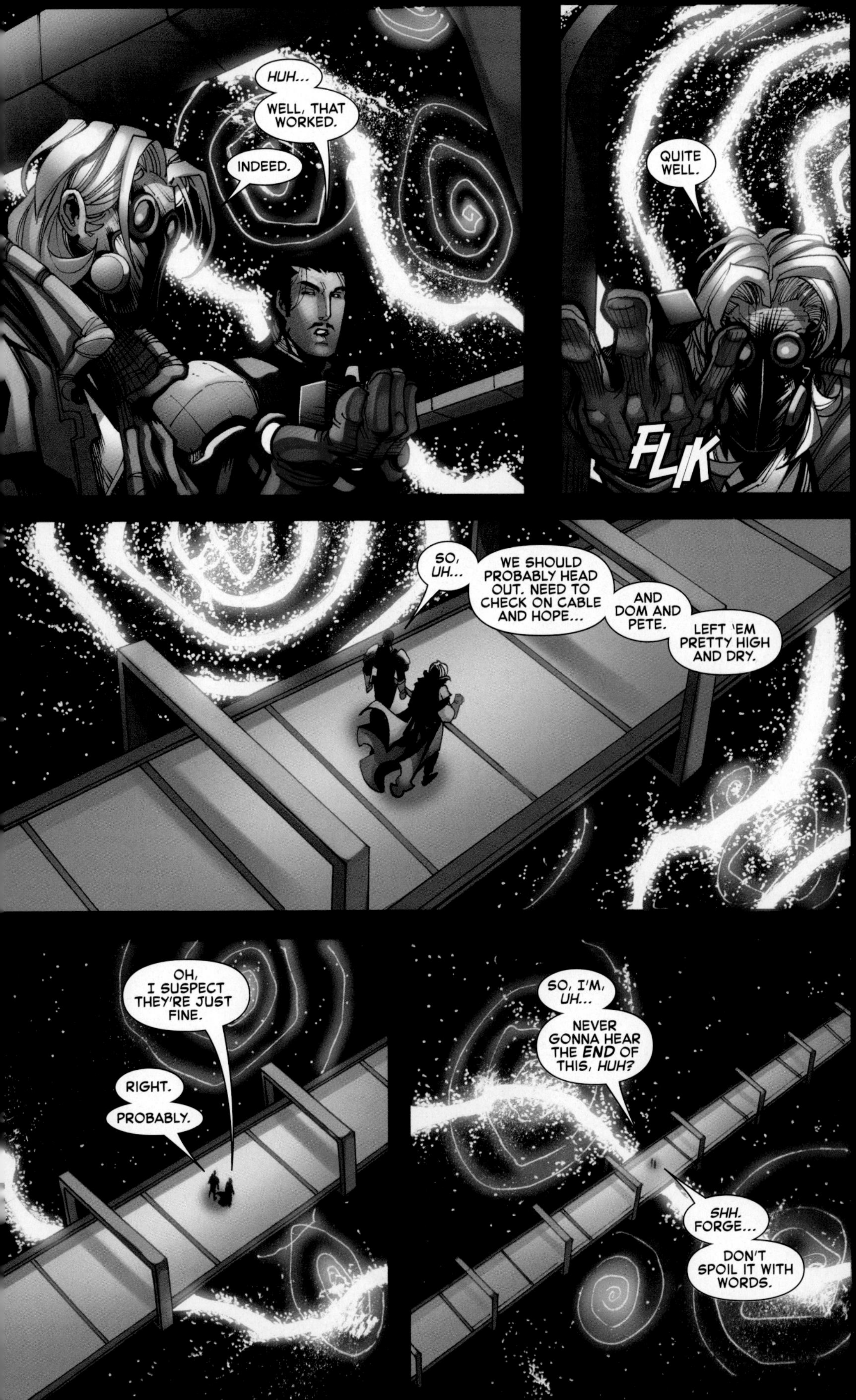

HUH...
WELL, THAT WORKED.
INDEED.
QUITE WELL.
FLIK
SO, UH...
WE SHOULD PROBABLY HEAD OUT. NEED TO CHECK ON CABLE AND HOPE...
AND DOM AND PETE.
LEFT 'EM PRETTY HIGH AND DRY.
OH, I SUSPECT THEY'RE JUST FINE.
RIGHT.
PROBABLY.
SO, I'M, UH...
NEVER GONNA HEAR THE END OF THIS, HUH?
SHH. FORGE...
DON'T SPOIL IT WITH WORDS.

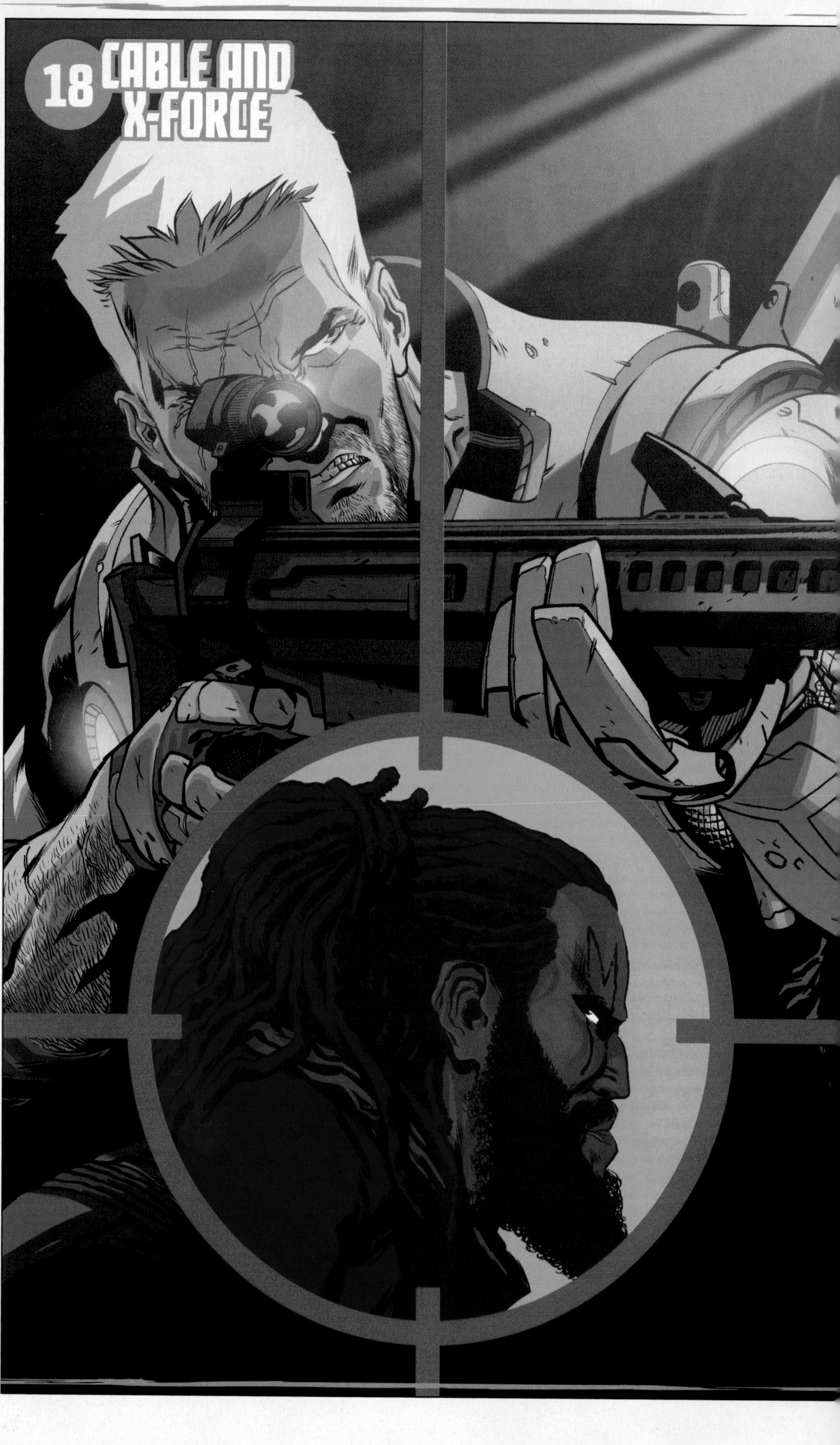
18
CABLE AND X-FORCE

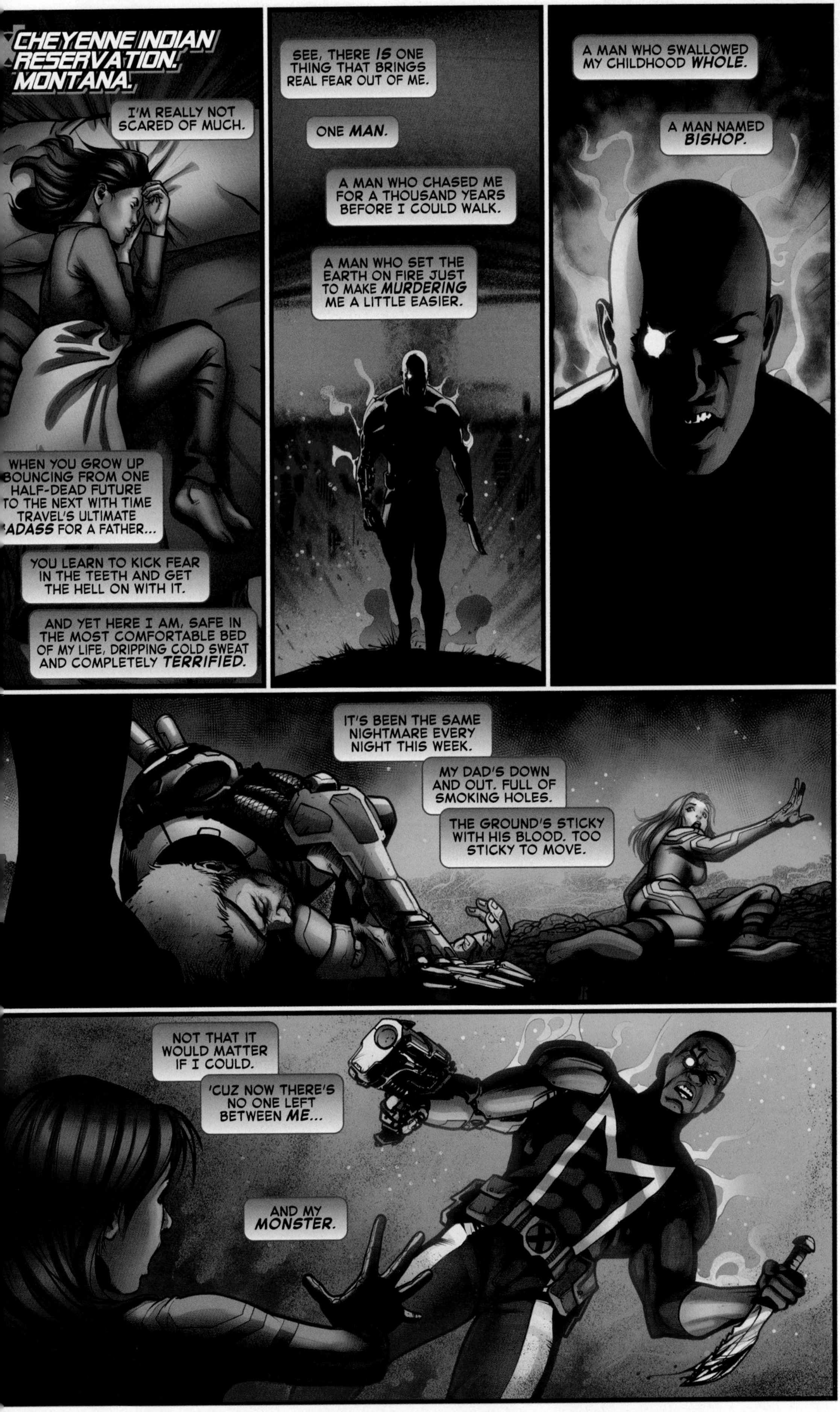
CHEYENNE INDIAN RESERVATION. MONTANA.
I'M REALLY NOT SCARED OF MUCH.
WHEN YOU GROW UP BOUNCING FROM ONE HALF-DEAD FUTURE TO THE NEXT WITH TIME TRAVEL'S ULTIMATE BADASS FOR A FATHER...
YOU LEARN TO KICK FEAR IN THE TEETH AND GET THE HELL ON WITH IT.
AND YET HERE I AM, SAFE IN THE MOST COMFORTABLE BED OF MY LIFE, DRIPPING COLD SWEAT AND COMPLETELY TERRIFIED.
SEE, THERE IS ONE THING THAT BRINGS REAL FEAR OUT OF ME.
ONE MAN.
A MAN WHO CHASED ME FOR A THOUSAND YEARS BEFORE I COULD WALK.
A MAN WHO SET THE EARTH ON FIRE JUST TO MAKE MURDERING ME A LITTLE EASIER.
A MAN WHO SWALLOWED MY CHILDHOOD WHOLE.
A MAN NAMED BISHOP.
IT'S BEEN THE SAME NIGHTMARE EVERY NIGHT THIS WEEK.
MY DAD'S DOWN AND OUT. FULL OF SMOKING HOLES.
THE GROUND'S STICKY WITH HIS BLOOD. TOO STICKY TO MOVE.
NOT THAT IT WOULD MATTER IF I COULD.
'CUZ NOW THERE'S NO ONE LEFT BETWEEN ME...
AND MY MONSTER.

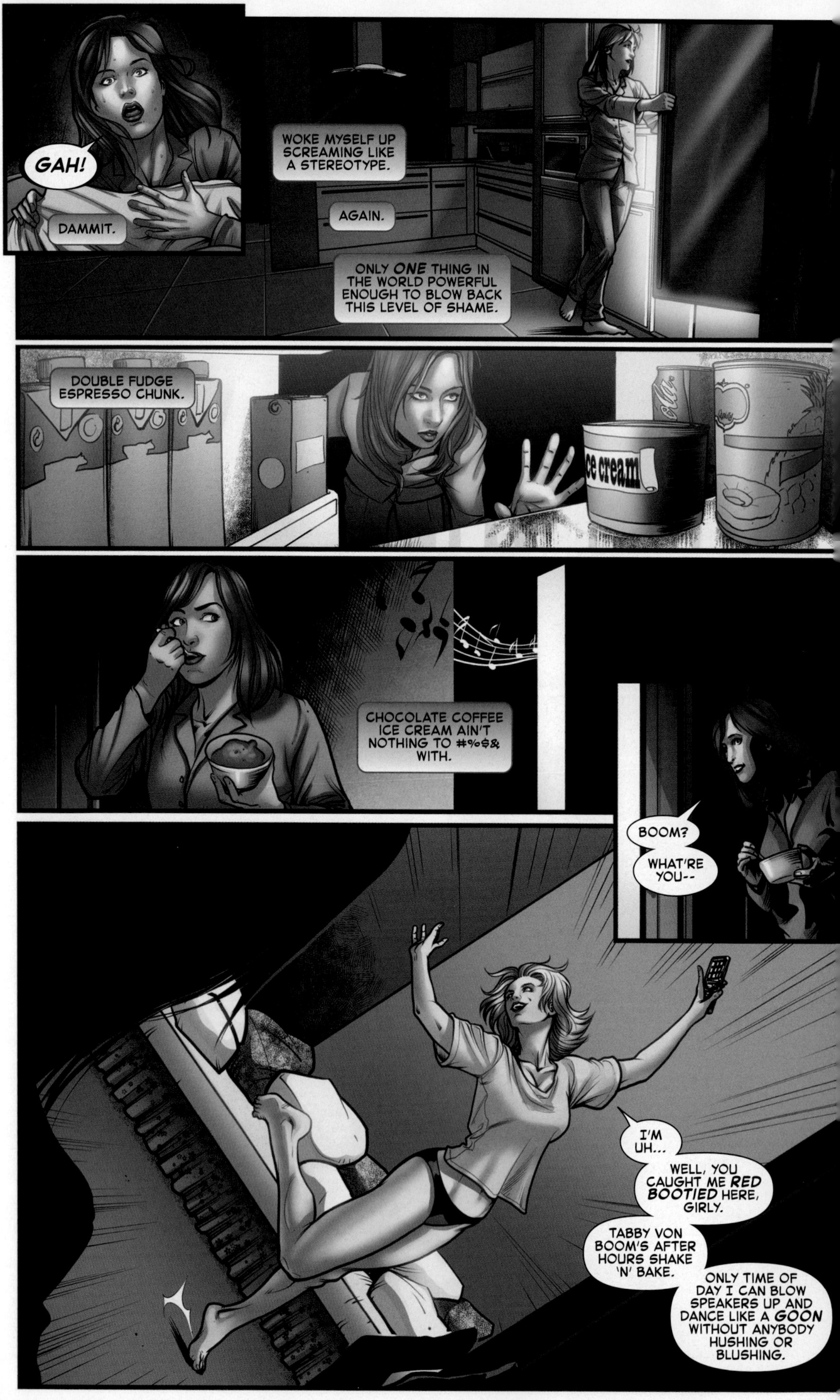

GAH!
DAMMIT.
WOKE MYSELF UP SCREAMING LIKE A STEREOTYPE.
AGAIN.
ONLY ONE THING IN THE WORLD POWERFUL ENOUGH TO BLOW BACK THIS LEVEL OF SHAME.
DOUBLE FUDGE ESPRESSO CHUNK.
ice cream
CHOCOLATE COFFEE ICE CREAM AIN'T NOTHING TO #%$& WITH.
BOOM?
WHAT'RE YOU--
I'M UH...
WELL, YOU CAUGHT ME RED BOOTIED HERE, GIRLY.
TABBY VON BOOM'S AFTER HOURS SHAKE 'N' BAKE.
ONLY TIME OF DAY I CAN BLOW SPEAKERS UP AND DANCE LIKE A GOON WITHOUT ANYBODY HUSHING OR BLUSHING.

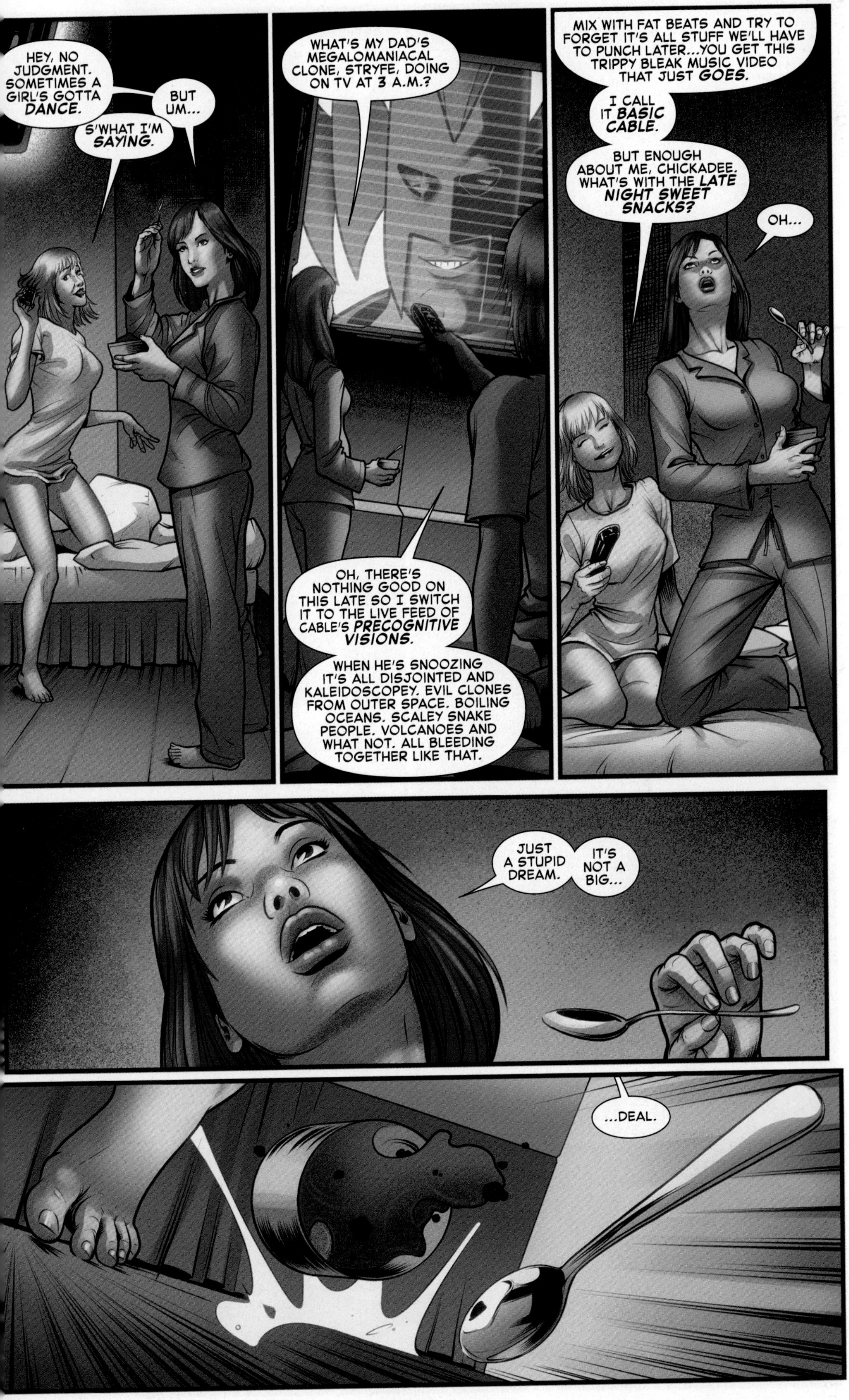

HEY, NO JUDGMENT. SOMETIMES A GIRL'S GOTTA DANCE.
BUT UM...
S'WHAT I'M SAYING.
WHAT'S MY DAD'S MEGALOMANIACAL CLONE, STRYFE, DOING ON TV AT 3 A.M.?
OH, THERE'S NOTHING GOOD ON THIS LATE SO I SWITCH IT TO THE LIVE FEED OF CABLE'S PRECOGNITIVE VISIONS.
WHEN HE'S SNOOZING IT'S ALL DISJOINTED AND KALEIDOSCOPEY. EVIL CLONES FROM OUTER SPACE. BOILING OCEANS. SCALEY SNAKE PEOPLE. VOLCANOES AND WHAT NOT. ALL BLEEDING TOGETHER LIKE THAT.
MIX WITH FAT BEATS AND TRY TO FORGET IT'S ALL STUFF WE'LL HAVE TO PUNCH LATER...YOU GET THIS TRIPPY BLEAK MUSIC VIDEO THAT JUST GOES.
I CALL IT BASIC CABLE.
BUT ENOUGH ABOUT ME, CHICKADEE. WHAT'S WITH THE LATE NIGHT SWEET SNACKS?
OH...
JUST A STUPID DREAM.
IT'S NOT A BIG...
...DEAL.

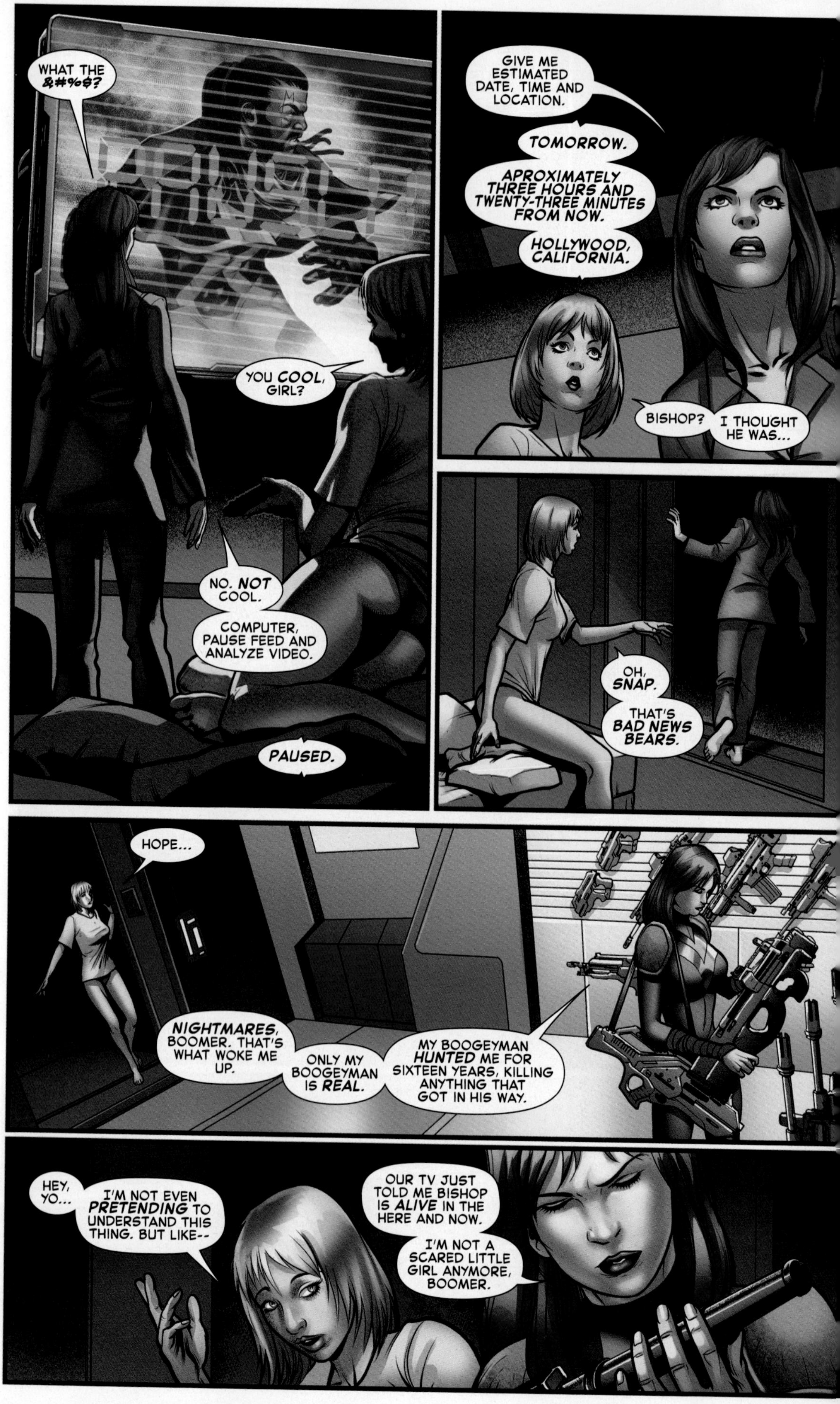
WHAT THE &#%$?
YOU COOL, GIRL?
NO. NOT COOL.
COMPUTER, PAUSE FEED AND ANALYZE VIDEO.
PAUSED.
GIVE ME ESTIMATED DATE, TIME AND LOCATION.
TOMORROW.
APROXIMATELY THREE HOURS AND TWENTY-THREE MINUTES FROM NOW.
HOLLYWOOD, CALIFORNIA.
BISHOP?
I THOUGHT HE WAS...
OH, SNAP.
THAT'S BAD NEWS BEARS.
HOPE...
NIGHTMARES, BOOMER. THAT'S WHAT WOKE ME UP.
ONLY MY BOOGEYMAN IS REAL.
MY BOOGEYMAN HUNTED ME FOR SIXTEEN YEARS, KILLING ANYTHING THAT GOT IN HIS WAY.
HEY, YO...
I'M NOT EVEN PRETENDING TO UNDERSTAND THIS THING. BUT LIKE--
OUR TV JUST TOLD ME BISHOP IS ALIVE IN THE HERE AND NOW.
I'M NOT A SCARED LITTLE GIRL ANYMORE, BOOMER.

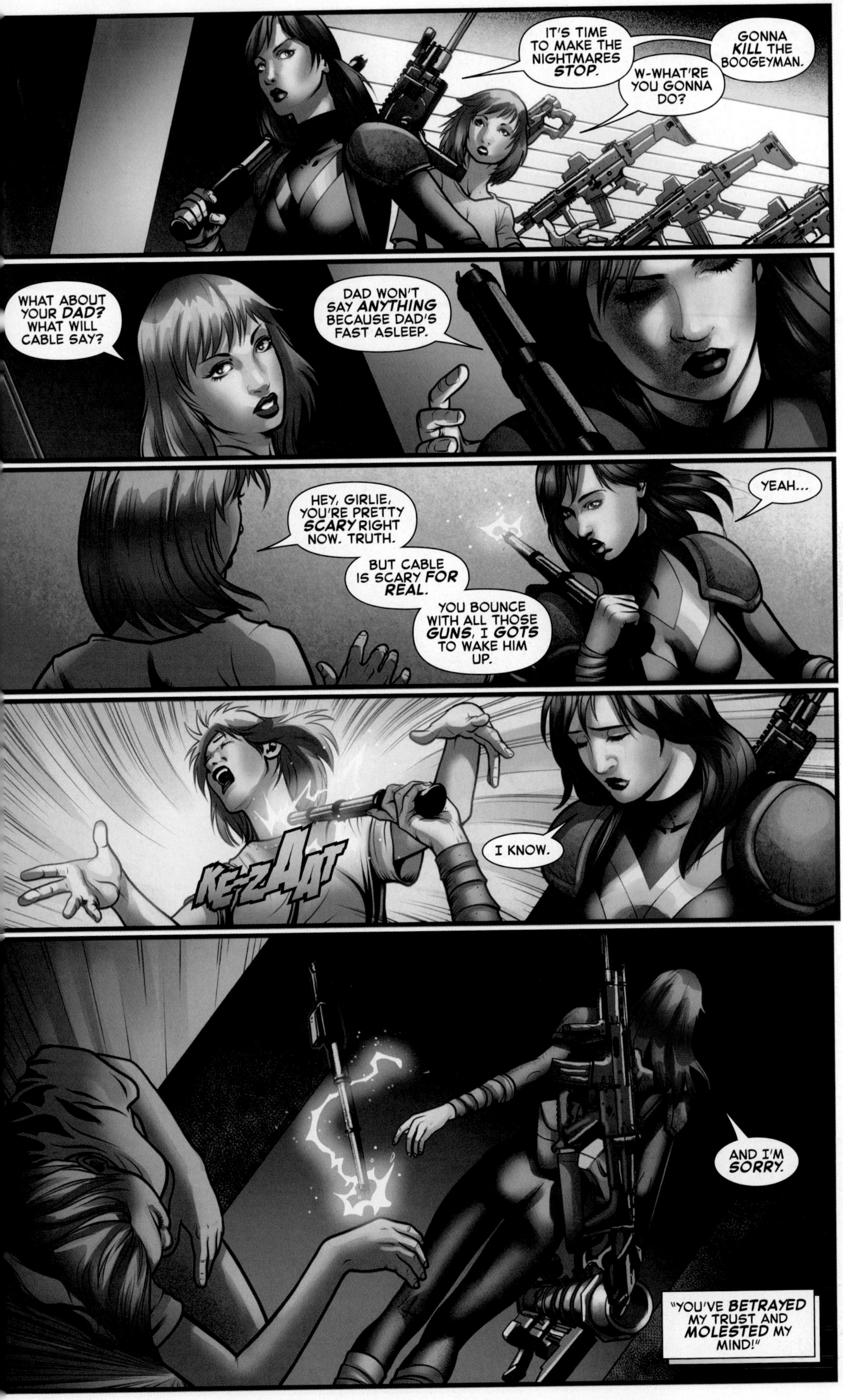

IT'S TIME TO MAKE THE NIGHTMARES STOP.
W-WHAT'RE YOU GONNA DO?
GONNA KILL THE BOOGEYMAN.
WHAT ABOUT YOUR DAD? WHAT WILL CABLE SAY?
DAD WON'T SAY ANYTHING BECAUSE DAD'S FAST ASLEEP.
HEY, GIRLIE, YOU'RE PRETTY SCARY RIGHT NOW. TRUTH.
BUT CABLE IS SCARY FOR REAL.
YOU BOUNCE WITH ALL THOSE GUNS, I GOTS TO WAKE HIM UP.
YEAH...
KE-ZAAT
I KNOW.
AND I'M SORRY.
"YOU'VE BETRAYED MY TRUST AND MOLESTED MY MIND!"

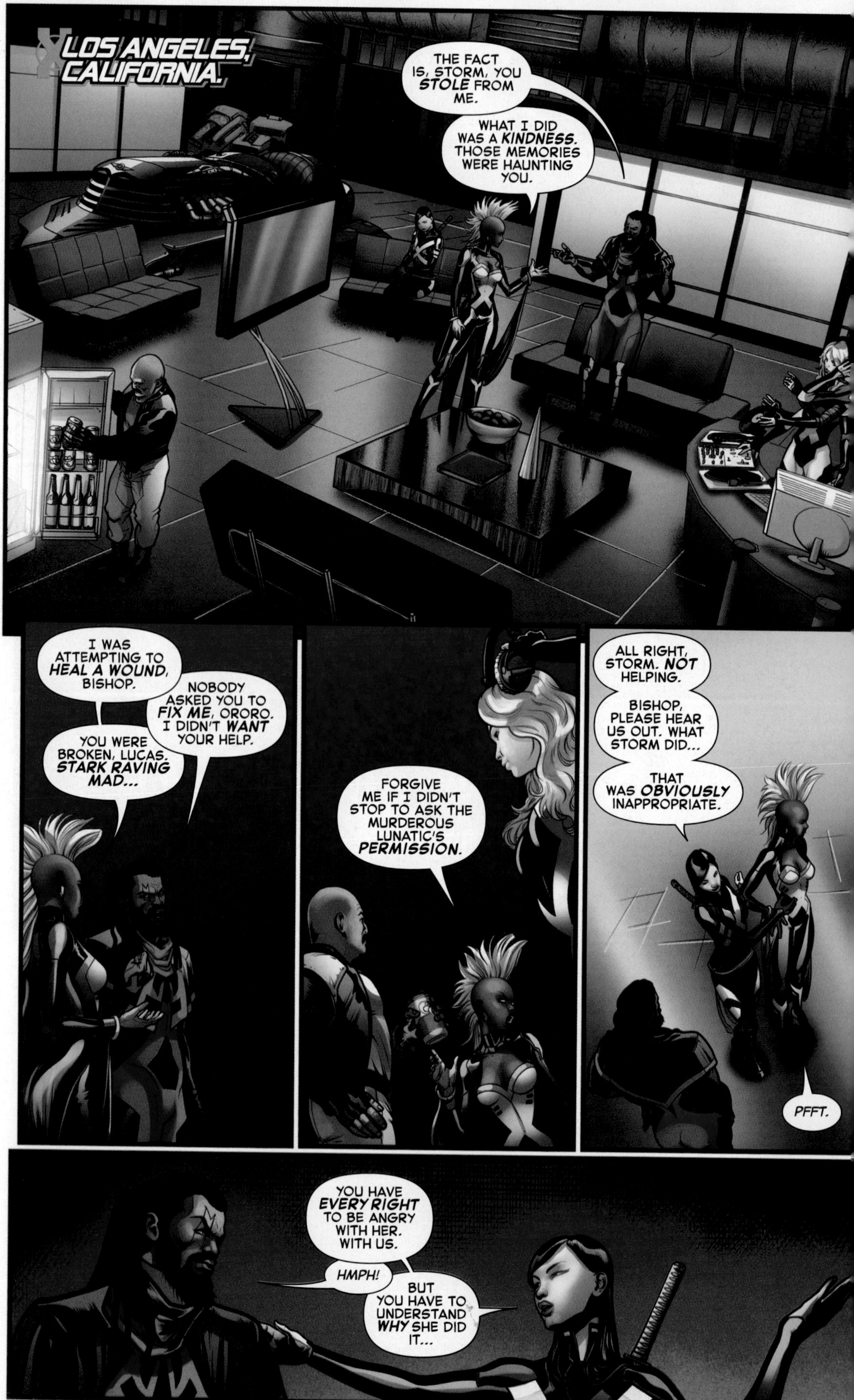
LOS ANGELES, CALIFORNIA.
THE FACT IS, STORM, YOU STOLE FROM ME.
WHAT I DID WAS A KINDNESS. THOSE MEMORIES WERE HAUNTING YOU.
I WAS ATTEMPTING TO HEAL A WOUND, BISHOP.
YOU WERE BROKEN, LUCAS. STARK RAVING MAD...
NOBODY ASKED YOU TO FIX ME, ORORO. I DIDN'T WANT YOUR HELP.
FORGIVE ME IF I DIDN'T STOP TO ASK THE MURDEROUS LUNATIC'S PERMISSION.
ALL RIGHT, STORM. NOT HELPING.
BISHOP, PLEASE HEAR US OUT. WHAT STORM DID...
THAT WAS OBVIOUSLY INAPPROPRIATE.
PFFT.
YOU HAVE EVERY RIGHT TO BE ANGRY WITH HER. WITH US.
HMPH!
BUT YOU HAVE TO UNDERSTAND WHY SHE DID IT...

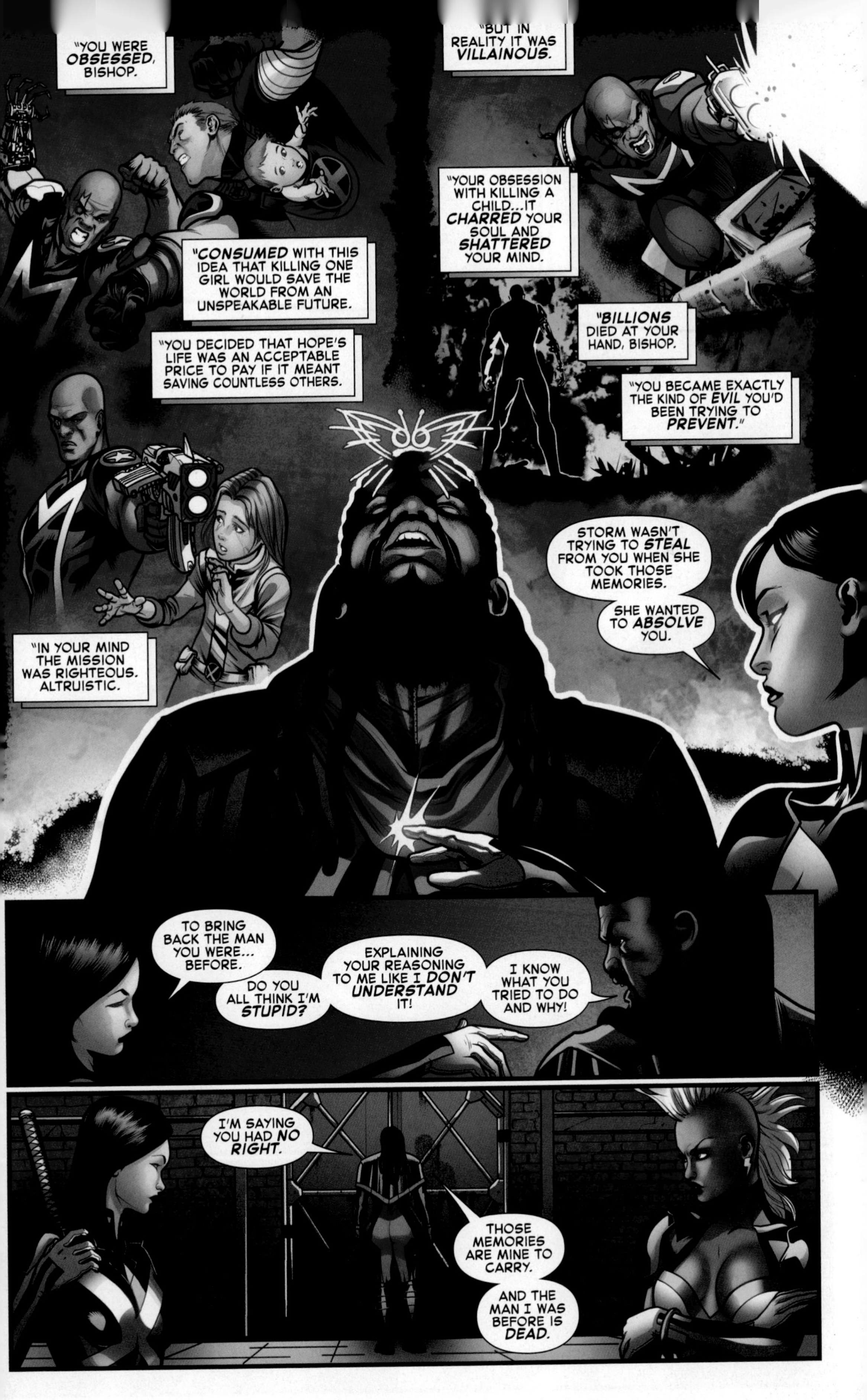
"YOU WERE OBSESSED, BISHOP.
"CONSUMED WITH THIS IDEA THAT KILLING ONE GIRL WOULD SAVE THE WORLD FROM AN UNSPEAKABLE FUTURE.
"YOU DECIDED THAT HOPE'S LIFE WAS AN ACCEPTABLE PRICE TO PAY IF IT MEANT SAVING COUNTLESS OTHERS.
"IN YOUR MIND THE MISSION WAS RIGHTEOUS. ALTRUISTIC.
"BUT IN REALITY IT WAS VILLAINOUS.
"YOUR OBSESSION WITH KILLING A CHILD...IT CHARRED YOUR SOUL AND SHATTERED YOUR MIND.
"BILLIONS DIED AT YOUR HAND, BISHOP.
"YOU BECAME EXACTLY THE KIND OF EVIL YOU'D BEEN TRYING TO PREVENT."
STORM WASN'T TRYING TO STEAL FROM YOU WHEN SHE TOOK THOSE MEMORIES.
SHE WANTED TO ABSOLVE YOU.
TO BRING BACK THE MAN YOU WERE... BEFORE.
DO YOU ALL THINK I'M STUPID?
EXPLAINING YOUR REASONING TO ME LIKE I DON'T UNDERSTAND IT!
I KNOW WHAT YOU TRIED TO DO AND WHY!
I'M SAYING YOU HAD NO RIGHT.
THOSE MEMORIES ARE MINE TO CARRY.
AND THE MAN I WAS BEFORE IS DEAD.

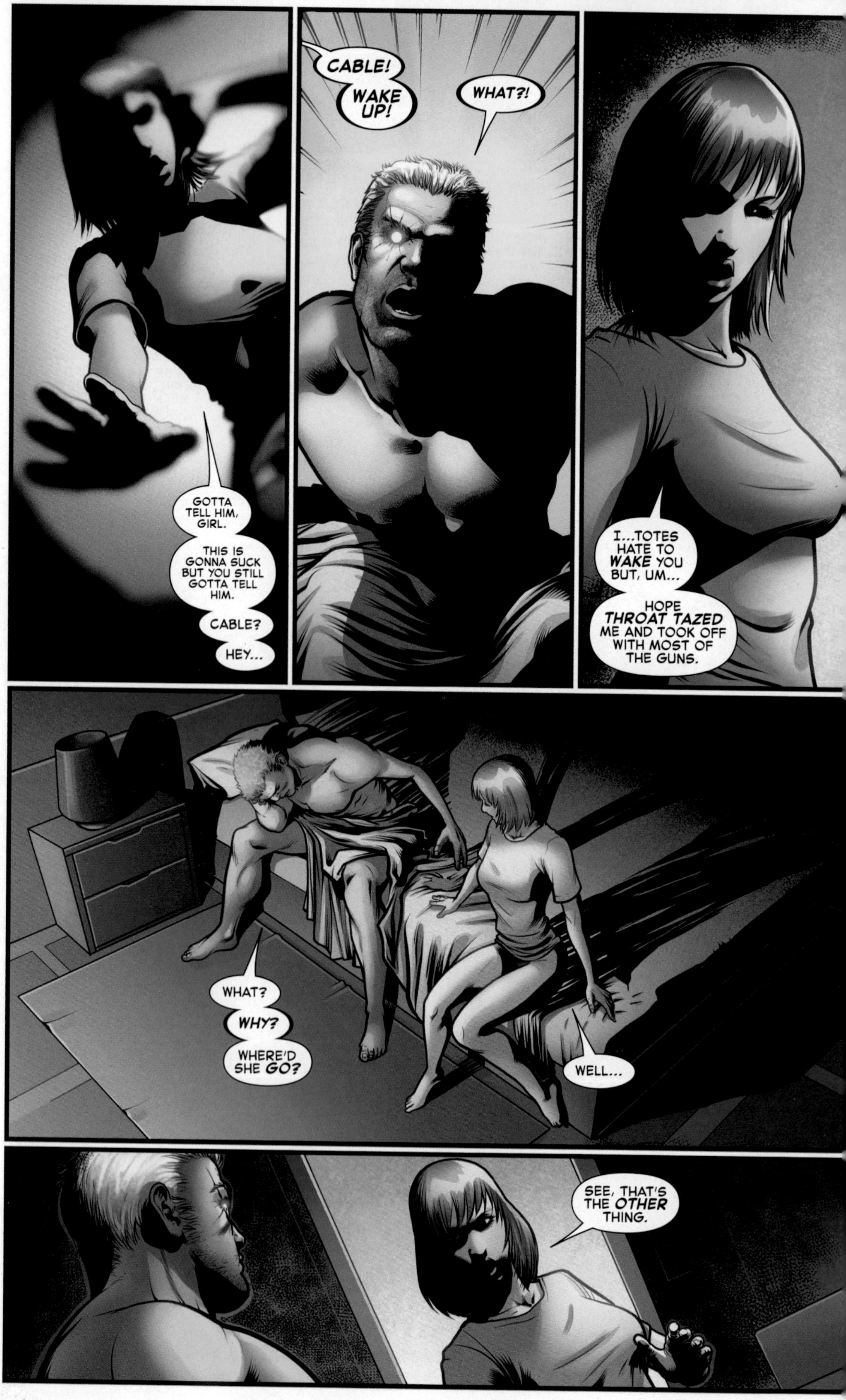

GOTTA TELL HIM, GIRL.
THIS IS GONNA SUCK BUT YOU STILL GOTTA TELL HIM.
CABLE?
HEY...
CABLE!
WAKE UP!
WHAT?!
I...TOTES HATE TO WAKE YOU BUT, UM...
HOPE THROAT TAZED ME AND TOOK OFF WITH MOST OF THE GUNS.
WHAT?
WHY?
WHERE'D SHE GO?
WELL...
SEE, THAT'S THE OTHER THING.

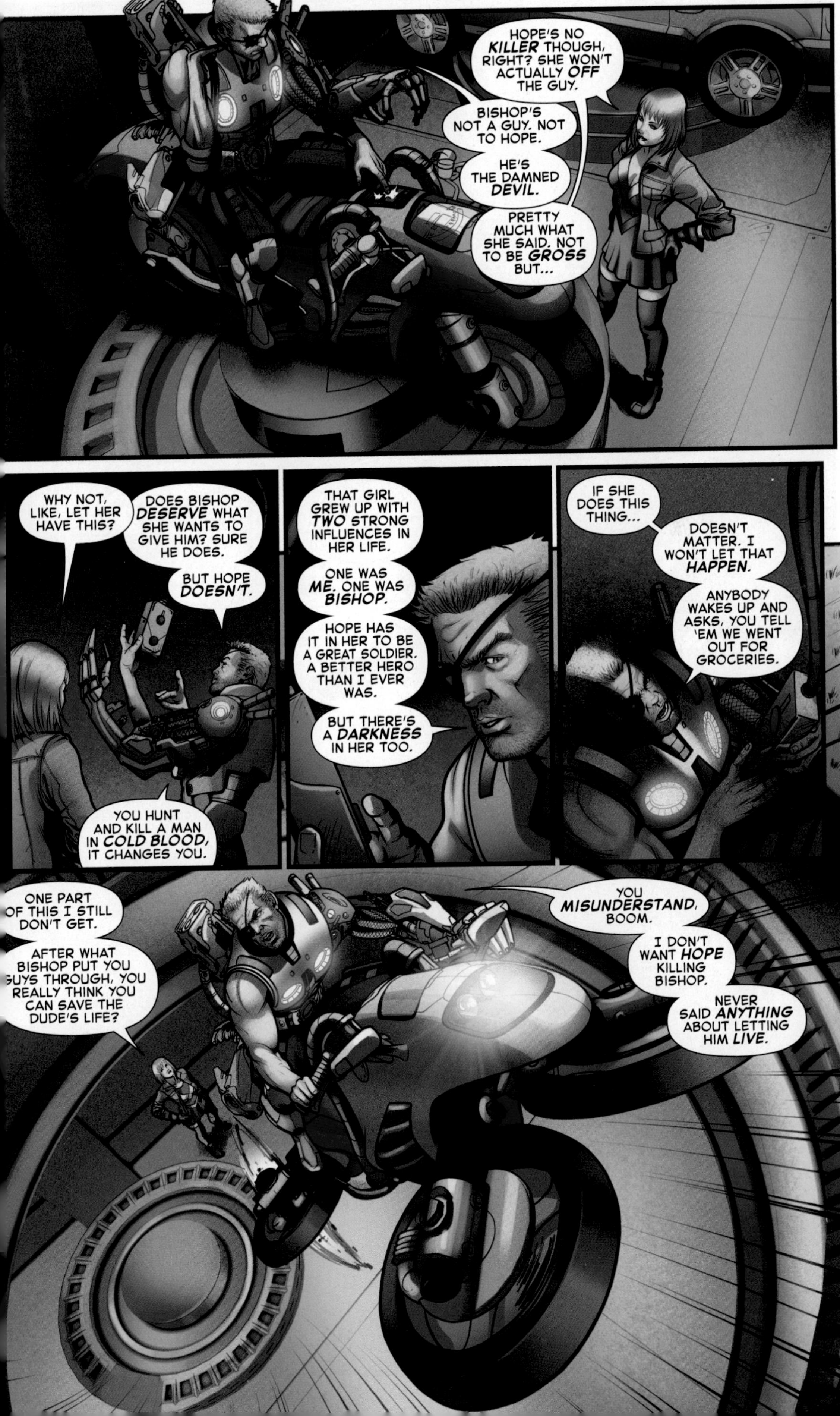
HOPE'S NO KILLER THOUGH, RIGHT? SHE WON'T ACTUALLY OFF THE GUY.
BISHOP'S NOT A GUY. NOT TO HOPE.
HE'S THE DAMNED DEVIL.
PRETTY MUCH WHAT SHE SAID. NOT TO BE GROSS BUT...
WHY NOT, LIKE, LET HER HAVE THIS?
DOES BISHOP DESERVE WHAT SHE WANTS TO GIVE HIM? SURE HE DOES.
BUT HOPE DOESN'T.
YOU HUNT AND KILL A MAN IN COLD BLOOD, IT CHANGES YOU.
THAT GIRL GREW UP WITH TWO STRONG INFLUENCES IN HER LIFE.
ONE WAS ME. ONE WAS BISHOP.
HOPE HAS IT IN HER TO BE A GREAT SOLDIER. A BETTER HERO THAN I EVER WAS.
BUT THERE'S A DARKNESS IN HER TOO.
IF SHE DOES THIS THING...
DOESN'T MATTER. I WON'T LET THAT HAPPEN.
ANYBODY WAKES UP AND ASKS, YOU TELL 'EM WE WENT OUT FOR GROCERIES.
ONE PART OF THIS I STILL DON'T GET.
AFTER WHAT BISHOP PUT YOU GUYS THROUGH, YOU REALLY THINK YOU CAN SAVE THE DUDE'S LIFE?
YOU MISUNDERSTAND, BOOM.
I DON'T WANT HOPE KILLING BISHOP.
NEVER SAID ANYTHING ABOUT LETTING HIM LIVE.

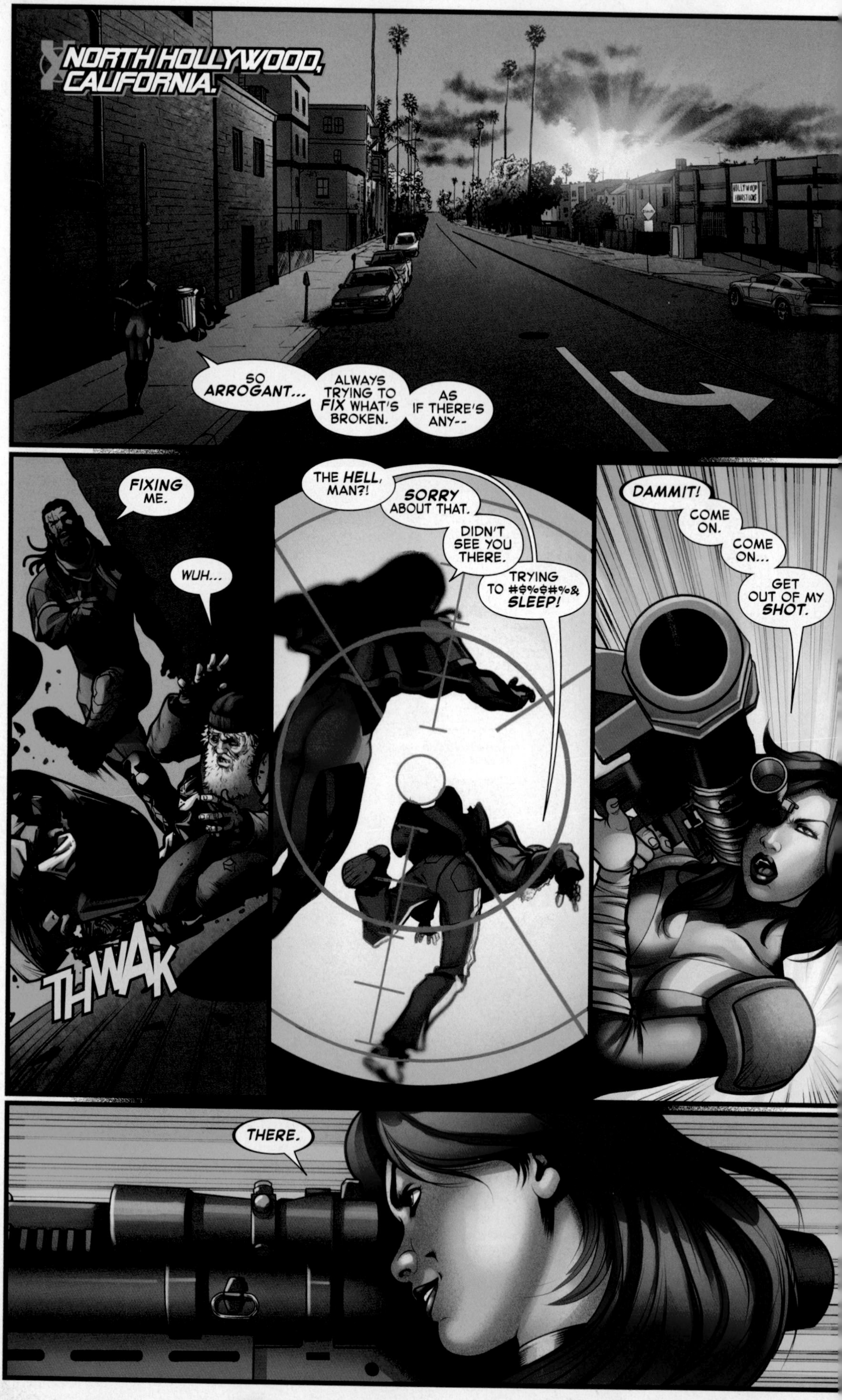
NORTH HOLLYWOOD, CALIFORNIA.
SO ARROGANT...
ALWAYS TRYING TO FIX WHAT'S BROKEN.
AS IF THERE'S ANY--
FIXING ME.
WUH...
THWAK
THE HELL, MAN?!
SORRY ABOUT THAT.
DIDN'T SEE YOU THERE.
TRYING TO #$%$#%& SLEEP!
DAMMIT!
COME ON.
COME ON...
GET OUT OF MY SHOT.
THERE.

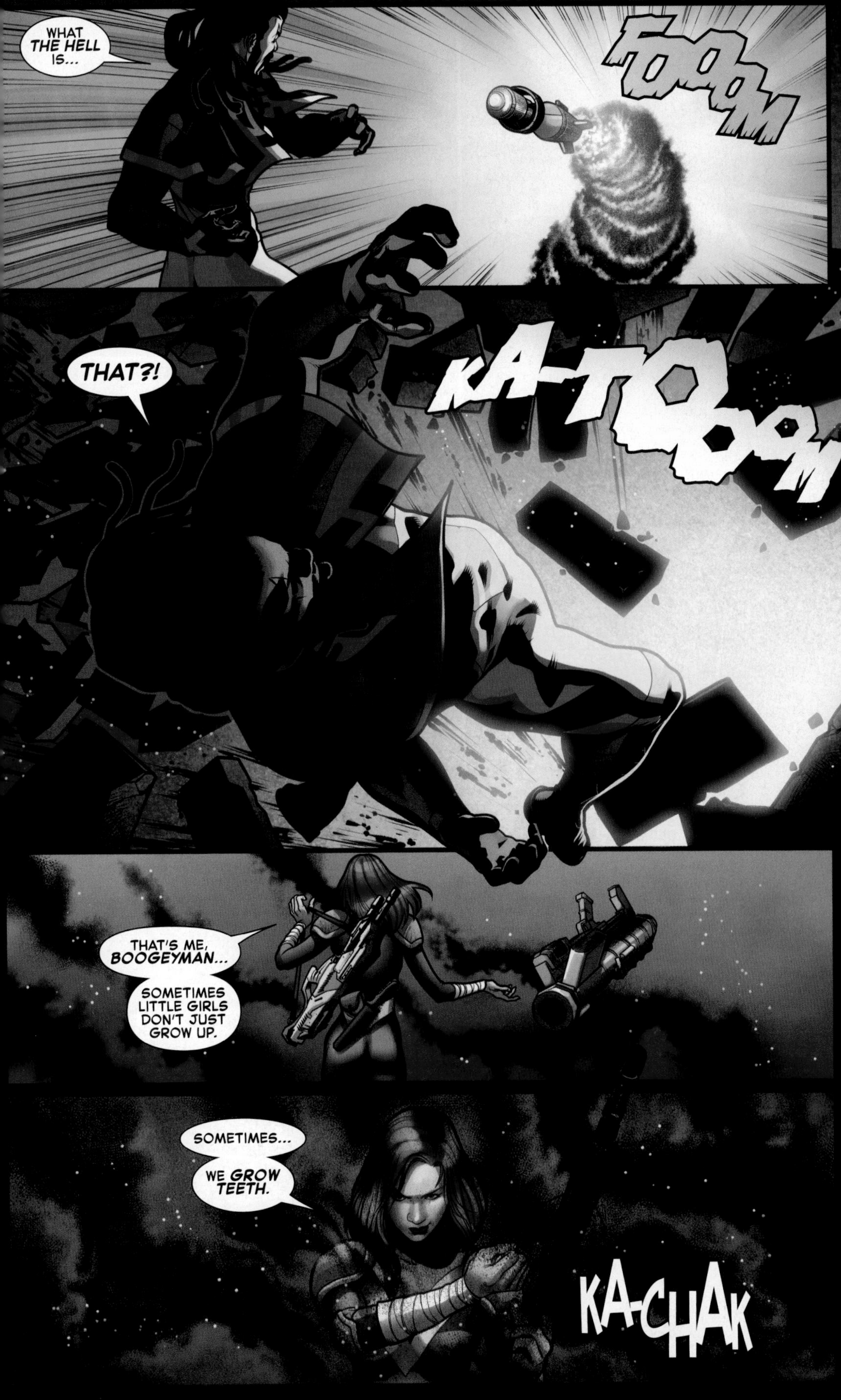
WHAT THE HELL IS...
FOOOOM
THAT?!
KA-TOOOM
THAT'S ME, BOOGEYMAN...
SOMETIMES LITTLE GIRLS DON'T JUST GROW UP.
SOMETIMES...
WE GROW TEETH.
KA-CHAK

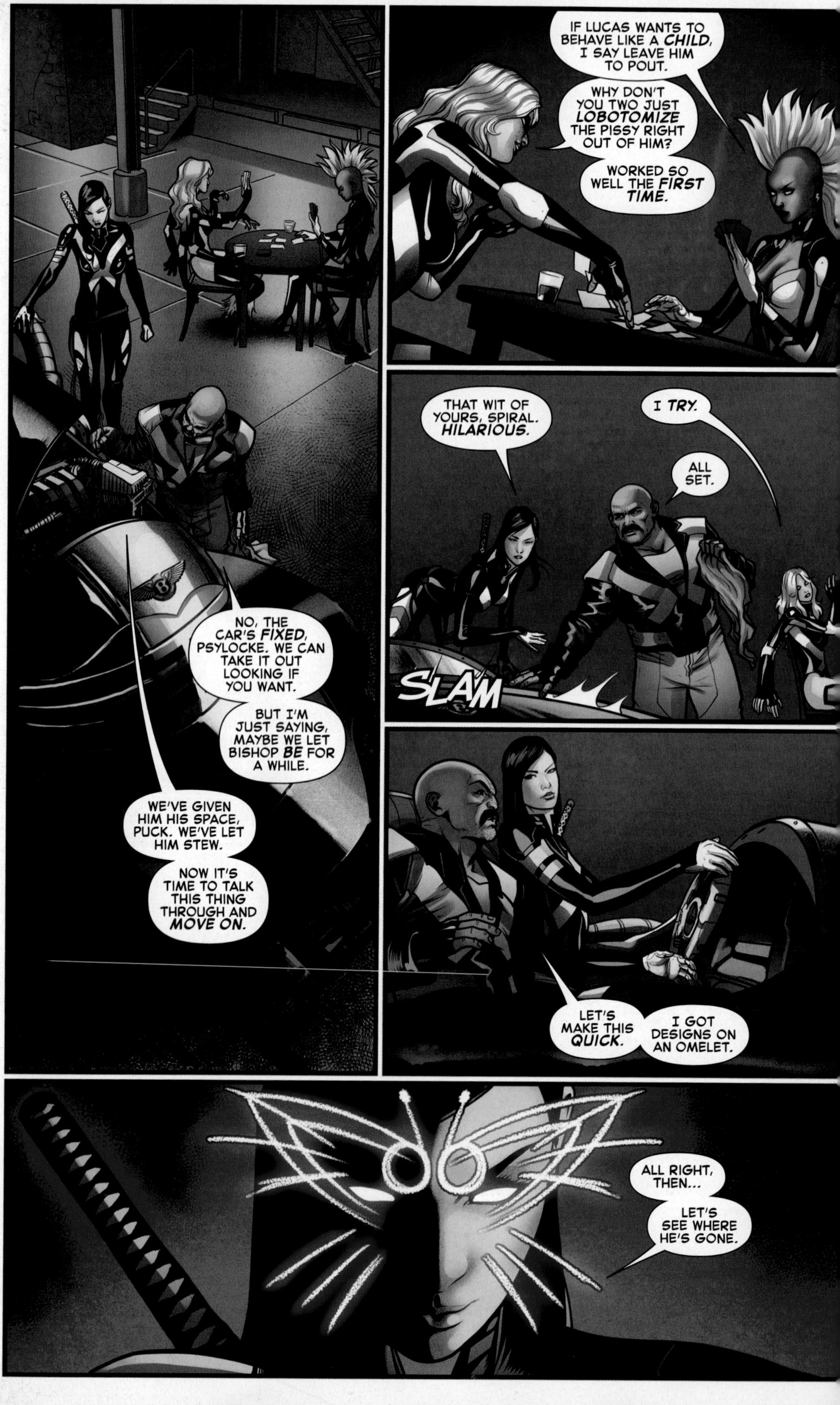
IF LUCAS WANTS TO BEHAVE LIKE A CHILD, I SAY LEAVE HIM TO POUT.
WHY DON'T YOU TWO JUST LOBOTOMIZE THE PISSY RIGHT OUT OF HIM?
WORKED SO WELL THE FIRST TIME.
NO, THE CAR'S FIXED, PSYLOCKE. WE CAN TAKE IT OUT LOOKING IF YOU WANT.
BUT I'M JUST SAYING, MAYBE WE LET BISHOP BE FOR A WHILE.
WE'VE GIVEN HIM HIS SPACE, PUCK. WE'VE LET HIM STEW.
NOW IT'S TIME TO TALK THIS THING THROUGH AND MOVE ON.
THAT WIT OF YOURS, SPIRAL. HILARIOUS.
I TRY.
ALL SET.
SLAM
LET'S MAKE THIS QUICK.
I GOT DESIGNS ON AN OMELET.
ALL RIGHT, THEN...
LET'S SEE WHERE HE'S GONE.

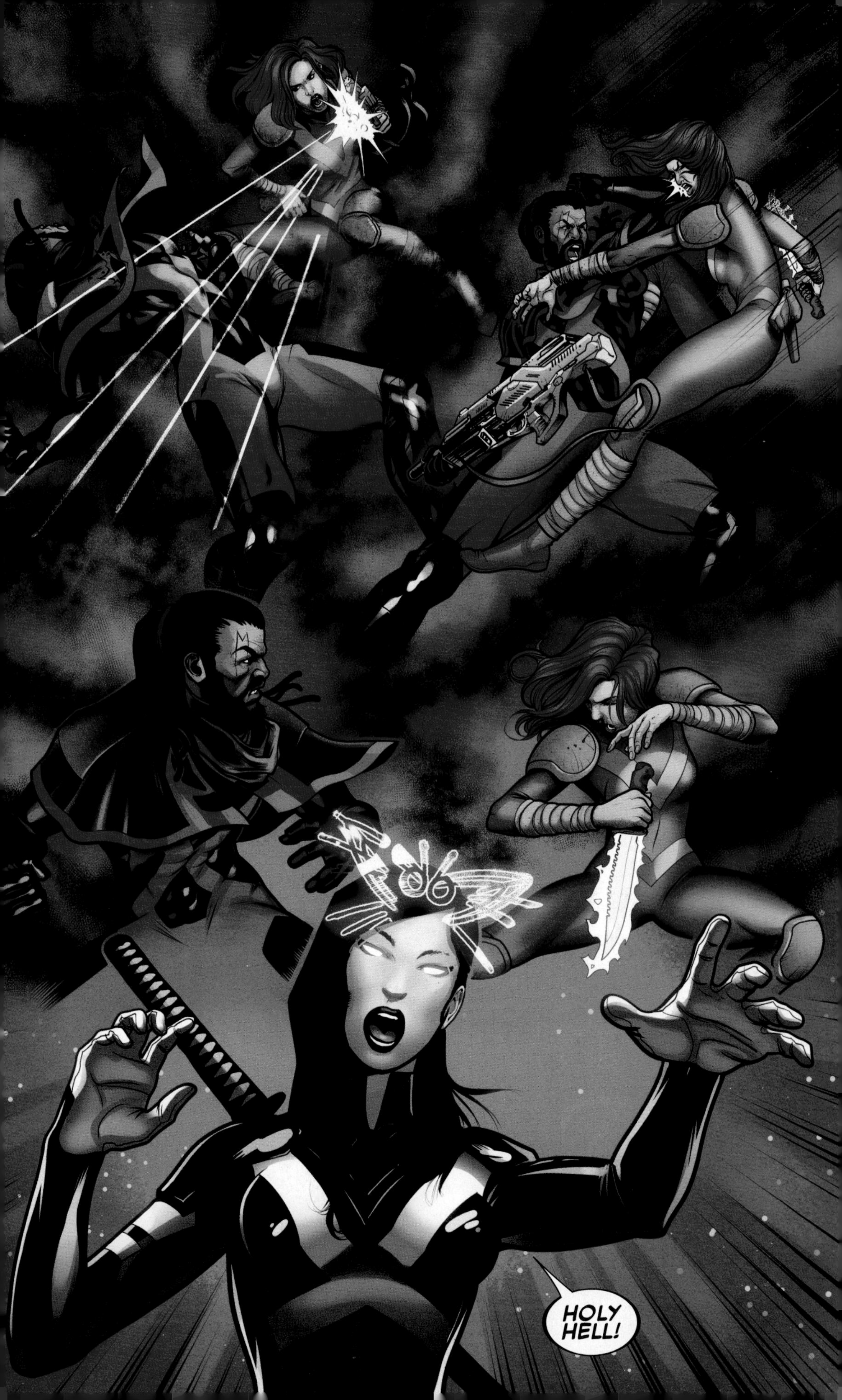
HOLY HELL!

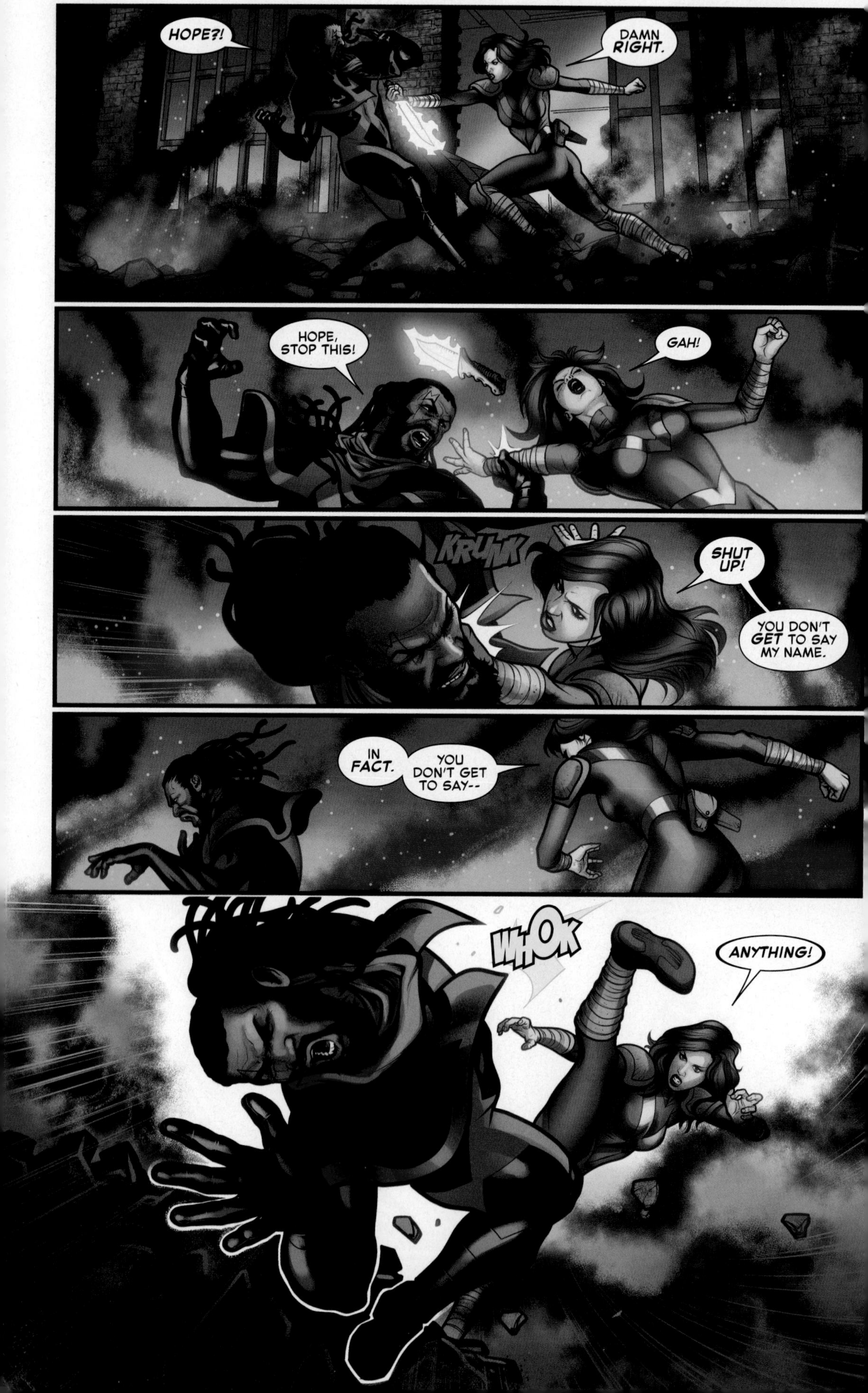

HOPE?!
DAMN RIGHT.
HOPE, STOP THIS!
GAH!
KRUNK
SHUT UP!
YOU DON'T GET TO SAY MY NAME.
IN FACT.
YOU DON'T GET TO SAY--
WHOK
ANYTHING!

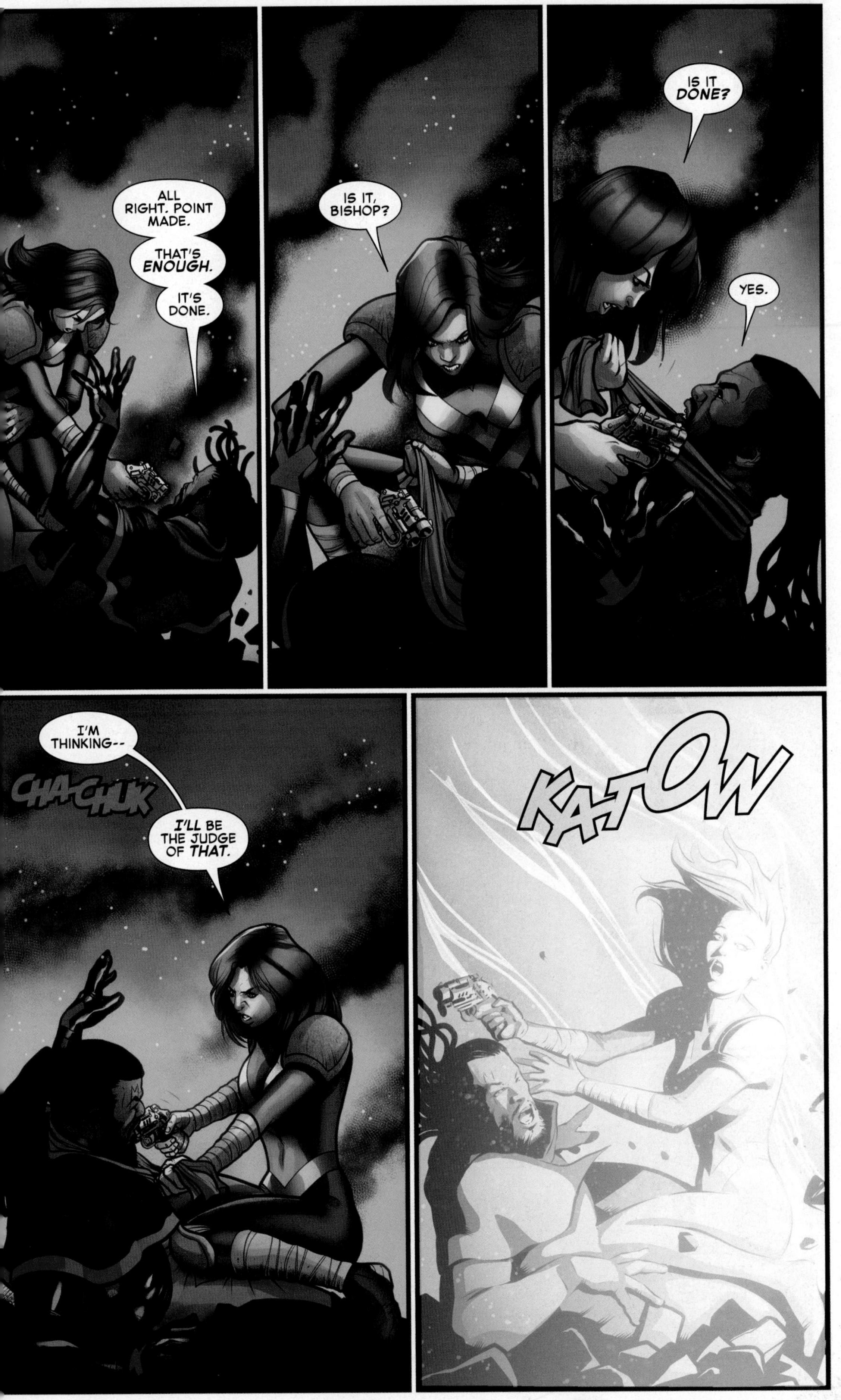
ALL RIGHT. POINT MADE.
THAT'S ENOUGH.
IT'S DONE.
IS IT, BISHOP?
IS IT DONE?
YES.
I'M THINKING--
CHA-CHUK
I'LL BE THE JUDGE OF THAT.
KATOW

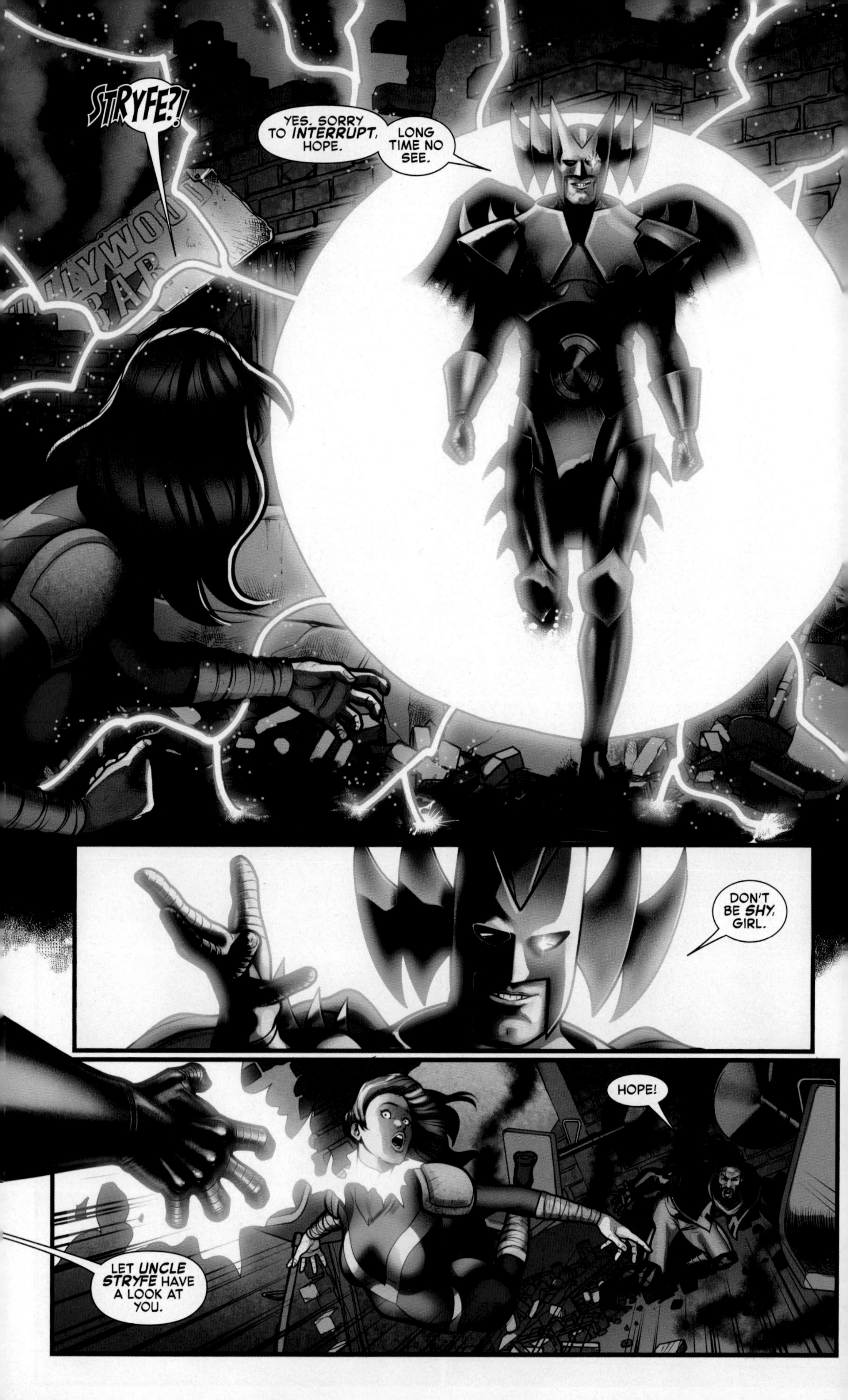
STRYFE?!
YES. SORRY TO INTERRUPT, HOPE.
LONG TIME NO SEE.
DON'T BE SHY, GIRL.
HOPE!
LET UNCLE STRYFE HAVE A LOOK AT YOU.

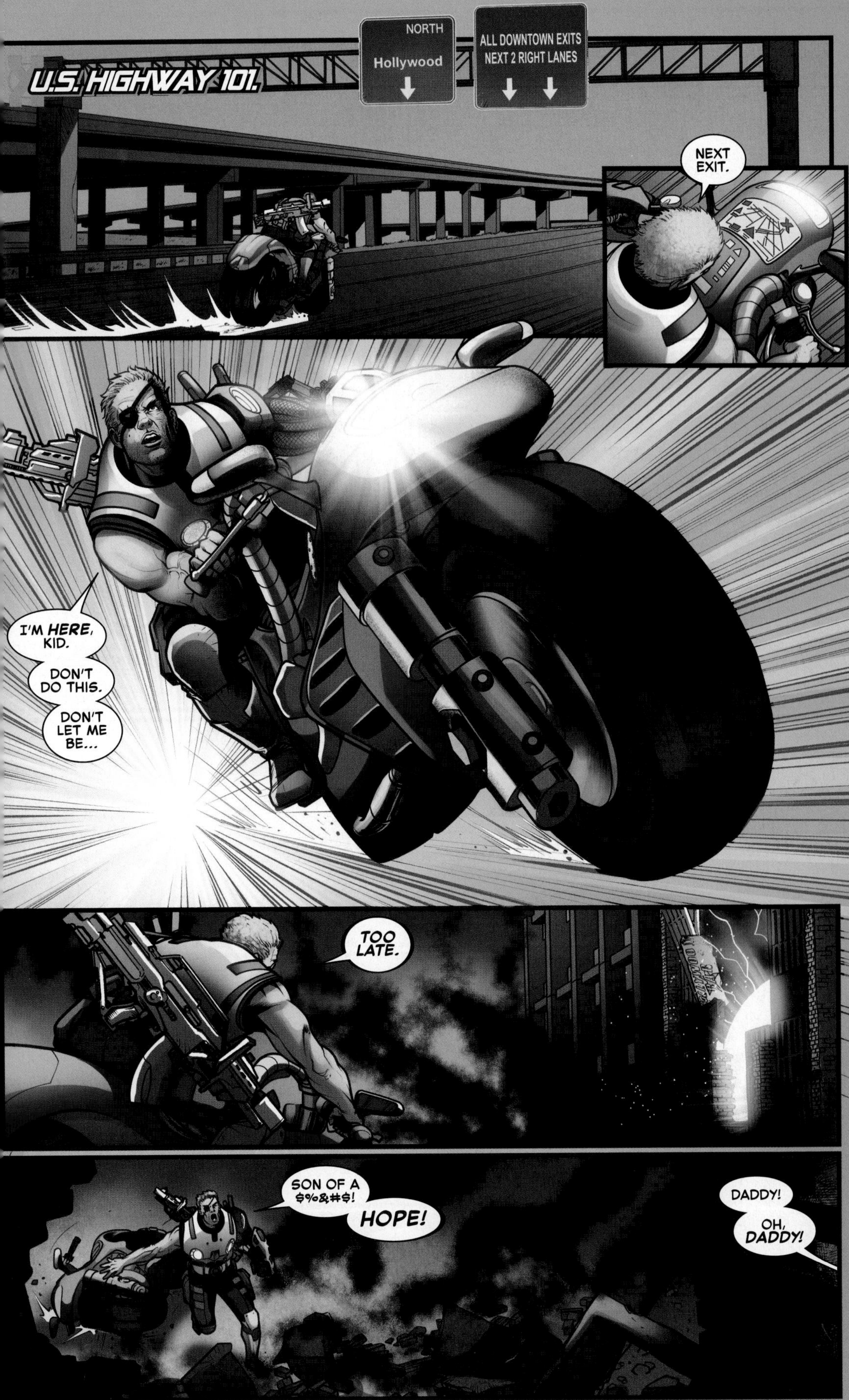
NORTH
Hollywood
ALL DOWNTOWN EXITS
NEXT 2 RIGHT LANES
U.S. HIGHWAY 101.
NEXT EXIT.
I'M HERE, KID.
DON'T DO THIS.
DON'T LET ME BE...
TOO LATE.
SON OF A $%&#$!
HOPE!
DADDY!
OH, DADDY!

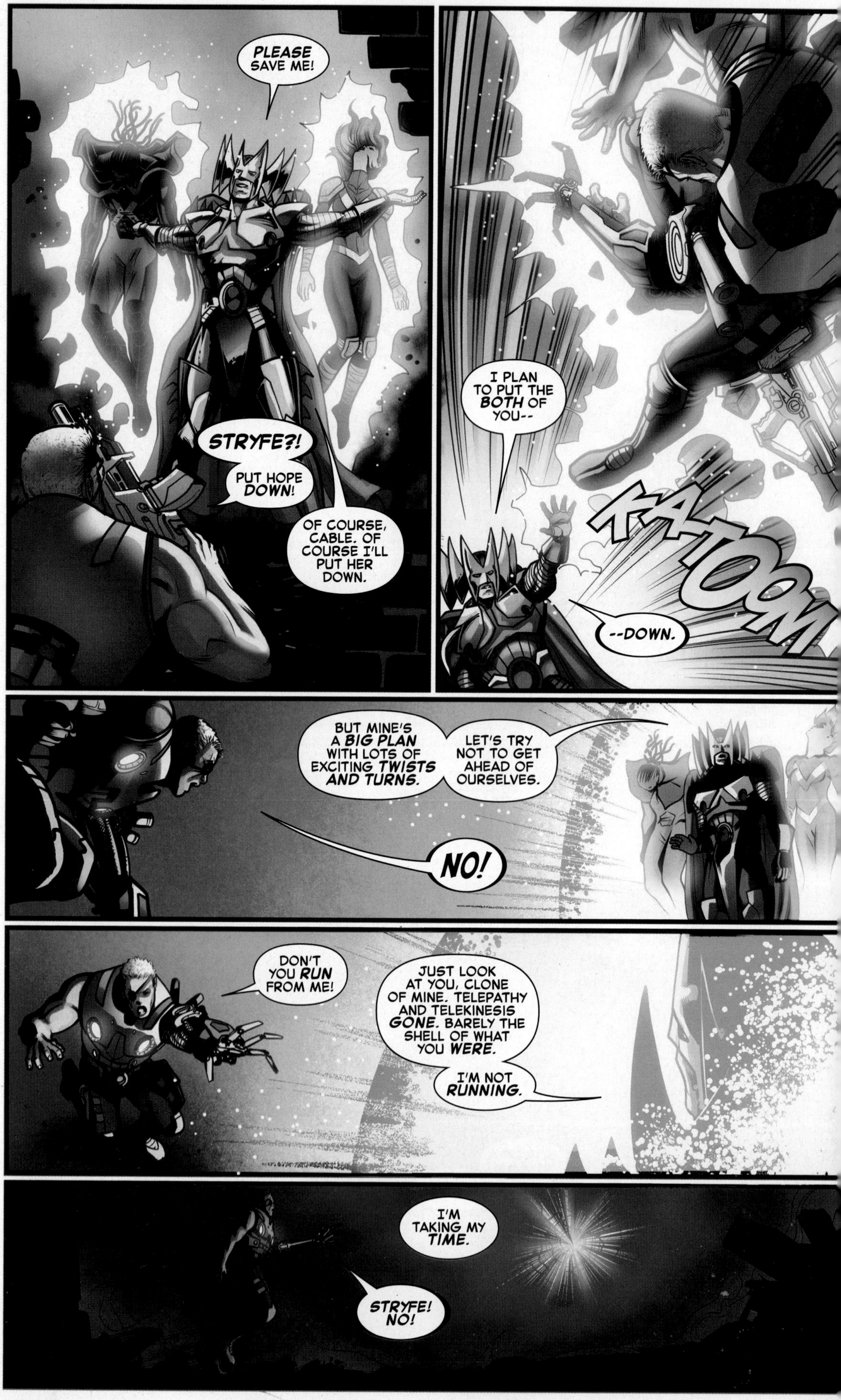
PLEASE SAVE ME!
STRYFE?!
PUT HOPE DOWN!
OF COURSE, CABLE. OF COURSE I'LL PUT HER DOWN.
I PLAN TO PUT THE BOTH OF YOU--
KA-TOOM
--DOWN.
BUT MINE'S A BIG PLAN WITH LOTS OF EXCITING TWISTS AND TURNS.
LET'S TRY NOT TO GET AHEAD OF OURSELVES.
NO!
DON'T YOU RUN FROM ME!
JUST LOOK AT YOU, CLONE OF MINE. TELEPATHY AND TELEKINESIS GONE. BARELY THE SHELL OF WHAT YOU WERE.
I'M NOT RUNNING.
I'M TAKING MY TIME.
STRYFE! NO!

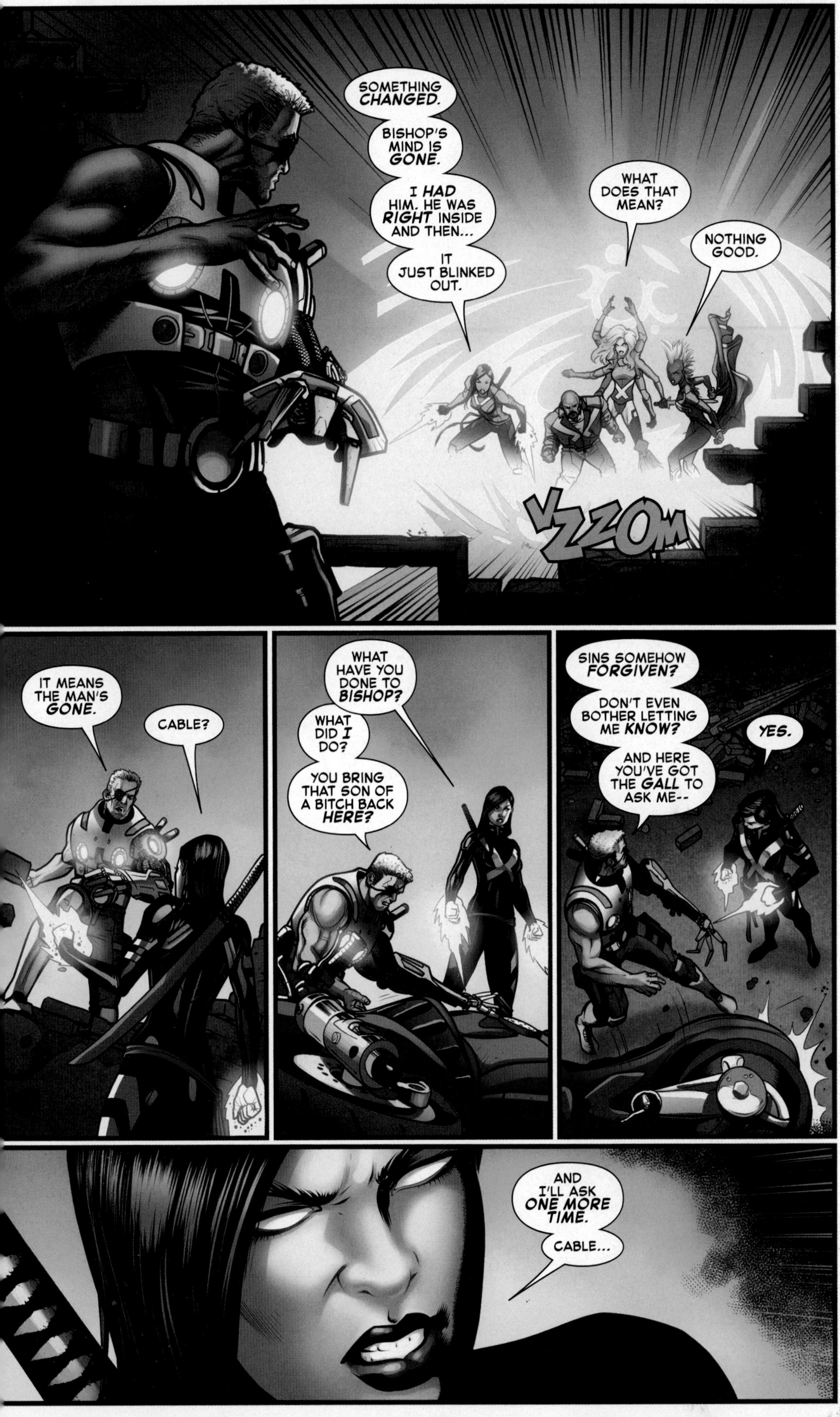
SOMETHING CHANGED.
BISHOP'S MIND IS GONE.
I HAD HIM. HE WAS RIGHT INSIDE AND THEN...
IT JUST BLINKED OUT.
WHAT DOES THAT MEAN?
NOTHING GOOD.
VZZOM
IT MEANS THE MAN'S GONE.
CABLE?
WHAT HAVE YOU DONE TO BISHOP?
WHAT DID I DO?
YOU BRING THAT SON OF A BITCH BACK HERE?
SINS SOMEHOW FORGIVEN?
DON'T EVEN BOTHER LETTING ME KNOW?
AND HERE YOU'VE GOT THE GALL TO ASK ME--
YES.
AND I'LL ASK ONE MORE TIME.
CABLE...

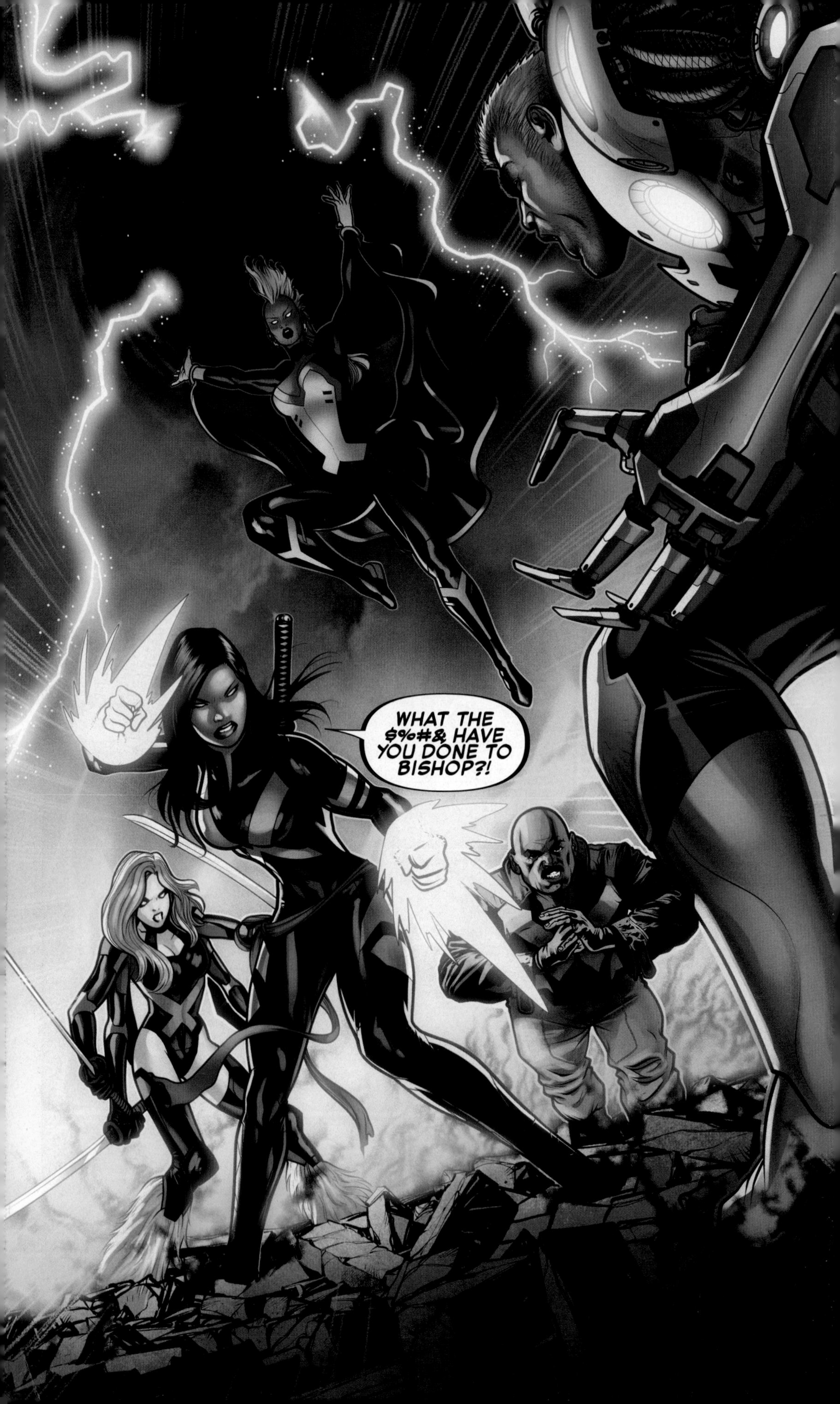
WHAT THE $%#& HAVE YOU DONE TO BISHOP?!

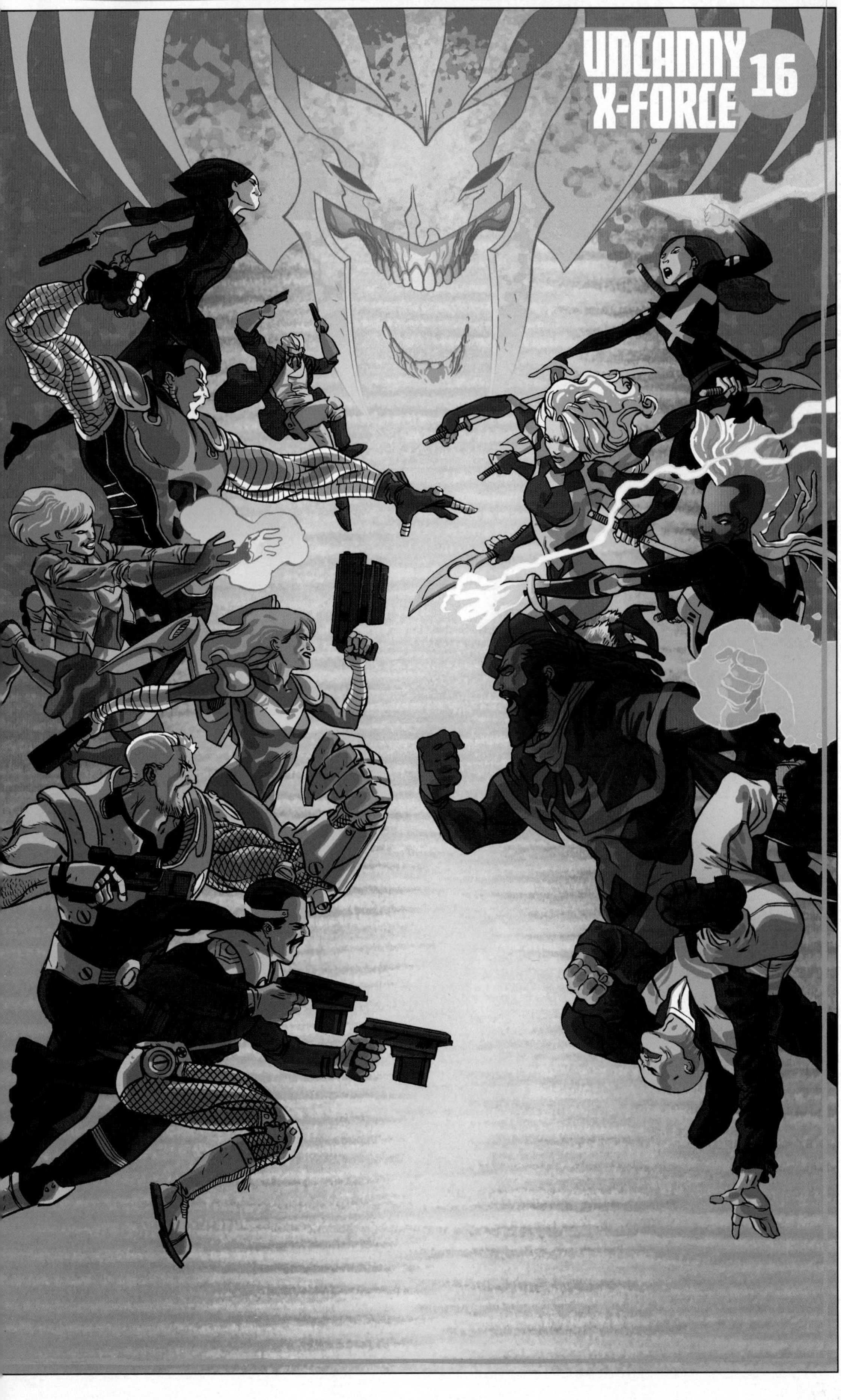
UNCANNY X-FORCE
16

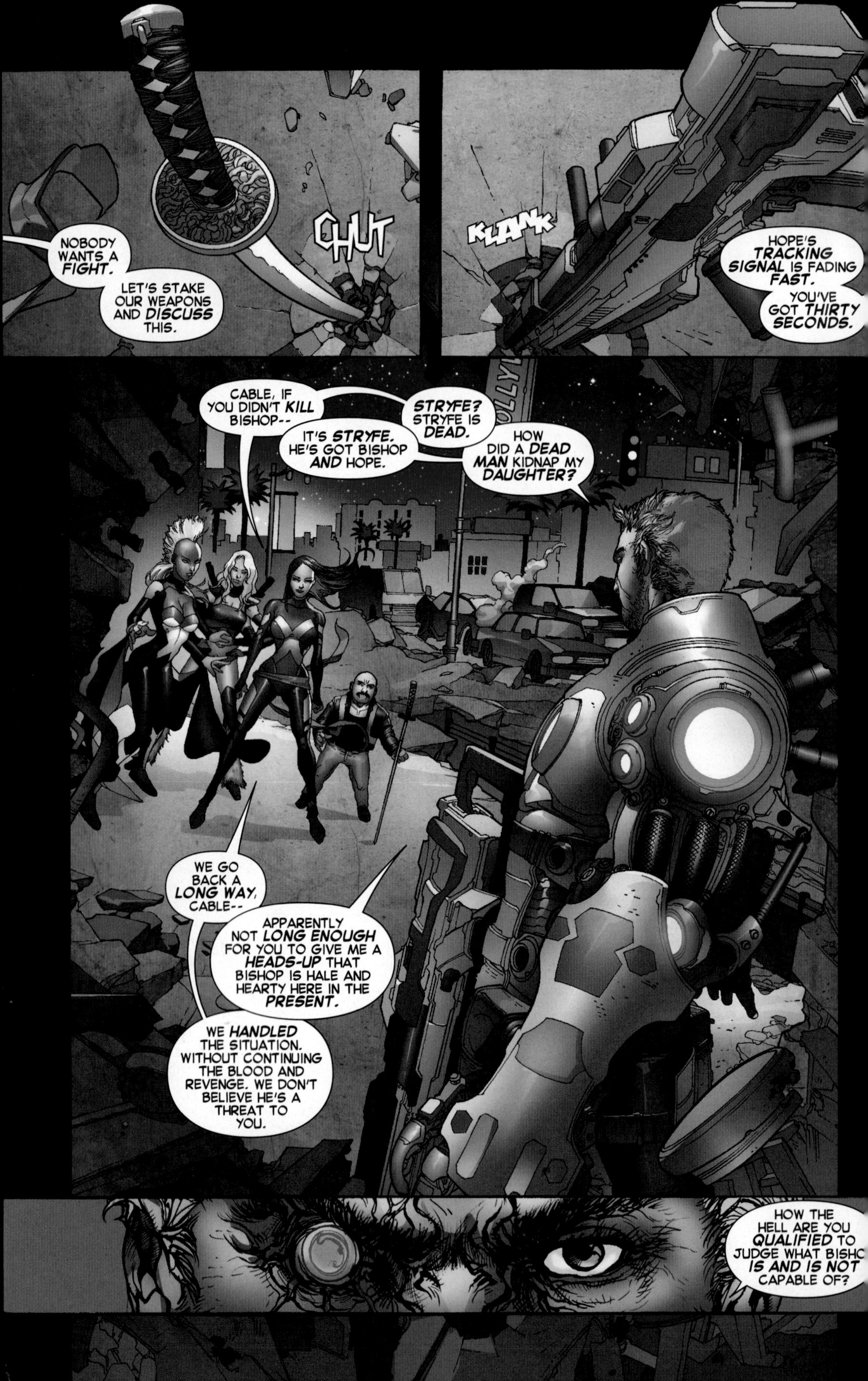
NOBODY WANTS A FIGHT.
LET'S STAKE OUR WEAPONS AND DISCUSS THIS.
CHUT
KLANK
HOPE'S TRACKING SIGNAL IS FADING FAST.
YOU'VE GOT THIRTY SECONDS.
CABLE, IF YOU DIDN'T KILL BISHOP--
IT'S STRYFE. HE'S GOT BISHOP AND HOPE.
STRYFE? STRYFE IS DEAD.
HOW DID A DEAD MAN KIDNAP MY DAUGHTER?
WE GO BACK A LONG WAY, CABLE--
APPARENTLY NOT LONG ENOUGH FOR YOU TO GIVE ME A HEADS-UP THAT BISHOP IS HALE AND HEARTY HERE IN THE PRESENT.
WE HANDLED THE SITUATION. WITHOUT CONTINUING THE BLOOD AND REVENGE. WE DON'T BELIEVE HE'S A THREAT TO YOU.
HOW THE HELL ARE YOU QUALIFIED TO JUDGE WHAT BISHC IS AND IS NOT CAPABLE OF?

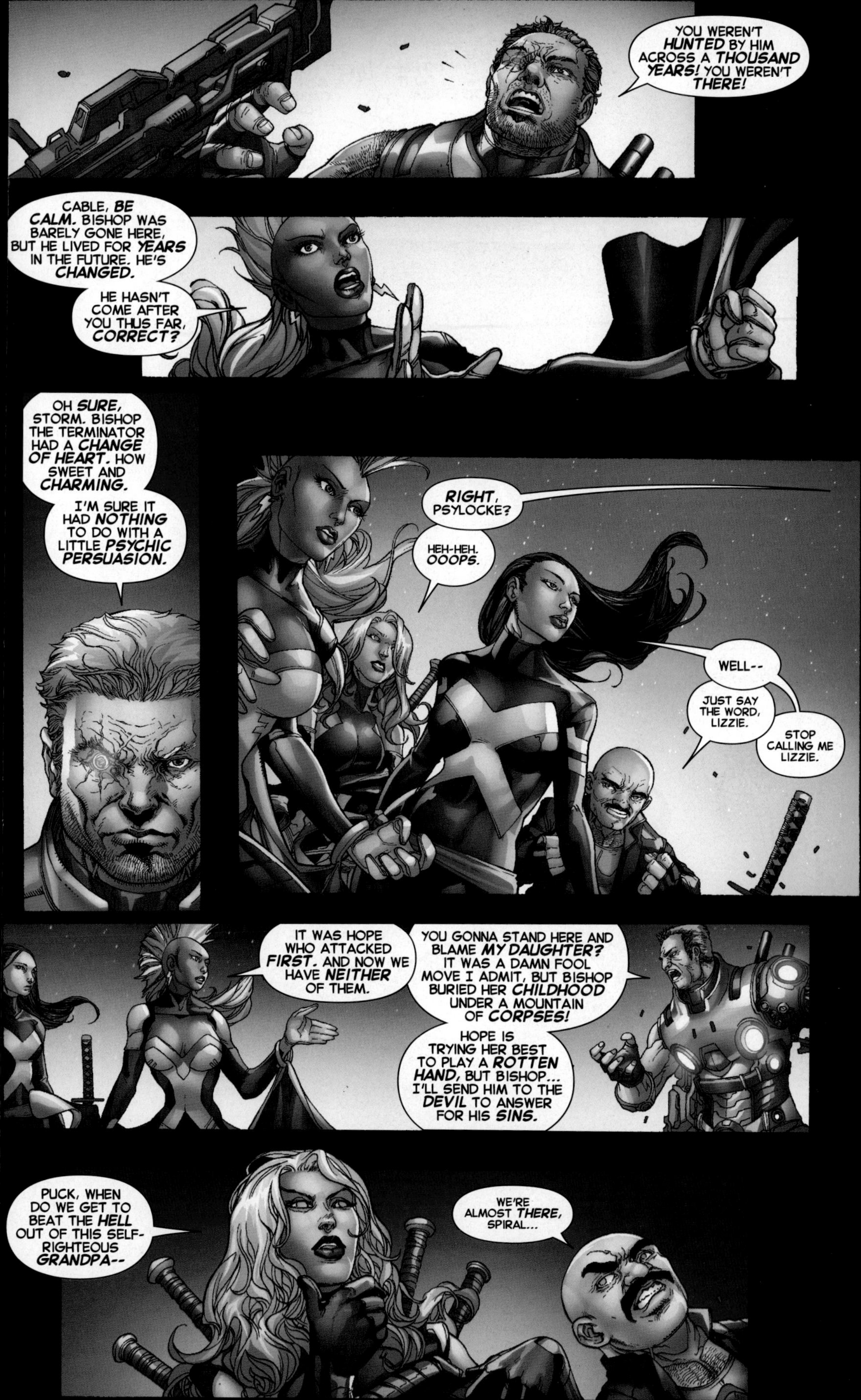
YOU WEREN'T HUNTED BY HIM ACROSS A THOUSAND YEARS! YOU WEREN'T THERE!
CABLE, BE CALM. BISHOP WAS BARELY GONE HERE, BUT HE LIVED FOR YEARS IN THE FUTURE. HE'S CHANGED.
HE HASN'T COME AFTER YOU THUS FAR, CORRECT?
OH SURE, STORM. BISHOP THE TERMINATOR HAD A CHANGE OF HEART. HOW SWEET AND CHARMING.
I'M SURE IT HAD NOTHING TO DO WITH A LITTLE PSYCHIC PERSUASION.
RIGHT, PSYLOCKE?
HEH-HEH. OOOPS.
WELL--
JUST SAY THE WORD, LIZZIE.
STOP CALLING ME LIZZIE.
IT WAS HOPE WHO ATTACKED FIRST. AND NOW WE HAVE NEITHER OF THEM.
YOU GONNA STAND HERE AND BLAME MY DAUGHTER? IT WAS A DAMN FOOL MOVE I ADMIT, BUT BISHOP BURIED HER CHILDHOOD UNDER A MOUNTAIN OF CORPSES!
HOPE IS TRYING HER BEST TO PLAY A ROTTEN HAND, BUT BISHOP... I'LL SEND HIM TO THE DEVIL TO ANSWER FOR HIS SINS.
PUCK, WHEN DO WE GET TO BEAT THE HELL OUT OF THIS SELF-RIGHTEOUS GRANDPA--
WE'RE ALMOST THERE, SPIRAL...

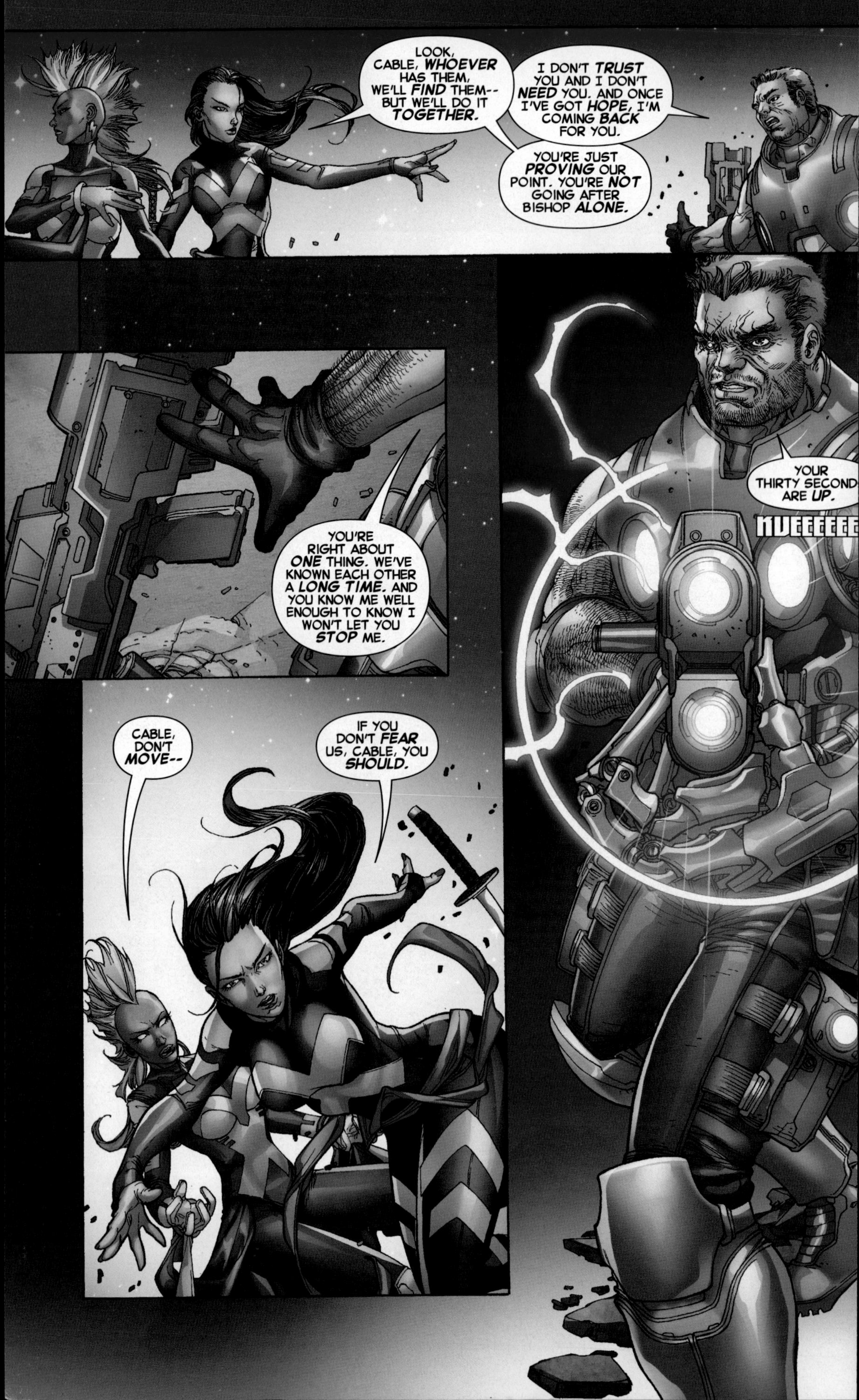
LOOK, CABLE, WHOEVER HAS THEM, WE'LL FIND THEM-- BUT WE'LL DO IT TOGETHER.
I DON'T TRUST YOU AND I DON'T NEED YOU. AND ONCE I'VE GOT HOPE, I'M COMING BACK FOR YOU.
YOU'RE JUST PROVING OUR POINT. YOU'RE NOT GOING AFTER BISHOP ALONE.
YOU'RE RIGHT ABOUT ONE THING. WE'VE KNOWN EACH OTHER A LONG TIME. AND YOU KNOW ME WELL ENOUGH TO KNOW I WON'T LET YOU STOP ME.
YOUR THIRTY SECONDS ARE UP.
KVEEEEEE
CABLE, DON'T MOVE--
IF YOU DON'T FEAR US, CABLE, YOU SHOULD.

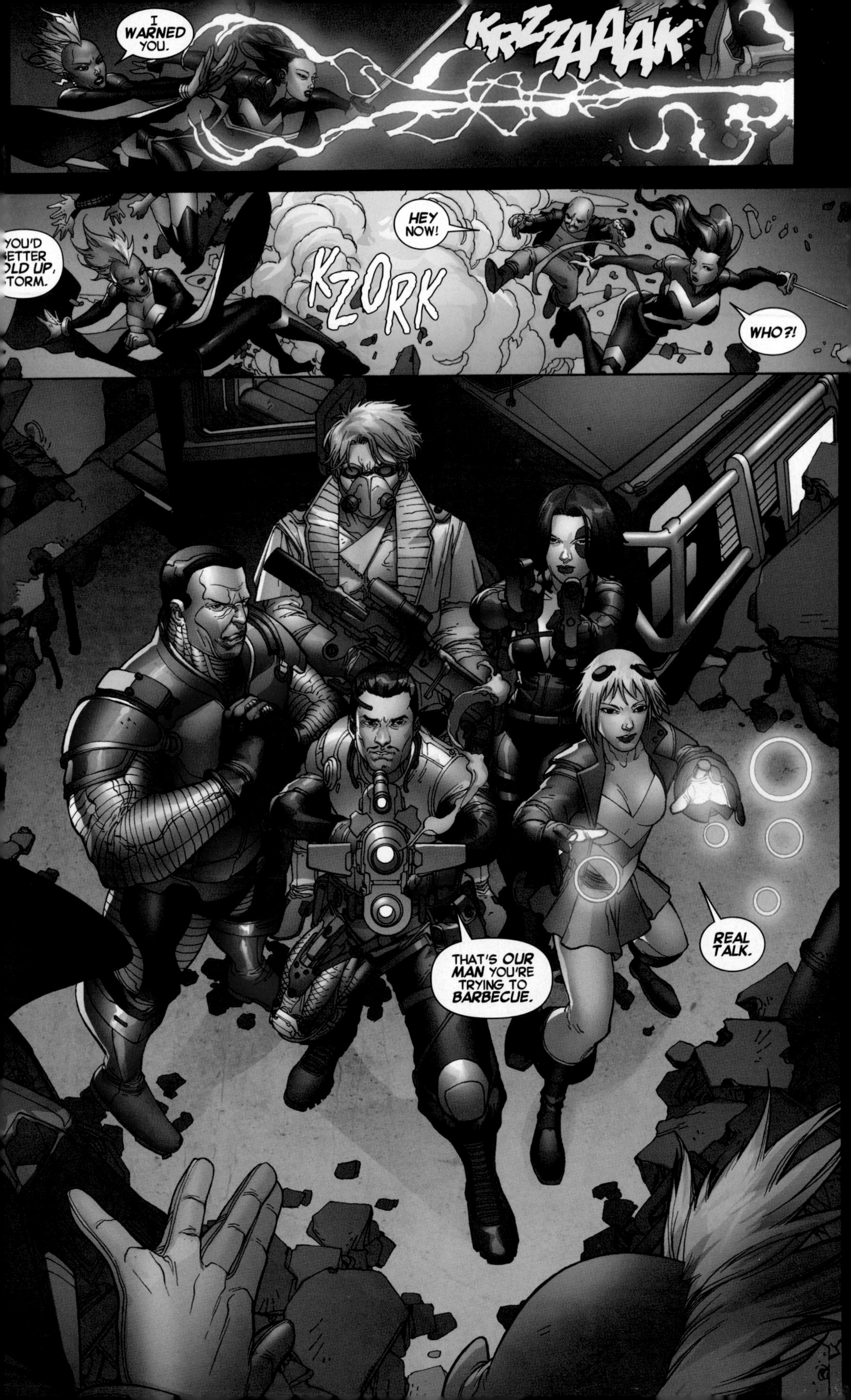
I WARNED YOU.
KRZZAAAK
YOU'D BETTER HOLD UP, STORM.
HEY NOW!
KZORK
WHO?!
THAT'S OUR MAN YOU'RE TRYING TO BARBECUE.
REAL TALK.

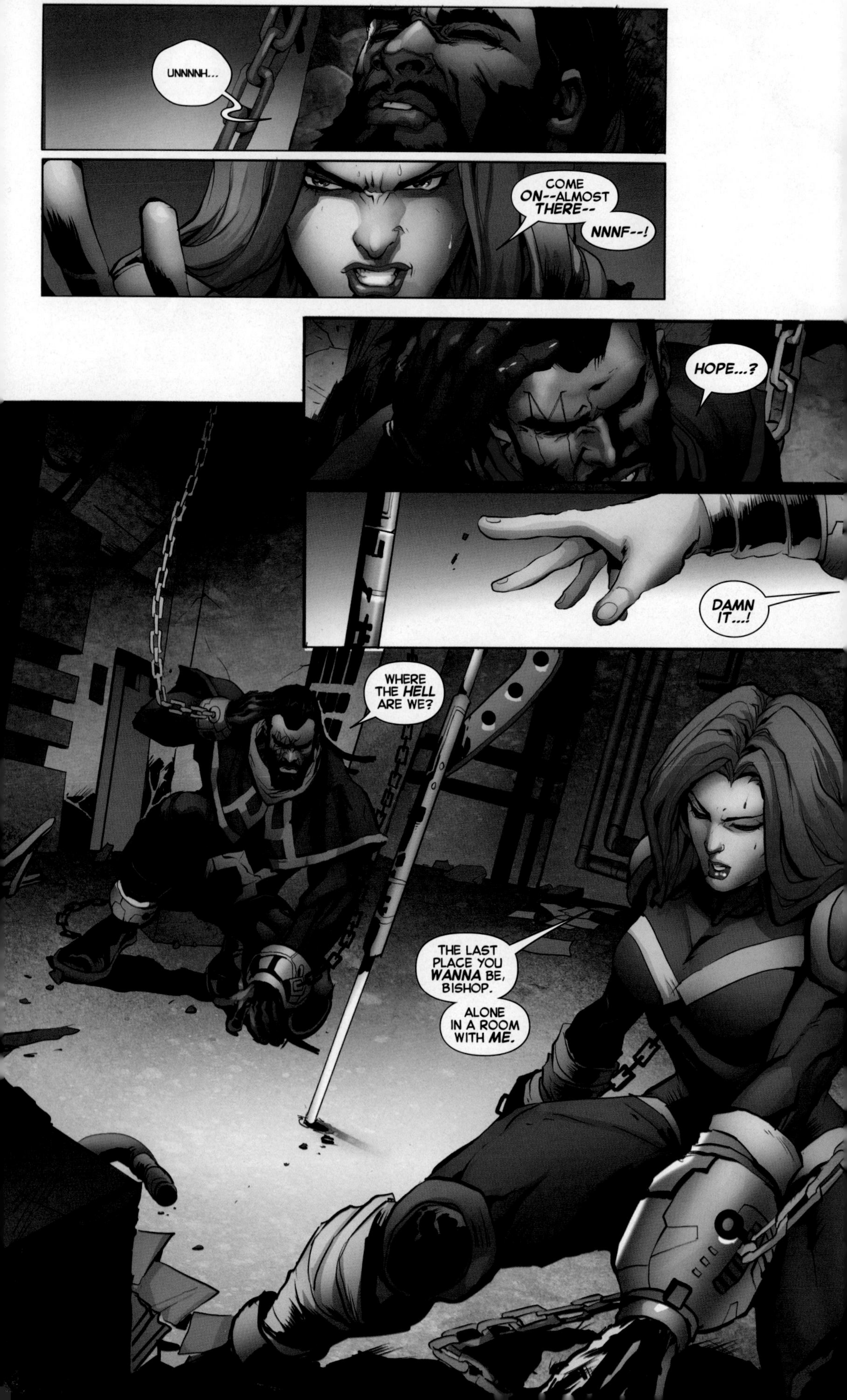
UNNNNH...
COME ON--ALMOST THERE--
NNNF--!
HOPE...?
DAMN IT...!
WHERE THE HELL ARE WE?
THE LAST PLACE YOU WANNA BE, BISHOP.
ALONE IN A ROOM WITH ME.

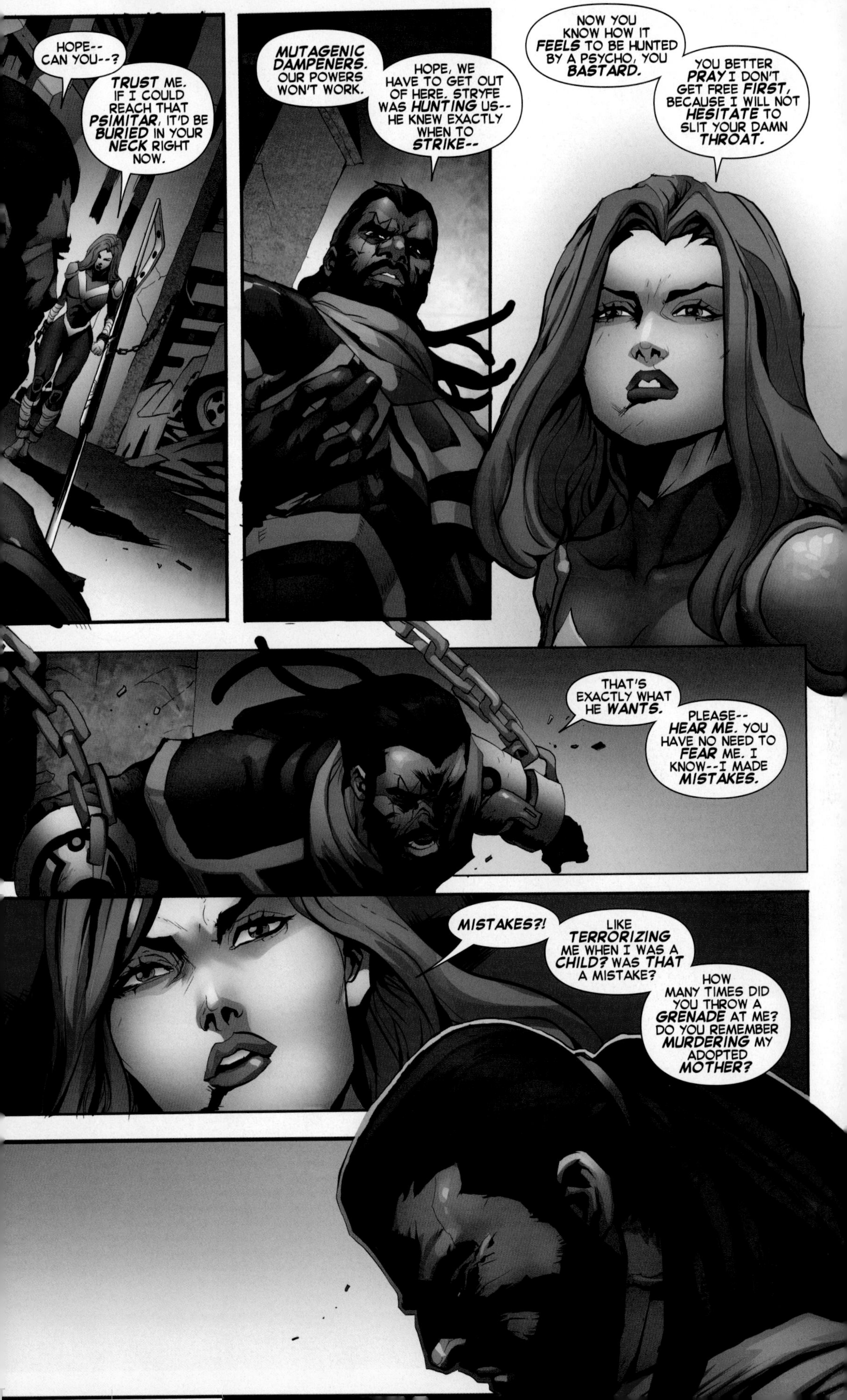
HOPE-- CAN YOU--?
TRUST ME. IF I COULD REACH THAT PSIMITAR, IT'D BE BURIED IN YOUR NECK RIGHT NOW.
MUTAGENIC DAMPENERS. OUR POWERS WON'T WORK.
HOPE, WE HAVE TO GET OUT OF HERE. STRYFE WAS HUNTING US-- HE KNEW EXACTLY WHEN TO STRIKE--
NOW YOU KNOW HOW IT FEELS TO BE HUNTED BY A PSYCHO, YOU BASTARD.
YOU BETTER PRAY I DON'T GET FREE FIRST, BECAUSE I WILL NOT HESITATE TO SLIT YOUR DAMN THROAT.
THAT'S EXACTLY WHAT HE WANTS.
PLEASE-- HEAR ME. YOU HAVE NO NEED TO FEAR ME. I KNOW--I MADE MISTAKES.
MISTAKES?!
LIKE TERRORIZING ME WHEN I WAS A CHILD? WAS THAT A MISTAKE?
HOW MANY TIMES DID YOU THROW A GRENADE AT ME? DO YOU REMEMBER MURDERING MY ADOPTED MOTHER?

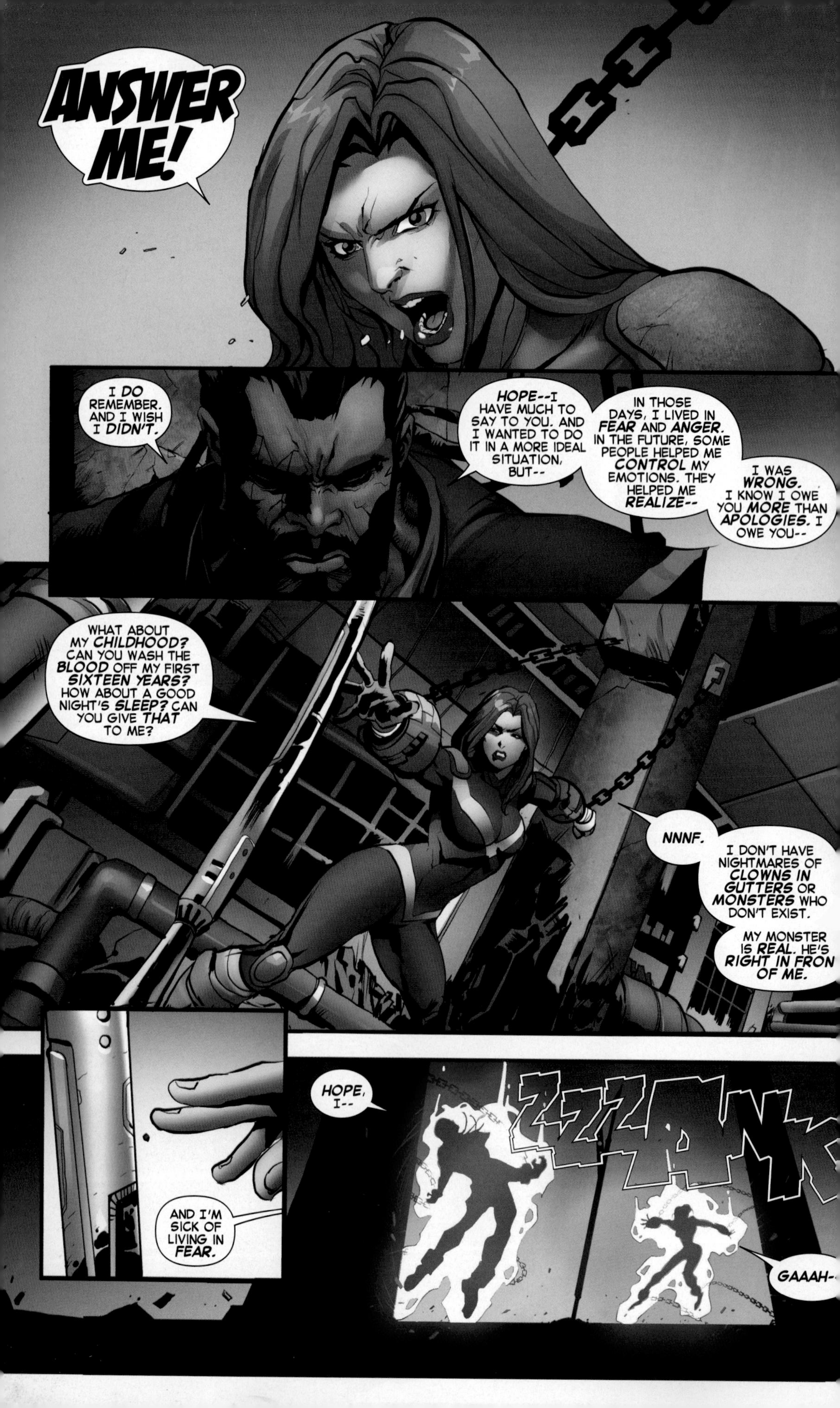
ANSWER ME!
I DO REMEMBER. AND I WISH I DIDN'T.
HOPE--I HAVE MUCH TO SAY TO YOU. AND I WANTED TO DO IT IN A MORE IDEAL SITUATION, BUT--
IN THOSE DAYS, I LIVED IN FEAR AND ANGER. IN THE FUTURE, SOME PEOPLE HELPED ME CONTROL MY EMOTIONS. THEY HELPED ME REALIZE--
I WAS WRONG. I KNOW I OWE YOU MORE THAN APOLOGIES. I OWE YOU--
WHAT ABOUT MY CHILDHOOD? CAN YOU WASH THE BLOOD OFF MY FIRST SIXTEEN YEARS? HOW ABOUT A GOOD NIGHT'S SLEEP? CAN YOU GIVE THAT TO ME?
NNNF.
I DON'T HAVE NIGHTMARES OF CLOWNS IN GUTTERS OR MONSTERS WHO DON'T EXIST.
MY MONSTER IS REAL. HE'S RIGHT IN FRON OF ME.
AND I'M SICK OF LIVING IN FEAR.
HOPE, I--
GAAAH--

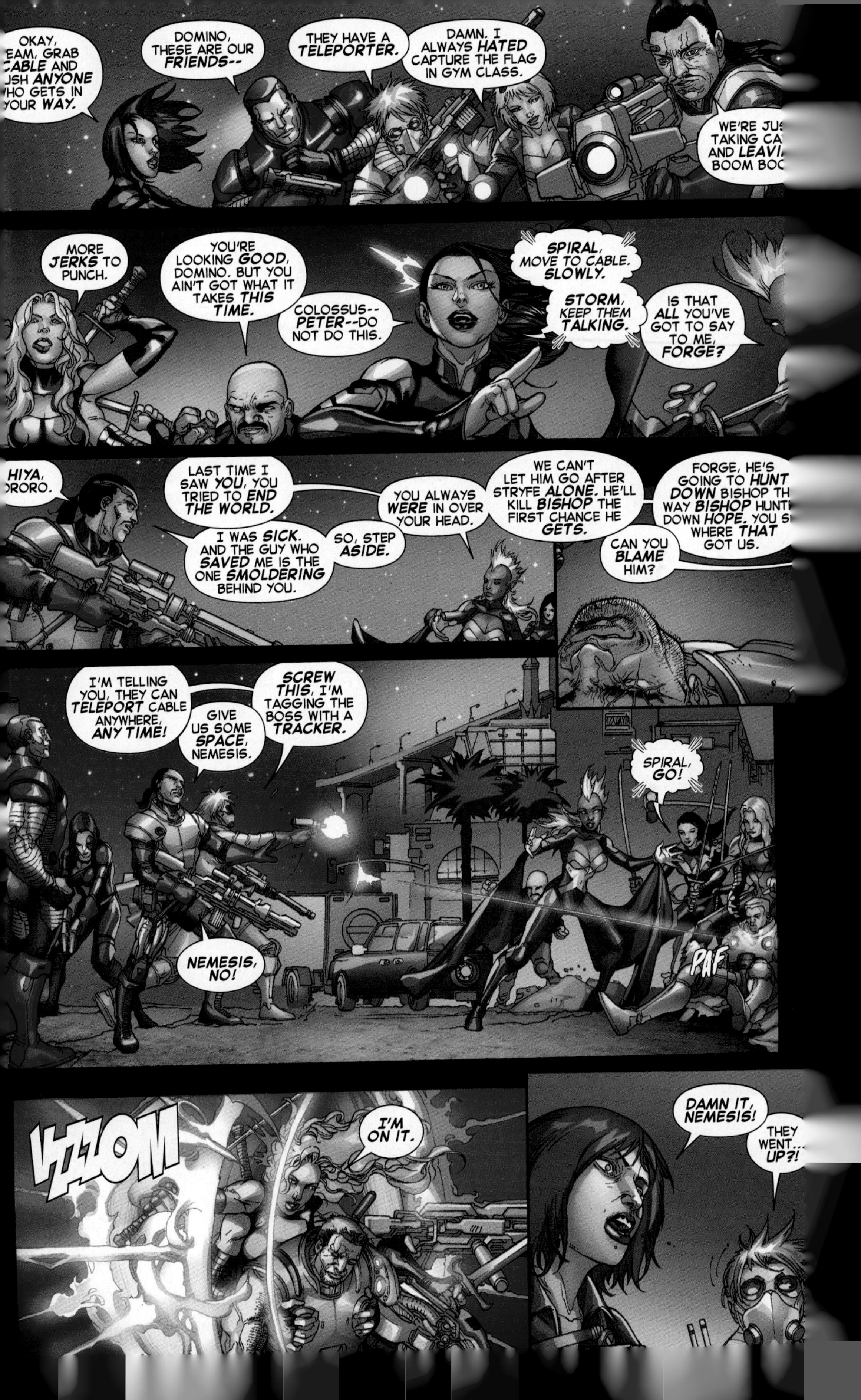
OKAY, EAM, GRAB CABLE AND USH ANYONE HO GETS IN YOUR WAY.
DOMINO, THESE ARE OUR FRIENDS--
THEY HAVE A TELEPORTER.
DAMN. I ALWAYS HATED CAPTURE THE FLAG IN GYM CLASS.
WE'RE JUS TAKING CA AND LEAVI BOOM BO
MORE JERKS TO PUNCH.
YOU'RE LOOKING GOOD, DOMINO. BUT YOU AIN'T GOT WHAT IT TAKES THIS TIME.
COLOSSUS-- PETER--DO NOT DO THIS.
SPIRAL, MOVE TO CABLE. SLOWLY.
STORM, KEEP THEM TALKING.
IS THAT ALL YOU'VE GOT TO SAY TO ME, FORGE?
HIYA, ORORO.
LAST TIME I SAW YOU, YOU TRIED TO END THE WORLD.
I WAS SICK. AND THE GUY WHO SAVED ME IS THE ONE SMOLDERING BEHIND YOU.
SO, STEP ASIDE.
YOU ALWAYS WERE IN OVER YOUR HEAD.
WE CAN'T LET HIM GO AFTER STRYFE ALONE. HE'LL KILL BISHOP THE FIRST CHANCE HE GETS.
FORGE, HE'S GOING TO HUNT DOWN BISHOP TH WAY BISHOP HUNT DOWN HOPE. YOU S WHERE THAT GOT US.
CAN YOU BLAME HIM?
I'M TELLING YOU, THEY CAN TELEPORT CABLE ANYWHERE, ANY TIME!
GIVE US SOME SPACE, NEMESIS.
SCREW THIS, I'M TAGGING THE BOSS WITH A TRACKER.
SPIRAL, GO!
NEMESIS, NO!
PAF
VZZOM
I'M ON IT.
DAMN IT, NEMESIS!
THEY WENT... UP?!

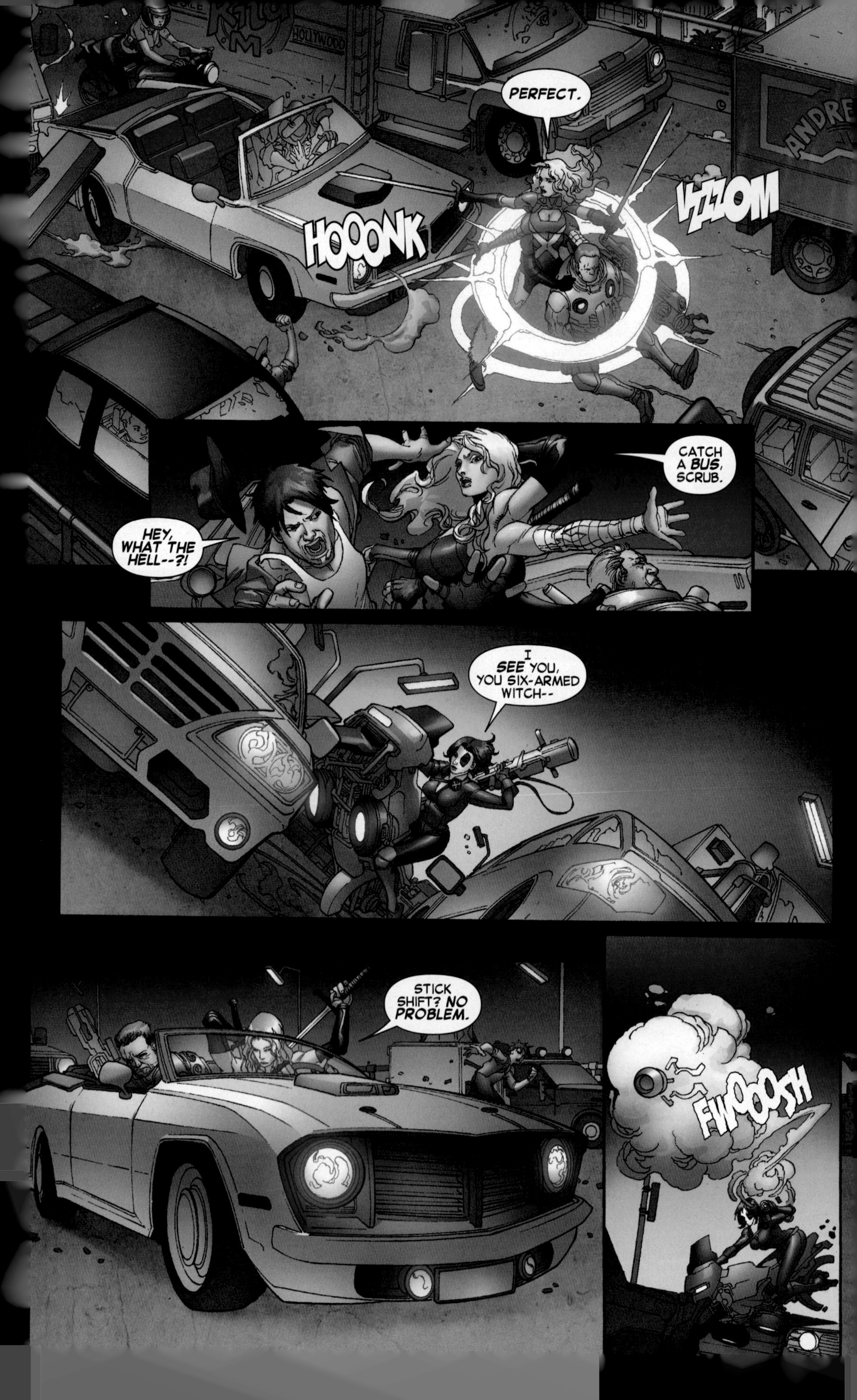
PERFECT.
HOOONK
VZZOM
CATCH A BUS, SCRUB.
HEY, WHAT THE HELL--?!
I SEE YOU, YOU SIX-ARMED WITCH--
STICK SHIFT? NO PROBLEM.
FWOOOSH

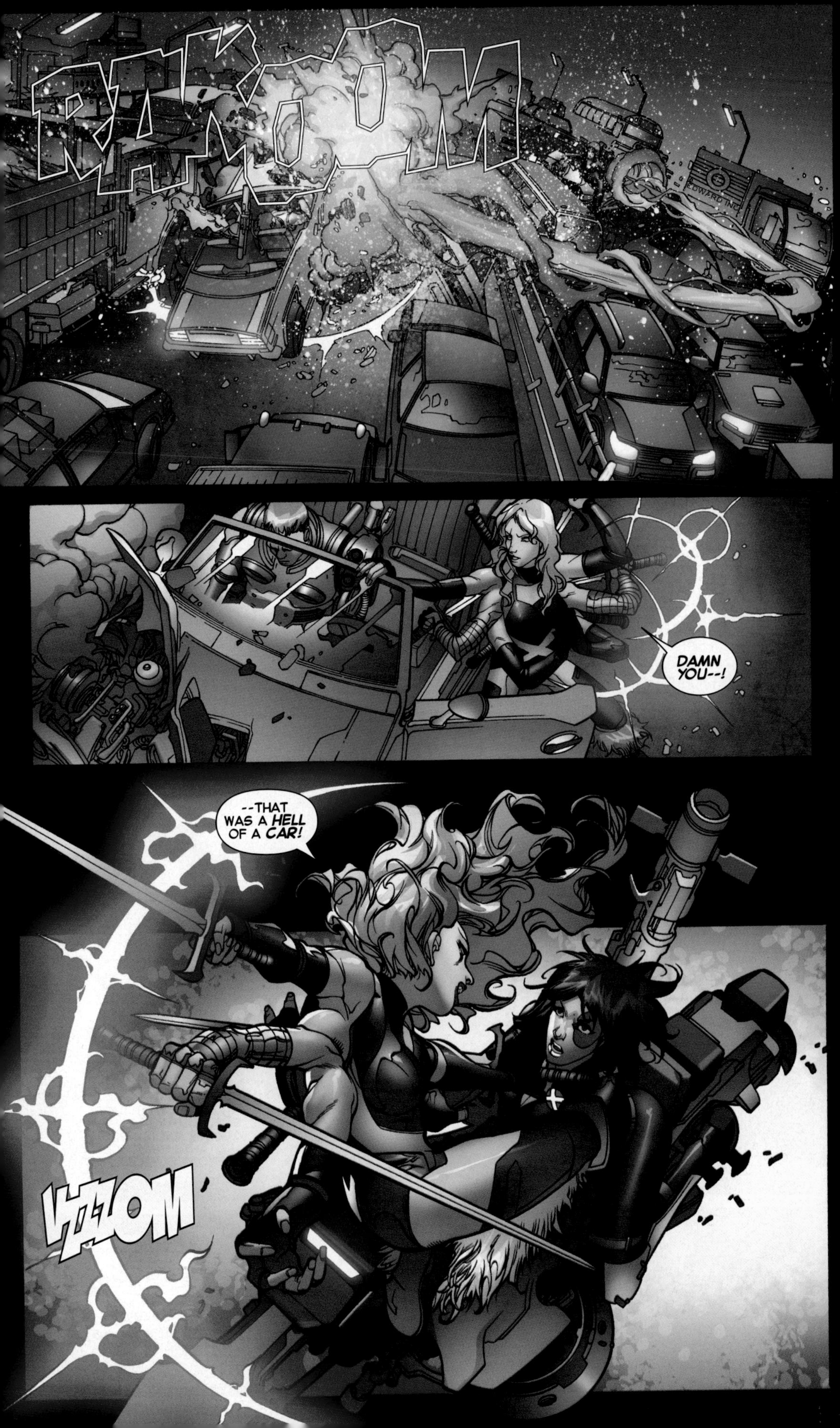
RAKOOM
DAMN YOU--!
--THAT WAS A HELL OF A CAR!
VZZOM

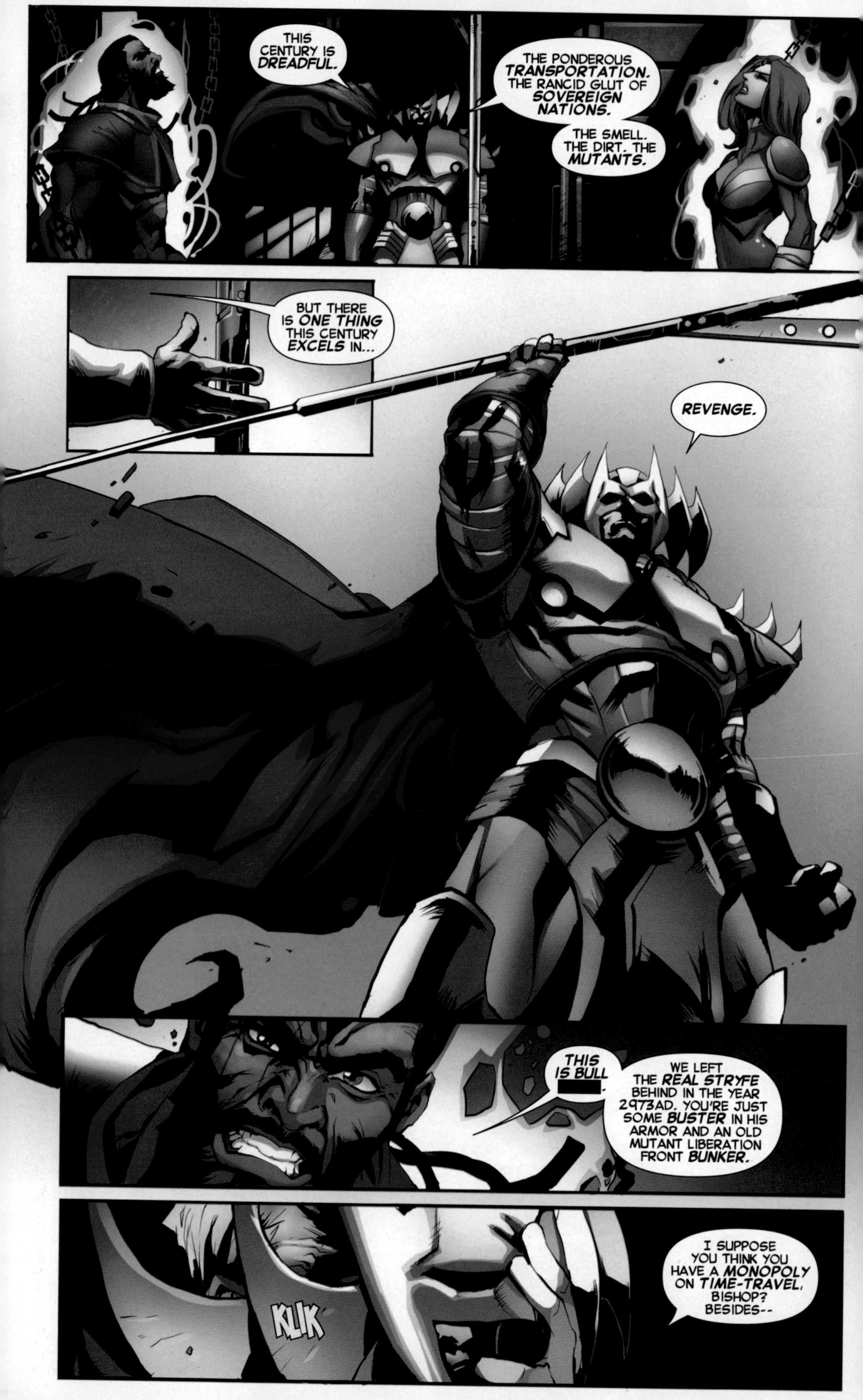
THIS CENTURY IS **DREADFUL.**
THE PONDEROUS **TRANSPORTATION.** THE RANCID GLUT OF **SOVEREIGN NATIONS.**
THE SMELL. THE DIRT. THE **MUTANTS.**
BUT THERE IS **ONE THING** THIS CENTURY **EXCELS** IN...
REVENGE.
THIS IS BULL [redacted]-.
WE LEFT THE **REAL STRYFE** BEHIND IN THE YEAR 2973AD. YOU'RE JUST SOME **BUSTER** IN HIS ARMOR AND AN OLD MUTANT LIBERATION FRONT **BUNKER.**
KLIK
I SUPPOSE YOU THINK YOU HAVE A **MONOPOLY** ON **TIME-TRAVEL,** BISHOP? BESIDES--

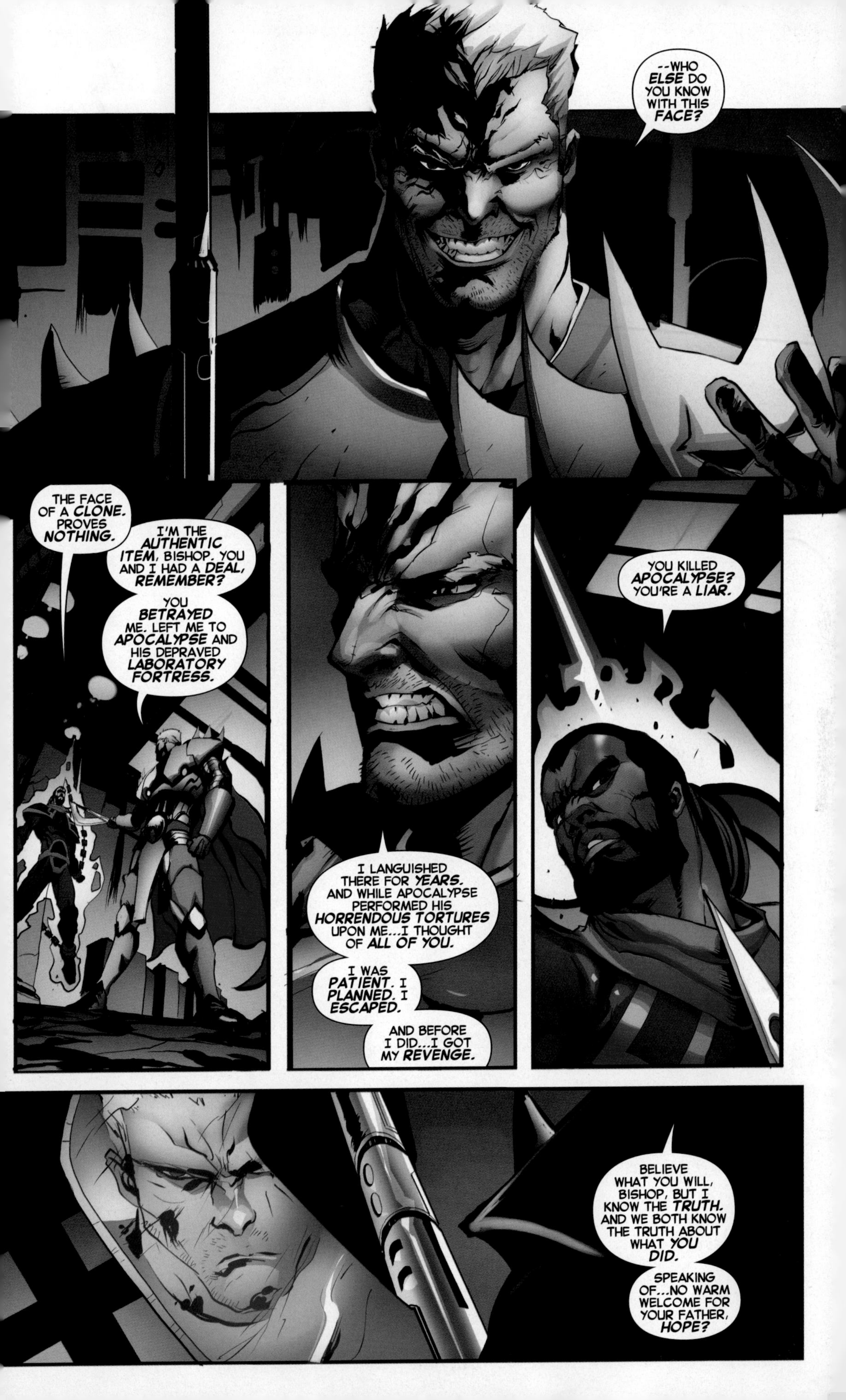
--WHO ELSE DO YOU KNOW WITH THIS FACE?
THE FACE OF A CLONE. PROVES NOTHING.
I'M THE AUTHENTIC ITEM, BISHOP. YOU AND I HAD A DEAL, REMEMBER?
YOU BETRAYED ME. LEFT ME TO APOCALYPSE AND HIS DEPRAVED LABORATORY FORTRESS.
I LANGUISHED THERE FOR YEARS. AND WHILE APOCALYPSE PERFORMED HIS HORRENDOUS TORTURES UPON ME...I THOUGHT OF ALL OF YOU.
I WAS PATIENT. I PLANNED. I ESCAPED.
AND BEFORE I DID...I GOT MY REVENGE.
YOU KILLED APOCALYPSE? YOU'RE A LIAR.
BELIEVE WHAT YOU WILL, BISHOP, BUT I KNOW THE TRUTH. AND WE BOTH KNOW THE TRUTH ABOUT WHAT YOU DID.
SPEAKING OF...NO WARM WELCOME FOR YOUR FATHER, HOPE?

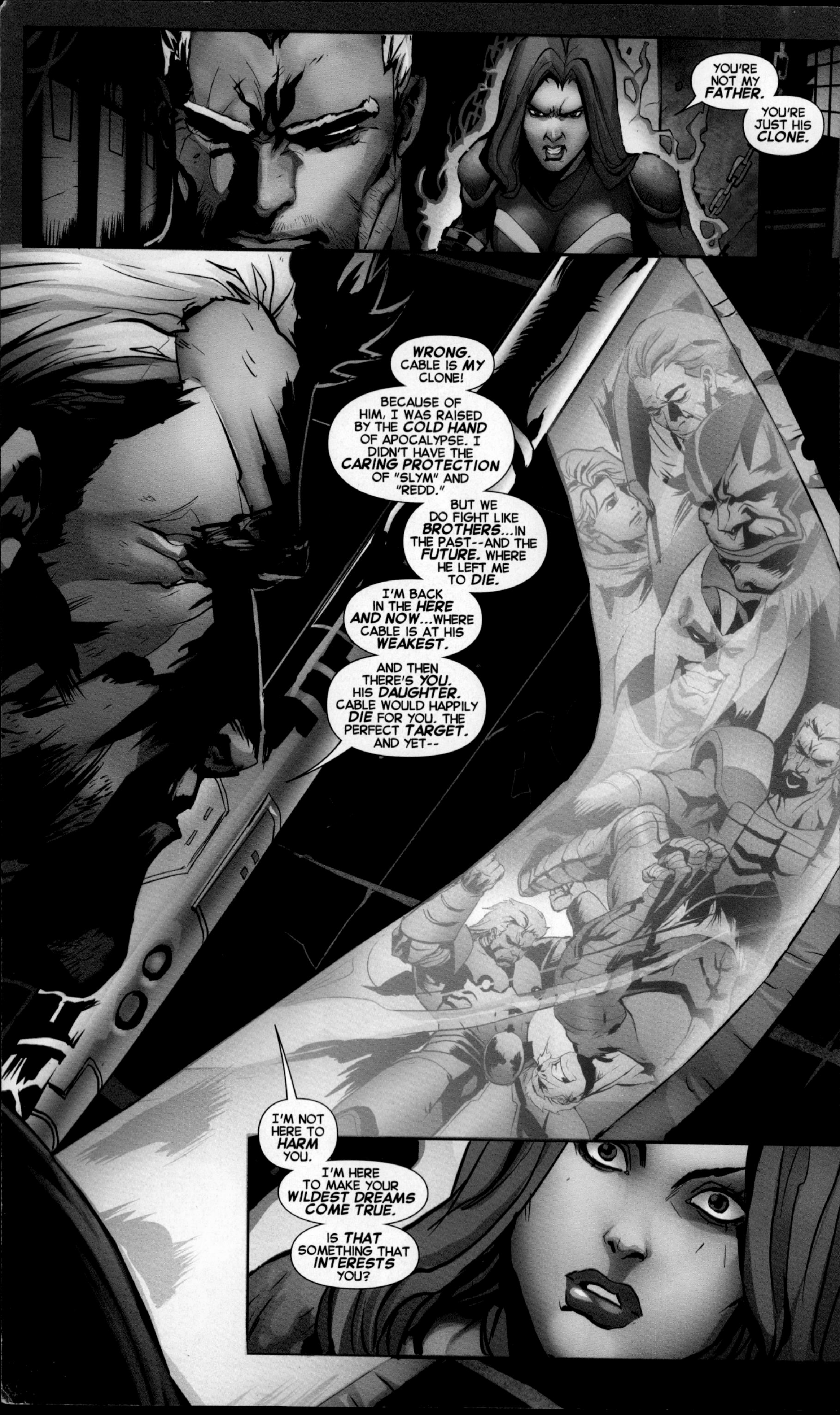

YOU'RE NOT MY FATHER.
YOU'RE JUST HIS CLONE.
WRONG. CABLE IS MY CLONE!
BECAUSE OF HIM, I WAS RAISED BY THE COLD HAND OF APOCALYPSE. I DIDN'T HAVE THE CARING PROTECTION OF "SLYM" AND "REDD."
BUT WE DO FIGHT LIKE BROTHERS...IN THE PAST--AND THE FUTURE. WHERE HE LEFT ME TO DIE.
I'M BACK IN THE HERE AND NOW...WHERE CABLE IS AT HIS WEAKEST.
AND THEN THERE'S YOU. HIS DAUGHTER. CABLE WOULD HAPPILY DIE FOR YOU. THE PERFECT TARGET. AND YET--
I'M NOT HERE TO HARM YOU.
I'M HERE TO MAKE YOUR WILDEST DREAMS COME TRUE.
IS THAT SOMETHING THAT INTERESTS YOU?

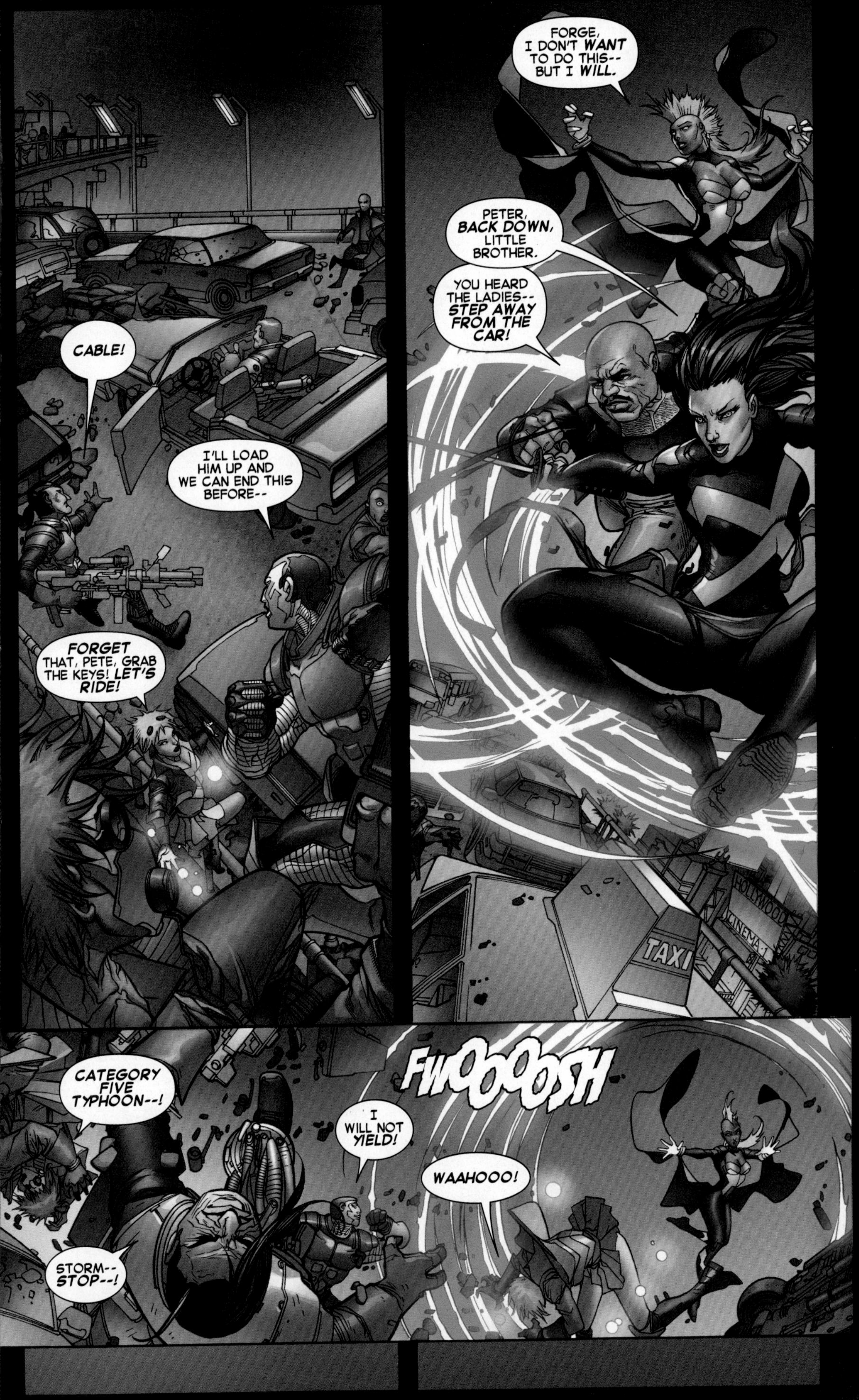
CABLE!
I'LL LOAD HIM UP AND WE CAN END THIS BEFORE--
FORGET THAT, PETE, GRAB THE KEYS! LET'S RIDE!
FORGE, I DON'T WANT TO DO THIS-- BUT I WILL.
PETER, BACK DOWN, LITTLE BROTHER.
YOU HEARD THE LADIES-- STEP AWAY FROM THE CAR!
HOLLYWOOD
CINEMA 1
TAXI
FWOOOOSH
CATEGORY FIVE TYPHOON--!
I WILL NOT YIELD!
WAAHOOO!
STORM-- STOP--!

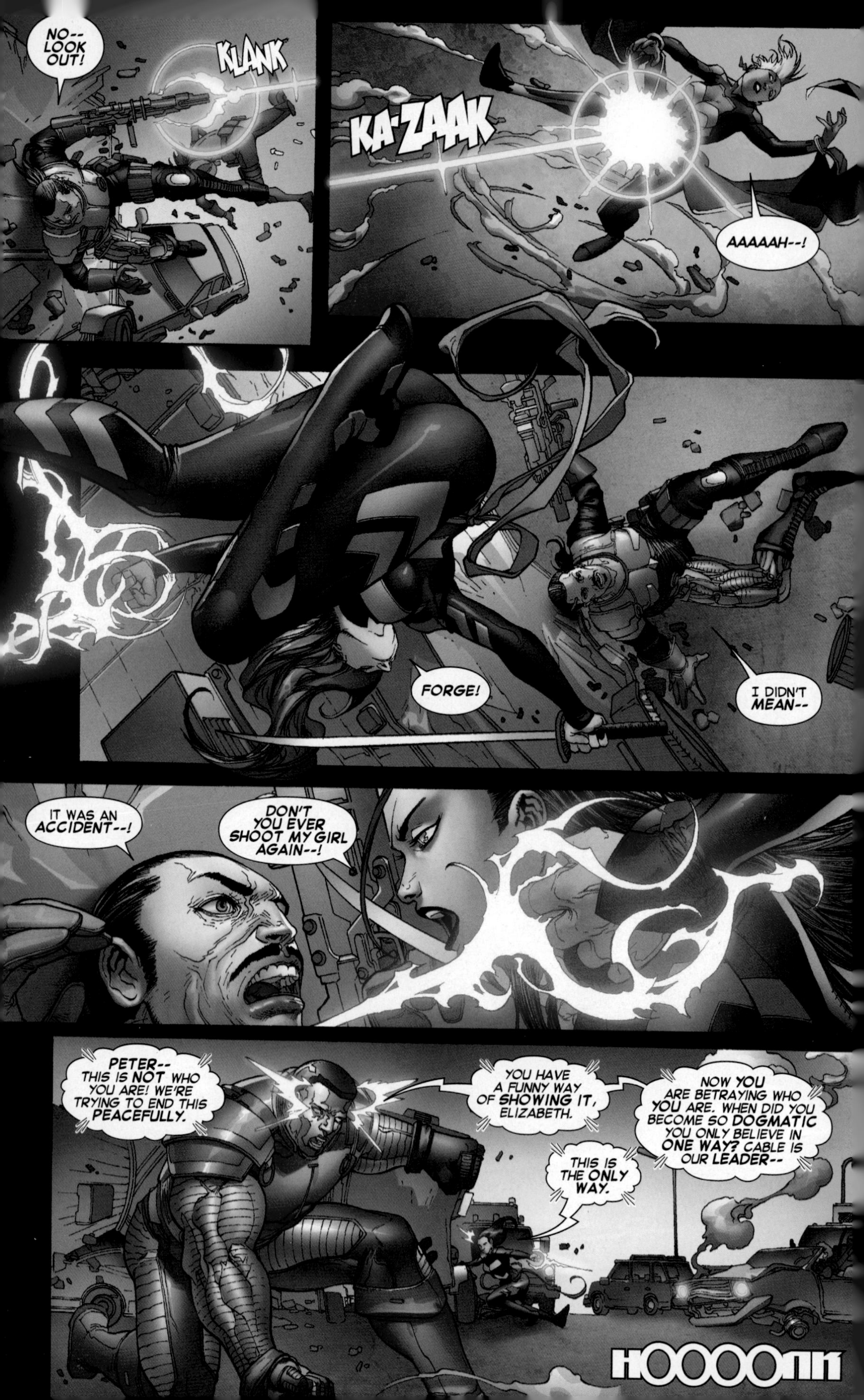
NO-- LOOK OUT!
KLANK
KA-ZAAK
AAAAAH--!
FORGE!
I DIDN'T MEAN--
IT WAS AN ACCIDENT--!
DON'T YOU EVER SHOOT MY GIRL AGAIN--!
PETER-- THIS IS NOT WHO YOU ARE! WE'RE TRYING TO END THIS PEACEFULLY.
YOU HAVE A FUNNY WAY OF SHOWING IT, ELIZABETH.
THIS IS THE ONLY WAY.
NOW YOU ARE BETRAYING WHO YOU ARE. WHEN DID YOU BECOME SO DOGMATIC YOU ONLY BELIEVE IN ONE WAY? CABLE IS OUR LEADER--
HOOOONK

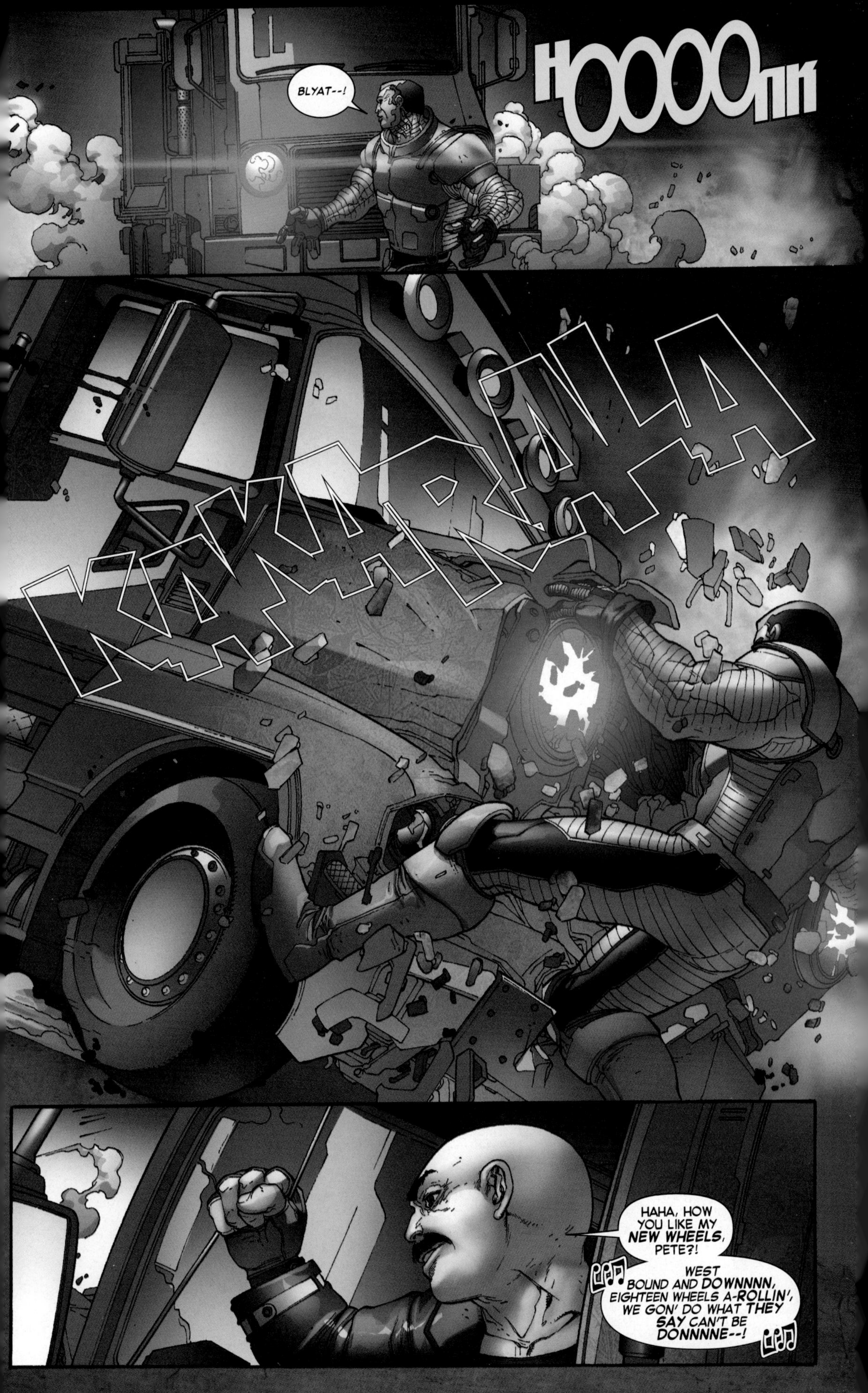
BLYAT--!
HOOOONK
KRAKRAKLA
HAHA, HOW YOU LIKE MY NEW WHEELS, PETE?!
WEST BOUND AND DOWNNNN, EIGHTEEN WHEELS A-ROLLIN', WE GON' DO WHAT THEY SAY CAN'T BE DONNNNE--!

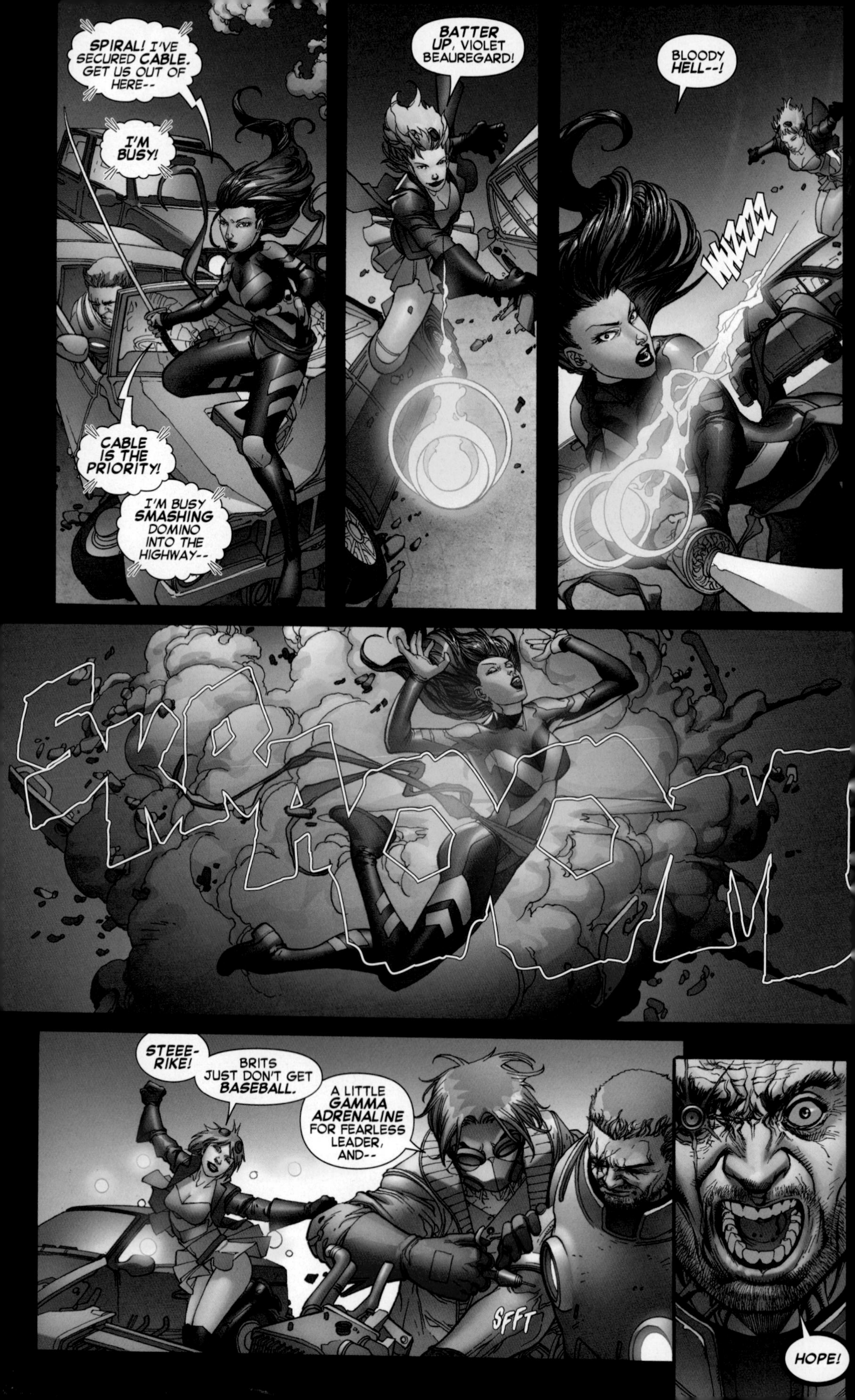
SPIRAL! I'VE SECURED CABLE. GET US OUT OF HERE--
I'M BUSY!
CABLE IS THE PRIORITY!
I'M BUSY SMASHING DOMINO INTO THE HIGHWAY--
BATTER UP, VIOLET BEAUREGARD!
BLOODY HELL--!
WHZZZZ
STEEE-RIKE!
BRITS JUST DON'T GET BASEBALL.
A LITTLE GAMMA ADRENALINE FOR FEARLESS LEADER, AND--
SFFT
HOPE!

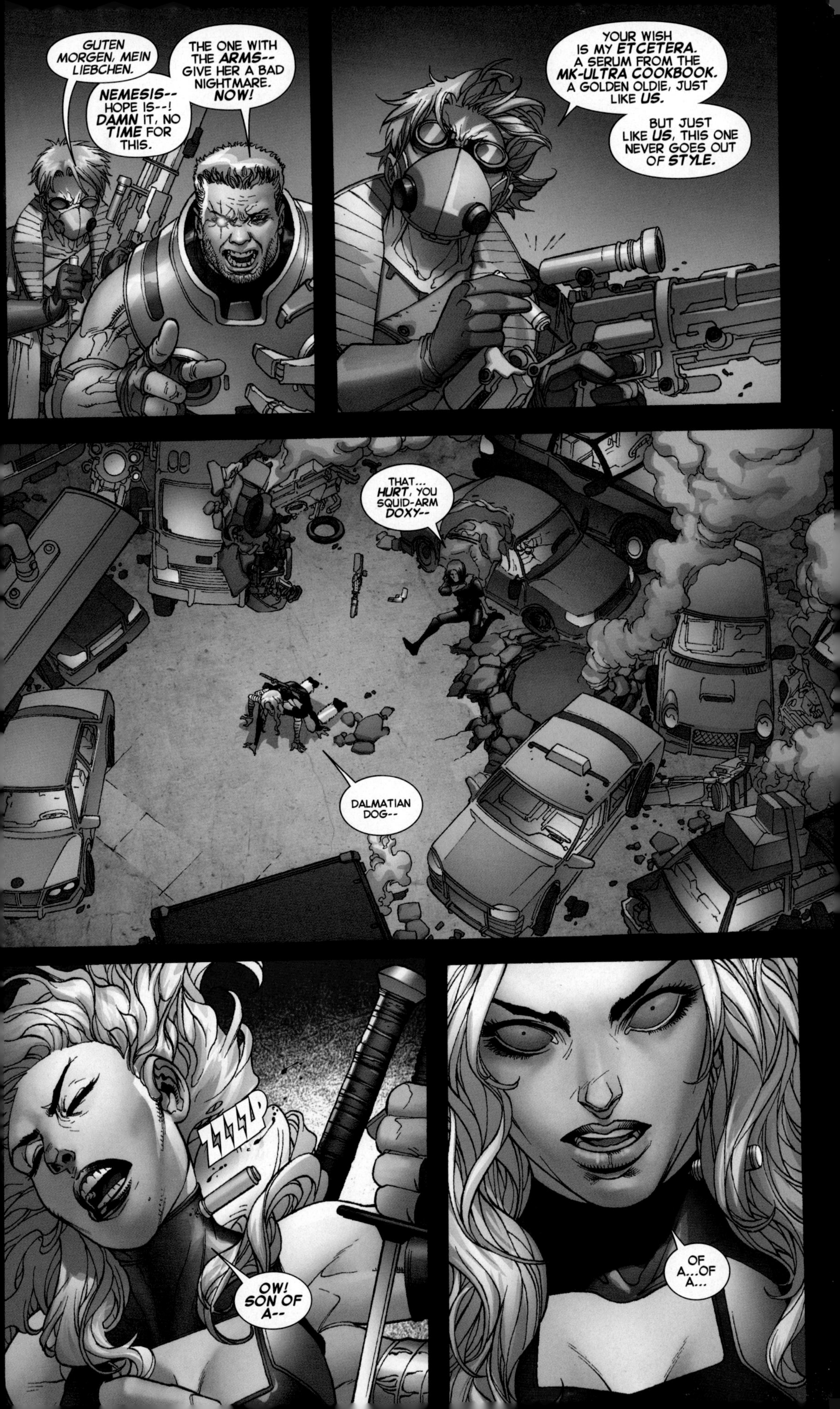
GUTEN MORGEN, MEIN LIEBCHEN.
NEMESIS-- HOPE IS--! DAMN IT, NO TIME FOR THIS.
THE ONE WITH THE ARMS-- GIVE HER A BAD NIGHTMARE. NOW!
YOUR WISH IS MY ETCETERA. A SERUM FROM THE MK-ULTRA COOKBOOK. A GOLDEN OLDIE, JUST LIKE US.
BUT JUST LIKE US, THIS ONE NEVER GOES OUT OF STYLE.
THAT... HURT, YOU SQUID-ARM DOXY--
DALMATIAN DOG--
ZZZZP
OW! SON OF A--
OF A...OF A...

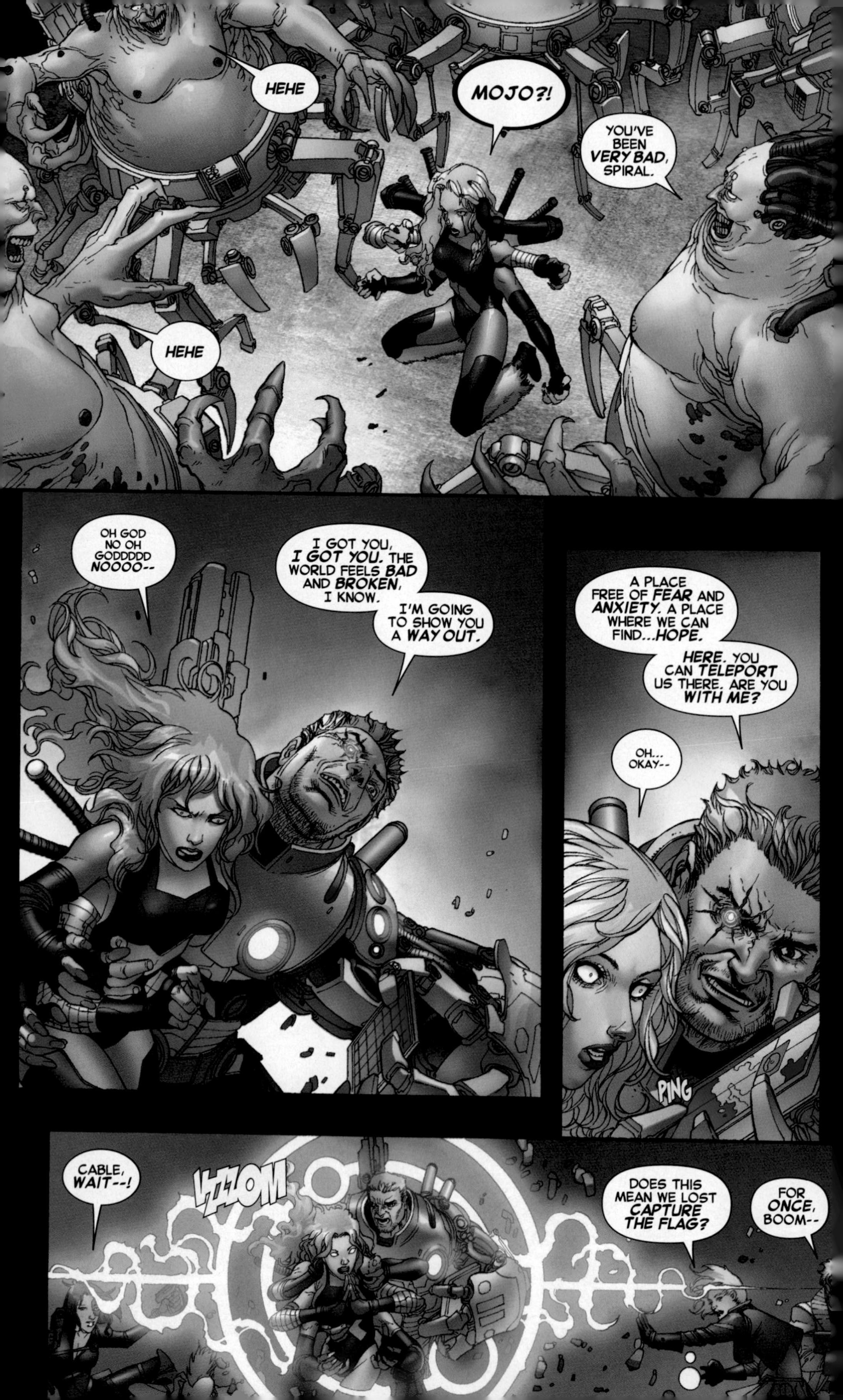
HEHE
MOJO?!
YOU'VE BEEN VERY BAD, SPIRAL.
HEHE
OH GOD NO OH GODDDDD NOOOO--
I GOT YOU, I GOT YOU. THE WORLD FEELS BAD AND BROKEN, I KNOW.
I'M GOING TO SHOW YOU A WAY OUT.
A PLACE FREE OF FEAR AND ANXIETY. A PLACE WHERE WE CAN FIND...HOPE.
HERE. YOU CAN TELEPORT US THERE. ARE YOU WITH ME?
OH... OKAY--
PING
CABLE, WAIT--!
VZZZOM
DOES THIS MEAN WE LOST CAPTURE THE FLAG?
FOR ONCE, BOOM--

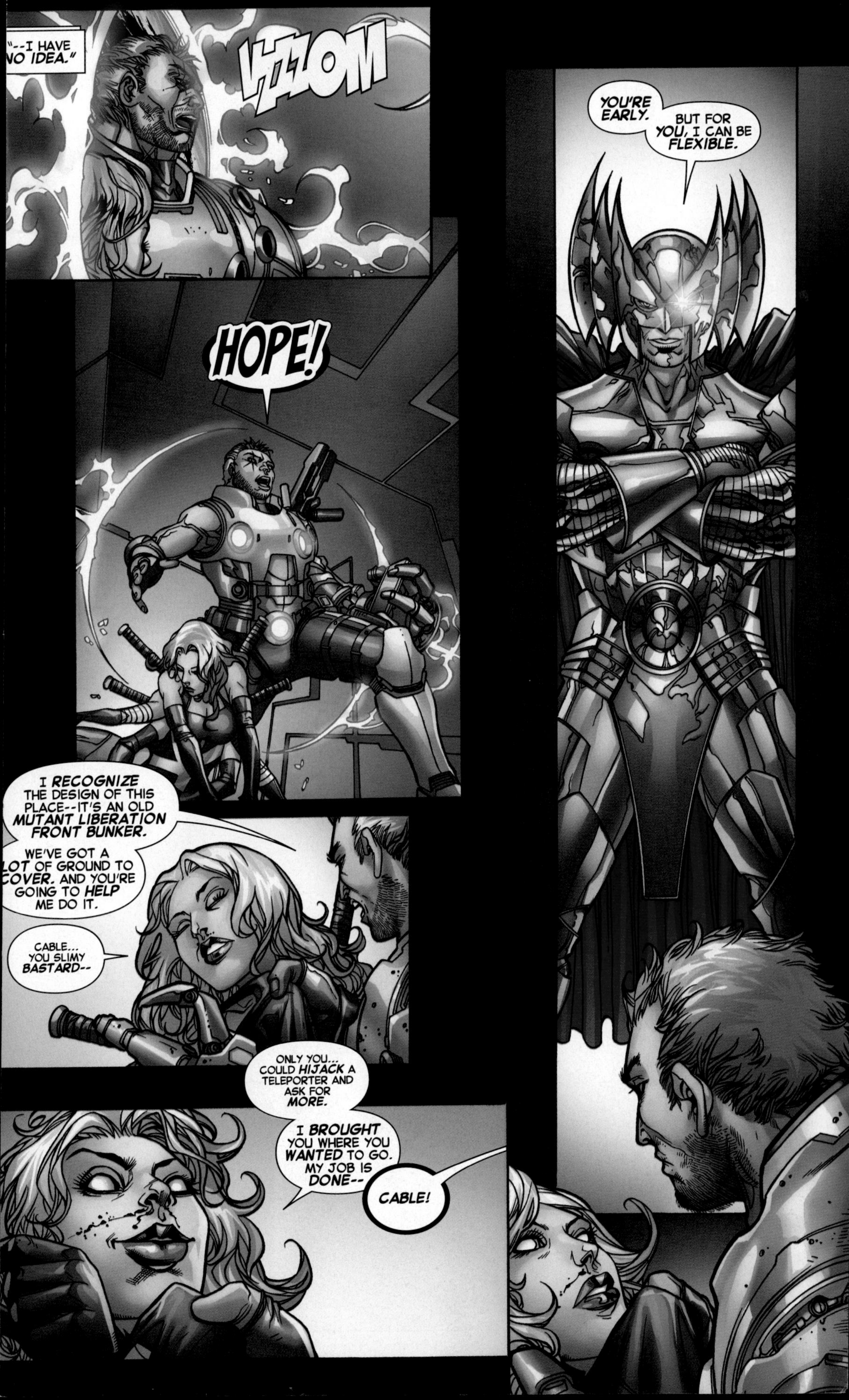
"--I HAVE NO IDEA."
VZZZOM
YOU'RE EARLY.
BUT FOR YOU, I CAN BE FLEXIBLE.
HOPE!
I RECOGNIZE THE DESIGN OF THIS PLACE--IT'S AN OLD MUTANT LIBERATION FRONT BUNKER.
WE'VE GOT A LOT OF GROUND TO COVER. AND YOU'RE GOING TO HELP ME DO IT.
CABLE... YOU SLIMY BASTARD--
ONLY YOU... COULD HIJACK A TELEPORTER AND ASK FOR MORE.
I BROUGHT YOU WHERE YOU WANTED TO GO. MY JOB IS DONE--
CABLE!

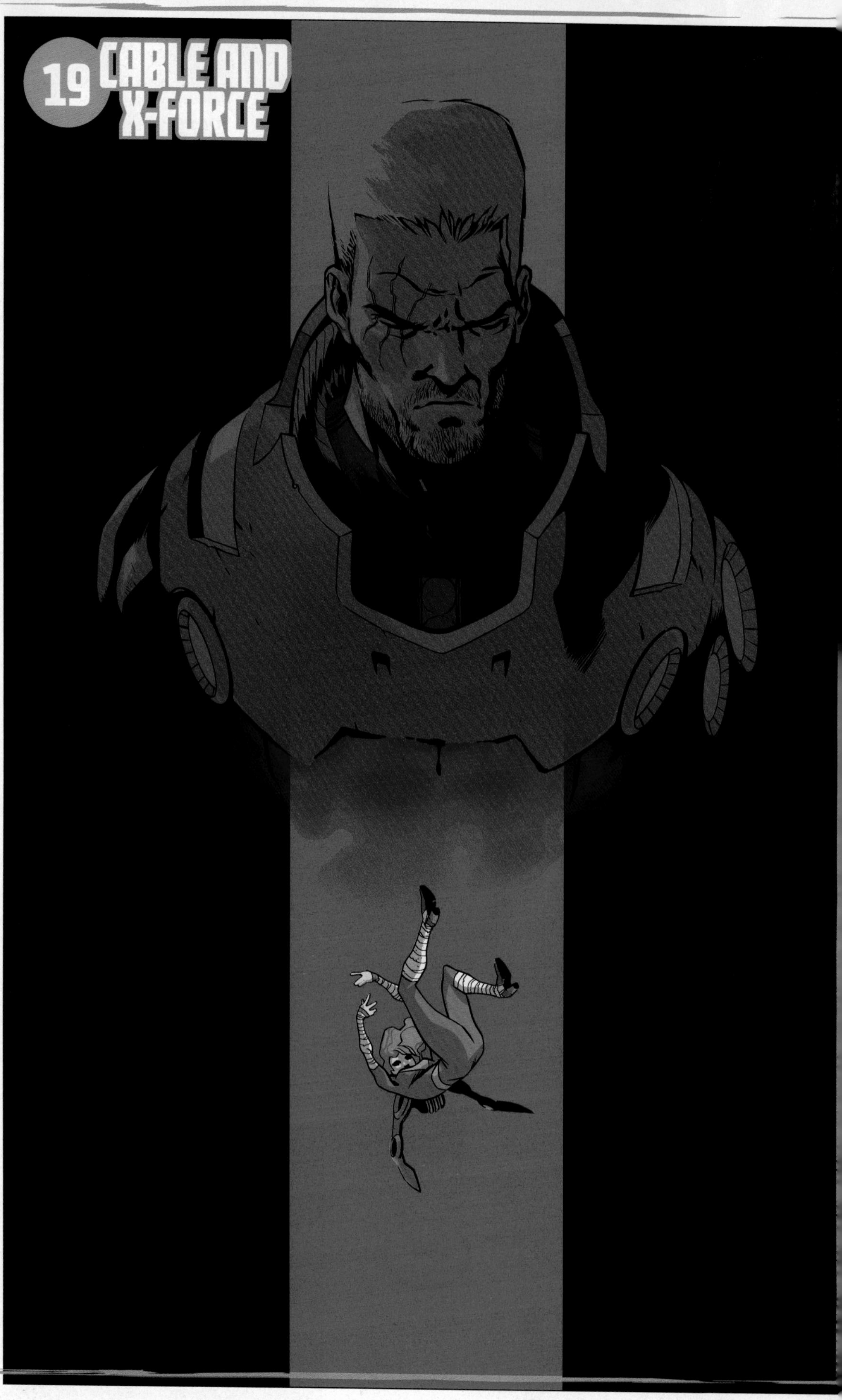
19
CABLE AND
X-FORCE

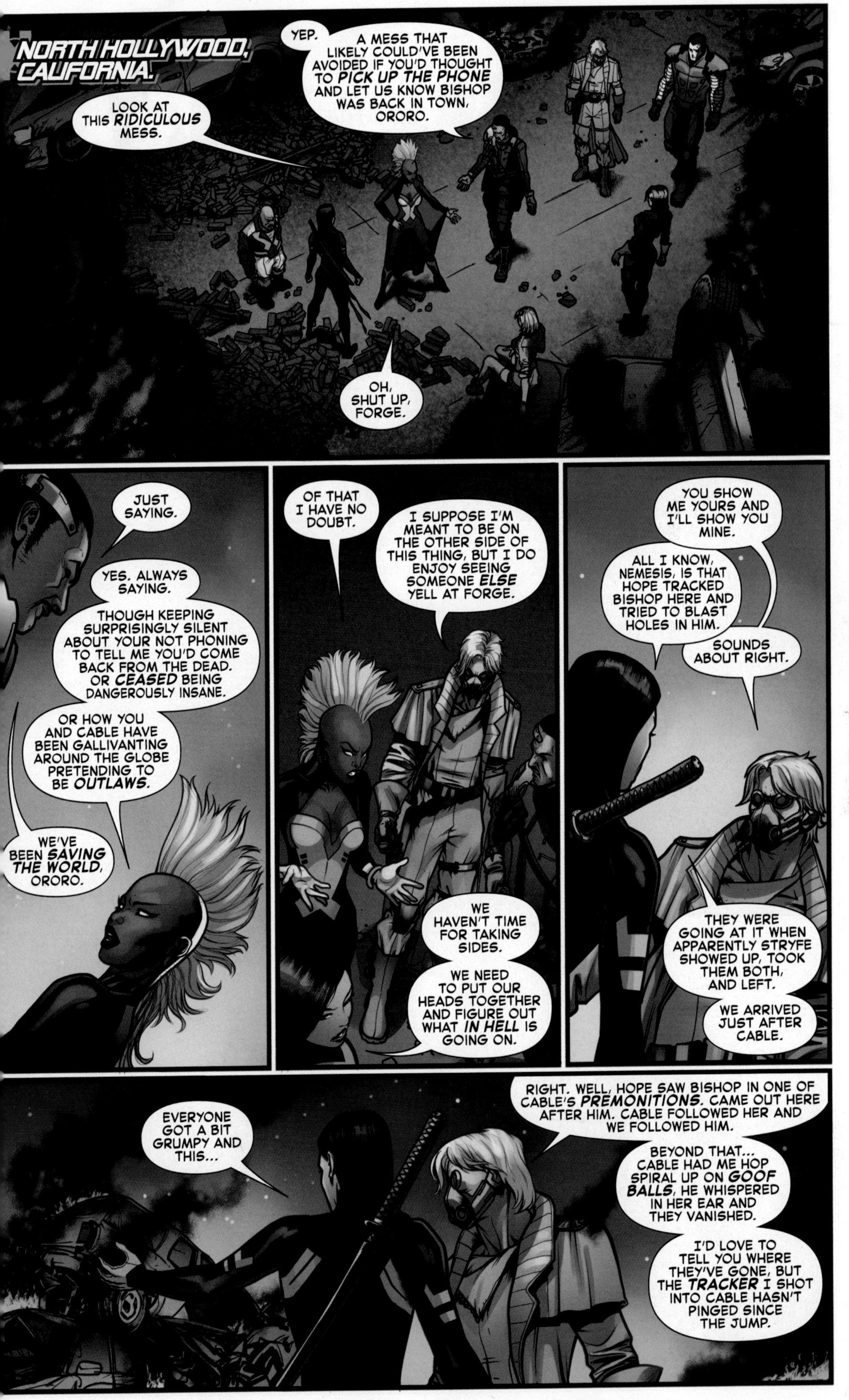
NORTH HOLLYWOOD, CALIFORNIA.
LOOK AT THIS RIDICULOUS MESS.
YEP.
A MESS THAT LIKELY COULD'VE BEEN AVOIDED IF YOU'D THOUGHT TO PICK UP THE PHONE AND LET US KNOW BISHOP WAS BACK IN TOWN, ORORO.
OH, SHUT UP, FORGE.
JUST SAYING.
YES. ALWAYS SAYING.
THOUGH KEEPING SURPRISINGLY SILENT ABOUT YOUR NOT PHONING TO TELL ME YOU'D COME BACK FROM THE DEAD. OR CEASED BEING DANGEROUSLY INSANE.
OR HOW YOU AND CABLE HAVE BEEN GALLIVANTING AROUND THE GLOBE PRETENDING TO BE OUTLAWS.
WE'VE BEEN SAVING THE WORLD, ORORO.
OF THAT I HAVE NO DOUBT.
I SUPPOSE I'M MEANT TO BE ON THE OTHER SIDE OF THIS THING, BUT I DO ENJOY SEEING SOMEONE ELSE YELL AT FORGE.
WE HAVEN'T TIME FOR TAKING SIDES.
WE NEED TO PUT OUR HEADS TOGETHER AND FIGURE OUT WHAT IN HELL IS GOING ON.
YOU SHOW ME YOURS AND I'LL SHOW YOU MINE.
ALL I KNOW, NEMESIS, IS THAT HOPE TRACKED BISHOP HERE AND TRIED TO BLAST HOLES IN HIM.
SOUNDS ABOUT RIGHT.
THEY WERE GOING AT IT WHEN APPARENTLY STRYFE SHOWED UP, TOOK THEM BOTH, AND LEFT.
WE ARRIVED JUST AFTER CABLE.
EVERYONE GOT A BIT GRUMPY AND THIS...
RIGHT. WELL, HOPE SAW BISHOP IN ONE OF CABLE'S PREMONITIONS. CAME OUT HERE AFTER HIM. CABLE FOLLOWED HER AND WE FOLLOWED HIM.
BEYOND THAT... CABLE HAD ME HOP SPIRAL UP ON GOOF BALLS, HE WHISPERED IN HER EAR AND THEY VANISHED.
I'D LOVE TO TELL YOU WHERE THEY'VE GONE, BUT THE TRACKER I SHOT INTO CABLE HASN'T PINGED SINCE THE JUMP.

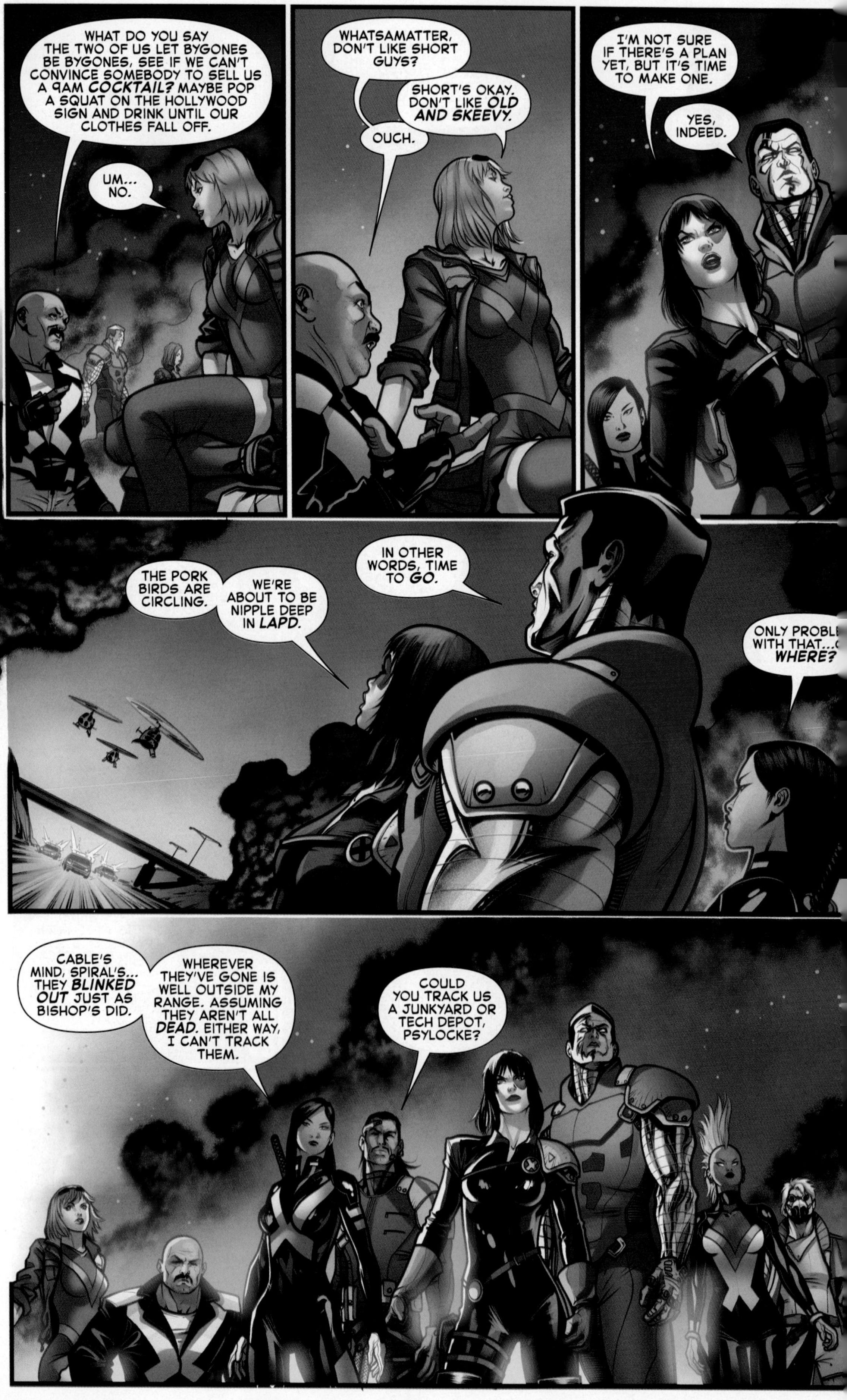
WHAT DO YOU SAY THE TWO OF US LET BYGONES BE BYGONES, SEE IF WE CAN'T CONVINCE SOMEBODY TO SELL US A 9AM COCKTAIL? MAYBE POP A SQUAT ON THE HOLLYWOOD SIGN AND DRINK UNTIL OUR CLOTHES FALL OFF.
UM... NO.
WHATSAMATTER, DON'T LIKE SHORT GUYS?
SHORT'S OKAY. DON'T LIKE OLD AND SKEEVY.
OUCH.
I'M NOT SURE IF THERE'S A PLAN YET, BUT IT'S TIME TO MAKE ONE.
YES, INDEED.
THE PORK BIRDS ARE CIRCLING.
WE'RE ABOUT TO BE NIPPLE DEEP IN LAPD.
IN OTHER WORDS, TIME TO GO.
ONLY PROBLE WITH THAT... WHERE?
CABLE'S MIND, SPIRAL'S... THEY BLINKED OUT JUST AS BISHOP'S DID.
WHEREVER THEY'VE GONE IS WELL OUTSIDE MY RANGE. ASSUMING THEY AREN'T ALL DEAD. EITHER WAY, I CAN'T TRACK THEM.
COULD YOU TRACK US A JUNKYARD OR TECH DEPOT, PSYLOCKE?

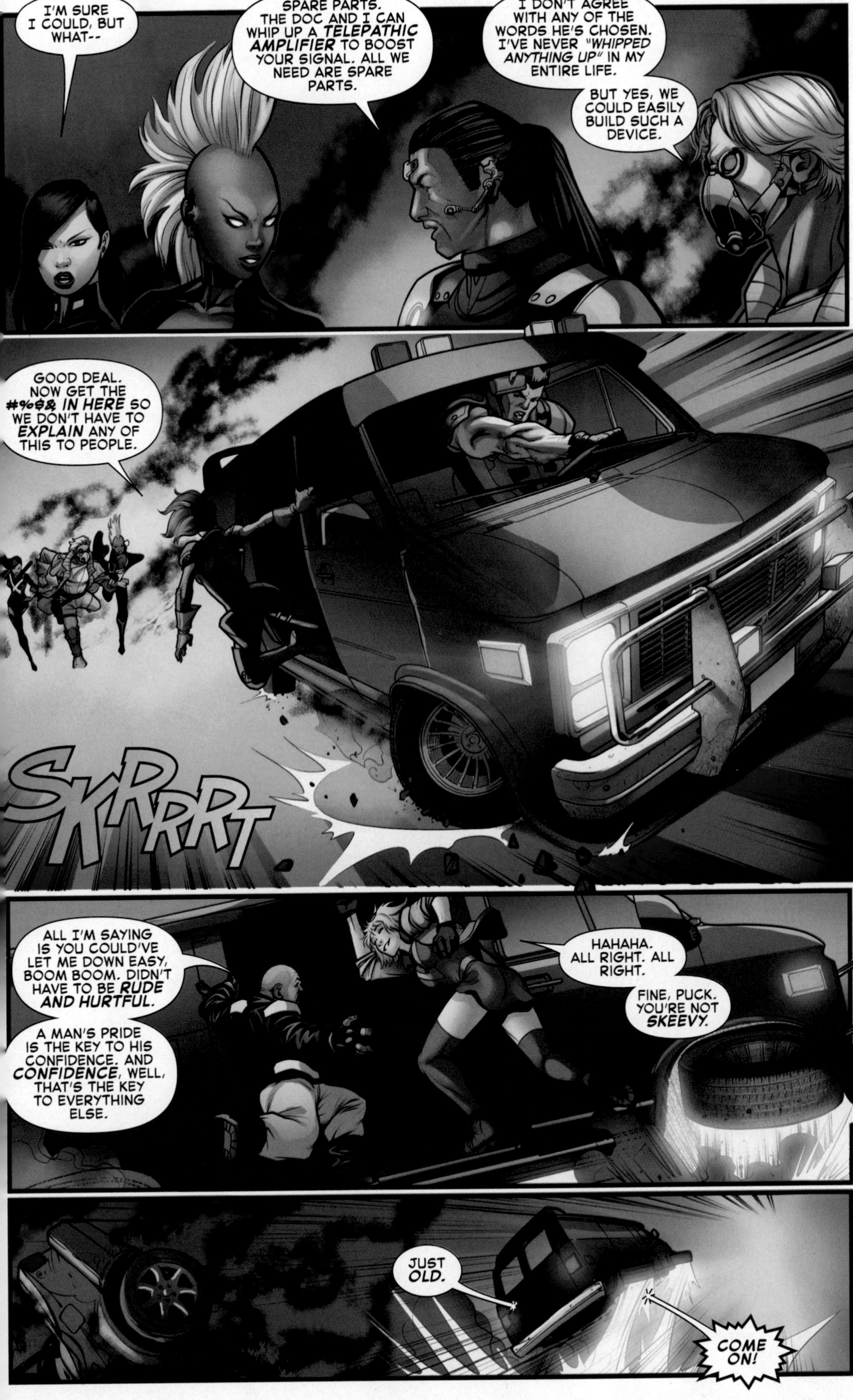

I'M SURE I COULD, BUT WHAT--
SPARE PARTS. THE DOC AND I CAN WHIP UP A *TELEPATHIC AMPLIFIER* TO BOOST YOUR SIGNAL. ALL WE NEED ARE SPARE PARTS.
I DON'T AGREE WITH ANY OF THE WORDS HE'S CHOSEN. I'VE NEVER "*WHIPPED ANYTHING UP*" IN MY ENTIRE LIFE.
BUT YES, WE COULD EASILY BUILD SUCH A DEVICE.
GOOD DEAL. NOW GET THE **#%$& IN HERE** SO WE DON'T HAVE TO ***EXPLAIN*** ANY OF THIS TO PEOPLE.
SKRRRT
ALL I'M SAYING IS YOU COULD'VE LET ME DOWN EASY, BOOM BOOM. DIDN'T HAVE TO BE ***RUDE AND HURTFUL.***
A MAN'S PRIDE IS THE KEY TO HIS CONFIDENCE. AND ***CONFIDENCE***, WELL, THAT'S THE KEY TO EVERYTHING ELSE.
HAHAHA. ALL RIGHT. ALL RIGHT.
FINE, PUCK. YOU'RE NOT ***SKEEVY.***
JUST ***OLD.***
COME ON!

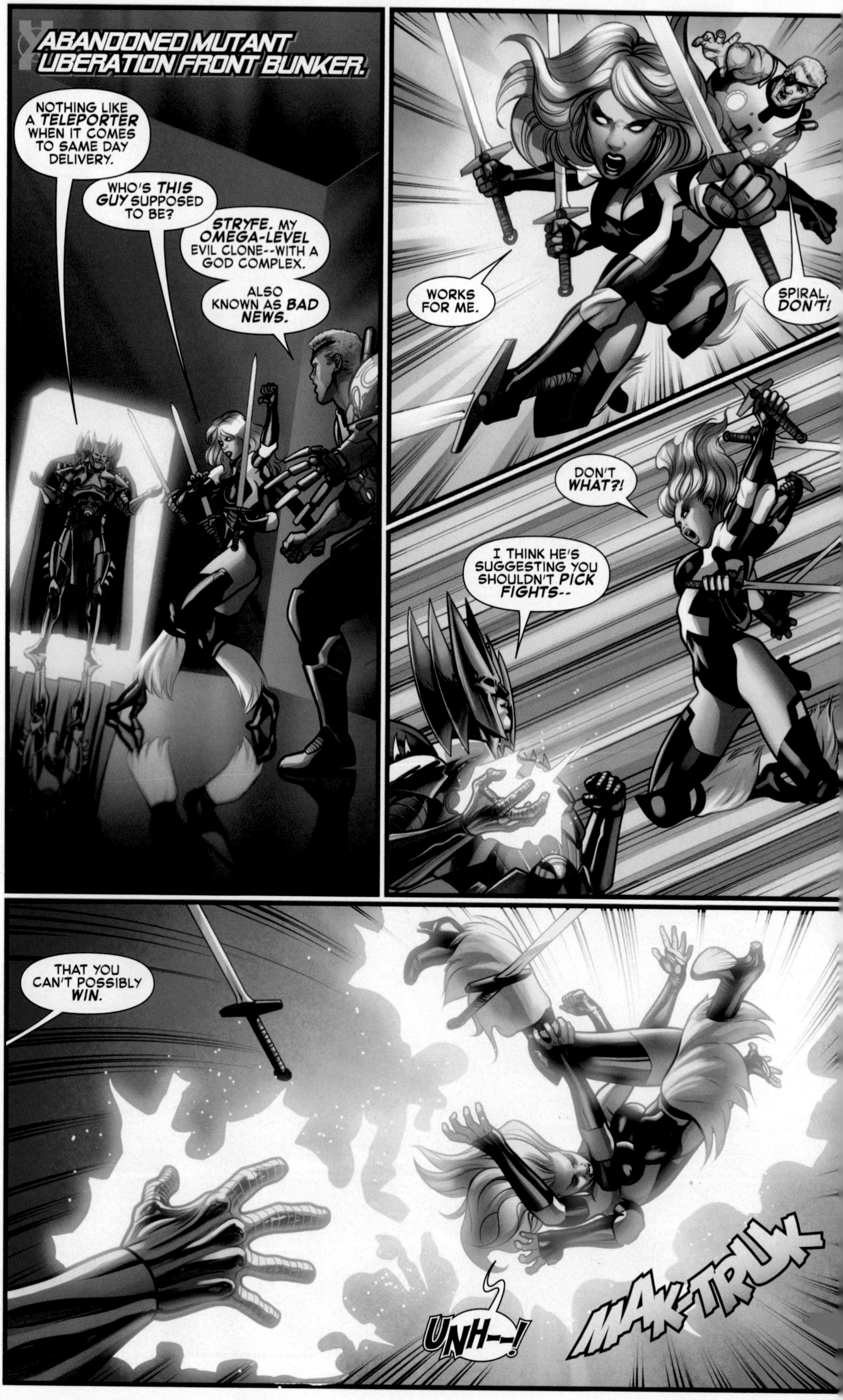
ABANDONED MUTANT LIBERATION FRONT BUNKER.
NOTHING LIKE A TELEPORTER WHEN IT COMES TO SAME DAY DELIVERY.
WHO'S THIS GUY SUPPOSED TO BE?
STRYFE. MY OMEGA-LEVEL EVIL CLONE--WITH A GOD COMPLEX.
ALSO KNOWN AS BAD NEWS.
WORKS FOR ME.
SPIRAL, DON'T!
DON'T WHAT?!
I THINK HE'S SUGGESTING YOU SHOULDN'T PICK FIGHTS--
THAT YOU CAN'T POSSIBLY WIN.
UNH--!
MAK-TRUK

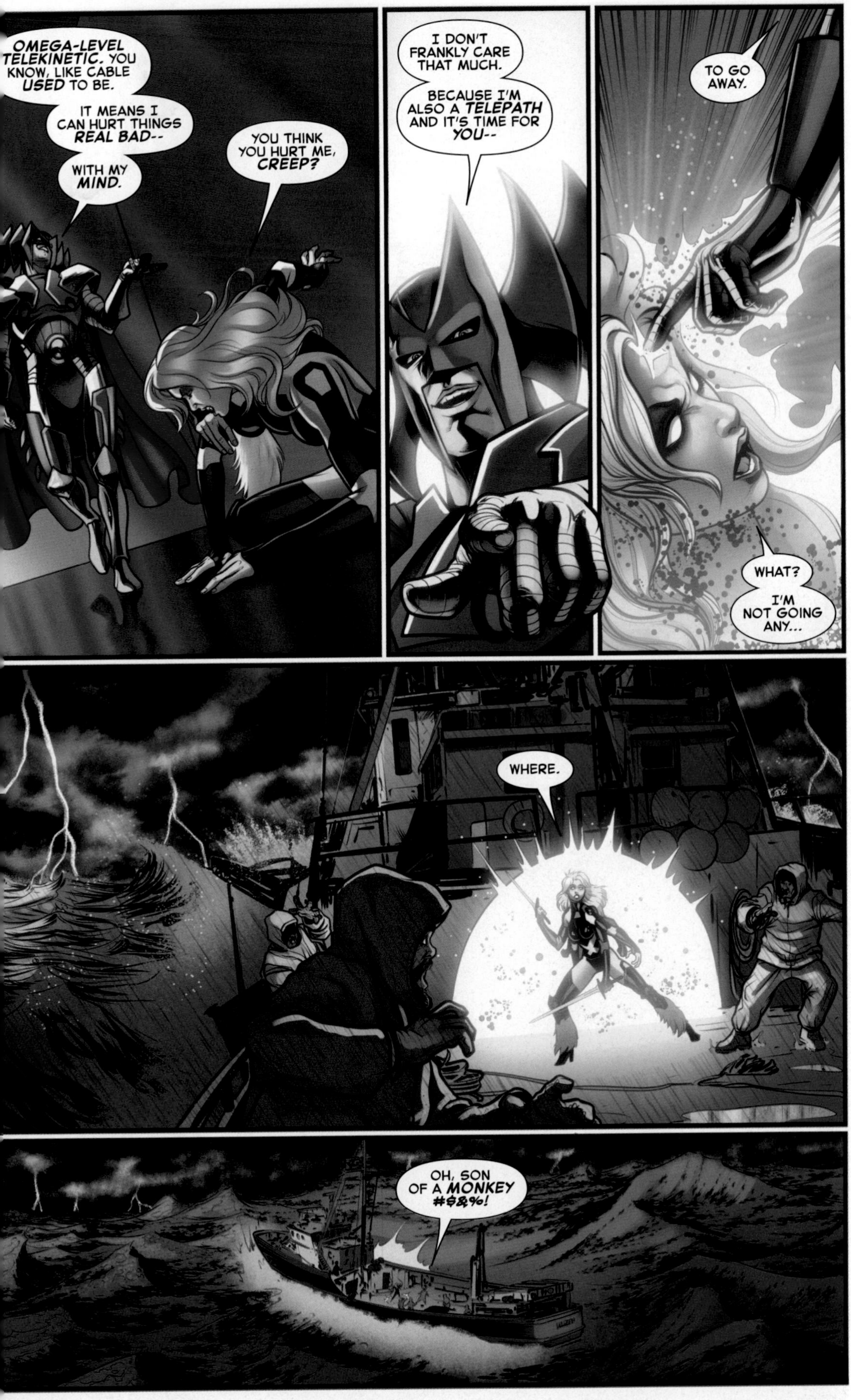

OMEGA-LEVEL TELEKINETIC. YOU KNOW, LIKE CABLE USED TO BE.
IT MEANS I CAN HURT THINGS REAL BAD--
WITH MY MIND.
YOU THINK YOU HURT ME, CREEP?
I DON'T FRANKLY CARE THAT MUCH.
BECAUSE I'M ALSO A TELEPATH AND IT'S TIME FOR YOU--
TO GO AWAY.
WHAT?
I'M NOT GOING ANY...
WHERE.
OH, SON OF A MONKEY #$&%!

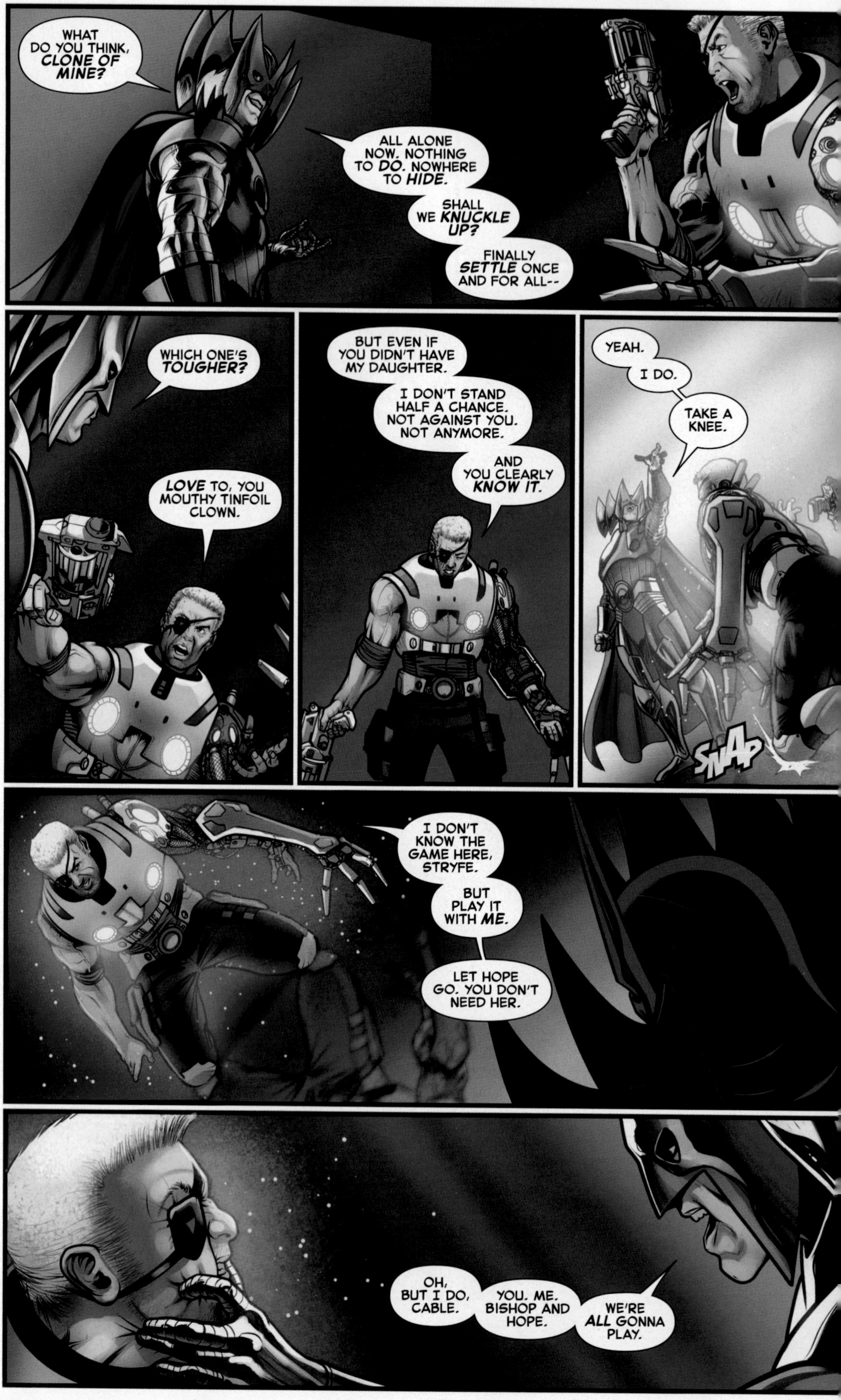

WHAT DO YOU THINK, CLONE OF MINE?
ALL ALONE NOW. NOTHING TO DO. NOWHERE TO HIDE.
SHALL WE KNUCKLE UP?
FINALLY SETTLE ONCE AND FOR ALL--
WHICH ONE'S TOUGHER?
LOVE TO, YOU MOUTHY TINFOIL CLOWN.
BUT EVEN IF YOU DIDN'T HAVE MY DAUGHTER.
I DON'T STAND HALF A CHANCE. NOT AGAINST YOU. NOT ANYMORE.
AND YOU CLEARLY KNOW IT.
YEAH.
I DO.
TAKE A KNEE.
SNAP
I DON'T KNOW THE GAME HERE, STRYFE.
BUT PLAY IT WITH ME.
LET HOPE GO. YOU DON'T NEED HER.
OH, BUT I DO, CABLE.
YOU. ME. BISHOP AND HOPE.
WE'RE ALL GONNA PLAY.

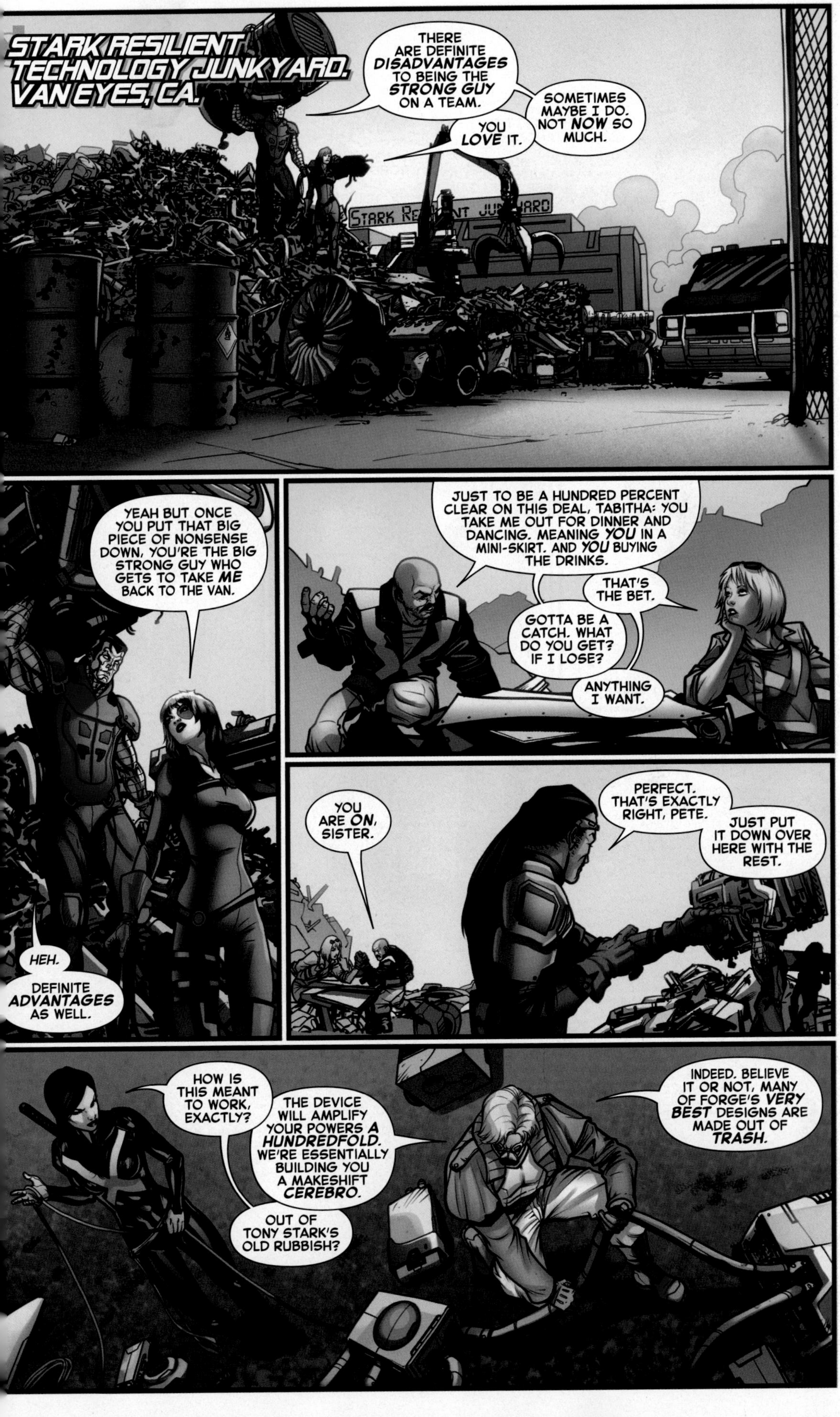
STARK RESILIENT TECHNOLOGY JUNKYARD. VAN EYES, CA.
THERE ARE DEFINITE DISADVANTAGES TO BEING THE STRONG GUY ON A TEAM.
YOU LOVE IT.
SOMETIMES MAYBE I DO. NOT NOW SO MUCH.
YEAH BUT ONCE YOU PUT THAT BIG PIECE OF NONSENSE DOWN, YOU'RE THE BIG STRONG GUY WHO GETS TO TAKE ME BACK TO THE VAN.
HEH.
DEFINITE ADVANTAGES AS WELL.
JUST TO BE A HUNDRED PERCENT CLEAR ON THIS DEAL, TABITHA: YOU TAKE ME OUT FOR DINNER AND DANCING. MEANING YOU IN A MINI-SKIRT. AND YOU BUYING THE DRINKS.
THAT'S THE BET.
GOTTA BE A CATCH. WHAT DO YOU GET? IF I LOSE?
ANYTHING I WANT.
YOU ARE ON, SISTER.
PERFECT. THAT'S EXACTLY RIGHT, PETE.
JUST PUT IT DOWN OVER HERE WITH THE REST.
HOW IS THIS MEANT TO WORK, EXACTLY?
THE DEVICE WILL AMPLIFY YOUR POWERS A HUNDREDFOLD. WE'RE ESSENTIALLY BUILDING YOU A MAKESHIFT CEREBRO.
OUT OF TONY STARK'S OLD RUBBISH?
INDEED. BELIEVE IT OR NOT, MANY OF FORGE'S VERY BEST DESIGNS ARE MADE OUT OF TRASH.

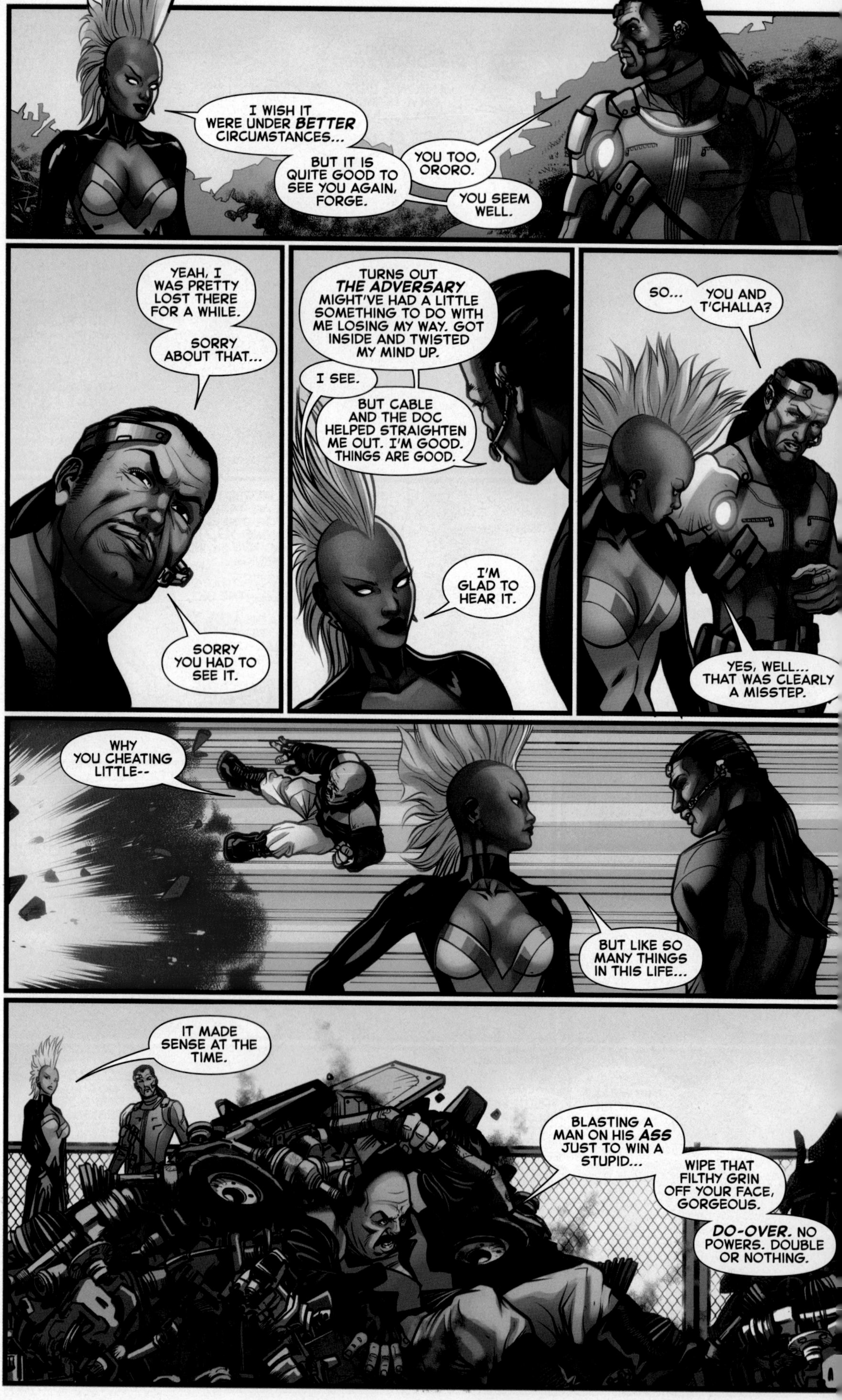
I WISH IT WERE UNDER BETTER CIRCUMSTANCES...
BUT IT IS QUITE GOOD TO SEE YOU AGAIN, FORGE.
YOU TOO, ORORO.
YOU SEEM WELL.
YEAH, I WAS PRETTY LOST THERE FOR A WHILE.
SORRY ABOUT THAT...
SORRY YOU HAD TO SEE IT.
TURNS OUT THE ADVERSARY MIGHT'VE HAD A LITTLE SOMETHING TO DO WITH ME LOSING MY WAY. GOT INSIDE AND TWISTED MY MIND UP.
I SEE.
BUT CABLE AND THE DOC HELPED STRAIGHTEN ME OUT. I'M GOOD. THINGS ARE GOOD.
I'M GLAD TO HEAR IT.
SO...
YOU AND T'CHALLA?
YES, WELL... THAT WAS CLEARLY A MISSTEP.
WHY YOU CHEATING LITTLE--
BUT LIKE SO MANY THINGS IN THIS LIFE...
IT MADE SENSE AT THE TIME.
BLASTING A MAN ON HIS ASS JUST TO WIN A STUPID...
WIPE THAT FILTHY GRIN OFF YOUR FACE, GORGEOUS.
DO-OVER. NO POWERS. DOUBLE OR NOTHING.

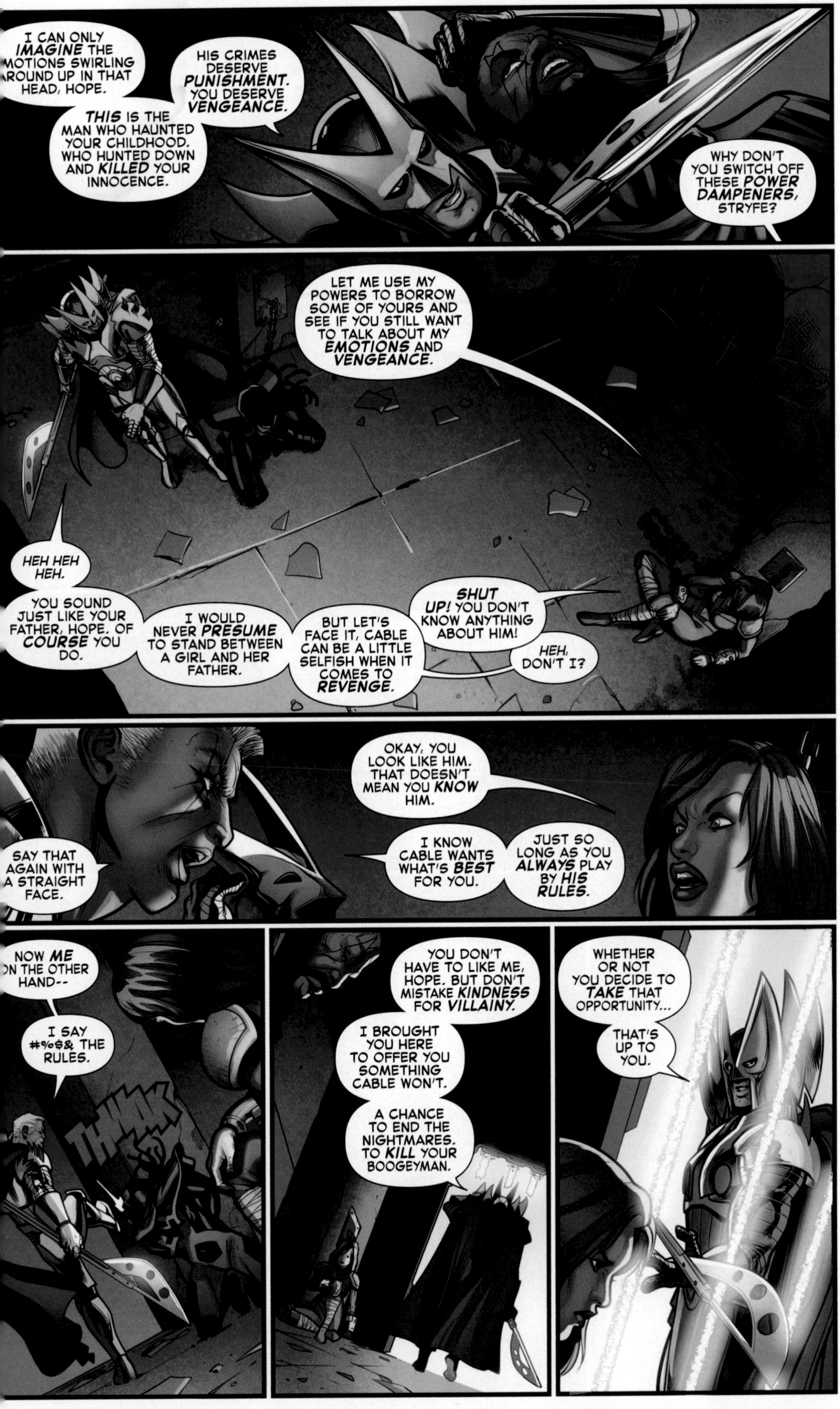
I CAN ONLY IMAGINE THE MOTIONS SWIRLING AROUND UP IN THAT HEAD, HOPE.
THIS IS THE MAN WHO HAUNTED YOUR CHILDHOOD. WHO HUNTED DOWN AND KILLED YOUR INNOCENCE.
HIS CRIMES DESERVE PUNISHMENT. YOU DESERVE VENGEANCE.
WHY DON'T YOU SWITCH OFF THESE POWER DAMPENERS, STRYFE?
LET ME USE MY POWERS TO BORROW SOME OF YOURS AND SEE IF YOU STILL WANT TO TALK ABOUT MY EMOTIONS AND VENGEANCE.
HEH HEH HEH.
YOU SOUND JUST LIKE YOUR FATHER, HOPE. OF COURSE YOU DO.
I WOULD NEVER PRESUME TO STAND BETWEEN A GIRL AND HER FATHER.
BUT LET'S FACE IT, CABLE CAN BE A LITTLE SELFISH WHEN IT COMES TO REVENGE.
SHUT UP! YOU DON'T KNOW ANYTHING ABOUT HIM!
HEH, DON'T I?
OKAY, YOU LOOK LIKE HIM. THAT DOESN'T MEAN YOU KNOW HIM.
I KNOW CABLE WANTS WHAT'S BEST FOR YOU.
JUST SO LONG AS YOU ALWAYS PLAY BY HIS RULES.
SAY THAT AGAIN WITH A STRAIGHT FACE.
NOW ME ON THE OTHER HAND--
I SAY #%$& THE RULES.
THWAK
YOU DON'T HAVE TO LIKE ME, HOPE. BUT DON'T MISTAKE KINDNESS FOR VILLAINY.
I BROUGHT YOU HERE TO OFFER YOU SOMETHING CABLE WON'T.
A CHANCE TO END THE NIGHTMARES. TO KILL YOUR BOOGEYMAN.
WHETHER OR NOT YOU DECIDE TO TAKE THAT OPPORTUNITY...
THAT'S UP TO YOU.

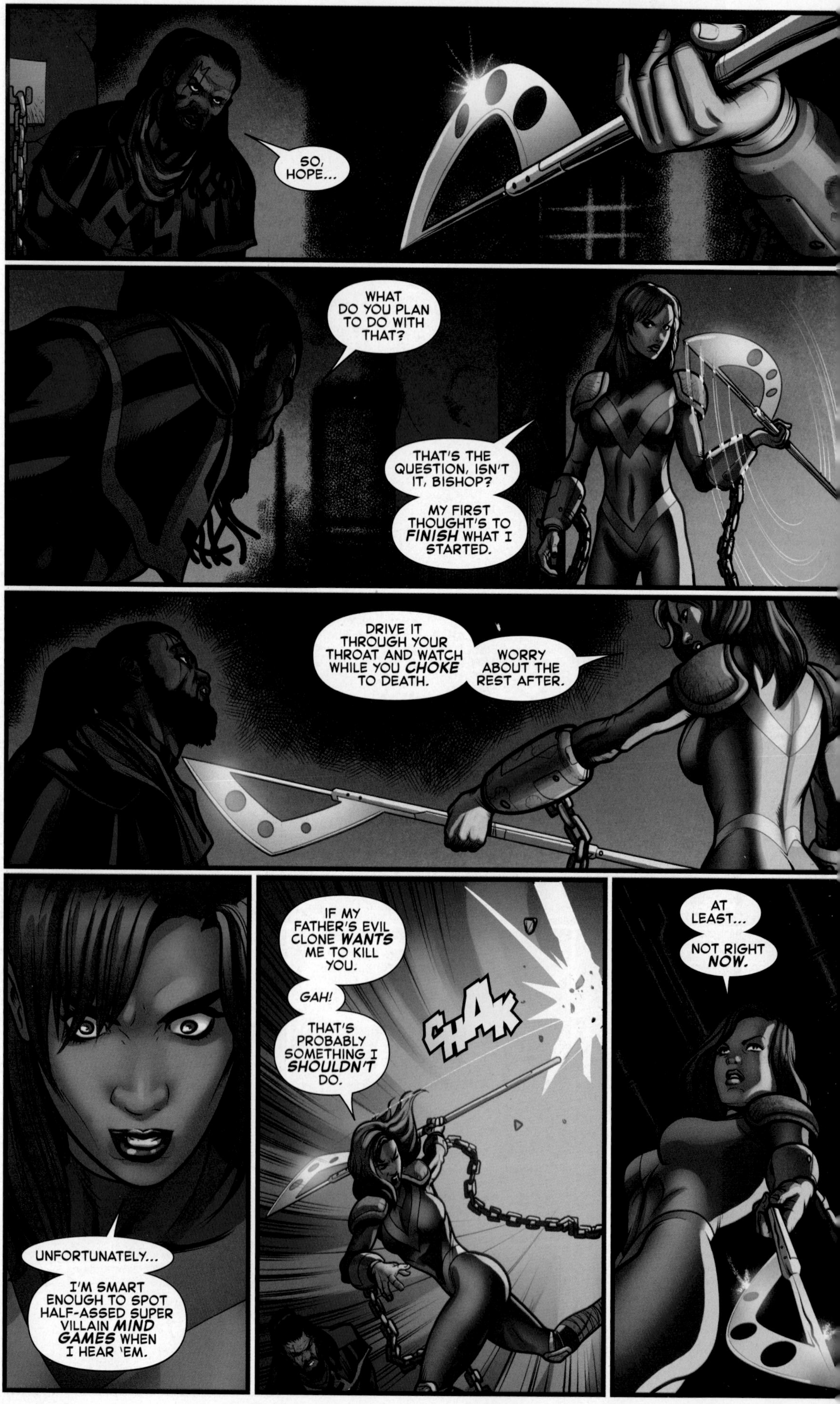
SO, HOPE...
WHAT DO YOU PLAN TO DO WITH THAT?
THAT'S THE QUESTION, ISN'T IT, BISHOP?
MY FIRST THOUGHT'S TO FINISH WHAT I STARTED.
DRIVE IT THROUGH YOUR THROAT AND WATCH WHILE YOU CHOKE TO DEATH.
WORRY ABOUT THE REST AFTER.
UNFORTUNATELY...
I'M SMART ENOUGH TO SPOT HALF-ASSED SUPER VILLAIN MIND GAMES WHEN I HEAR 'EM.
IF MY FATHER'S EVIL CLONE WANTS ME TO KILL YOU.
GAH!
THAT'S PROBABLY SOMETHING I SHOULDN'T DO.
CHAK
AT LEAST...
NOT RIGHT NOW.

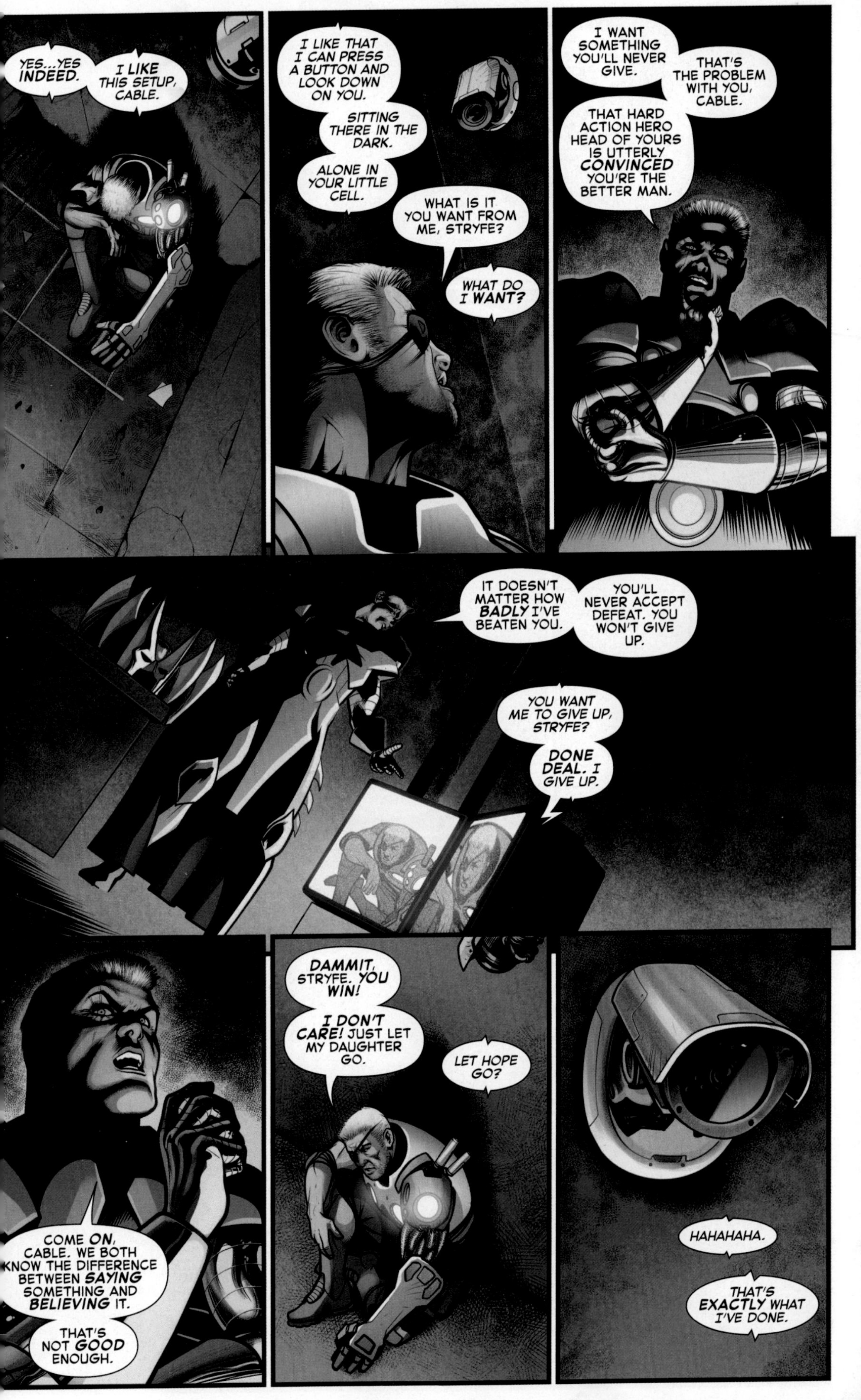
YES...YES INDEED.
I LIKE THIS SETUP, CABLE.
I LIKE THAT I CAN PRESS A BUTTON AND LOOK DOWN ON YOU.
SITTING THERE IN THE DARK.
ALONE IN YOUR LITTLE CELL.
WHAT IS IT YOU WANT FROM ME, STRYFE?
WHAT DO I WANT?
I WANT SOMETHING YOU'LL NEVER GIVE.
THAT'S THE PROBLEM WITH YOU, CABLE.
THAT HARD ACTION HERO HEAD OF YOURS IS UTTERLY CONVINCED YOU'RE THE BETTER MAN.
IT DOESN'T MATTER HOW BADLY I'VE BEATEN YOU.
YOU'LL NEVER ACCEPT DEFEAT. YOU WON'T GIVE UP.
YOU WANT ME TO GIVE UP, STRYFE?
DONE DEAL. I GIVE UP.
COME ON, CABLE. WE BOTH KNOW THE DIFFERENCE BETWEEN SAYING SOMETHING AND BELIEVING IT.
THAT'S NOT GOOD ENOUGH.
DAMMIT, STRYFE. YOU WIN!
I DON'T CARE! JUST LET MY DAUGHTER GO.
LET HOPE GO?
HAHAHAHA.
THAT'S EXACTLY WHAT I'VE DONE.

JUST GET IT OVER WITH, HOPE.

WHAT?

YOU'RE PACING BACK AND FORTH OVER THERE, STARING *HOLES* THROUGH ME. HOPING STRYFE WILL COME BACK AND *FORCE* YOUR HAND.

ENOUGH. EITHER *USE* THAT PSIMITAR OR PUT IT *AWAY.*

DO YOU REALLY THINK *POKING ME* IS A GOOD IDEA RIGHT NOW?

YOU DESERVE THIS BLADE AND *WORSE.*

LOOK...I UNDERSTAND THAT.

I'M MORE THAN SORRY FOR WHAT I DID TO YOU. FOR WHO I WAS.

YOU'RE *SORRY*?

YES. AND I UNDERSTAND MY APOLOGY WILL *NEVER* BE ENOUGH, HOPE.

UNFORTUNATELY, IT'S ALL I HAVE TO GIVE.

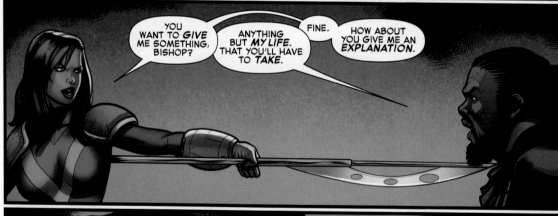

YOU WANT TO *GIVE* ME SOMETHING, BISHOP?

ANYTHING BUT *MY LIFE.* THAT YOU'LL HAVE TO *TAKE.*

FINE.

HOW ABOUT YOU GIVE ME AN *EXPLANATION.*

EXPLAIN HOW YOU COULD HUNT A *LITTLE GIRL.*

OR *NUKE THE WORLD* JUST TO GET AT ME.

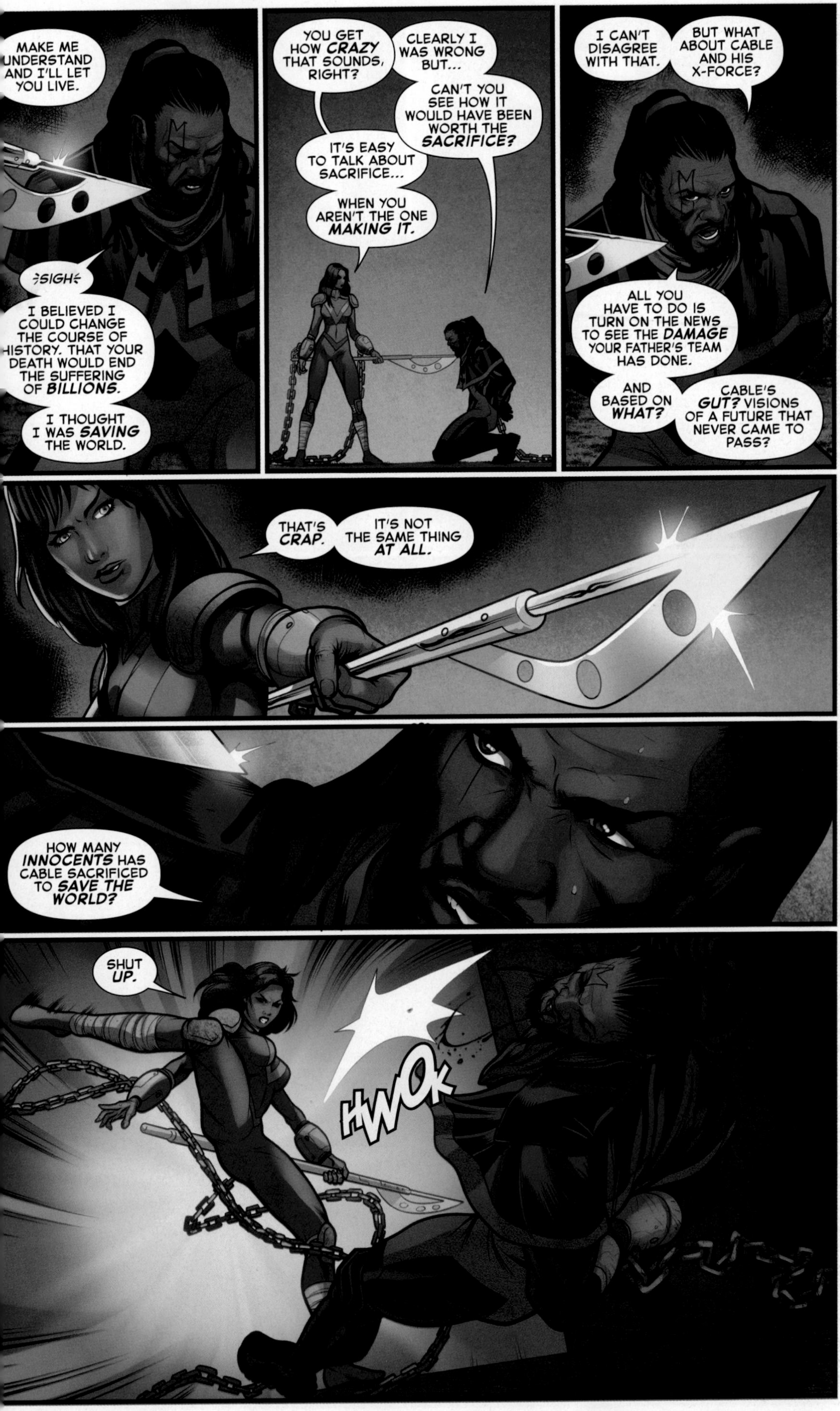
MAKE ME UNDERSTAND AND I'LL LET YOU LIVE.
SIGH
I BELIEVED I COULD CHANGE THE COURSE OF HISTORY. THAT YOUR DEATH WOULD END THE SUFFERING OF BILLIONS.
I THOUGHT I WAS SAVING THE WORLD.
YOU GET HOW CRAZY THAT SOUNDS, RIGHT?
CLEARLY I WAS WRONG BUT...
CAN'T YOU SEE HOW IT WOULD HAVE BEEN WORTH THE SACRIFICE?
IT'S EASY TO TALK ABOUT SACRIFICE...
WHEN YOU AREN'T THE ONE MAKING IT.
I CAN'T DISAGREE WITH THAT.
BUT WHAT ABOUT CABLE AND HIS X-FORCE?
ALL YOU HAVE TO DO IS TURN ON THE NEWS TO SEE THE DAMAGE YOUR FATHER'S TEAM HAS DONE.
AND BASED ON WHAT?
CABLE'S GUT? VISIONS OF A FUTURE THAT NEVER CAME TO PASS?
THAT'S CRAP.
IT'S NOT THE SAME THING AT ALL.
HOW MANY INNOCENTS HAS CABLE SACRIFICED TO SAVE THE WORLD?
SHUT UP.
HWOK

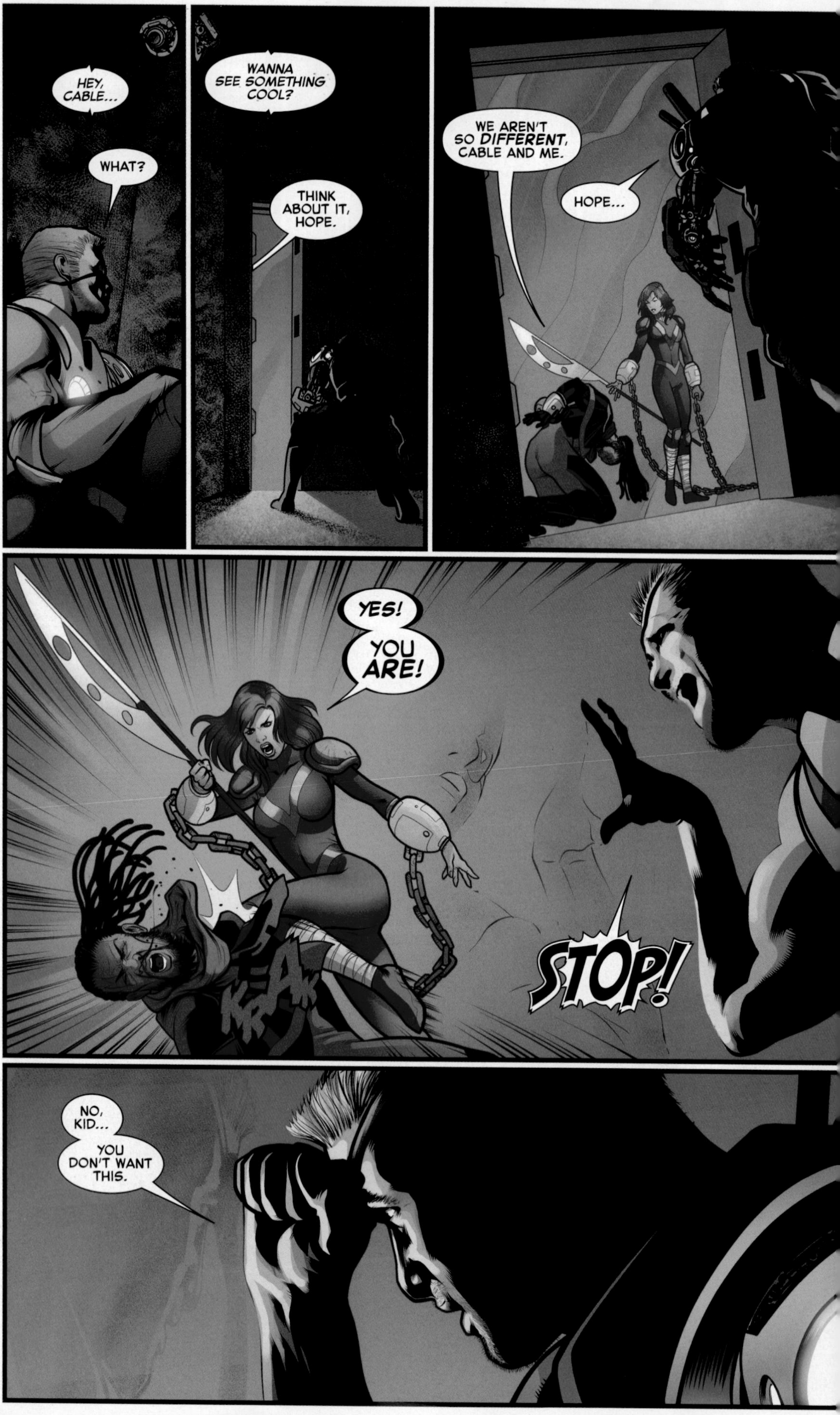
HEY, CABLE...
WHAT?
WANNA SEE SOMETHING COOL?
THINK ABOUT IT, HOPE.
WE AREN'T SO DIFFERENT, CABLE AND ME.
HOPE...
YES!
YOU ARE!
KRAK
STOP!
NO, KID...
YOU DON'T WANT THIS.

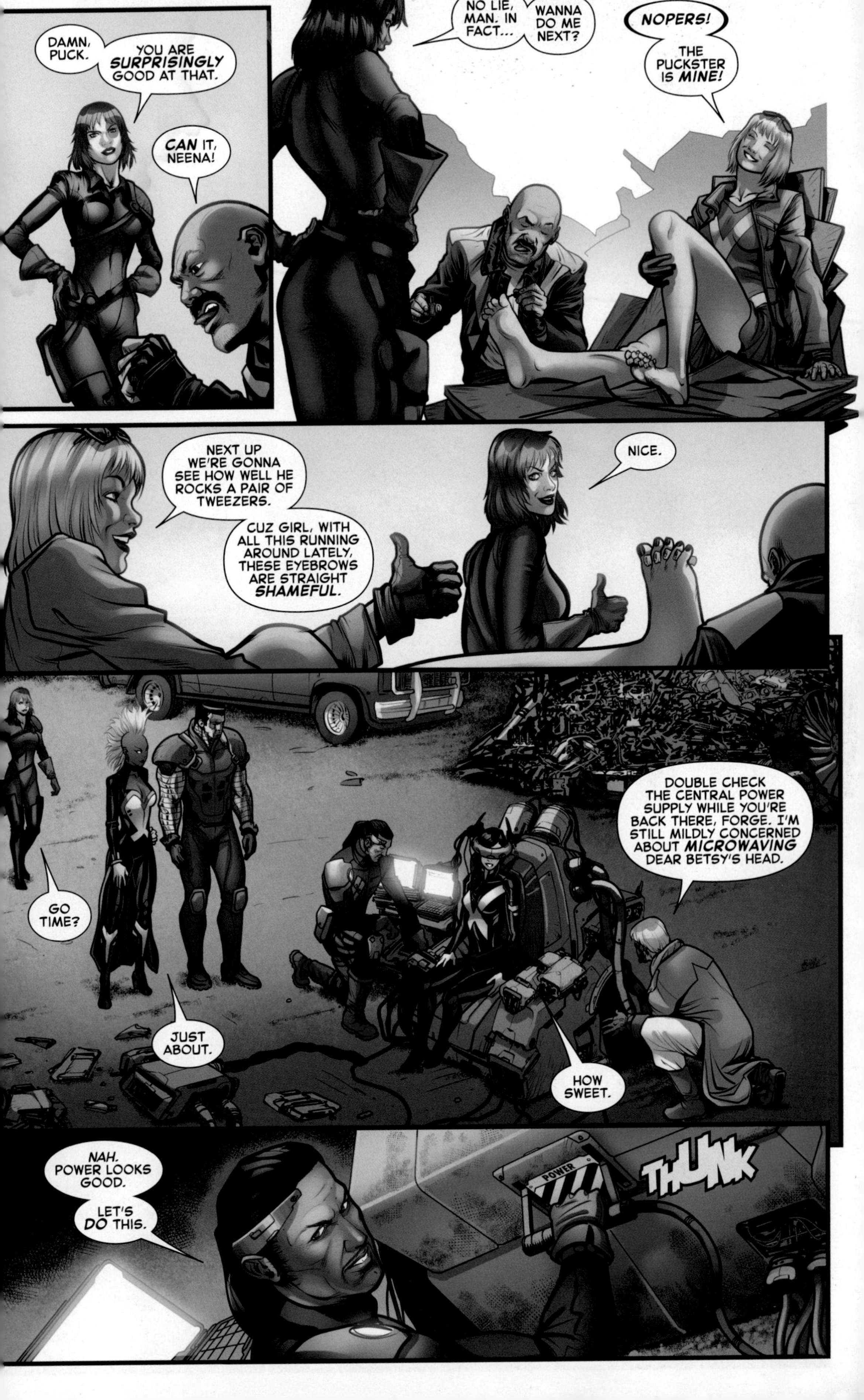
DAMN, PUCK.
YOU ARE SURPRISINGLY GOOD AT THAT.
CAN IT, NEENA!
NO LIE, MAN. IN FACT...
WANNA DO ME NEXT?
NOPERS!
THE PUCKSTER IS MINE!
NEXT UP WE'RE GONNA SEE HOW WELL HE ROCKS A PAIR OF TWEEZERS.
CUZ GIRL, WITH ALL THIS RUNNING AROUND LATELY, THESE EYEBROWS ARE STRAIGHT SHAMEFUL.
NICE.
GO TIME?
JUST ABOUT.
DOUBLE CHECK THE CENTRAL POWER SUPPLY WHILE YOU'RE BACK THERE, FORGE. I'M STILL MILDLY CONCERNED ABOUT MICROWAVING DEAR BETSY'S HEAD.
HOW SWEET.
NAH. POWER LOOKS GOOD.
LET'S DO THIS.
POWER
THUNK

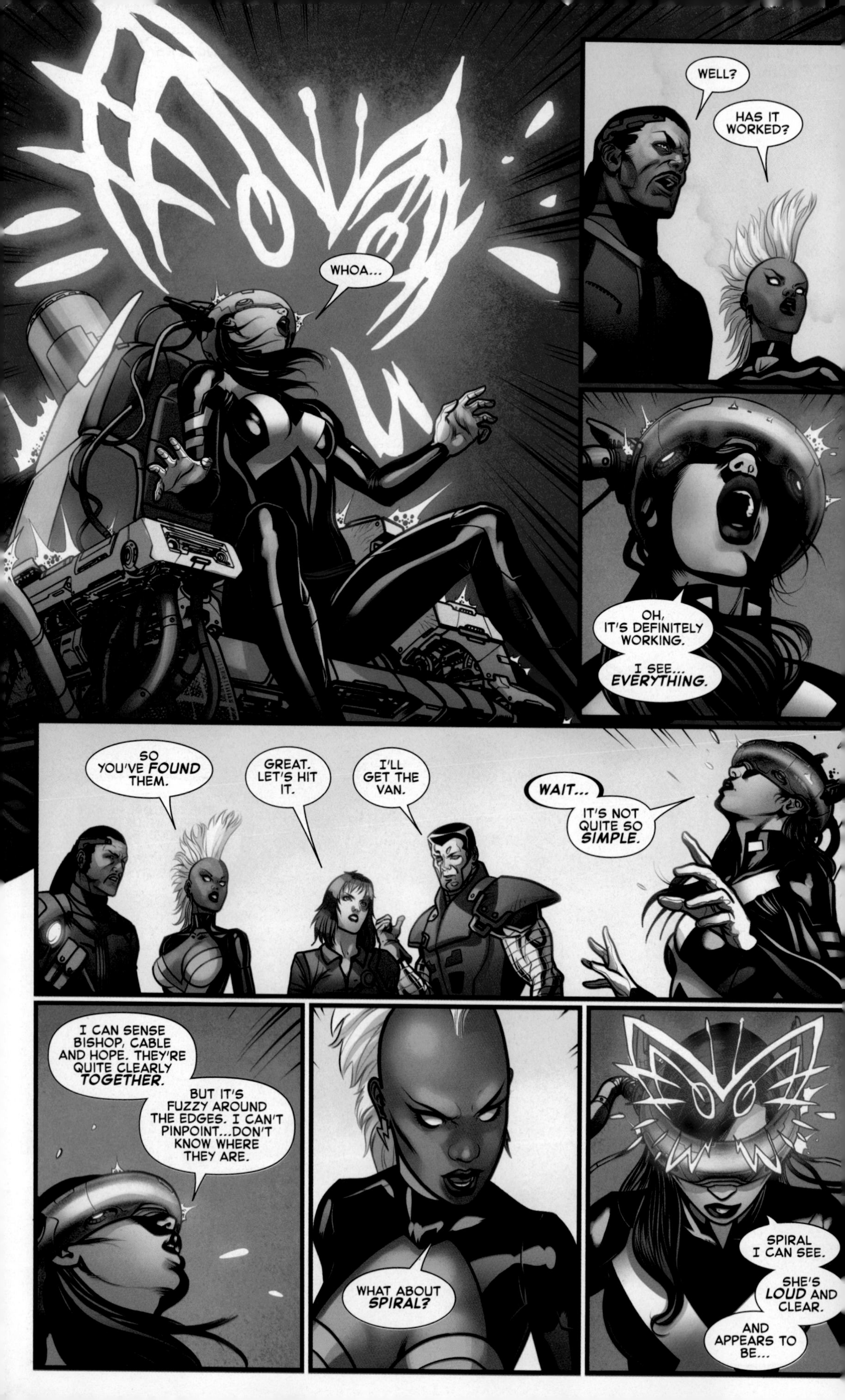

WHOA...
WELL?
HAS IT WORKED?
OH, IT'S DEFINITELY WORKING.
I SEE... EVERYTHING.
SO YOU'VE FOUND THEM.
GREAT. LET'S HIT IT.
I'LL GET THE VAN.
WAIT...
IT'S NOT QUITE SO SIMPLE.
I CAN SENSE BISHOP, CABLE AND HOPE. THEY'RE QUITE CLEARLY TOGETHER.
BUT IT'S FUZZY AROUND THE EDGES. I CAN'T PINPOINT...DON'T KNOW WHERE THEY ARE.
WHAT ABOUT SPIRAL?
SPIRAL I CAN SEE.
SHE'S LOUD AND CLEAR.
AND APPEARS TO BE...

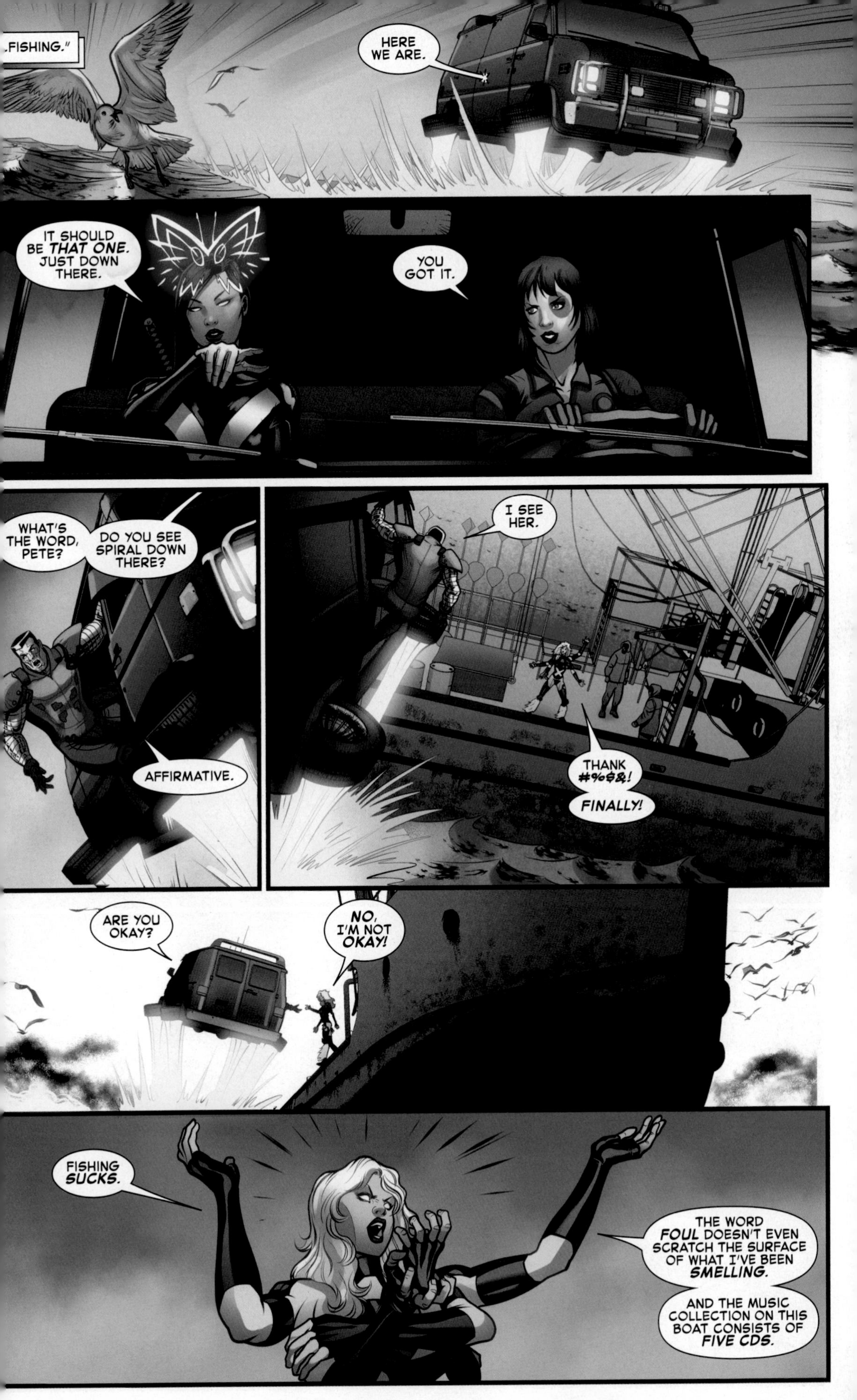
...FISHING."
HERE WE ARE.
IT SHOULD BE THAT ONE. JUST DOWN THERE.
YOU GOT IT.
WHAT'S THE WORD, PETE?
DO YOU SEE SPIRAL DOWN THERE?
AFFIRMATIVE.
I SEE HER.
THANK #%$&!
FINALLY!
ARE YOU OKAY?
NO, I'M NOT OKAY!
FISHING SUCKS.
THE WORD FOUL DOESN'T EVEN SCRATCH THE SURFACE OF WHAT I'VE BEEN SMELLING.
AND THE MUSIC COLLECTION ON THIS BOAT CONSISTS OF FIVE CDS.

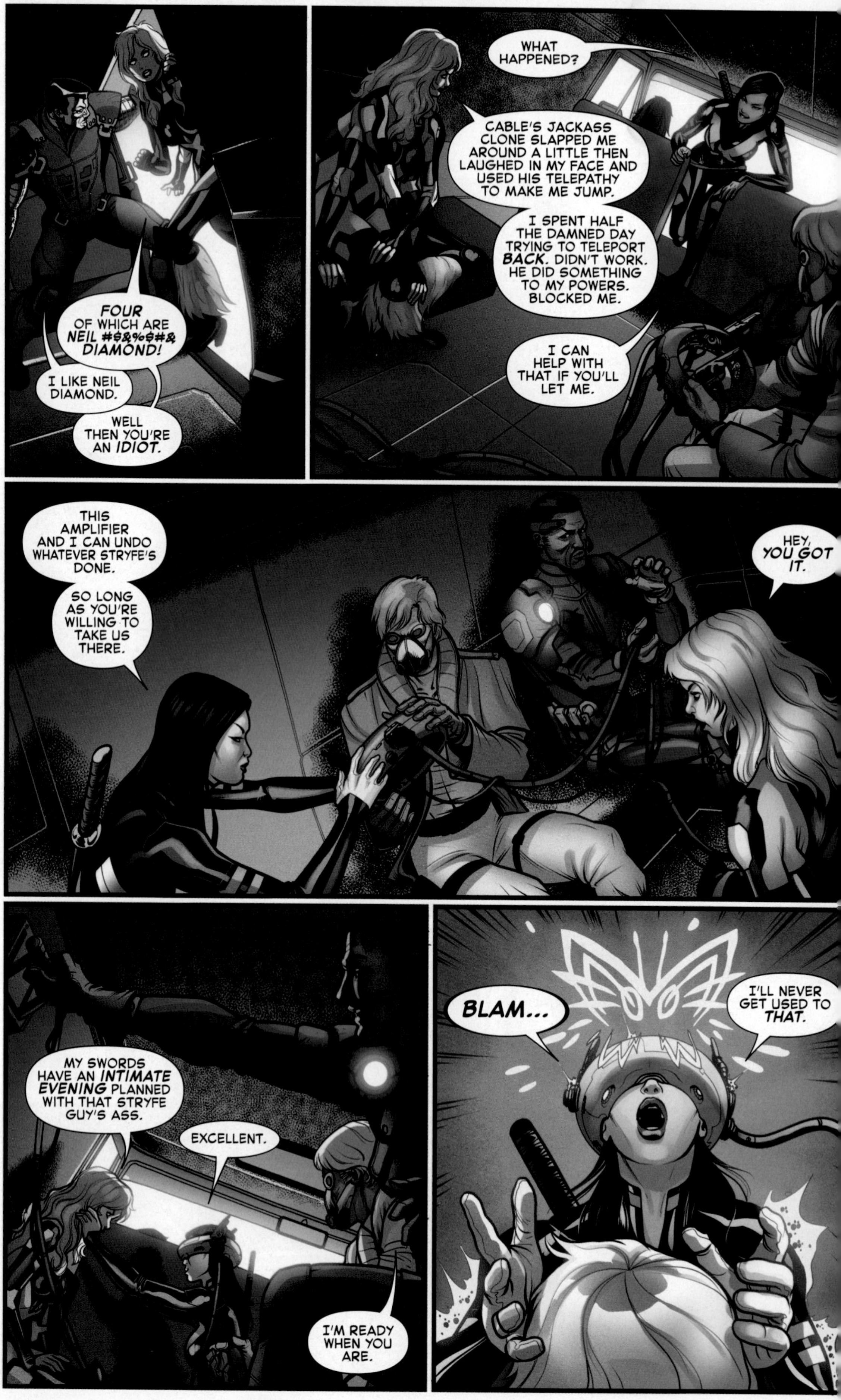
FOUR OF WHICH ARE NEIL #$&%$#& DIAMOND!
I LIKE NEIL DIAMOND.
WELL THEN YOU'RE AN IDIOT.
WHAT HAPPENED?
CABLE'S JACKASS CLONE SLAPPED ME AROUND A LITTLE THEN LAUGHED IN MY FACE AND USED HIS TELEPATHY TO MAKE ME JUMP.
I SPENT HALF THE DAMNED DAY TRYING TO TELEPORT BACK. DIDN'T WORK. HE DID SOMETHING TO MY POWERS. BLOCKED ME.
I CAN HELP WITH THAT IF YOU'LL LET ME.
THIS AMPLIFIER AND I CAN UNDO WHATEVER STRYFE'S DONE.
SO LONG AS YOU'RE WILLING TO TAKE US THERE.
HEY, YOU GOT IT.
MY SWORDS HAVE AN INTIMATE EVENING PLANNED WITH THAT STRYFE GUY'S ASS.
EXCELLENT.
I'M READY WHEN YOU ARE.
BLAM...
I'LL NEVER GET USED TO THAT.

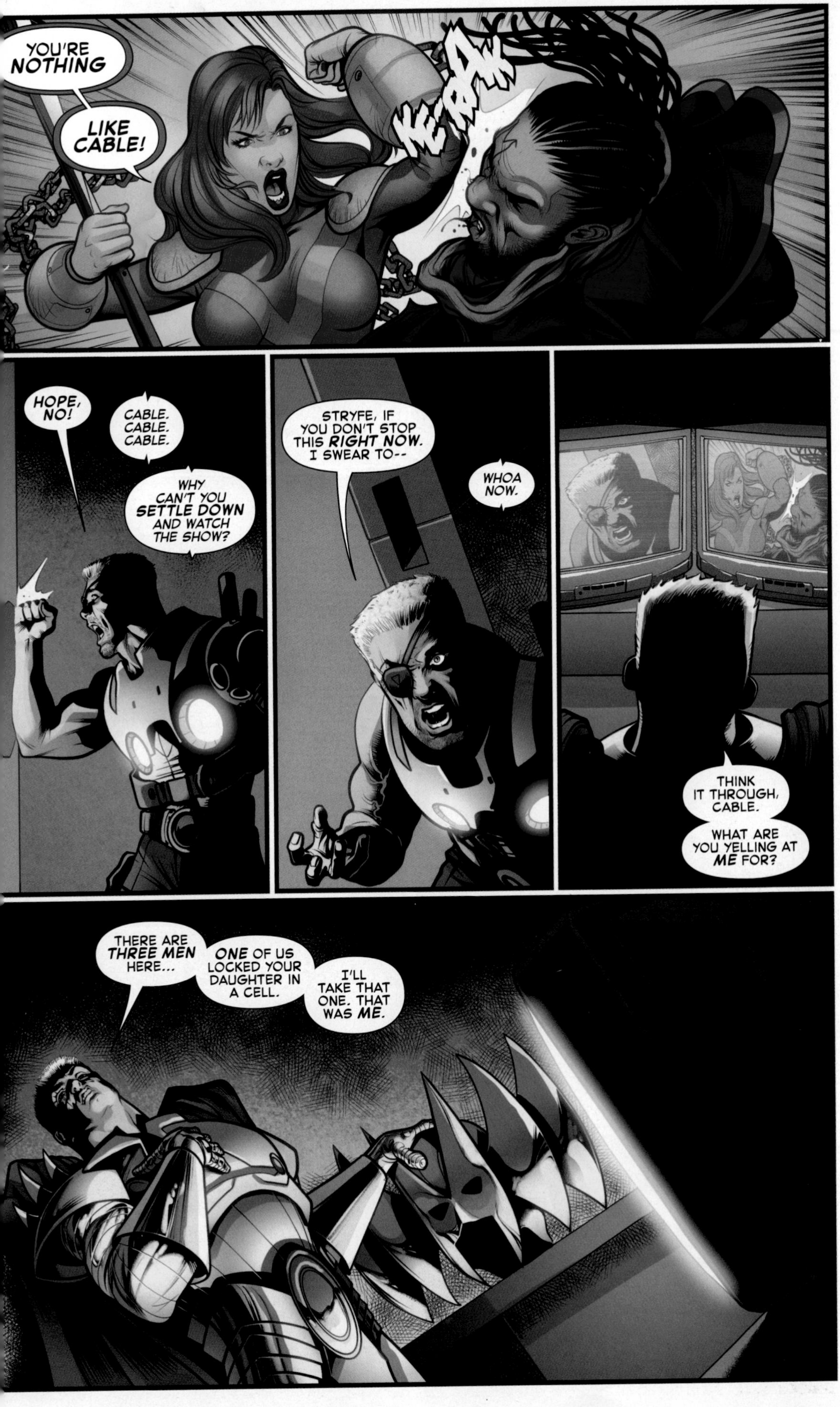

YOU'RE NOTHING
LIKE CABLE!
HOPE, NO!
CABLE. CABLE. CABLE.
WHY CAN'T YOU SETTLE DOWN AND WATCH THE SHOW?
STRYFE, IF YOU DON'T STOP THIS RIGHT NOW. I SWEAR TO--
WHOA NOW.
THINK IT THROUGH, CABLE.
WHAT ARE YOU YELLING AT ME FOR?
THERE ARE THREE MEN HERE...
ONE OF US LOCKED YOUR DAUGHTER IN A CELL.
I'LL TAKE THAT ONE. THAT WAS ME.

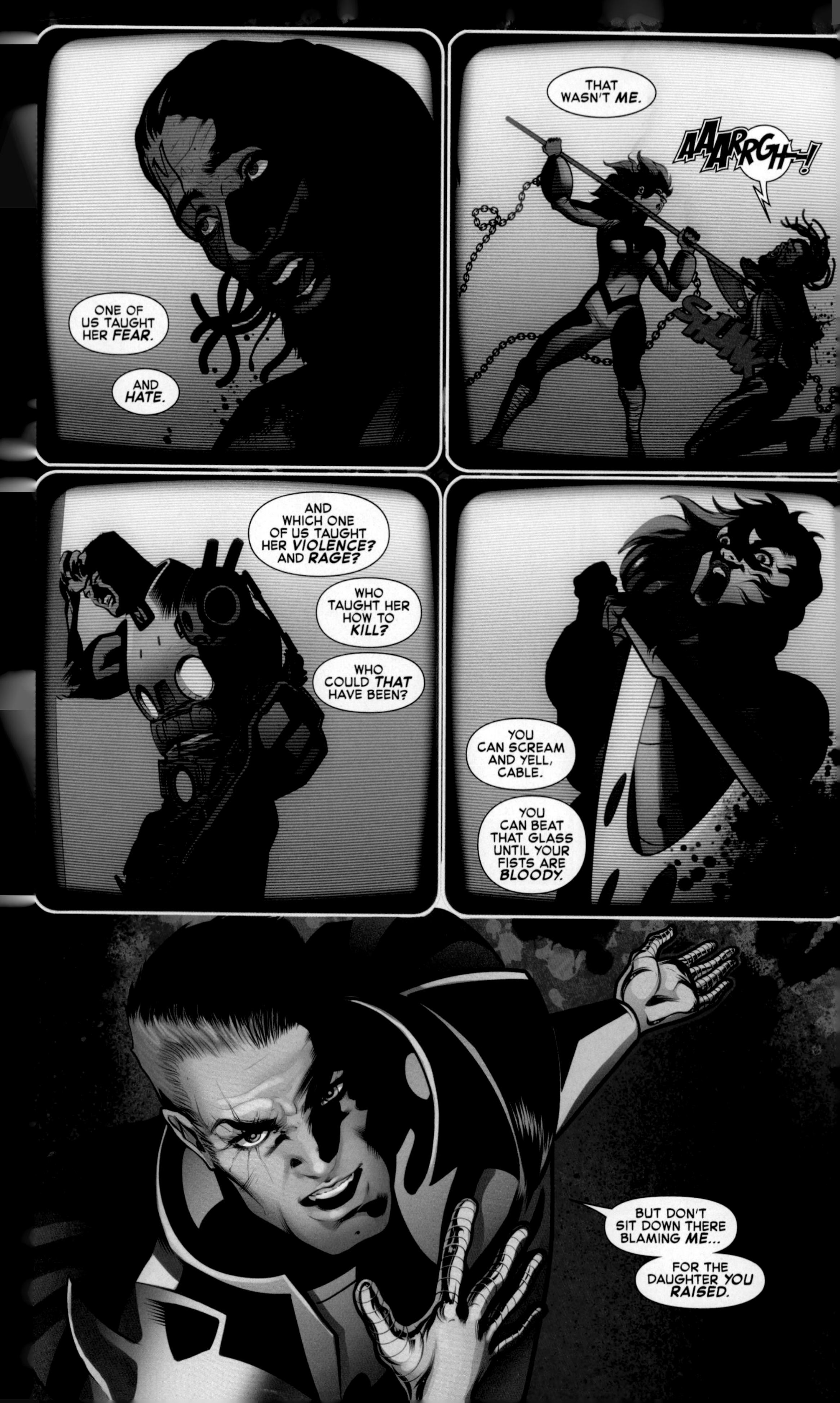

ONE OF US TAUGHT HER FEAR.
AND HATE.
THAT WASN'T ME.
AAARRGH--!
SHUNK
AND WHICH ONE OF US TAUGHT HER VIOLENCE? AND RAGE?
WHO TAUGHT HER HOW TO KILL?
WHO COULD THAT HAVE BEEN?
YOU CAN SCREAM AND YELL, CABLE.
YOU CAN BEAT THAT GLASS UNTIL YOUR FISTS ARE BLOODY.
BUT DON'T SIT DOWN THERE BLAMING ME...
FOR THE DAUGHTER YOU RAISED.

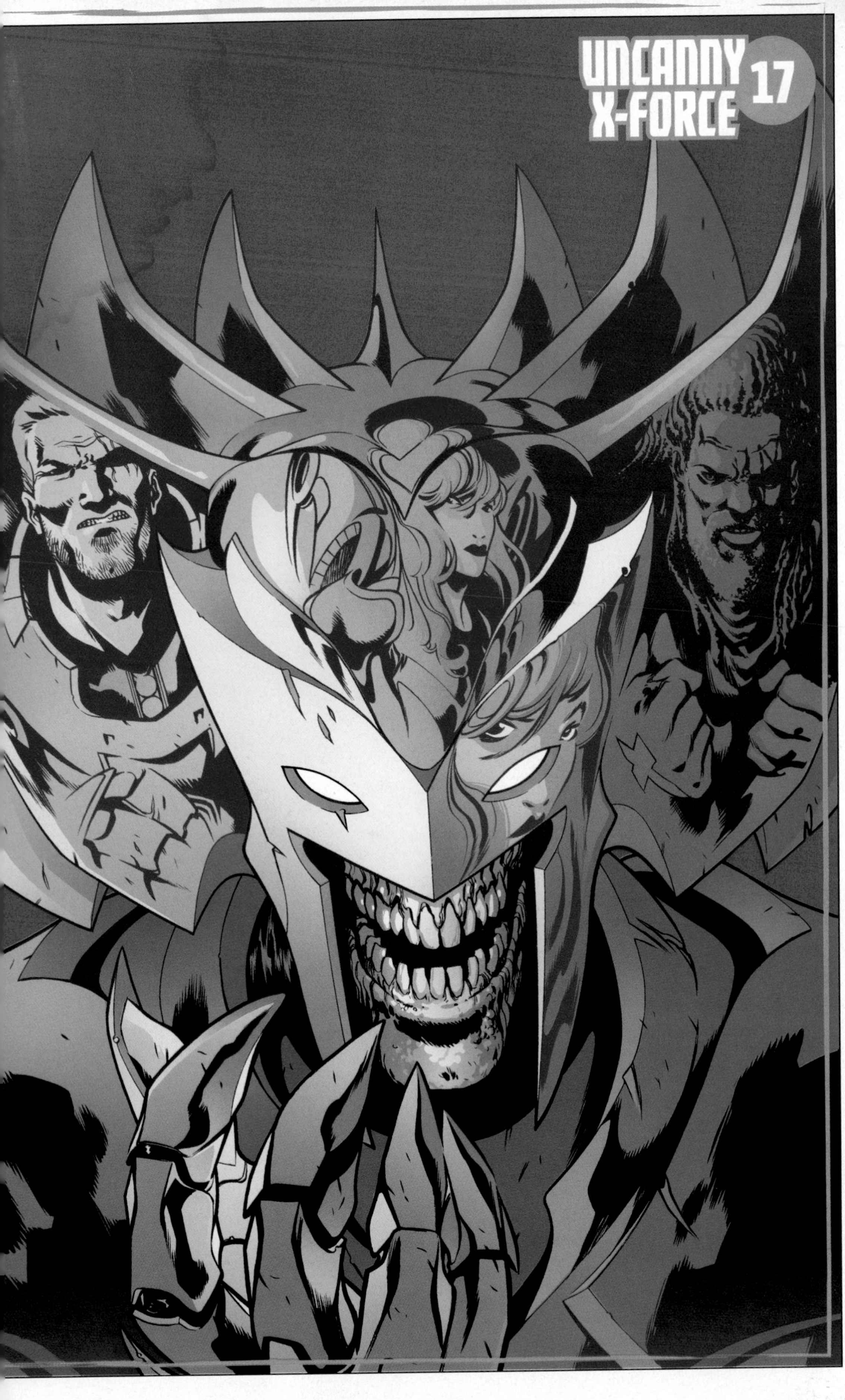
UNCANNY X-FORCE
17

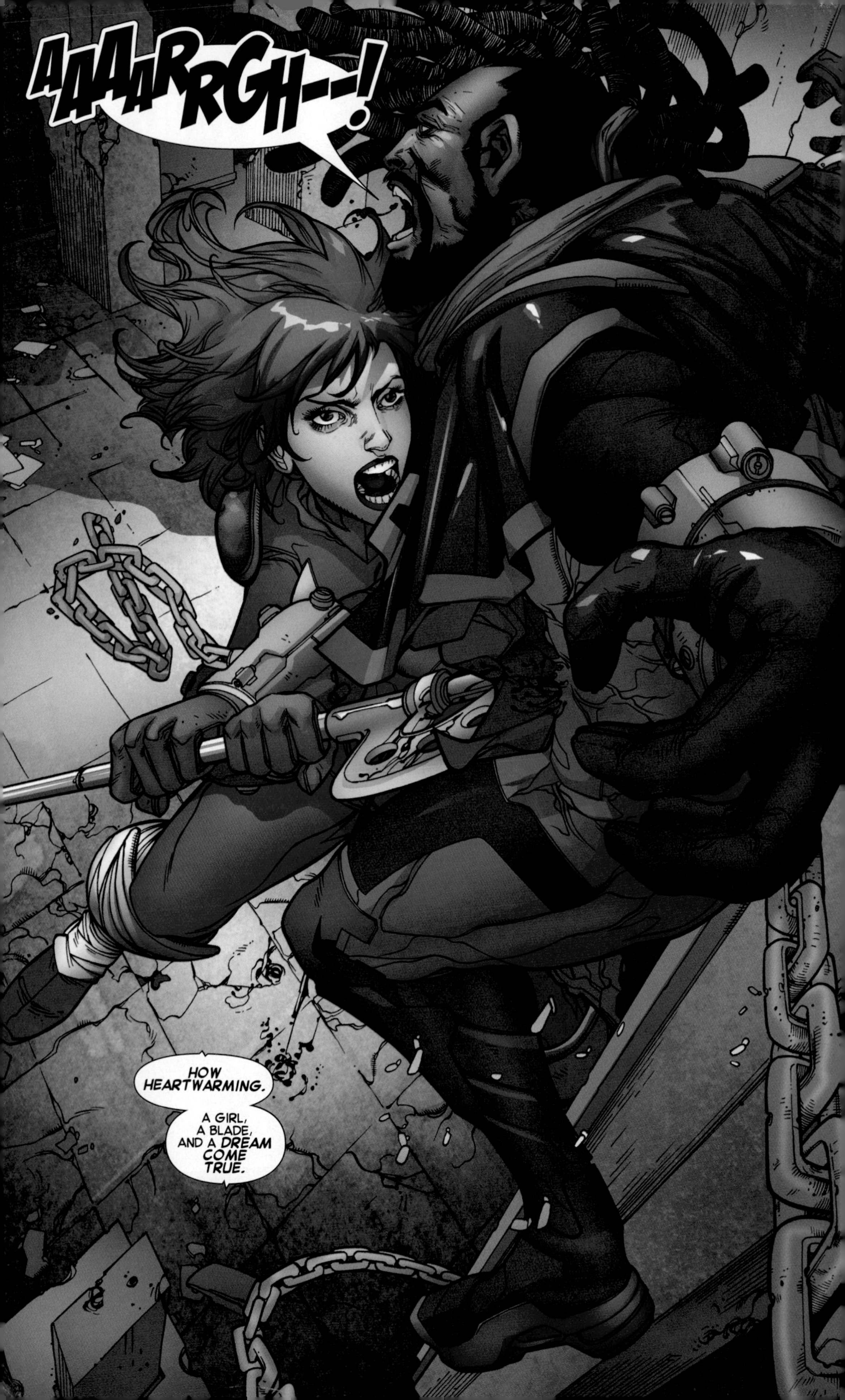
AAAARRGH--!
HOW HEARTWARMING.
A GIRL, A BLADE, AND A DREAM COME TRUE.

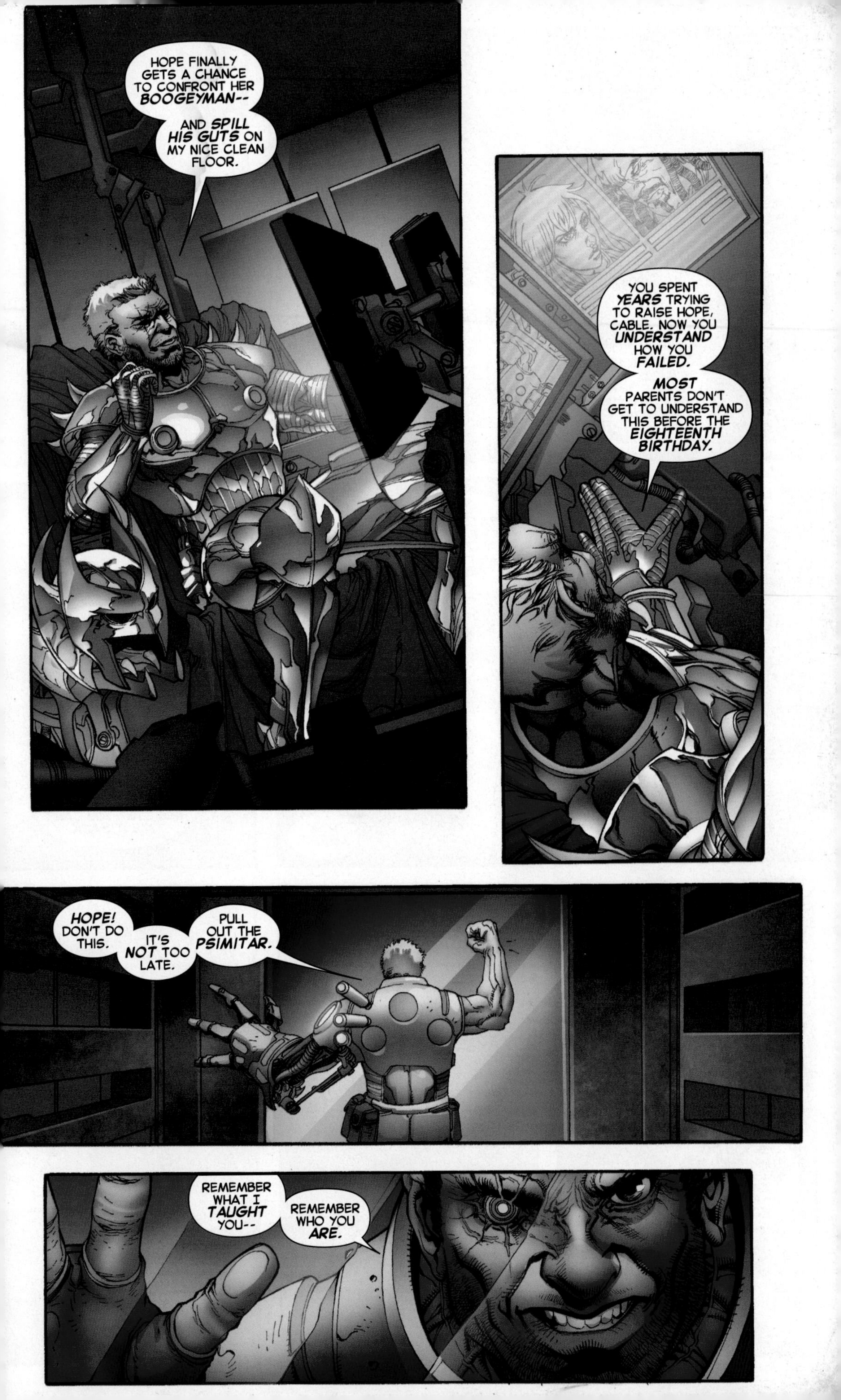
HOPE FINALLY GETS A CHANCE TO CONFRONT HER BOOGEYMAN--
AND SPILL HIS GUTS ON MY NICE CLEAN FLOOR.
YOU SPENT YEARS TRYING TO RAISE HOPE, CABLE. NOW YOU UNDERSTAND HOW YOU FAILED.
MOST PARENTS DON'T GET TO UNDERSTAND THIS BEFORE THE EIGHTEENTH BIRTHDAY.
HOPE! DON'T DO THIS.
IT'S NOT TOO LATE.
PULL OUT THE PSIMITAR.
REMEMBER WHAT I TAUGHT YOU--
REMEMBER WHO YOU ARE.

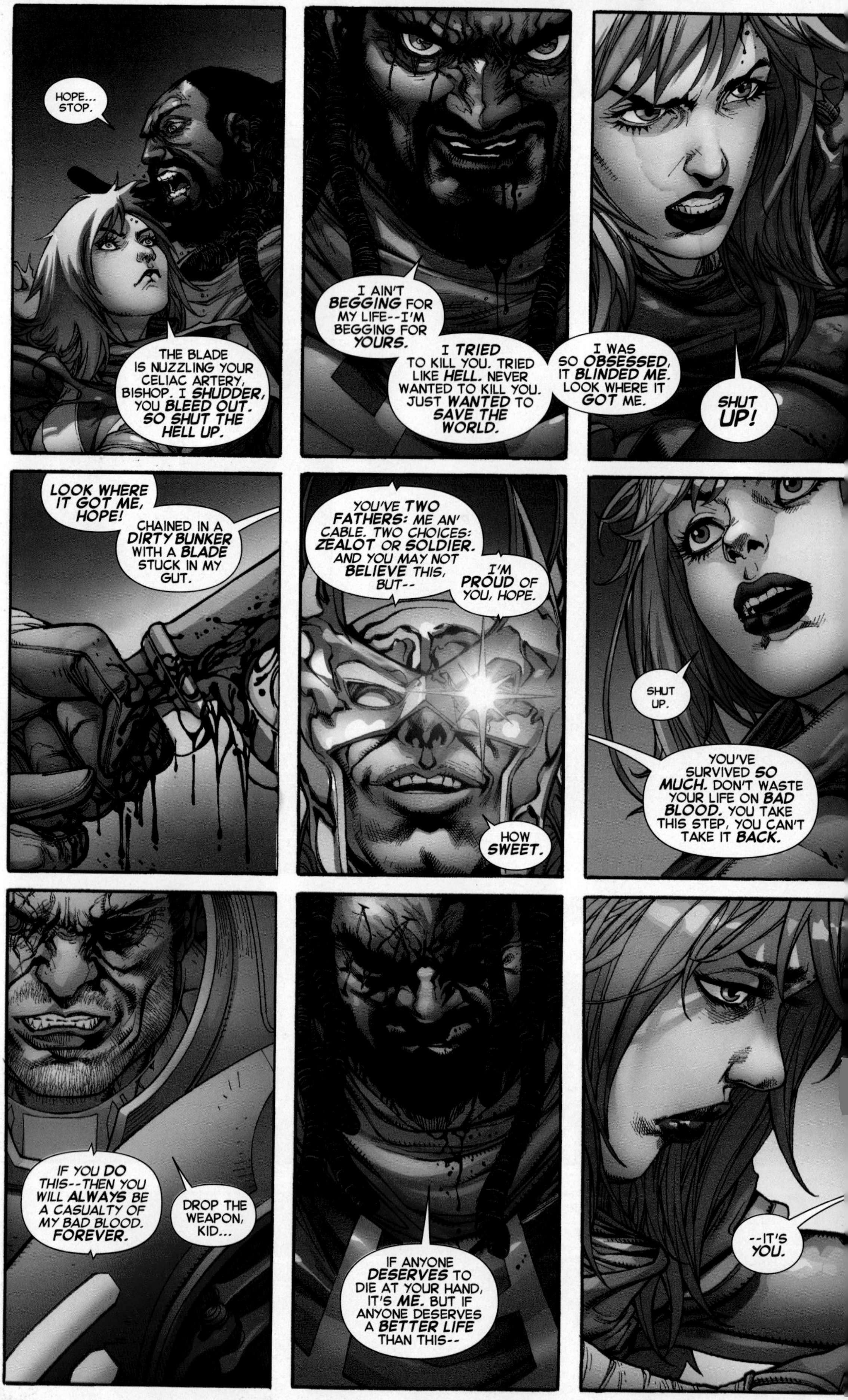
HOPE... STOP.
THE BLADE IS NUZZLING YOUR CELIAC ARTERY, BISHOP. I SHUDDER, YOU BLEED OUT. SO SHUT THE HELL UP.
I AIN'T BEGGING FOR MY LIFE--I'M BEGGING FOR YOURS.
I TRIED TO KILL YOU. TRIED LIKE HELL. NEVER WANTED TO KILL YOU. JUST WANTED TO SAVE THE WORLD.
I WAS SO OBSESSED, IT BLINDED ME. LOOK WHERE IT GOT ME.
SHUT UP!
LOOK WHERE IT GOT ME, HOPE!
CHAINED IN A DIRTY BUNKER WITH A BLADE STUCK IN MY GUT.
YOU'VE TWO FATHERS: ME AN' CABLE. TWO CHOICES: ZEALOT OR SOLDIER. AND YOU MAY NOT BELIEVE THIS, BUT--
I'M PROUD OF YOU, HOPE.
HOW SWEET.
SHUT UP.
YOU'VE SURVIVED SO MUCH. DON'T WASTE YOUR LIFE ON BAD BLOOD. YOU TAKE THIS STEP, YOU CAN'T TAKE IT BACK.
IF YOU DO THIS--THEN YOU WILL ALWAYS BE A CASUALTY OF MY BAD BLOOD. FOREVER.
DROP THE WEAPON, KID...
IF ANYONE DESERVES TO DIE AT YOUR HAND, IT'S ME. BUT IF ANYONE DESERVES A BETTER LIFE THAN THIS--
--IT'S YOU.

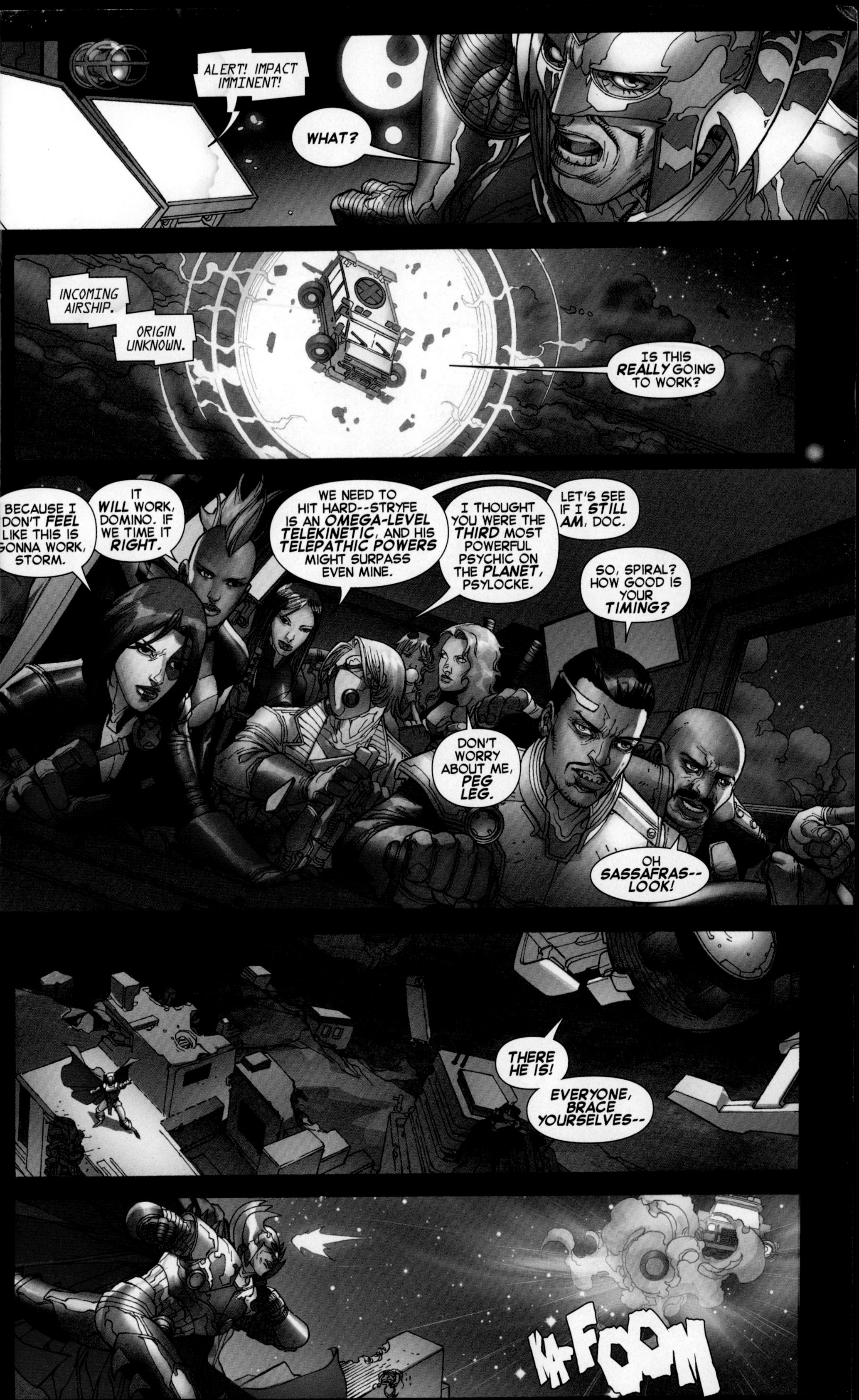
ALERT! IMPACT IMMINENT!
WHAT?
INCOMING AIRSHIP.
ORIGIN UNKNOWN.
IS THIS REALLY GOING TO WORK?
BECAUSE I DON'T FEEL LIKE THIS IS GONNA WORK, STORM.
IT WILL WORK, DOMINO. IF WE TIME IT RIGHT.
WE NEED TO HIT HARD--STRYFE IS AN OMEGA-LEVEL TELEKINETIC, AND HIS TELEPATHIC POWERS MIGHT SURPASS EVEN MINE.
I THOUGHT YOU WERE THE THIRD MOST POWERFUL PSYCHIC ON THE PLANET, PSYLOCKE.
LET'S SEE IF I STILL AM, DOC.
SO, SPIRAL? HOW GOOD IS YOUR TIMING?
DON'T WORRY ABOUT ME, PEG LEG.
OH SASSAFRAS-- LOOK!
THERE HE IS!
EVERYONE, BRACE YOURSELVES--
KA-FOOM

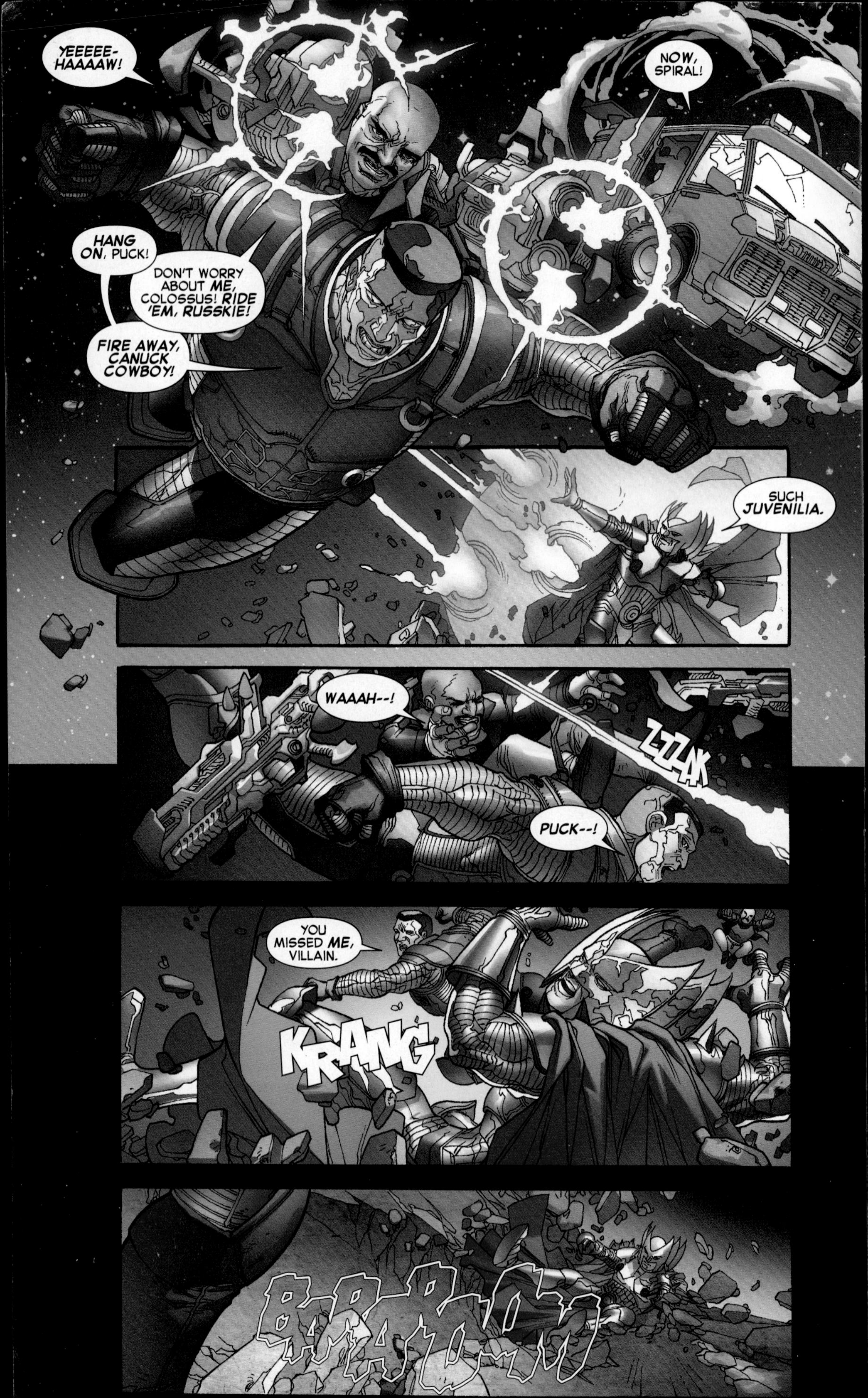
YEEEEE-HAAAAW!
NOW, SPIRAL!
HANG ON, PUCK!
DON'T WORRY ABOUT ME, COLOSSUS! RIDE 'EM, RUSSKIE!
FIRE AWAY, CANUCK COWBOY!
SUCH JUVENILIA.
WAAAH--!
ZZZAK
PUCK--!
YOU MISSED ME, VILLAIN.
KRANG

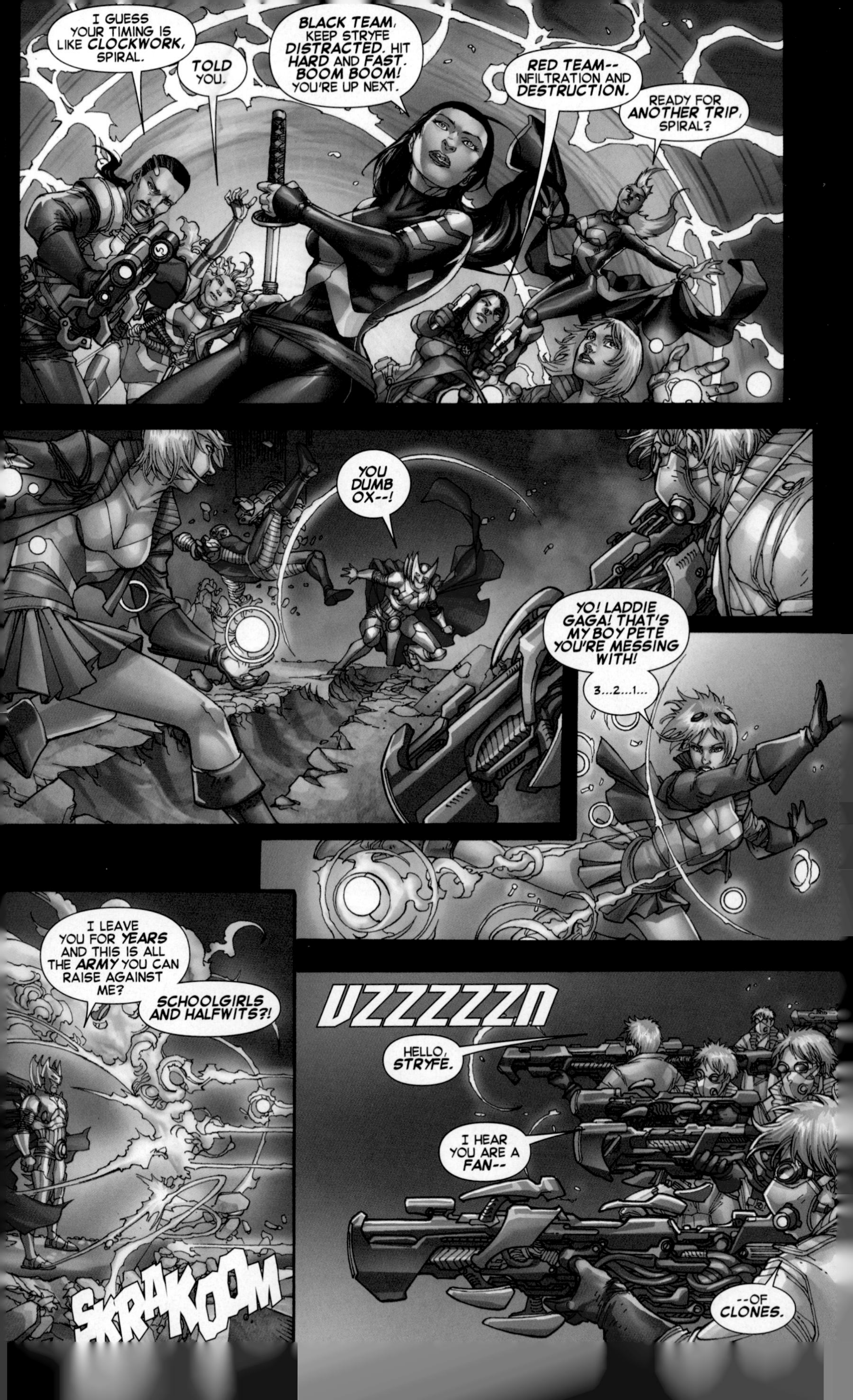
I GUESS YOUR TIMING IS LIKE CLOCKWORK, SPIRAL.
TOLD YOU.
BLACK TEAM, KEEP STRYFE DISTRACTED. HIT HARD AND FAST. BOOM BOOM! YOU'RE UP NEXT.
RED TEAM-- INFILTRATION AND DESTRUCTION.
READY FOR ANOTHER TRIP, SPIRAL?
YOU DUMB OX--!
YO! LADDIE GAGA! THAT'S MY BOY PETE YOU'RE MESSING WITH!
3...2...1...
I LEAVE YOU FOR YEARS AND THIS IS ALL THE ARMY YOU CAN RAISE AGAINST ME?
SCHOOLGIRLS AND HALFWITS?!
SKRAKOOM
VZZZZZN
HELLO, STRYFE.
I HEAR YOU ARE A FAN--
--OF CLONES.

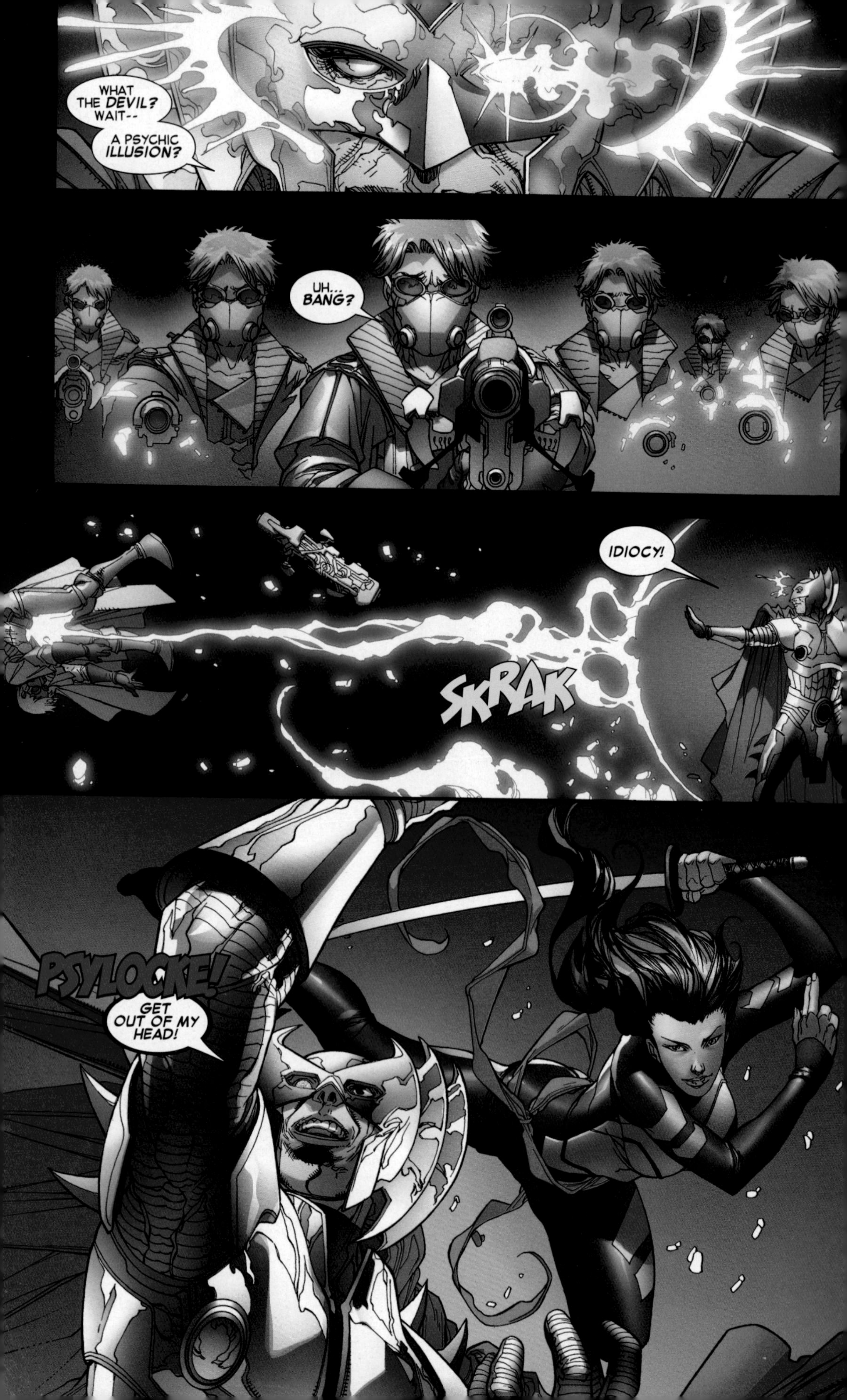
WHAT THE DEVIL? WAIT--
A PSYCHIC ILLUSION?
UH... BANG?
IDIOCY!
SKRAK
PSYLOCKE!
GET OUT OF MY HEAD!

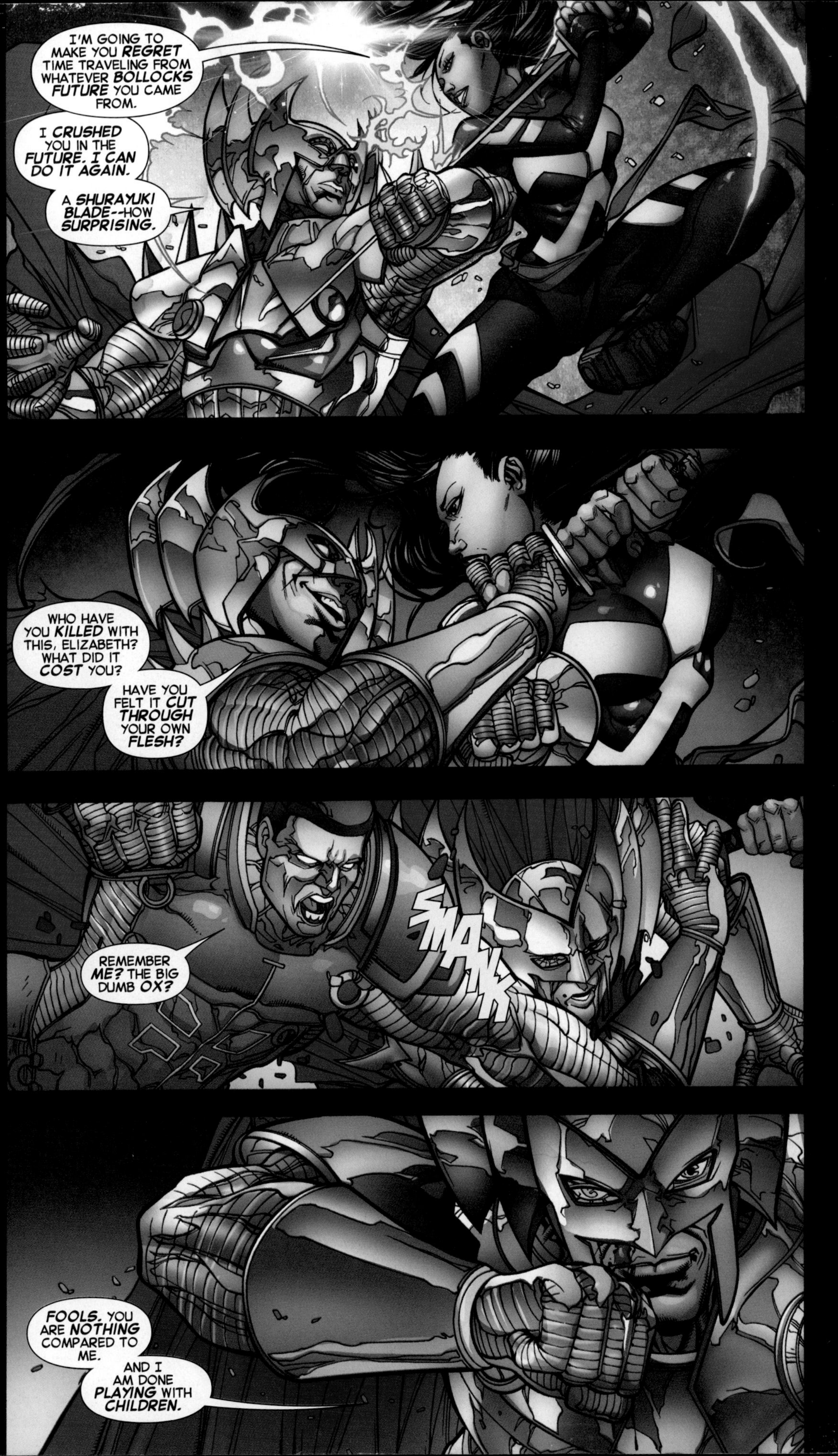
I'M GOING TO MAKE YOU REGRET TIME TRAVELING FROM WHATEVER BOLLOCKS FUTURE YOU CAME FROM.
I CRUSHED YOU IN THE FUTURE. I CAN DO IT AGAIN.
A SHURAYUKI BLADE--HOW SURPRISING.
WHO HAVE YOU KILLED WITH THIS, ELIZABETH? WHAT DID IT COST YOU?
HAVE YOU FELT IT CUT THROUGH YOUR OWN FLESH?
REMEMBER ME? THE BIG DUMB OX?
SMANK
FOOLS. YOU ARE NOTHING COMPARED TO ME.
AND I AM DONE PLAYING WITH CHILDREN.

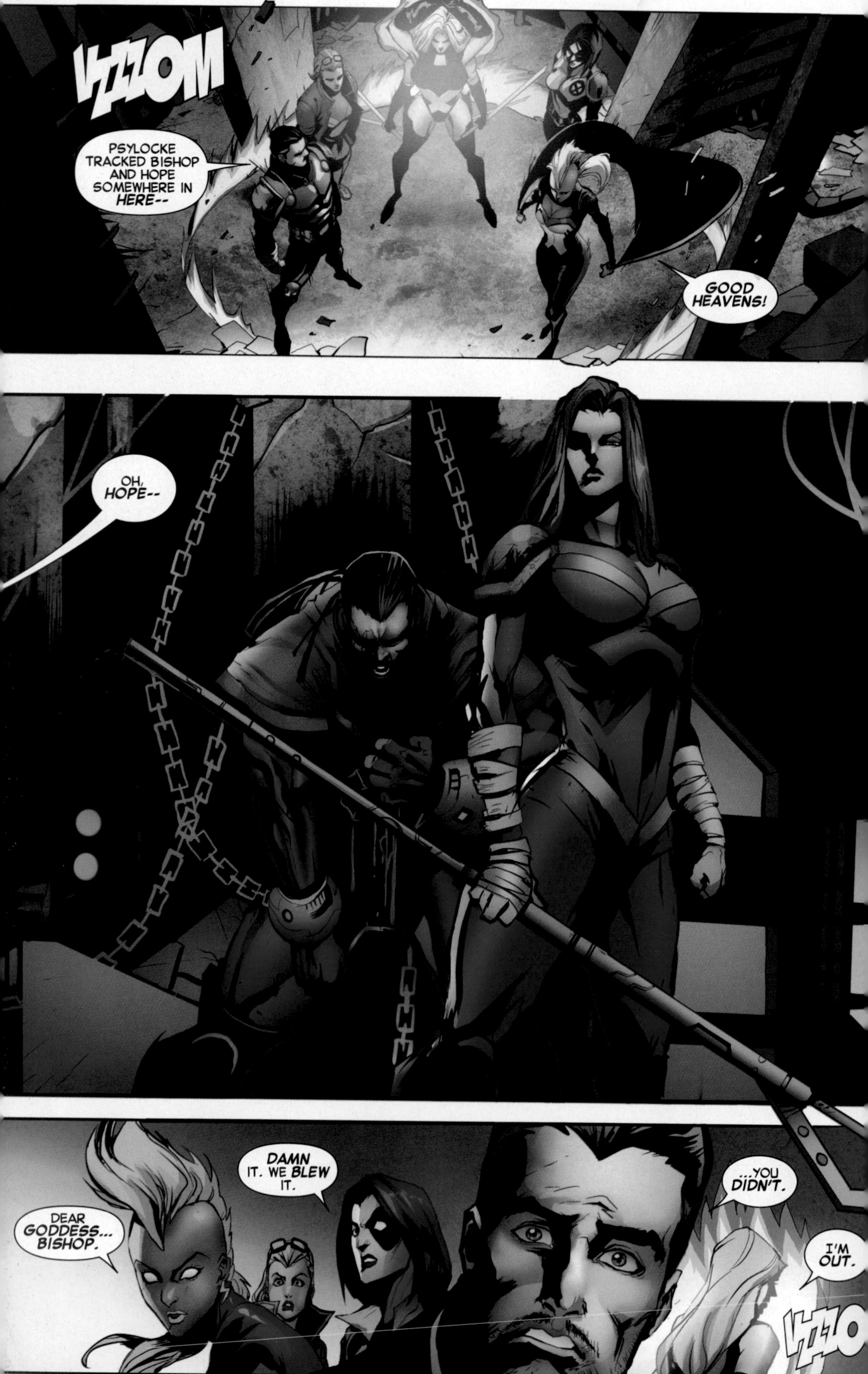

VZZZOM
PSYLOCKE TRACKED BISHOP AND HOPE SOMEWHERE IN HERE--
GOOD HEAVENS!
OH, HOPE--
DEAR GODDESS... BISHOP.
DAMN IT. WE BLEW IT.
...YOU DIDN'T.
I'M OUT.
VZZZO

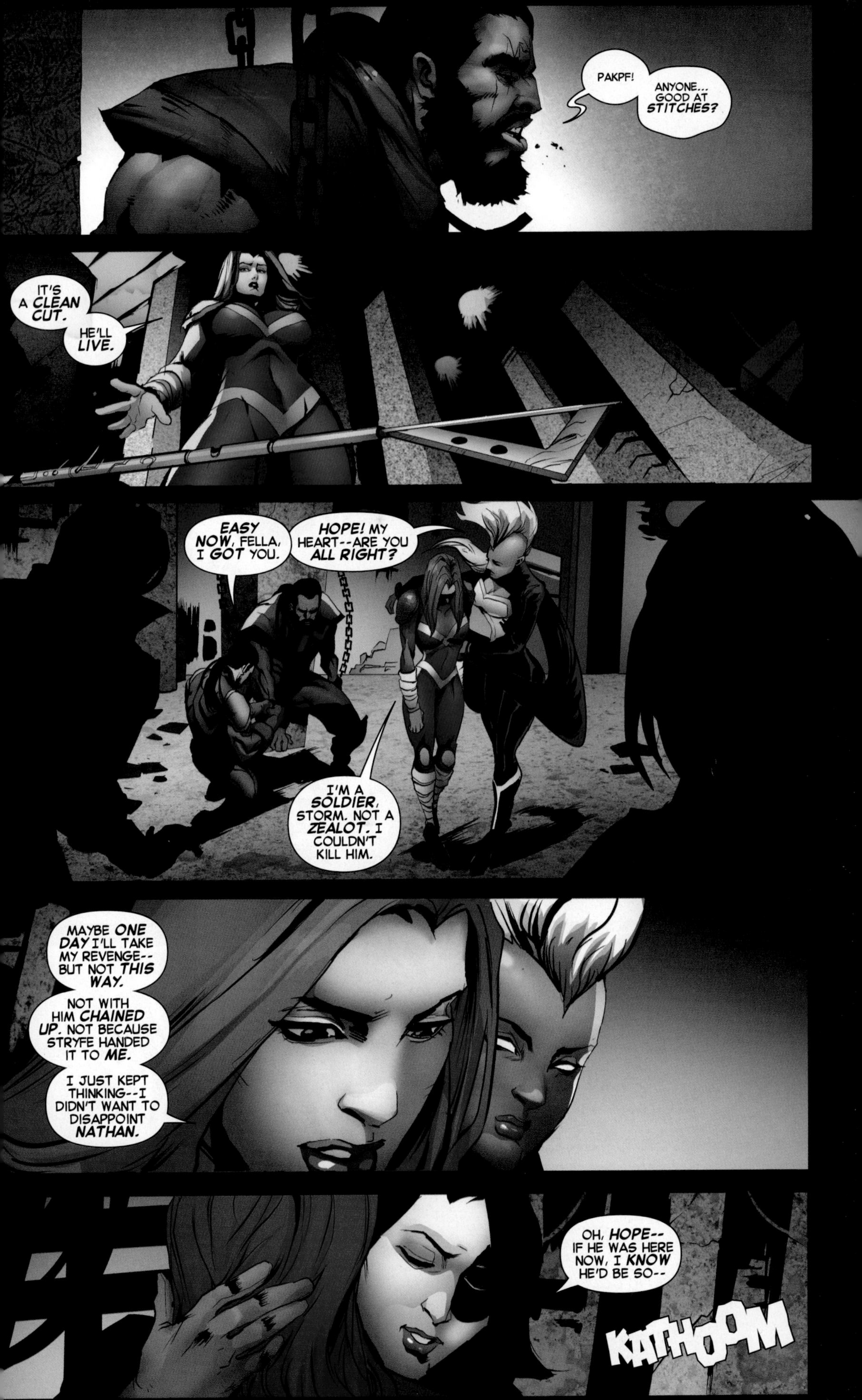
PAKPF!
ANYONE... GOOD AT STITCHES?
IT'S A CLEAN CUT.
HE'LL LIVE.
EASY NOW, FELLA, I GOT YOU.
HOPE! MY HEART--ARE YOU ALL RIGHT?
I'M A SOLDIER, STORM. NOT A ZEALOT. I COULDN'T KILL HIM.
MAYBE ONE DAY I'LL TAKE MY REVENGE-- BUT NOT THIS WAY.
NOT WITH HIM CHAINED UP. NOT BECAUSE STRYFE HANDED IT TO ME.
I JUST KEPT THINKING--I DIDN'T WANT TO DISAPPOINT NATHAN.
OH, HOPE-- IF HE WAS HERE NOW, I KNOW HE'D BE SO--
KATHOOM

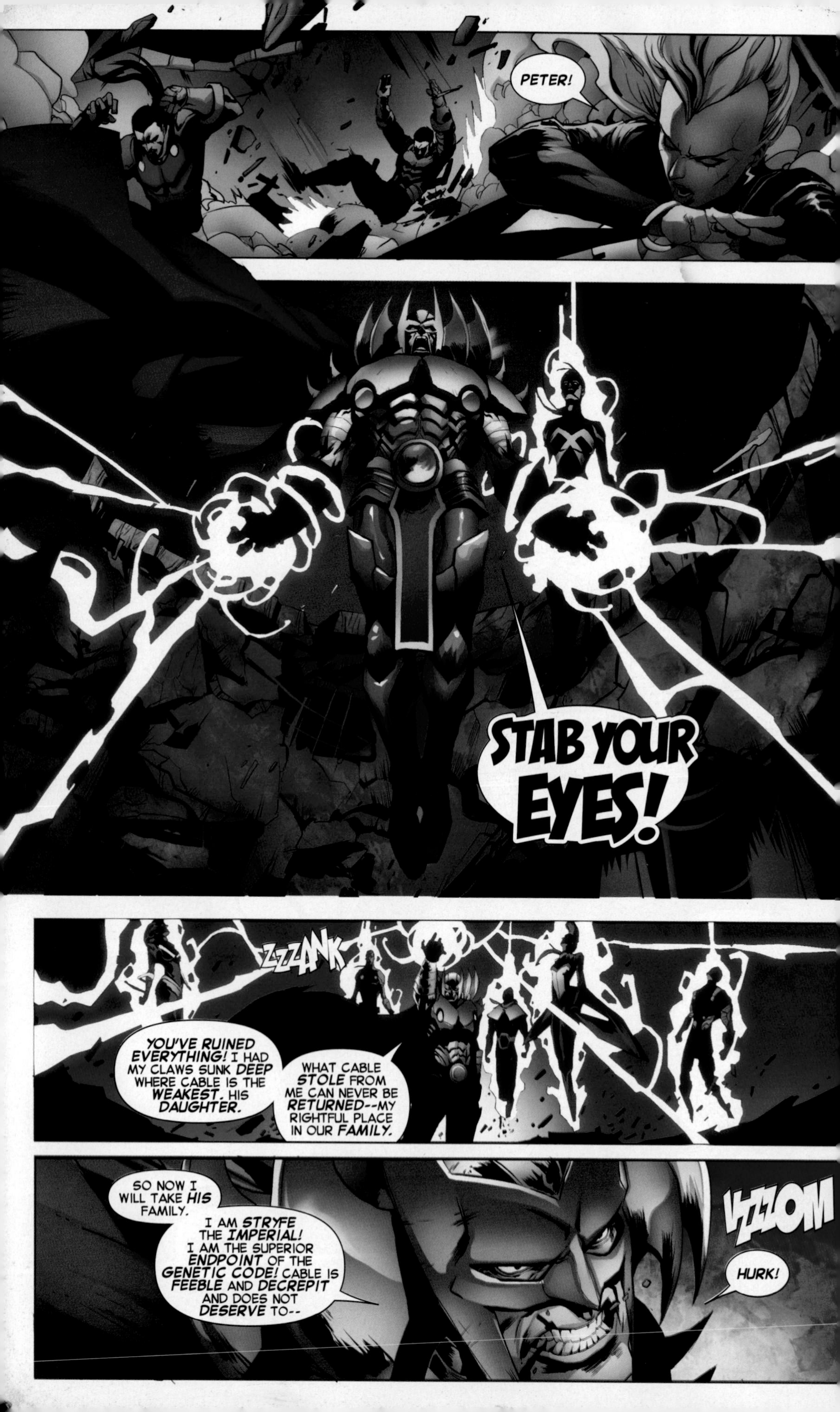
PETER!
STAB YOUR EYES!
ZZZZANK
YOU'VE RUINED EVERYTHING! I HAD MY CLAWS SUNK DEEP WHERE CABLE IS THE WEAKEST. HIS DAUGHTER.
WHAT CABLE STOLE FROM ME CAN NEVER BE RETURNED--MY RIGHTFUL PLACE IN OUR FAMILY.
SO NOW I WILL TAKE HIS FAMILY.
I AM STRYFE THE IMPERIAL! I AM THE SUPERIOR ENDPOINT OF THE GENETIC CODE! CABLE IS FEEBLE AND DECREPIT AND DOES NOT DESERVE TO--
VZZOM
HURK!

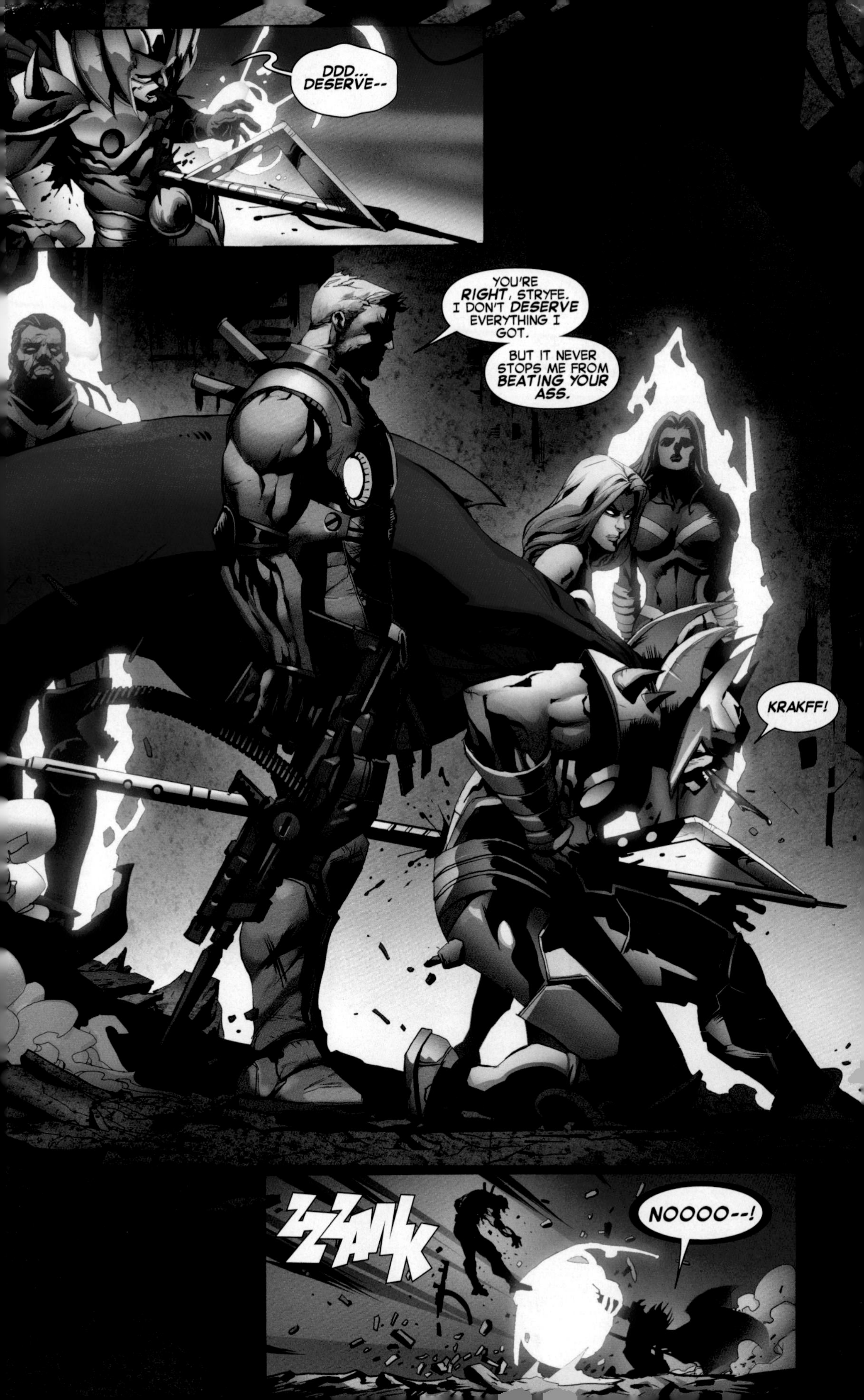
DDD... DESERVE--
YOU'RE RIGHT, STRYFE. I DON'T DESERVE EVERYTHING I GOT.
BUT IT NEVER STOPS ME FROM BEATING YOUR ASS.
KRAKFF!
ZZZANK
NOOOO--!

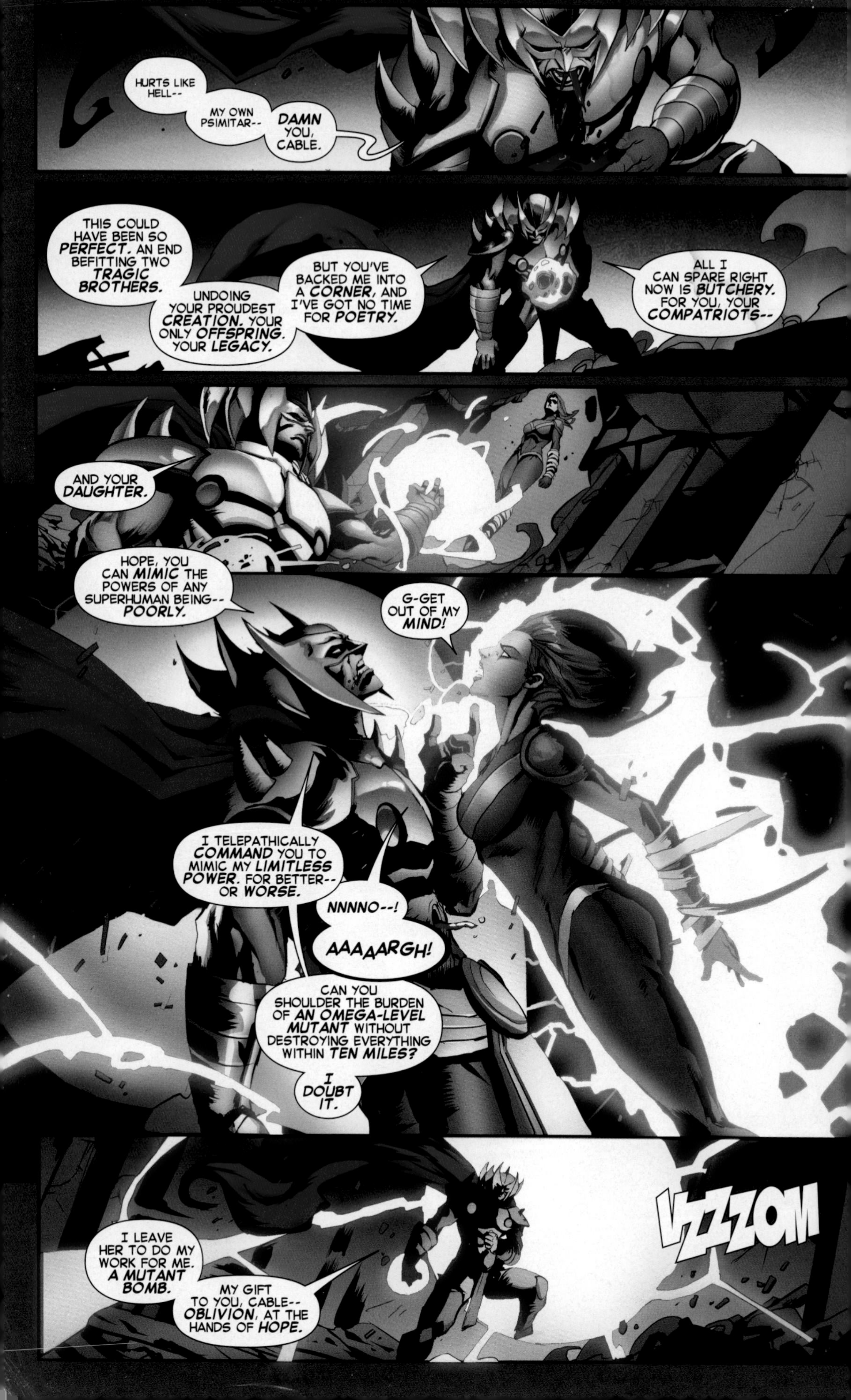

HURTS LIKE HELL--
MY OWN PSIMITAR--
DAMN YOU, CABLE.
THIS COULD HAVE BEEN SO PERFECT. AN END BEFITTING TWO TRAGIC BROTHERS.
UNDOING YOUR PROUDEST CREATION. YOUR ONLY OFFSPRING. YOUR LEGACY.
BUT YOU'VE BACKED ME INTO A CORNER, AND I'VE GOT NO TIME FOR POETRY.
ALL I CAN SPARE RIGHT NOW IS BUTCHERY. FOR YOU, YOUR COMPATRIOTS--
AND YOUR DAUGHTER.
HOPE, YOU CAN MIMIC THE POWERS OF ANY SUPERHUMAN BEING-- POORLY.
G-GET OUT OF MY MIND!
I TELEPATHICALLY COMMAND YOU TO MIMIC MY LIMITLESS POWER. FOR BETTER-- OR WORSE.
NNNNO--!
AAAAARGH!
CAN YOU SHOULDER THE BURDEN OF AN OMEGA-LEVEL MUTANT WITHOUT DESTROYING EVERYTHING WITHIN TEN MILES?
I DOUBT IT.
VZZZOM
I LEAVE HER TO DO MY WORK FOR ME. A MUTANT BOMB.
MY GIFT TO YOU, CABLE-- OBLIVION, AT THE HANDS OF HOPE.

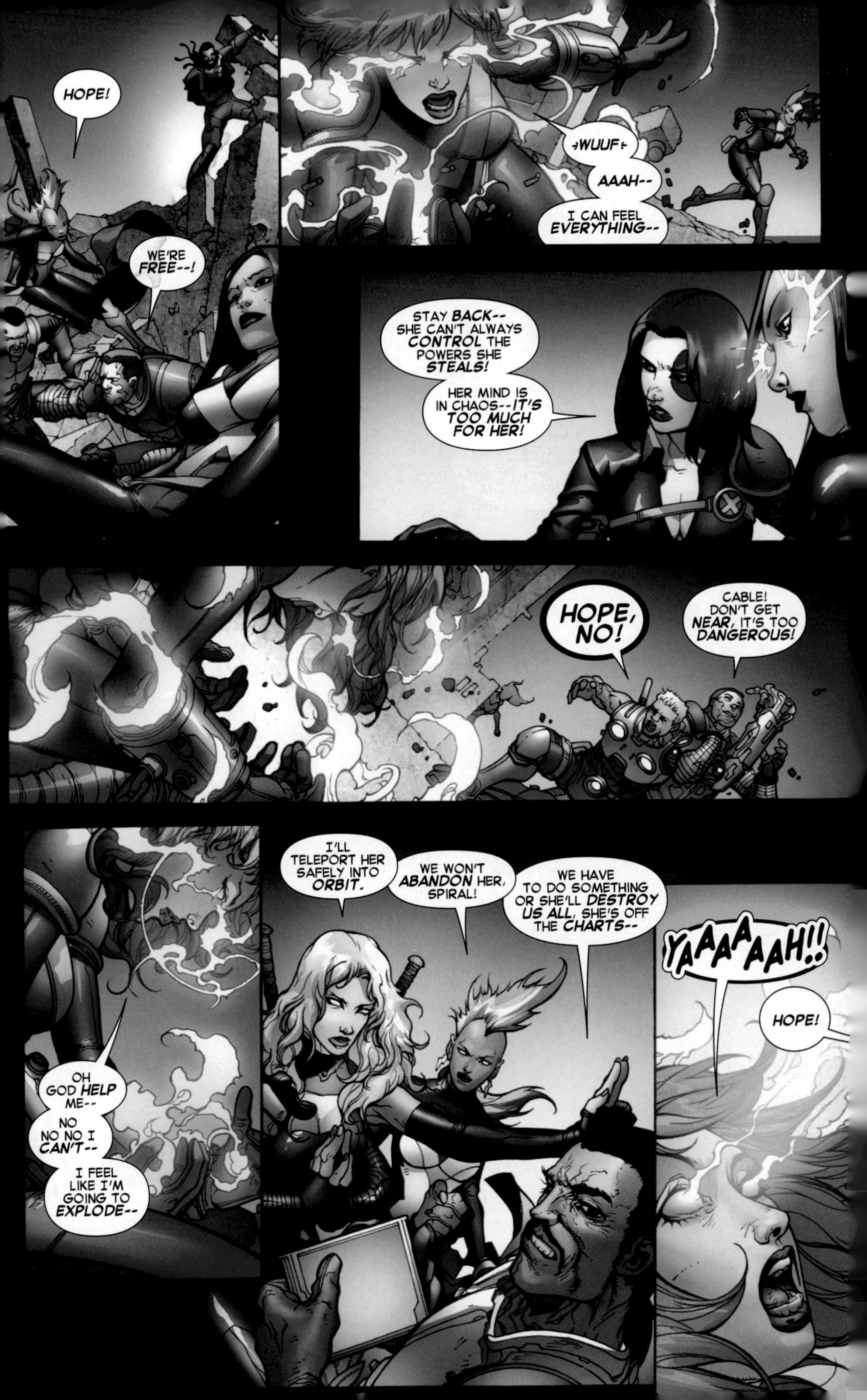
HOPE!
WE'RE FREE--!
-WUUF-
AAAH--
I CAN FEEL EVERYTHING--
STAY BACK-- SHE CAN'T ALWAYS CONTROL THE POWERS SHE STEALS!
HER MIND IS IN CHAOS--IT'S TOO MUCH FOR HER!
HOPE, NO!
CABLE! DON'T GET NEAR, IT'S TOO DANGEROUS!
OH GOD HELP ME--
NO NO NO I CAN'T--
I FEEL LIKE I'M GOING TO EXPLODE--
I'LL TELEPORT HER SAFELY INTO ORBIT.
WE WON'T ABANDON HER, SPIRAL!
WE HAVE TO DO SOMETHING OR SHE'LL DESTROY US ALL, SHE'S OFF THE CHARTS--
YAAAAAAH!!
HOPE!

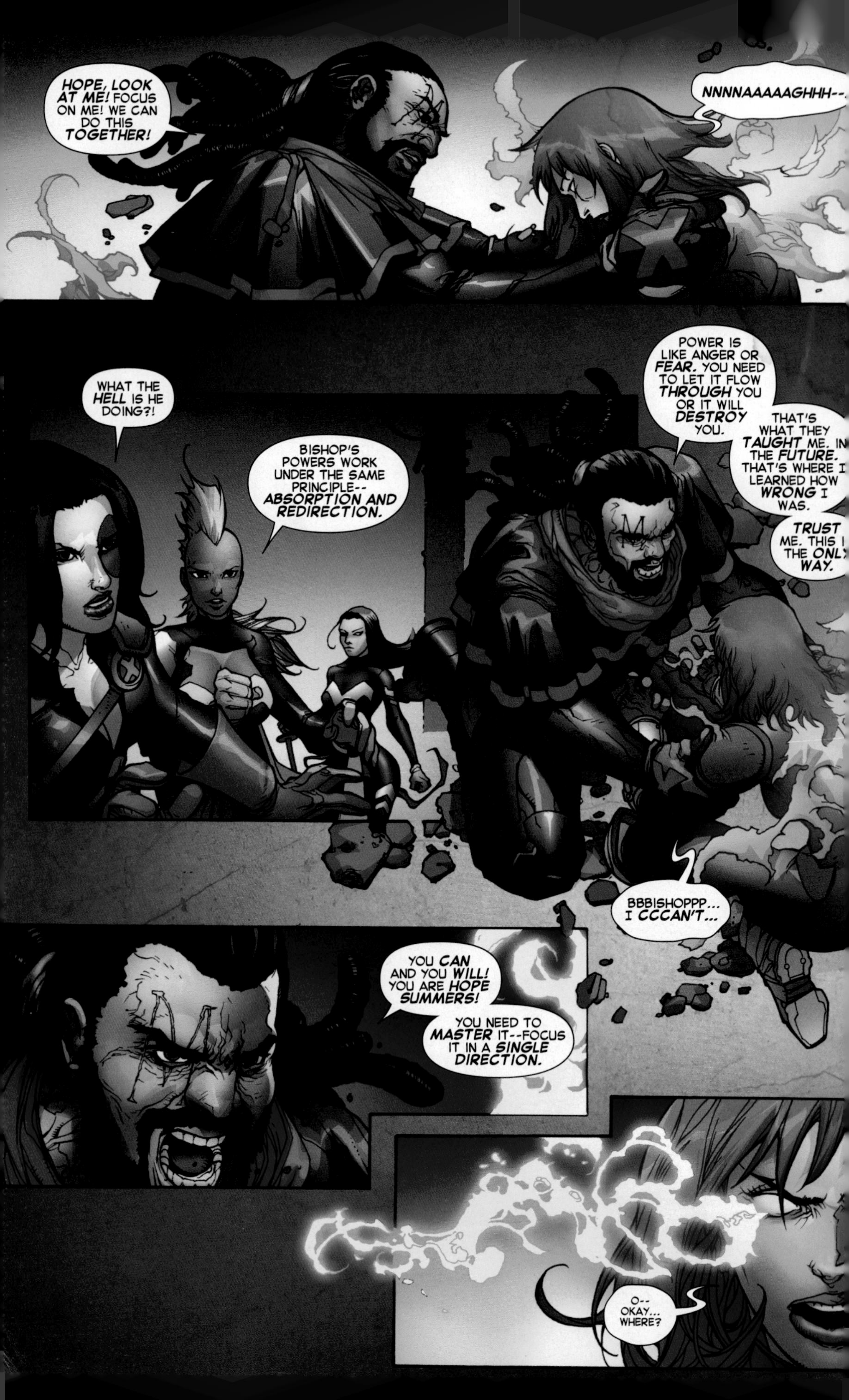
HOPE, LOOK AT ME! FOCUS ON ME! WE CAN DO THIS TOGETHER!
NNNNAAAAAGHHH--
WHAT THE HELL IS HE DOING?!
BISHOP'S POWERS WORK UNDER THE SAME PRINCIPLE-- ABSORPTION AND REDIRECTION.
POWER IS LIKE ANGER OR FEAR. YOU NEED TO LET IT FLOW THROUGH YOU OR IT WILL DESTROY YOU.
THAT'S WHAT THEY TAUGHT ME. IN THE FUTURE. THAT'S WHERE I LEARNED HOW WRONG I WAS.
TRUST ME. THIS I THE ONLY WAY.
BBBISHOPPP... I CCCAN'T...
YOU CAN AND YOU WILL! YOU ARE HOPE SUMMERS!
YOU NEED TO MASTER IT--FOCUS IT IN A SINGLE DIRECTION.
O-- OKAY... WHERE?

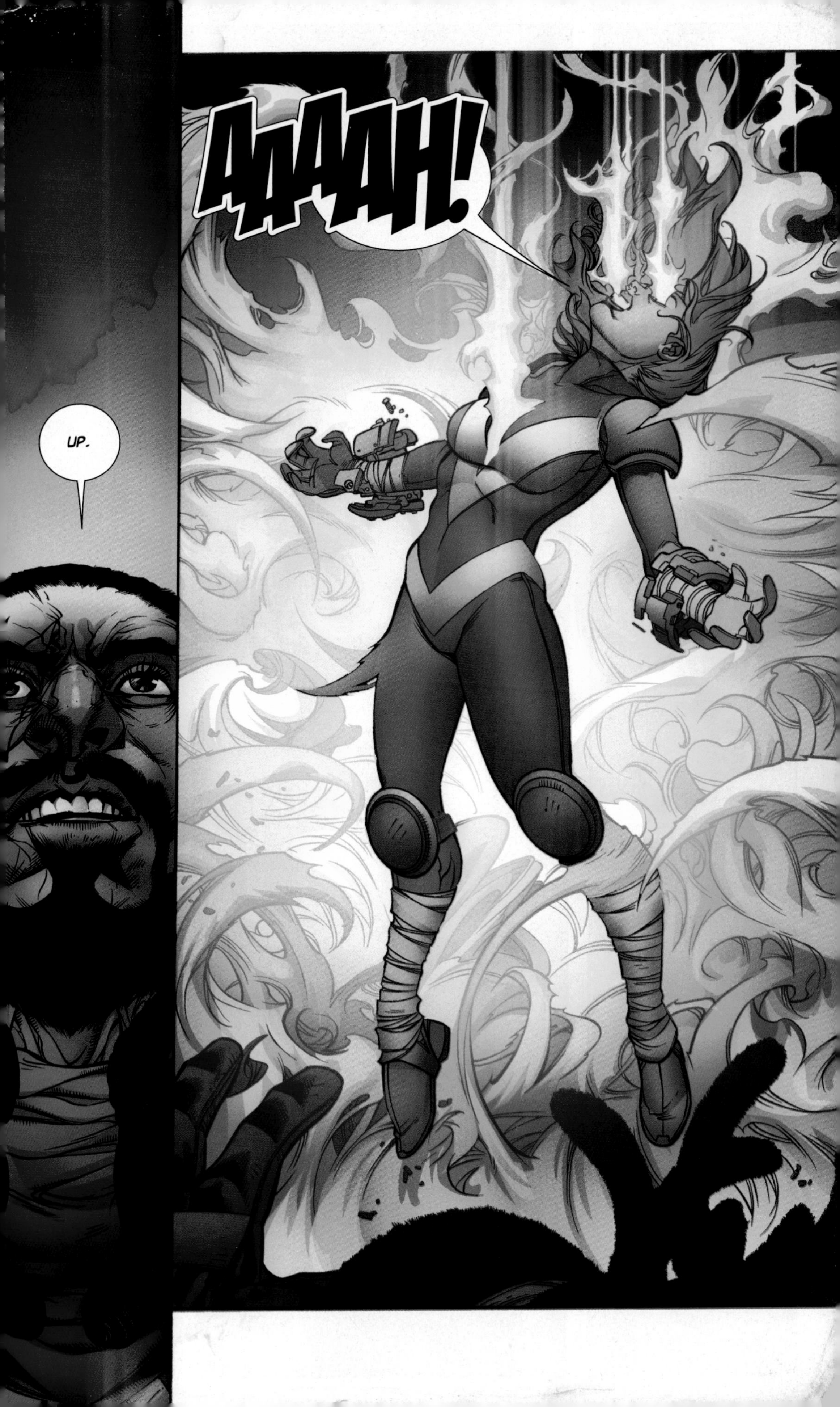
UP.
AAAAH!

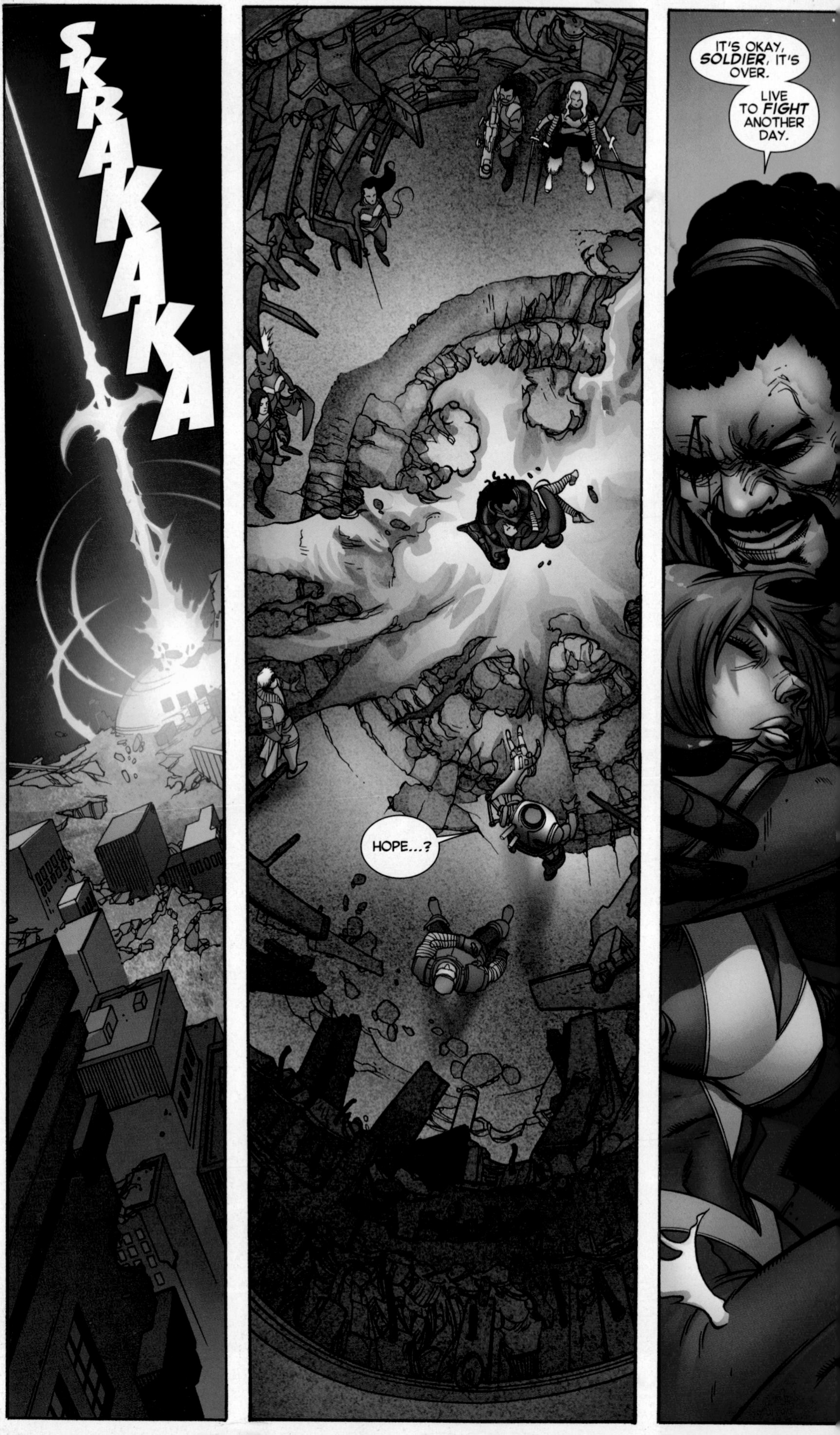
SKRAKAKA
HOPE...?
IT'S OKAY, SOLDIER, IT'S OVER.
LIVE TO FIGHT ANOTHER DAY.

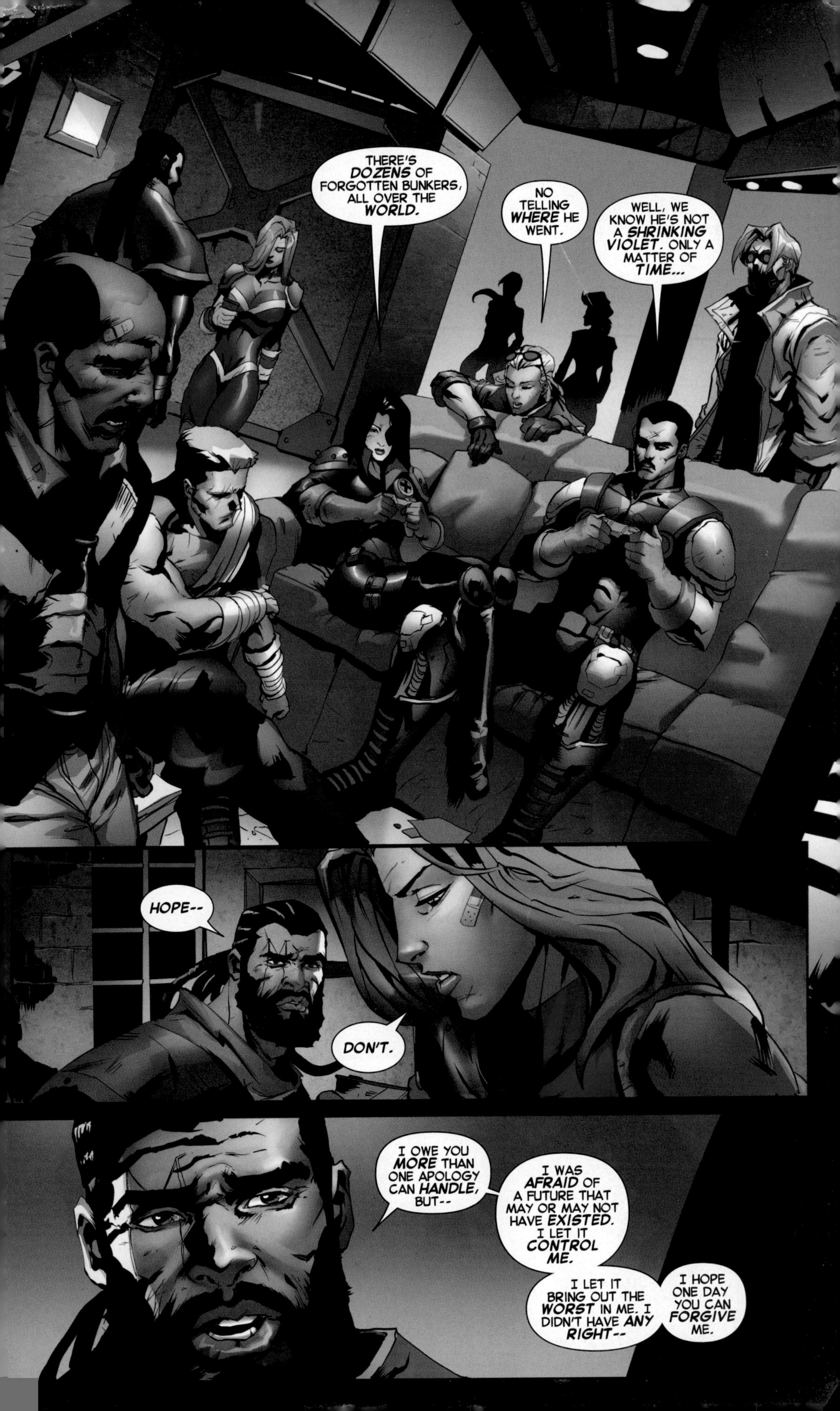
THERE'S DOZENS OF FORGOTTEN BUNKERS, ALL OVER THE WORLD.
NO TELLING WHERE HE WENT.
WELL, WE KNOW HE'S NOT A SHRINKING VIOLET. ONLY A MATTER OF TIME...
HOPE--
DON'T.
I OWE YOU MORE THAN ONE APOLOGY CAN HANDLE, BUT--
I WAS AFRAID OF A FUTURE THAT MAY OR MAY NOT HAVE EXISTED. I LET IT CONTROL ME.
I LET IT BRING OUT THE WORST IN ME. I DIDN'T HAVE ANY RIGHT--
I HOPE ONE DAY YOU CAN FORGIVE ME.

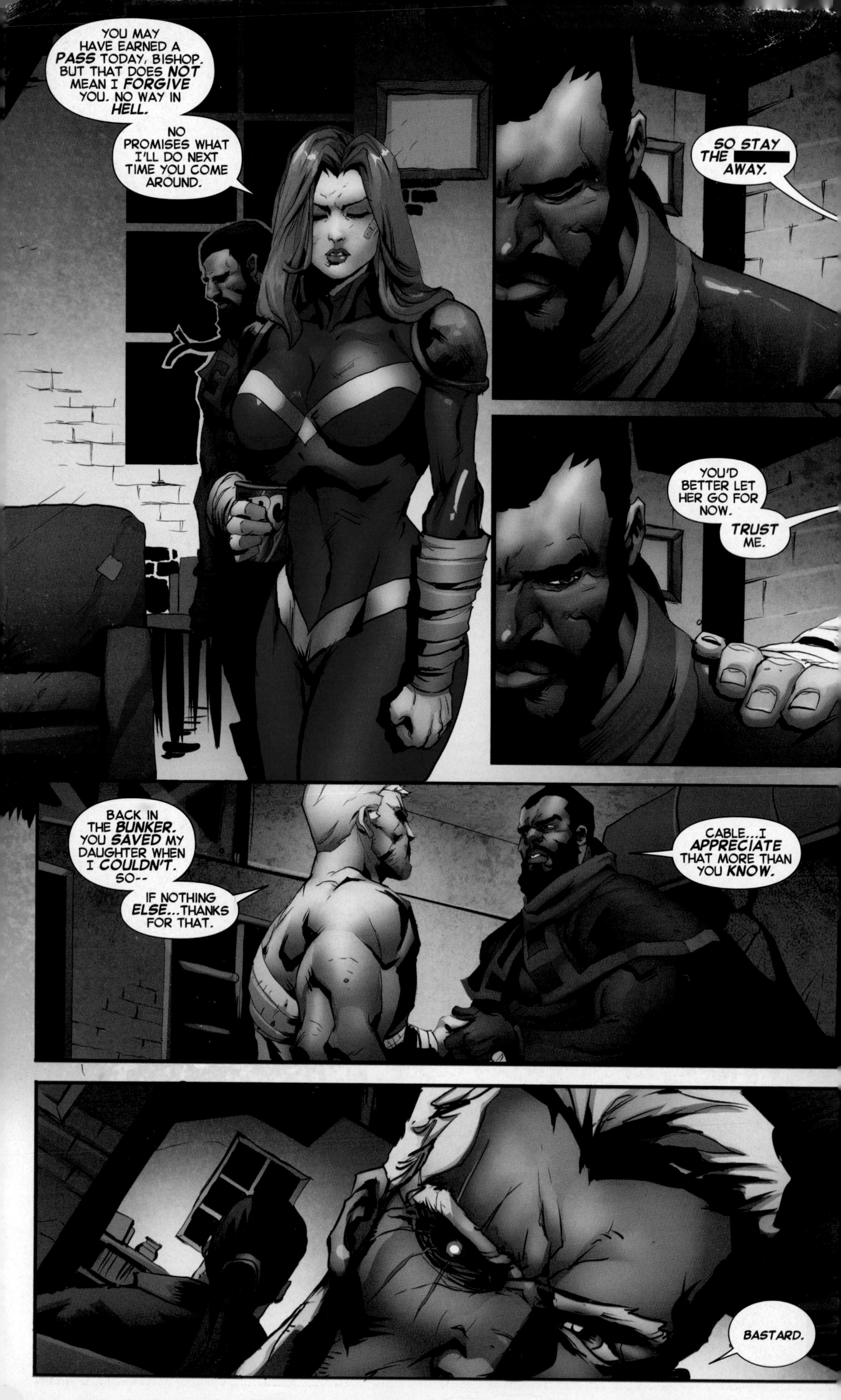
YOU MAY HAVE EARNED A PASS TODAY, BISHOP. BUT THAT DOES NOT MEAN I FORGIVE YOU. NO WAY IN HELL.
NO PROMISES WHAT I'LL DO NEXT TIME YOU COME AROUND.
SO STAY THE [redacted] AWAY.
YOU'D BETTER LET HER GO FOR NOW.
TRUST ME.
BACK IN THE BUNKER. YOU SAVED MY DAUGHTER WHEN I COULDN'T. SO--
IF NOTHING ELSE...THANKS FOR THAT.
CABLE...I APPRECIATE THAT MORE THAN YOU KNOW.
BASTARD.

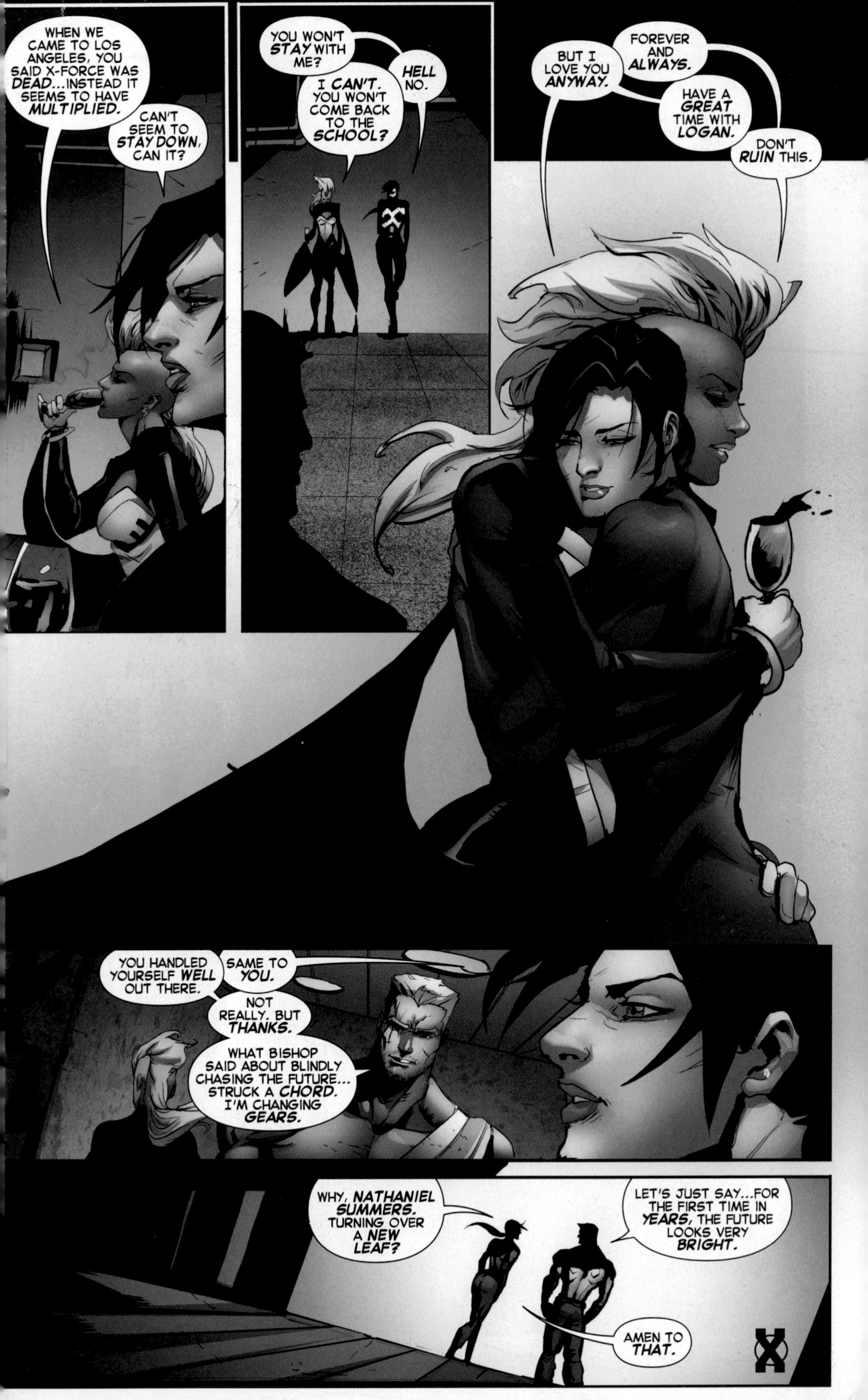

WHEN WE CAME TO LOS ANGELES, YOU SAID X-FORCE WAS DEAD...INSTEAD IT SEEMS TO HAVE MULTIPLIED.
CAN'T SEEM TO STAY DOWN, CAN IT?
YOU WON'T STAY WITH ME?
HELL NO.
I CAN'T. YOU WON'T COME BACK TO THE SCHOOL?
BUT I LOVE YOU ANYWAY.
FOREVER AND ALWAYS.
HAVE A GREAT TIME WITH LOGAN.
DON'T RUIN THIS.
YOU HANDLED YOURSELF WELL OUT THERE.
SAME TO YOU.
NOT REALLY. BUT THANKS.
WHAT BISHOP SAID ABOUT BLINDLY CHASING THE FUTURE... STRUCK A CHORD. I'M CHANGING GEARS.
WHY, NATHANIEL SUMMERS. TURNING OVER A NEW LEAF?
LET'S JUST SAY...FOR THE FIRST TIME IN YEARS, THE FUTURE LOOKS VERY BRIGHT.
AMEN TO THAT.

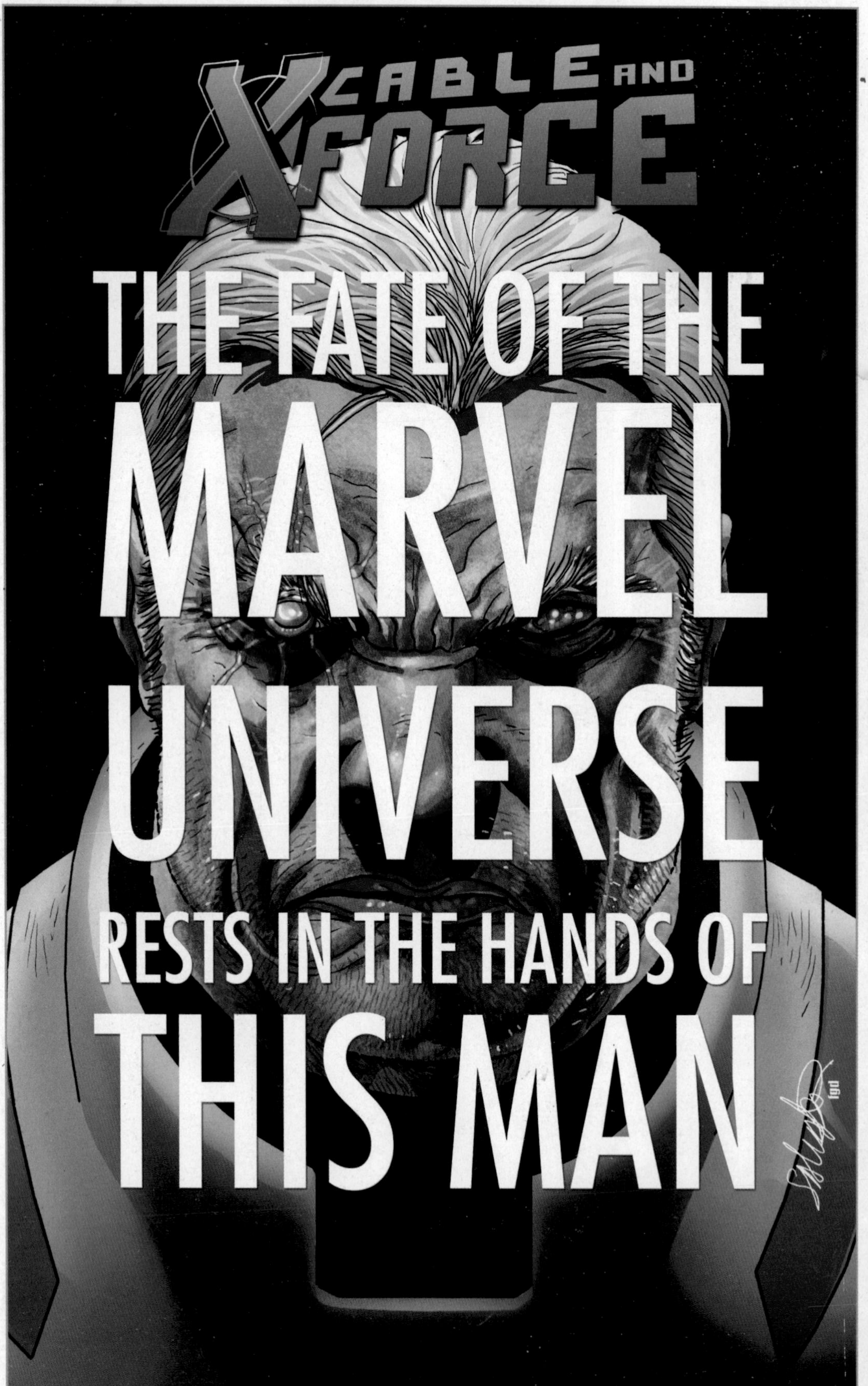
CABLE AND
X-FORCE
THE FATE OF THE
MARVEL
UNIVERSE
RESTS IN THE HANDS OF
THIS MAN

CABLE AND X-FORCE #16 COVER WITH TRADE DRESS